LAW AND
ECONOMIC
REGULATION
IN
TRANSPORTATION

Recent Titles from QUORUM BOOKS

LAW AND
ECONOMIC
REGULATION
IN
TRANSPORTATION

Paul Stephen Dempsey and
William E. Thoms

Q

QUORUM BOOKS
NEW YORK
WESTPORT, CONNECTICUT
LONDON

Library of Congress Cataloging-in-Publication Data

Dempsey, Paul Stephen.
  Law and economic regulation in transportation.

  Includes index.
  1. Transportation—Law and legislation—
United States.   I. Thoms, William E.   II. Title.
KF2179.D46   1986   343.73′093   85–9593
                         347.30393
ISBN 0–89930–138–X (lib. bdg. : alk. paper)

Library of Congress Catalog Card Number: 85–9593
ISBN: 0–89930–138–X

First published in 1986 by Quorum Books

Greenwood Press, Inc.
88 Post Road West, Westport, Connecticut 06881

Printed in the United States of America

The paper used in this book complies with the
Permanent Paper Standard issued by the National
Information Standards Organization (Z39.48–1984).

10 9 8 7 6 5 4 3 2 1

Copyright Acknowledgments

The authors and publishers gratefully acknowledge permission to reprint the following:

All articles by William E. Thoms that appeared in *Passenger Train Journal* are reprinted and adapted by permission of *Passenger Train Journal*.

"Patching Up the Amtrak Statute" (May 1975 *Trains*); "The Return of Section 13a" (January 1976 *Trains*); "New Rules for Bankrupt Rails" (May 1980 *Trains*); "Those Directed-service Orders" (September 1981 *Trains*); "What Price Labor Protection" (June 1982 *Trains*) are reprinted and adapted by permission of *Trains*. Copyright 1975, 1975, 1980, 1981, 1982 Kalmbach Publishing Company.

"The Contemporary Evolution of Intermodal and International Transport Regulation under the Interstate Commerce Act: Land, Sea, and Air Coordination of Foreign Commerce Movements," 10 *Vanderbilt Journal of Transnational Law* 505–555 (1977) by Paul Stephen Dempsey, is reprinted and adapted by permission of the publisher.

"Entry Control under the Interstate Commerce Act: A Comparative Analysis of the Statutory Criteria Governing Entry in Transportation," 13 *Wake Forest Law Review* 729–772 (1977), by Paul Stephen Dempsey, is reprinted and adapted by permission of the publisher.

"Foreign Commerce Regulation under the Interstate Commerce Act: Intermodal Coordination of International Transportation in the United States," 5 *Syracuse Journal of International Law and Commerce* 53–92 (1977), by Paul Stephen Dempsey, is reprinted and adapted by permission of the publisher.

"The International Rate and Route Revolution in North Atlantic Passenger Transportation," 17 *Columbia Journal of Transnational Law* 393–449 (1978), by Paul Stephen Dempsey, is reprinted and adapted by permission of the publisher.

"Rate Regulation and Antitrust Immunity in Transportation: The Genesis and Evolution of This Endangered Species," 32 *American University Law Review* 335–375 (1983), by Paul Stephen Dempsey, is reprinted and adapted by permission of the publisher.

"The Experience of Deregulation: Erosion of the Common Carrier System," 13 *Transportation Law Institute* 121–176 (1980), by Paul Stephen Dempsey, is reprinted and adapted by permission of the publisher.

"Congressional Intent and Agency Discretion—Never the Twain Shall Meet: The Motor Carrier Act of 1980," 58 *Chicago-Kent Law Review* 1–58 (1982), by Paul Stephen Dempsey, is reprinted and adapted by permission of the publisher.

"Entry Control and the Federal Motor Carrier Act of 1980," 12 *Transportation Law Journal* 51 (1980); "The Rise and Fall of the Civil Aeronautics Board—Opening Wide the Floodgates of Entry," 9 *Transportation Law Journal* 91 (1979); "Plotting the Return of Isbrandsten: The Illegality of Interconference Rate Arguments," 9 *Transportation Law Journal* 337 (1978); "The Airline Merger Cases: CAB Application of Clayton Section 7 after Deregulation," 12 *Transportation Law Journal* 139 (1980); "Clear Track for Deregulation," 12 *Transportation Law Journal* 183 (1982); and "Proposed Regulatory Reform in the Area of Railroad Abandonment," 11 *Transportation Law Journal* 213 (1979) are reprinted and adapted by permission of the publisher.

Economic Principles Commission of the National Association of Manufacturers, *The American Individual Enterprise System*, vol. 1 (New York: McGraw-Hill, 1946), pp. 531–544, is reprinted and adapted by permission of the publisher.

James C. Hardman, Transportation Law: An Introductory Study (1978), is reprinted and adapted by permission of the author.

William J. Augello, "Cargo Liability Changes Resulting from the Motor Carrier Act of 1980," found at the Westminster Law Library, University of Denver, Denver, Colorado, is reprinted and adapted by permission of the author.

Contents

6.   Government Operation of Rail Transportation Systems   277

     I.   Traditional Approach   277
     II. Statelization of the Rail Industry   277
     III. Amtrak   281
     IV. Commuter Railroads   287
     V.   Conrail   288
     VI. Benign Neglect: The Bankrupt Railroads   291
     VII. Directed-Service Orders   293

7.   Labor Relations in the Transportation Industry   297

     I.   The Railway Labor Act   297
     II. Compulsory Arbitration   299
     III. Labor Protection for Railroad Employees   301
     IV. Labor Protection for Airline Employees   306
     V.   Labor Protection for Transit Employees   306
     VI. National Labor Relations Act   308

8.   Urban Mass Transit   311

     I.   Emergence of the Urban Mass Transportation Act   311
     II. Structure of the Urban Mass Transportation Act   312
     III. The Future of Urban Mass Transit   335

     INDEX   345

Preface

Why a book about the regulation of transportation when the press regularly informs us about the triumph of deregulation? Why should the law student, business student, practitioner or attorney care to concern himself with this ostensibly arcane area of the law?

We have written this book and used it in our courses in transportation law because we agree that it is a fascinating subject to teach and an effective way to learn how the political, legal and economic forces converge to make national policy.

—Transportation is the most important industry in the United States so far as employment, investment and impact on other industries is concerned. It is the fundamental infrastructure which facilitates the free flow of commerce. Its influence is so pervasive that special laws have been promulgated to govern its operation.

—Transportation was the first industry to be regulated and, a century later, the first to be significantly deregulated. Most schemes for government regulation of industry in the United States are based upon those originally developed for railroads in 1887 and, subsequently, for airlines and motor carriers. The contemporary pattern of deregulation for financial institutions, communications and energy is again following the lead of the transportation field.

—The reports of regulation's death, like that of Mark Twain, are highly exaggerated. The Civil Aeronautics Board may have met its demise at the end of 1984, but its functions in international aviation, local service airlines, antitrust and consumer protection have been assumed by the Department of Transportation. The Interstate Commerce Commission still exercises important functions concerning surface transportation. State regulatory bodies continue to exercise jurisdiction over aspects of local service.

It appears that even with the diminution of economic regulation of airlines, safety regulation by the Federal Aviation Administration continues to play a major role. Regulation of landing slots by local airport authorities seems to be even more important, and antitrust regulation is growing in all directions.

—The United States has followed a unique pattern in development of its transportation facilities. Most nations have opted for government ownership of railways and the rest of the transportation infrastructure. Canada has followed a pattern of government corporations competing with large private companies. The United States, however, proceeded from a completely free market during the developmental years of the industry to a regulatory scheme designed to curb the excesses of the robber-baron era. Within the past decade, the United States has come almost full circle—returning to a reliance on the marketplace. Some observers fear that the reasons for which regulation was instituted in the first place may be ignored in the rush to dismantle the regulatory structure.

—In addition to the free entry and more or less free competition that characterized the postregulatory era, in the United States the government has moved to take over services which the private market was unable to supply. This has been most evident for the rail industry in the 1970s when first Amtrak relieved the railroads of the duty to provide passenger service and then Conrail was established to prevent the collapse of eastern railroading. In the 1980s there has been a move away from this nationalizing trend, characterized by the pending sale of Conrail to private interests. In some instances, these unprofitable services have been unloaded onto the states. Branch lines and whole main lines, like the Milwaukee, are now under state ownership, and the Alaska Railroad has been sold to that state. The Northeast Rail Service Act of 1981 provided for the transfer of commuter train service to the states involved. Urban mass transit is exclusively a local governmental function.

We have organized the book to give the general reader an idea of the growth of transportation law in America in the past century. It addresses *all* modes of domestic transportation. Chapter 1 contains a history of the industry and its regulators. Chapters 2, 3 and 4 examine economic regulations: (a) the policing of entry and exit from transportation, (b) efforts to keep rates just, reasonable and nondiscriminatory, and (c) mergers, consolidations, antitrust and other financial issues, respectively. Chapter 5 examines loss and damage and other tort suits against carriers, and their limitation by regulation. Chapter 6 deals with government operations of railroads—Amtrak, Conrail and state and local operation of commuter and local freight lines. Chapter 7 reviews the Railway Labor Act and other labor legislation pertinent to the transportation industry, while Chapter 8 is concerned with urban mass transit and its sponsorship by the federal government.

Many people assisted in the preparation of this book. We particularly thank Deans Daniel S. Hoffman, William M. Beaney, and Edward A. Dauer of the University of Denver and W. Jeremy Davis of the University of North Dakota for their support of this project. Director Gene C. Griffin of North Dakota State University arranged for the typing of the manuscript by computer and allowed us to reprint materials from the Transportation Law Series of the Upper Great Plains Transportation Institute. Editors Mike Schafer of *Passenger Train Journal* and David P. Morgan of *Trains* graciously gave permission to reprint materials published in the magazines. The National Association of Manufacturers extended permission to reproduce portions of "The American Individual Enterprise System." We also acknowledge the support and assistance of the *Transportation Law Journal*, published at the University of Denver in conjunction with the Transportation Lawyers Association, in which journal several portions of this book first saw the light of day.

So as to make this volume of material manageable, to the extent that the literature authored by third parties (*e.g.*, court opinion, law review articles, government documents) has been reproduced, the authors have taken some literary license to delete paragraphs, reword sentences and omit or renumber footnotes. Also, the 1978 recodification of the Interstate Commerce Act in title 49 of the United States Code rendered obsolete the prior section numbering system. Throughout this book, we have employed five-digit post–1978 section references, even where the material we have quoted used the now obsolete pre–1978 section numbers. Care has been taken to ensure that the meaning of the author's work has not been significantly altered. But most of these changes appear in this book without brackets or ellipsis. To the extent the reader intends to use this book as a research source and quote the materials reproduced herein, he may wish to examine the primary reference source, footnoted at the end of each chapter.

In addition, we thank the people responsible for the final editing and typesetting of this book. While many were the helping hands, we particularly thank Charlotte Dupree and Michael Luse of the University of Denver, Lisa Beckstrom Gibbens, Linda Kohoutek and Robert Stroup of the University of North Dakota, Jody Ufer of the Upper Great Plains Transportation Institute, North Dakota State University, and Lynn Kendall of Greenwood Press. The Institute also sponsored the work of Transportation Law Fellows Paul Kerian and Susan C. Lein, who were instrumental in research, writing and editing this material. Besides reviewing the entire manuscript in 1982–83, Mrs. Lein assisted in the preparation of Chapter 8, dealing with urban mass transit. Rodney D. Peterson, Professor of Economics at Colorado State University, was kind enough to review the manuscript and make suggestions as to economic aspects.

This work has taken a few years, and things have moved more rapidly in the field of regulatory law than either of us had envisioned. In that respect, we would like to thank our friends and relatives for their patient support and encouragement during the many years that this nebulous monster was taking shape.

Paul Stephen Dempsey
William E. Thoms

LAW AND
ECONOMIC
REGULATION
IN
TRANSPORTATION

A Historical Survey of Transportation and the Origins of Economic Regulation

I. INTRODUCTION

The progress of civilized man is frequently described in terms of his accomplishments in transportation: the invention of the wheel; the voyages of Leif Erickson and Christopher Columbus; the explorations of Cook, Drake, Magellan, Marco Polo and the rest; the construction by Charlemagne of the canal system of Europe; the driving of the golden spike into the tracks at Promontory Point, Utah, linking the American east with its west; the construction of the Suez and Panama Canals; the Wright Brothers' flight at Kitty Hawk; the assembly lines of Henry Ford; the transatlantic flight of Colonel Charles Lindbergh; the construction of the German Autobahn and the American Interstate Highway System; and Neil Armstrong's "giant leap for mankind."[1] Each of these events enabled man first to explore and then to conquer the planet. Man now stands on the threshold of outer-space exploration, to be logically followed by the exploitation of its infinite resources. Transportation has been a fundamental, essential criterion in the growth of civilization and the industrial revolution. And, in a circular fashion, technological innovations in transportation have been a by-product of the growth of civilization and the industrial revolution.

So, too, has transportation had a profound effect upon the collective economic growth and intellectual development of man. The birth of civilization in Mesopotamia has, to some extent, been attributed to the existence of trade routes crossing the Tigris and the Euphrates, permitting intellectual intercourse between people of different cultures. Many cities owe their existence and growth to their geographic proximity to trade routes. For example, European cities such as Rotterdam, Copenhagen, Vienna and Hamburg and American cities such as New York, Chicago, Atlanta, Denver and

New Orleans owe much of their economic growth to their geographic proximity to natural trade routes.

Conversely, many cities owe their economic decline to the relocation of
trade routes: Bruges in Belgium and Rothenburg ob der Tauber in Germany
were important centers for trade and commerce which have since been
"frozen in time" because of changing trade patterns. Similarly, some of the
major American ports of the colonial era (e.g., Alexandria, Virginia; Charles-
ton, South Carolina; and Savannah, Georgia) have experienced an economic
decline because of the loss of traffic to other ports or because of the shift of
traffic to non-maritime modes of transportation.

At some point, man recognized that there are certain industries which
are essential to economic growth and industrial development: transportation,
communications (telephone and telegraph, radio and television) and energy
(electric and gas companies). Without these, prosperity is unattainable. Hence,
he began to treat them differently than other industries—to allow the public
interest to prevail over individual economic interests. Because they constitute essential components of economic growth, these industries have traditionally been deemed to be too important to be left to the vicissitudes of
the marketplace.

It is difficult to delineate the precise point at which the regulation of
transportation began. There is some literature which indicates that barge
traffic on the Nile was regulated by the pharaohs. Certainly, the German
robber-barons regulated commerce on the Rhine and the Mosel by demanding the payment of tolls. And common carriers were regulated in England during the reign of William and Mary.

The regulation of American business began with the regulation of the
transportation industry. Indeed, in 1887, the U.S. government created its
first independent regulatory agency, the Interstate Commerce Commission,
and conferred to it jurisdiction to regulate the rates and practices of the
railroads.

During the ensuing century, there has been an astounding proliferation
in the number, size and scope of federal regulatory agencies. Although
several agencies (i.e., the Interstate Commerce Commission, the Federal
Maritime Commission, the Civil Aeronautics Board, the Federal Energy
Regulatory Commission and the numerous components of the Department
of Transportation) regulate the several modes of transportation (i.e., rail,
motor, air and water carriage, as well as freight forwarding and pipelines),
each mode has a single common characteristic—it is engaged in the business
of selling the service of movement of passengers or commodities from one
point to another.

Nevertheless, there are substantive differences between the types and
scope of regulation in which the various agencies are engaged. The differences in types of regulation reflect, *inter alia*, (a) the inherent economic
differences between the modes of transportation; (b) the legislative history

of regulation in the area and the language of the specific statutory provisions; (c) the philosophical and political composition of the individuals serving on the independent regulatory commissions; and (d) the role of the judiciary in either circumscribing or encouraging regulatory activity.

Moreover, the objectives in regulating transportation have changed radically since 1887. Although Congress initially instituted regulation under the ICC essentially in order to protect the public from the monopolistic abuses of the railroads, between 1920 and 1975 the national transportation policy sought to protect the transportation industry from the deleterious consequences of unrestrained competition, and thereby brought into focus the relationship of antitrust *vis-á-vis* other federal regulatory policies. Since the early 1980s, regulatory policy has sought to stimulate competition in order to achieve the inherent free market attributes of economy and efficiency of operations by diminishing the federal regulatory role in the areas of entry and pricing.

A. Historical Survey of American Transportation

The United States has sometimes been called an "experiment in transportation."[2] Only through amazing improvements in transportation during the nineteenth century was conquest of the North American continent achieved.

Our modern transportation system is little more than a century old. The invention of the steam engine marked the turning point in its history by giving man a moving power that was tireless and virtually unlimited in quantity. In recent years, development of the electric motor and the internal-combustion engine has led to the highway motor vehicle, the airplane, and the rapid-transit system.

We can divide our transportation history into five periods: (1) public and toll roads, (2) canals and improved rivers, (3) steam railroads, (4) motor vehicles and (5) airplanes.

We now have such a highly developed system of improved highways throughout the United States that it is difficult to believe that there was a time when most land transportation was provided by pack horses, because few roads were suitable for use by wagons or coaches. Early roads were poorly constructed and often clogged with snow and mud during the winter and spring months. The absence of bridges in many places added to the inconvenience.

A rapidly growing population created a demand for a more extensive and efficient system. The demand became so great that private companies, with or without the aid of the government, found it profitable to build turnpikes. One of the earliest and most successful was the 66–mile toll road built in 1792 from Philadelphia to Lancaster. During that time, the federal government did little to aid road construction, but it did construct one famous highway. This was the Cumberland Road or National Pike, which began in Cumberland, Maryland, and extended to Vandalia, Illinois. In a few instances local, state or federal government subsidized private roads. For example, Pennsylvania had contributed nearly $2 million to the construction of turnpikes, and other states were almost as generous. Local governments also made heavy contributions, and for a while, even the federal government bought stock in privately owned turnpikes. Federal participation was brought to an end by President Jackson, when he vetoed a bill providing for the purchase of stock in a turnpike company organized to construct a road in Kentucky. By that time, however, the turnpike era was drawing near an end, and the public was turning to canals.

The canal era is generally regarded as beginning with the Erie Canal. Completed in 1825, it extended 360 miles from Albany to Buffalo, New York. The Erie Canal reduced the time and the shipping costs between New York and the West to such an extent that New York had a distinct advantage over its competitors, especially Baltimore and Philadelphia. This success induced Pennsylvania to construct a system of canals and portages from Philadelphia to Pittsburgh and led to an effort to build a canal from the Potomac to the Ohio River. Other canals were built in the East, and considerable development also took place in the West, particularly in Ohio, Indiana, and Michigan.

Many canals were financial failures because their volume of business was small, because they were mismanaged, or because they had been too expensive to construct. Despite the outcome of the early ventures, belief in the efficacy of canal transportation persisted. Much interest in canal transportation was aroused by the Inland Waterways Commission, appointed by Theodore Roosevelt in 1907, to prepare a plan for improvement of the U.S. river systems. Extensive improvements of the Ohio River, construction of a "Lakes-to-Gulf Deep Waterway,"and reconstruction of the old Erie Canal were advocated. The state of New York spent millions improving its barge canal system, but at no time did the volume of traffic meet the expectations of those who had promoted the project.

Although the experience of the states and the United States with inland waterway transportation has not been altogether encouraging, river improvements in the interest of flood control, promotion of irrigation, and development of hydroelectric power have been worthwhile. But few inland waterways constructed solely as transportation facilities have justified the expenditures made on them. Despite this fact, many ardent believers in inland waterway transportation urge construction of a comprehensive system of canals and river improvements. It may be that the time will come when establishment of such a system will be advisable, but experience indicates that river and canal transportation is, at the present time, greatly inferior to transportation on our railroads and highways.

The first common-carrier railroad in the United States, the Baltimore and Ohio, was begun barely two years after the Erie Canal was opened. In the course of a few years, every canal and navigable river in the country was challenged by a parallel steam railroad. The railroad provided a better answer than the canal to the country's demand for cheaper, more efficient, more reliable and, above all, speedier transportation.

Although our railroads were built largely by private enterprise, some early lines were constructed by state governments. Those constructed by the states did not achieve satisfactory results, and many were soon surrendered to private companies. It early became the practice for private companies to own track, vehicle and motive power and to provide a complete transportation service. Tolls disappeared, and carriers charged rates designed to cover costs of both ownership and operation. Essential differences between rail and other forms of transportation made different methods of operation necessary. Because trains operate on track, they could not meet and pass at will (without the aid of sidings), as boats and highway vehicles could. This fundamental distinction between railroads and other kinds of transportation persists to the present day. The railroad is the only important carrier which owns the highway, the vehicle and the motive power. Ships and motor vehicles operate on highways which their operators do not own; even their terminal facilities are often owned and operated by other agencies. Airplanes find the air to be free, but their paths are marked by beacons and signs usually provided by public authority, and airports, likewise, are seldom owned by the organizations that fly the planes.

Once the superiority of the railroads as a carrier of freight and passengers had been demonstrated, railroad companies experienced little difficulty raising needed capital in areas with dense population and advanced economic development. But in the more sparsely settled Middle and Far West, the returns promised were too meager to make railroad construction an attractive venture to those who had capital to invest. The people of these districts, familiar with the benefits railroads had brought to other regions and realizing the need of access to markets for the products of their fields and small industries, began to demand public aid for railroad corporations. As a result, government aid accounted for the construction of thousands of miles of railroad lines long before they would have been built had reliance been placed entirely upon the voluntary investment of private capital.

This aid was given not only by the federal and state governments, but also by local governments. Local government aid appeared primarily as (a) subscriptions to railroad stock, (b) guaranteeing of railroad bond issues, (c) exchange of their own obligations for those of the railroads, either with or without security, and (d) donations to rail construction costs. State aid was similar, but in addition, states often granted the right of eminent domain, monopoly, and gave banking privileges, tax exemptions and direct financial assistance.

Federal assistance differed somewhat in form from the assistance of the state governments. The federal government advanced loans to railroads having projected routes to the Pacific Coast, remitted duties on imported railway iron and granted land for rights of way and sites for depots and terminals. The most significant form of federal aid was the land grant. These federal grants to railway corporations totaled more than 132 million acres, later reduced to about 130 million by readjustments.

The land grants benefited not only the railroads, but also the government. The value of public land along railways increased. The building of the roads encouraged economic development and increased the wealth of the country. In addition, the railroads were required to provide transportation for the movement of troops, mail and government property at rates below the regular rates.

Railroad mileage has increased tremendously since the days when federal land grants were used in many parts of the country to encourage the building of new roads. But by 1910, railway development had reached the point where the mileage was more than adequate to take care of the needs in all except a few sections of the country. By 1943, the number of miles of railway owned in the United States had dropped. This decline in mileage did not mean a decline in efficiency. The development of refrigerator cars, improved Pullman service, air-conditioned trains, diesel engines and improved methods for handling both freight and passenger traffic have created a more efficient system.

The greatest challenge to steam railroads and to city and suburban electric railways has come from the rapid development of motor vehicle transportation. The motor truck has become almost as important an agency of passenger transportation as the private car. Thousands of taxicabs carry passengers. The bus has largely supplanted the street railway, and it competes with Amtrak passenger trains as well. Hundreds of intercity bus lines offer frequent and convenient services, which are heavily patronized. Cross-country bus lines give service from coast to coast.

The motor truck has also become a common carrier of undeniable importance, in many places boldly challenging and overcoming in a competitive struggle the long-dominant railroad. At the close of World War I, it was frequently said that the motor truck could never profitably carry anything but high-class, valuable merchandise, and not even that for distances in excess of 50 miles. In less than a score of years, it demonstrated its ability to carry all kinds of freight, with no limit to the distance over which it could operate. The railroad is still an important carrier of both passengers and freight, but it no longer occupies the dominating position in our transportation system that it held at the close of the nineteenth century.

The production of cars, trucks and buses has been financed by private capital, just as the railroads were. But the government—local, state and federal—had contributed heavily to the development of transportation by motor vehicles by providing and maintaining the highways over which these vehicles operate. State and local authorities have used bond issues and general taxes to finance highway construction. Gasoline taxes and motor car license fees have also provided substantial funds and at the same time have shifted the costs to the users of the highways in considerable degree.

The most recent form of transportation developed on a national basis in the United States is air transport, chiefly used to carry mail, passengers and express. Its development has followed the pattern set by highway transportation rather than that set by rail. Private enterprise has funded the manufacture of planes and equipment and the operation of air services. On the other hand, government has constructed and maintained the airports. The federal government has aided the development of air transportation with payments for mail service and lighted airstrips.

Although air transport's primary advantage over other forms of transportation is speed, it cannot provide economical transport for most types of freight and express. Air transport's expansion and growth have been rapid in recent years, but the traffic carried by air transport is still small in comparison with that carried by other transportation modes.

II. STATE AND FEDERAL REGULATION

A. Origins of Rail Regulation

Government regulation of industry in the United States owes its origin to the problems encountered as a result of laissez faire rate manipulation by the transportation industry.[3] Indeed, the trend toward creation of independent federal administrative agencies has a common genesis.

Rail expansion into the Middle West and western United States in the nineteenth century owes much of its growth and development to the role played by government in encouraging such expansion. The desire for transportation led many governments (local, state and federal) to provide construction capital in the forms of loans, bonds, purchases of stock and grants of real estate. State and local governments contributed to such growth through their conference of tax exemptions, stock subscriptions, loans, and loan guarantees. Similarly, the federal government offered incentives for rail expansion including loans, remissions of the duty on imported iron and the land grant system. For example, during the decade preceding the War Between the States, the states granted 32 million acres of land to the rail industry. Between 1862 and 1871, the states granted 17 million acres to railroads, and the federal government granted 130 million acres. Clearly, government played a major role in the promotion and development of the nation's rail system.

The railroad promoters also turned to private individuals along the rights of way, particularly farmers who would be served by the new road. Farmers invested in rail stock by mortgaging their farms in anticipation of lucrative dividends and the ability to secure reasonably priced transportation with which to ship their crops to eastern markets. They were frequently disappointed on both counts, for they were often paid no dividends, and the cost of rail service was excessive. Many railroads went through bankruptcy and reorganization, effectively wiping out the value of the stock sold to investors. Farmers who had invested would be left with a mortgage, worthless stock and exorbitantly priced or nonexistent transportation. Moreover, the farmer's taxes would be raised to cover the parallel investment or donation made by his local government. Quite naturally, this led many farmers to strongly resent the railroads.

It was at first the state governments which attacked the abuses of the rail industry. Such abuses included the bribery of public officials, the sale of worthless securities and rate and service discrimination between places and persons. The rate irregularities were perhaps the most significant in prompting government to regulate this industry. Preferred shippers enjoyed special rates, underbilling and rebates. Although points at which rail carrier competition existed enjoyed fiercely competitive rates, those which were served only by a single rail carrier paid comparatively high rates, even then they were located at points closer to destination than the competitive markets. Indeed, it was not uncommon for the transportation prices to be higher on a shorter haul than on a longer haul on the same line in the same direction.

One commentator summarized the high level of price competition between carriers serving common points as follows:

Rate wars become rampant, each carrier trying to underbid the other with little regard for cost considerations. Much traffic was carried at a loss in the hope that the fierce competition would drive the other carriers out of the business leaving the entire field to the victor, who could then make its own terms with the shipper.

Thus, it was reported that in the late 1860's, cattle were moved from Buffalo to New York City for $1.00 per car. Also during this period, the first class rate for shipments from Chicago to New York varied between twenty-five cents and $2.15 per hundred pounds. It has even been reported that in the late 1870's cattle were carried free of charge from Chicago to Pittsburgh and for $5.00 per car from Chicago to New York.

An example of such excessive competition was that practiced between the Erie and the New York Central railroads on traffic between Chicago and New York. After a series of rate reductions which lowered the price of shipping cattle to less than $1.00 per car, Jim Fisk, president of the Erie, purchased all the cattle available and shipped them aboard the New York Central.

Midwestern farmers assailed the excessively high rates charged by railroads in the carriage of midwestern agricultural products from the carriers' monopoly origins to eastern markets:

Farmers, the primary victims of the rail carriers, needed the carrying capacity of railroads to transport their products to market or processing areas. The cost of transportation directly influenced the profitability of farm operations. In the opinion of farmers, rail carriers were reaping unreasonably high profits. This exploitation was particularly severe when only one rail carrier served a geographic area.[4]

Dissatisfaction with excessively high and discriminatory rail rates and practices led midwestern farmers to object vehemently to the abuses of market power prevalent in the rail industry. Under the aegis of the "Patrons of Husbandry," the Granger movement succeeded in persuading numerous states to promulgate legislation constricting the ability of rail carriers to engage in such activity. Illinois initiated the legislative momentum with a statute passed in 1869, which insisted that railroads offer just, reasonable and uniform rates. Minnesota followed suit in 1871 with a law that regulated maximum rates and prohibited unjust discrimination.[5] During the subsequent 15 years, Iowa, Wisconsin, Missouri, California, Nebraska, Kansas, Oregon and several southern states promulgated similar litigation.

Many states discovered that their legislatures were not particularly well suited to perform the complex task of regulating rates, for legislators had neither the time, the talent nor the expertise to adjudicate rate disputes or otherwise regulate the intricacies of this complex industry. Hence, several states established independent commissions to develop such expertise and protect the public interest in transportation matters.[6] In the West, these state commissions were given power to regulate rail rates; in the East, these governmental bodies usually held only advisory powers.

Rail carriers were, quite naturally, dissatisfied with the regulatory schemes imposed upon them by the states and opposed their constitutionality before the courts. They contended that such laws were fundamentally inconsistent with Article I, Section 8 of the U.S. Constitution, which confers upon Congress the power to "regulate Commerce with foreign Nations, and among the several States." Among the most famous of the decisions rendered in response thereto was that of *Munn v. Illinois.*[7]

Munn involved an Illinois law promulgated in 1871 which required managers of public warehouses to obtain licenses and to observe maximum rate levels as established by the state. The defendants were managers and lessees of terminal grain storage elevators in Chicago. They ignored the state licensing and rate provisions and argued that the state had no right to infringe upon their economic freedom. After all, did not the grain elevator constitute the defendants' private property, to be enjoyed and operated at the owners' exclusive discretion? The U.S. Supreme Court thought not:

Property does become clothed with a public interest when used in a manner to make it of public consequence, and affect the community at large. When, therefore, one devotes his property to a use in which the public has an interest, he, in effect, grants to the public an interest in that use, and must submit to be controlled by the public for the common good, to the extent of the interest he has thus created. He may withdraw his grant by discontinuing the use; but, so long as he maintains the use, he must submit to the control.[8]

Hence, government may lawfully regulate private property dedicated to a public use.

As to the argument that the state law was fundamentally inconsistent with the commerce clause of the U.S. Constitution, the Supreme Court concluded that such

regulation is a thing of domestic concern, and certainly, until Congress acts in reference to their interstate regulations, the State may exercise all the powers of government over them, even though in so doing it may indirectly operate upon commerce outside its immediate jurisdiction.[9]

Numerous bills involving rail regulation were introduced in the U.S. Congress after the Civil War. Indeed, between 1868 and 1886, some 150 bills and resolutions were considered by the Congress. But it was a decision of the U.S. Supreme Court which finally prompted Congress to act, for the decision left a void in the comprehensive scheme of regulation which had been established by the several states.

In *Wabash v. Illinois*,[10] the U.S. Supreme Court reversed itself on the second premise of *Munn*—the effect of the dormant commerce clause in an area in which Congress had not yet enacted legislation. The Court held unconstitutional a state statute which prohibited a rival carrier from charging the same or higher rate for transportation for the same commodity over a lesser distance than for a greater distance in the same direction:

It is not the railroads themselves that are regulated by this act of the Illinois legislature so much as the charge for transportation, and . . . if each one of the States through whose territories these goods are transported can fix its own rules for prices, for modes of transit, for time and modes of delivery, and all other incidents of trans-portation to which the word "regulation" can be applied, it is readily seen that the embarrassments upon interstate commerce, might be too oppressive to be submitted to. "It was . . . to meet just such a case that the commerce clause of the Constitution was adopted."

It cannot be too strongly insisted upon that the right of continuous transportation from one end of the country to the other is essential in modern times to that freedom of commerce from the restraints which the State might chose to impose upon it, that the commerce clause intended to secure. This clause, giving to Congress the power to regulate commerce among the States and with foreign nations, . . . was among the most important of the subjects which prompted the formation of the Constitution . . . . And it would be a very feeble and almost useless provision, but poorly adapted to secure the entire freedom of commerce among the States which was deemed essential to a more perfect union by the framers of the Constitution, if, at every stage of the transportation of goods and chattels through the country, the State within whose limits a part of this transportation must be done could impose regulations concerning the price, compensation, or taxation, or any other restrictive regulation interfering with and seriously embarrassing this commerce. . . .

We must, therefore, hold that it is not, and never has been, the deliberate opinion of a majority of this court that a statute of a State which attempts to regulate the fares and charges by railroad companies within its limits, for a transportation which constitutes a part of commerce among the States, is a valid law.[11]

Thus, even when Congress has not exercised its jurisdiction under Article I, Section 8 of the Constitution, the states may not impose economic regulation upon businesses operating in interstate or foreign commerce. Because approximately 75 percent of the commodities shipped at the time were transported in interstate commerce, the *Wabash* decision effectively left the bulk of rail traffic unregulated.

This result provided a major impetus for Congress to act favorably upon the legislative proposals then before it—to provide federal regulation of interstate transportation. This it did in 1887, by passing the Act to Regulate Commerce, which established the first independent federal agency, the Interstate Commerce Commission, and conferred upon it jurisdiction to regulate what was then (and now) one of the nation's principal industries.

Congress had already passed two bills which had imposed constraints upon the rail industry. The first, enacted in 1886, authorized state-chartered railroads to carry passengers in interstate commerce and to connect with other rail carriers in order to form continuous carriage. The second, passed in 1873, required humane treatment of animals transported by rail. Hence, Congress had exercised its powers to regulate interstate transportation prior to 1887, although only to a limited extent.

However, the Act to Regulate Commerce of 1887 was the first significant effort made by Congress to regulate the rail industry. It was a rather succinct piece of legislation. Most important, the Commission was given jurisdiction to regulate the interstate rates charged by railroads to ensure that they were just and reasonable. Rail carriers were not permitted to discriminate in rates or services between persons, localities or traffic. They were no longer allowed to charge a greater compensation for a shorter haul than for a longer haul over the same line in the same direction, the shorter distance being included within the longer. Nor could they pool freight or revenues. And under the 1887 Act, railroads were required to make their rates public, file them with the newly formed Commission and adhere to such published tariffs.[12] Legislation promulgated in 1903, 1906 and 1910, ultimately conferred upon the ICC jurisdiction to suspend questionable rates pending their investigation.

The promulgation of the Act to Regulate Commerce in 1887 established an important precedent in American public law. The federal government may freely regulate a major industry when the public interest so requires. And, in the creation of the Interstate Commerce Commission, the Congress began what would become the establishment of a wide variety of specialized federal administrative agencies, many of which would be patterned after that original model—the ICC.

By the time the United States entered World War I, in 1917, the problems of the railroads were severe, since profits were unevenly distributed and costs were beginning to increase at a much greater rate than income. Faced with the industry's inability to handle the wartime surge in traffic, President Wilson ordered government operation of the railroads on December 28, 1917, and it lasted until March 1, 1920.

Unified operation under federal control was intended to alleviate the car shortages, port congestion, and labor disputes that had been plaguing the railroads, and thereby ensure the coordinated, efficient and dependable transportation of commodities needed for the conduct of the war. Shortages of track materials and funds, aggravated by the terms of the contract between the government and the railroads, resulted in the continuation, during 1918 and 1919, of the inadequate pretakeover maintenance levels for railroad track. The condition of passenger equipment eroded somewhat, and freight car condition deteriorated severely, but locomotive maintenance actually improved. The continuation of inadequate maintenance levels for track and equipment left the railroads with a badly deteriorated physical plant by the end of the war.

As a response to this physical deterioration and to the completely inadequate rail rate structures that emerged from the war (aggravated by the generally poor postwar economic climate), the Transportation Act of 1920 was preoccupied with the financial well-being of the railroads, a concern not expressed in the earlier legislation.

The Transportation Act of 1920 introduced the "rule of ratemaking," which, in its original form, directed the ICC to provide a climate in which the railroad companies, in the aggregate, could earn a fair rate of return on a fair valuation of their rail property.

Prior to 1920, the ICC had been concerned primarily with unreasonably high rates and with discrimination, preference, and prejudice. As one manifestation of the concern about the railroads' financial well-being and about the long controversial rate reduction practices of the railroads, the Act of 1920 gave the ICC, for the first time, the authority to determine minimum as well as maximum rates.[13]

The ICC had no authority over entry of new railroads until the Transportation Act of 1920. Thus, prior to 1920, new lines continued to be constructed, further contributing to the severe overcapacity problem that had existed since 1887. The Rock Island Railroad, for example, consisted of 3,408 miles of railroad in 1891 but operated 14,270 miles of track in 1907 (acquired partly through merger, partly through construction). The Milwaukee Railroad built its western extension in 1909, running almost within sight of the Northern Pacific route for many miles and competing directly with three other roads.

In 1920, the Congress recognized the problems associated with continued expansion of the railroad system in a climate of pervasive regulation and granted the ICC authority over additional construction. A test of "public convenience and necessity" had to be met before new lines could be built. The ICC was also granted authority to compel new construction when the public interest demanded it. Prior to 1920, the states had some control over abandonment of lines. This control was generally exercised to protect local communities and businesses that were dependent on rail services. The 1920 Act gave the ICC full control over abandonments and provided another public convenience and necessity test. Given the concern of the 1920 Act for the financial health of the railroads, this provision was intended to allow the ICC to balance the local need for continued service against the railroads' need to cease operating unprofitable lines. Control over intercorporate relationships and the issuance of securities were also vested in the ICC in the 1920 Act so as to ensure a sound railroad financial structure.

The Transportation Act of 1940 introduced the concept of a national transportation policy—the first serious attempt to deal with the problems of intermodal competition. The ICC was to administer the Act in a fair and impartial manner so as to "recognize and preserve the inherent advantages of each (mode)." This provision was often used to protect the other modes from railroad competition. Finally, in recognition that the consolidation efforts of the Transportation Act of 1920 had not worked, the 1940 Act eliminated the requirement that consolidations conform to the plans drawn up by the ICC. The ICC was, instead, required to take certain factors into consideration when judging a consolidation proposal, including (a) the effect of the proposed transaction upon adequate transportation service to the public; (b) the effect upon the public interest of the inclusion of, or the failure to include, other railroads in the proposed transactions; (c) the total fixed charges resulting from the proposed transaction; and (d) the interest of the company employees affected.

The Reed-Bulwinkle Act of 1948 allowed the ICC, at its discretion, to grant rate bureaus (collective rate-setting organizations) antitrust immunity. That is, this Act allowed carriers to agree among themselves on rates, charges and divisions.

Ever since passage of the Sherman Antitrust Act in 1890, collective rate making by the railroads had been subject to challenge. The Supreme Court outlawed two rate bureau agreements in 1897 and 1898.[14] Collective rate setting went on, nonetheless. In the 1940s after litigation that challenged the lawfulness of rate bureaus was brought once again, Congress moved to legalize the function of the bureaus. Recognizing the unique characteristics of joint service, among other considerations, the Congress promulgated the Reed-Bulwinkle Act, which permits the ICC, at its discretion and under certain conditions, to exempt rate bureau operations from the antitrust laws.

By 1958, the railroads' financial condition had declined significantly as a result of intense water and motor carrier competition, deteriorated physical plant, economic recession, increasing losses from passenger operations and the resultant difficulty in attracting capital. The Transportation Act of 1958 gave the ICC greater authority over discontinuance of passenger service, since state authorities had been reluctant to accede to discontinuance of unprofitable operations. In the 1958 Act, the ICC was given the authority to determine whether unprofitable passenger operations constituted a burden on interstate commerce, even if the railroad's overall operations were profitable. The rule of rate making was again amended, directing the ICC not to keep the rates of one mode high in order to protect the traffic of another mode. In addition, because of an earlier Supreme Court decision, the ICC had lost all practical authority over intrastate rates.[15] In the 1958 Act, Congress permitted the ICC to find that a particular intrastate rate was so low as to impose a burden on interstate commerce, without having to investigate whether other intrastate rates were cross-subsidizing the low rate.

Despite the long history of regulation, many problems remained unresolved in the early 1970s. Indeed, the U.S. Railway Association remarked, in its Preliminary and Final System Plans, that further regulatory change would be required for the industry to be fully efficient. In 1976, Congress considered and passed the 4R Act.

The 4R Act (the Railroad Revitalization and Regulatory Reform Act of 1976) was the first comprehensive attempt in many years to reexamine the need for the assumptions underlying the economic regulation of the railroad industry. The 4R Act made fundamental changes in the regulatory system administered by the ICC, including minimum and maximum rate regulation; establishment of demand-sensitive rates, separate rates for distinct rail services; operations of rate bureaus; merger and abandonment procedures; and accounting and costing methods.

Railroads are a fully regulated industry. The ICC is responsible for deciding whether a proposed rail rate is too high, too low or discriminatory. The ICC may, temporarily or permanently, prohibit any rate from taking effect and may set the rate it thinks appropriate. Even intrastate rail rates are subject to some ICC control. The ICC also has authority to enforce the "common carrier obligation" that requires a railroad to provide service to anyone who seeks it and who is willing to pay the charge contained in a tariff filed with the ICC.

In addition to authority over rates, the ICC has regulatory control over the construction and abandonment of railroad lines, mergers, acquisitions and related activities, rail accounting and costing procedures and issuance of rail securities. The Act, as continuously amended over the years, also gives the ICC the power to exempt railroad rate-making activities from the jurisdiction of the anti-trust laws.

In 1887, when the railroad companies first came under regulation, they generally exercised monopoly control over the individual markets they served. The system of regulation that was established was a reflection of that economic fact. The economic conditions of the railroads, however, changed rapidly and dramatically in the twentieth century. The regulatory system changed much more slowly. The 4R Act was the first comprehensive attempt in decades to match rail regulation with the current financial and competitive condition of the rail industry.

The 4R Act modifies significantly the standards the ICC applies in determining the reasonableness of proposed rates, so as to assure greater rate-making flexibility for rail management and an enhanced ability to compete effectively against other, largely unregulated transportation modes.

The 4R Act provided new standards and procedures for determining whether rates charged by railroads are just and reasonable and removed ICC authority to determine whether proposed rates are too high on traffic for which effective competition exists. Additional changes provide that a proposed rate that contributes to the "going concern value" of the carrier proposing the rate cannot be found unjustly or unreasonably low. A rate that equals or exceeds the carrier's variable cost of providing the service to which the rate pertains is presumed, absent clear and convincing evidence to the contrary, to contribute to the carrier's going concern value. The 4R Act also changes, fundamentally, the so-called rule of rate making that sets forth the general policy standards to be applied to the ICC in judging the reasonableness of the proposed rate.

The 4R Act insists, however, that none of these rate-making changes are to be construed to modify the provisions of the Interstate Commerce Act (prohibiting undue discrimination, preference or prejudice), to make lawful predatory or other anticompetitive practices or to affect existing law governing rate relationships between ports and equalization of rates within a port. The revisions also created a 7 percent, no-suspend rate zone for an experimental period of two years (now elapsed), prescribed time limits for ICC investigations of proposed rates, modified the power of the ICC to suspend rates and reallocated the burden of proof in suspension cases.

Other provisions of the 4R Act require the ICC to establish procedures assuring the railroads adequate revenue levels, modify the provisions governing collective rate making, and set new procedures and standards to be followed in abandonment and merger proceedings and authorize the ICC to exempt from regulation those persons and transportation services that are found not to be necessary "to effectuate the national transportation policy." Each of these areas constitutes a part of the regulatory system. The intent of the 4R Act revisions to that system is to subject railroad rates and other regulated activities to more competition and less government regulation.

The Conference Report on the 4R Act states that the changes in rate regulation embodied in the Act "are intended to inaugurate a new era of competitive pricing." The legislative history makes clear that this new era is to be marked by less reliance on rates set by ICC regulation and greater reliance on rates set by market forces. Congress recognized that the passage of time had dramatically changed the competitive position of the railroads.

Thus, the legislation resulting from these concerns had two major premises: that the dominant position of the railroads had been severely eroded; and that in order to compete for existing traffic, the railroads needed enough rate-making flexibility to compete effectively with unregulated carriers. From these conclusions came the mandate in the 4R Act for a substantial diminution of the ICC's rate-making powers and for greater railroad freedom to set rates.

The Staggers Rail Act was promulgated in September of 1980. President Carter described this legislation as "the capstone of my efforts to get rid of needless and burdensome federal regulations which benefit nobody and harm all of us." The purpose of this legislation has been described by the congressional committee which adopted it as follows:

Earnings by the railroad industry are the lowest of any transportation mode and are insufficient to generate funds for necessary capital improvements.... The overall purpose of the Act is to provide, through financial assistance and freedom from unnecessary regulation, the opportunity for railroads to obtain adequate earnings to restore, maintain and improve their physical facilities while achieving the financial stability of the national rail system.

The Staggers Rail Act creates a new congressional declaration of policy for railroads in Section 10101(a) of the Interstate Commerce Act. Indeed, competition is mentioned as a policy objective throughout Section 10101(a). In order to accomplish the objective of increased competition, the ICC is directed "to reduce regulatory barriers to entry . . . and exit" and "to minimize the need for federal regulatory control." The ICC is further encouraged to allow "carriers to earn adequate revenues" and to eliminate "noncompensatory rates." Nevertheless, it is encouraged to "prohibit predatory pricing . . . to avoid undue concentrations of market power and to prohibit unlawful discrimination" and to "maintain reasonable rates where there is an absence of effective competition and where rail rates provide revenues which exceed the amount necessary to maintain the rail system and to attract capital." Further, the legislative history reveals that it was Congress' purpose that the ICC should encourage and promote the transportation of coal, with the objective of enhancing our national energy policy of relieving dependence upon foreign energy resources "at rates which do not exceed a reasonable maximum where there is an absence of effective competition." As is indicated by the new congressional statement of policy, the principal focus of the new legislation is rail rate making.

B. Origins of Motor Carrier Regulation

The Motor Carrier Act of 1935[16,17] was not generated by the Depression, but by the decision of the Supreme Court of the United States in *Buck v. Kuykendall*.[18] After that decision, bills for the regulation of interstate motor carriers of passengers were introduced in and actively considered by six successive Congresses, beginning with the 69th Congress in 1926.

Buck proposed to operate between Seattle, Washington, and Portland, Oregon, as a common carrier exclusively for the transportation of interstate passengers and express. Buck's application for a certificate of public convenience and necessity was denied by the state of Washington on the grounds that existing rail and motor passenger transportation service between Seattle and Portland was adequate.

The Supreme Court held that the state of Washington could not require a certificate of public convenience and necessity to operate in interstate commerce. The primary purpose of controlling entry was to limit or prohibit competition in interstate commerce, a purpose which the Court found to be forbidden by the Commerce Clause of the Constitution. State action in determining whether competition should be prohibited was determined by a standard which the Court found to be essentially federal in nature—the existence of adequate facilities for conducting interstate commerce. Oregon would have permitted the operation proposed by Buck, a circumstance which aggravated the obstruction to interstate commerce by the state of Washington.

As generally interpreted, *Buck v. Kuykendall* not only wiped out state controls on entry for motor carriers engaged in interstate commerce, but also invalidated state requirements respecting insurance and standards of service. Thus, the net effect of the decision was to confine regulation of interstate motor carrier transportation to the area of state police powers: motor vehicle safety and highway construction.

At the time of the decision in *Buck v. Kuykendall*, some 40 states prohibited motor common carriers of passengers from using their highways without a certificate obtained by a showing that the involved service is required by the present or future public convenience and necessity. In general, state requirements for certification were imposed not only on carriers engaged in intrastate commerce, but also on those engaged exclusively in interstate commerce.

In drafting what became the Motor Carrier Act of 1935, the Congress and the Commission, in one sense, were not plowing new ground. They were filling a gap created by the Supreme Court in a long-established pattern of regulation. For that reason, perhaps, supporters of federal regulation did not produce detailed economic data or studies showing that control of entry was an essential feature of regulation. However, the legislation history of the Motor Carrier Act of 1935 contains an adequate explanation. The reasons advanced to justify entry controls are listed below in descending order of importance.

In hearings before the Senate Interstate Commerce Committee on bills which became the Motor Carrier Act of 1935, Commissioner Eastman, testifying as the Federal Coordinator of Transportation, said:

The most important thing, I think, is the prevention of an oversupply of transportation; in other words, an oversupply which will sap and weaken the transportation system rather than strengthen it. . . . The States have, I think, in all cases, found the necessity in their regulation of motor transportation to provide for that prevention of an oversupply by . . . the granting of certificates or permits.[19]

The Motor Carrier Act of 1935 provided that no motor carrier may lawfully engage in operations in interstate or foreign commerce "unless there is in force with respect to such carrier a certificate of public convenience and necessity issued by the Commission authorizing such operations."[20]

In 1935, the railroads were fully regulated and recognized to be a sick industry. Many argued that it was unfair to burden the railroads with comprehensive regulation, while turning the trucks loose to take the cream of their commerce, and then expect them to offer comparable service.

In *Coordination of Motor Transportation*,[21] the Commission concluded:

1. That there is substantial competition between rail and water carriers on the one hand and motor carriers on the other for the transportation of both passengers and freight and that this competition is increasing;

2. That such competition is conducted under conditions of inequality, particularly in regard to regulation.[22]

It was obviously unfair to continue to regulate rail carriers without enacting a similar system of regulation for motor carriers of passengers.

Proponents of regulation also stressed the inequity in subjecting intrastate motor carriers to full economic regulation while permitting interstate carriers to be wholly unregulated.

At various times in the debate on federal regulation of interstate motor carriers, the value of a certificate of public convenience and necessity as an enforcement tool was recognized. State regulatory commissions, for example, could suspend or revoke the operating authority of a carrier for failure to provide reasonable, adequate service or for wanton disregard of safety regulations. Prior to 1935, the public was frequently victimized by unscrupulous brokers of passenger transportation acting in concert with unregulated interstate carriers. The solution adopted in the Motor Carrier Act of 1935 was to prohibit brokers from using carriers not authorized by a certificate of public convenience and necessity to engage in interstate commerce.

Congress was concerned about the failure of unregulated interstate carriers to observe schedules; to perform the service promised to the public; to provide liability insurance; to make restitution for loss of baggage; and generally to provide reasonably adequate service. The Commission, however, found in its report in 1928, in *Motor Bus and Motor Truck Operation*,[23] that intercity bus service "on regularly certified routes is generally satisfactory throughout the country." The Commission also found that "wildcatters" were cutting fares below compensatory levels and engaging in reprehensible practices which discredited bus travel in the eyes of the general public. Congress and the Commission concluded that these reprehensible practices would be eliminated by federal legislation of the type eventually enacted as the Motor Carrier Act of 1935, but neither body considered whether such practices could be prevented if virtually unrestricted entry were permitted. In any event, the Commission and Congress believed that entry controls were a useful adjunct to regulation, having as their ultimate objective a reliable and efficient system of motor transport.

1. Legislative History of the 1935 Act

The concern of the states with respect to the failure of the federal government to regulate motor carrier transportation was significant in prompting the Congress to promulgate the Motor Carrier Act of 1935 and pervaded the debates in both the Senate and the House of Representatives.[24] In explaining the effect of the lack of federal regulation of motor carriers, Senator Wheeler reported that "the absence of such regulations has in some instances created chaotic conditions beyond the control of any state or municipal body."[25] In discussing the controls or restraints placed upon the Commission, Senator Wheeler advised the Senate that "section 202 (a) of the pending bill . . . makes clear that the policy of the Congress is to deal fairly and impartially with transportation by motor carriers and to preserve the natural advantages of such transportation."[26] He also described the fear on the part of some bus and truck operators that the Commission would not deal with them fairly and said that to safeguard these operators:

we specifically wrote into the bill, in the declaration of policy provision, and at other places throughout the bill, that the peculiar features of transportation by truck and by bus should be taken into consideration at all times by the declaration of policy.
  The exercise of authority by the Commission under certain sections of the bill is directly related to the declaration of policy and in the added provisions with respect to discrimination, preference, and unfair or destructive competitive practices lay a stronger and more definite basis for administrative action.[27]

The debate concerning Senate Bill 1629 in the House of Representatives was led by Representative Sadowski. He described the hearings and the testimony taken by the Interstate and Foreign Commerce Committee of the House and the reports of the state utility commissions and stated:

It is self-evident that there is a positive need for interstate regulation of motor carriers. Legislation over interstate motor carriers, to be practical, must conform with the principles of regulation now in effect in the 48 States which regulate contract carriers. The State commissions have asked Congress to pass this bill so that there may be harmony between states as to motor carrier regulation and since 1926 Congress has had before it legislation of this character.[28]

Representative Sadowski acknowledged that "the purpose of this bill is to provide for transportation that will foster and develop sound economic conditions in the industry, together with other forms of transportation so that highway transportation will always progress."[29]

Finally, Representative Sadowski noted that states are empowered to grant or deny the use of their public highways but cannot regulate operations of interstate motor carriers. The hiatus of regulation resulted in abuses and problems for the state and federally regulated transportation services. He stated:

In the case of *Buck v. Kuykendall* the court held that a State could not regulate motor carriers operating in interstate commerce, and that the matter of control of carriers in interstate commerce was entirely in the hands of Congress to provide for Federal regulation.

Their decision left the door wide open. It permitted all sorts of abuses by irresponsible operators at the expense of the intrastate motor carriers and other transportation agencies who were under strict State and Federal regulation.[30]

Not surprisingly, it was evident throughout the debate that strong pressure for the enactment of the legislation was coming from the states that were affected by the absence of regulation over the interstate transportation. It was observed that "the regulatory bodies of the various states which are grouped together in a national organization, composed of the 48 state commissions, have investigated this subject. All of the state commissions out of vast experience they have had, are now calling upon this Congress to pass this bill."

BUCK V. KUYKENDALL

267 U. S. 307 (1925)

Mr. Justice Brandeis delivered the opinion of the Court.

Buck, a citizen of Washington, wished to operate an auto stage line over the Pacific Highway between Seattle, Washington and Portland, Oregon, as a common carrier for hire exclusively for through interstate passengers and express. He obtained from Oregon the license prescribed by its laws. Having complied with the laws of Washington relating to motor vehicles, their owners and drivers (*Carlsen v. Cooney*, 123 Wash. 441), and alleging willingness to comply with all applicable regulations concerning common carriers, Buck applied there for the prescribed certificate of public convenience and necessity. It was refused. The ground for refusal was that, under the laws of the State, the certificate may not be granted for any territory which is already being adequately served by the holder of a certificate; and that, in addition to frequent steam railroad service, adequate transportation facilities between Seattle and Portland were already being provided by means of four connecting auto stage lines, all of which held such certificates from the State of Washington. . . . To enjoin interference by its officials with the operation of the projected line, Buck brought this suit against Kuykendall, the Director of Public Works.

A citizen may have, under the Fourteenth Amendment, the right to travel and transport his property upon [state highways] by auto vehicle. But he has no right to make the highways his place of business by using them as a common carrier for hire. Such use is a privilege which may be granted or withheld by the State in its discretion, without violating either the due process clause or the equal protection clause. *Packare v. Banton*, 264 U.S. 140, 144. The highways belong to the State. It may make provision appropriate for securing the safety and convenience of the public in the use of them. *Kane v. New Jersey*, 242 U.S. 160. It may impose fees with a view both to raising funds to defray the cost of supervision and maintenance and to obtaining compensation for the use of the road facilities provided. *Hendrick v. Maryland*, 235 U.S. 610. See also *Pierce Oil Corporation v. Hopkins*, 264 U.S. 137. With the increase in number and size of the vehicles used upon a highway, both the danger and the wear and tear grow. To exclude unnecessary vehicles—particularly the large ones commonly used by carriers for hire—promotes both safety and economy. State regulation of that character is valid even as applied to interstate commerce, in the absence of legislation by Congress which deals specifically with the subject.

The primary purpose of provision here in question is not regulation with a view to safety or to conservation of the highways, but the prohibition of competition. It determines not the manner of use, but the persons by whom the highways may be used. It prohibits such use to some persons while permitting it to others for the same purpose and in the same manner. Moreover, it determines whether the prohibition shall be applied by resort, through state officials, to a test which is peculiarly within the province of federal action—the existence of adequate facilities for conducting interstate commerce. The vice of the legislation is dramatically exposed by the fact that the State of Oregon had issued its certificate which may be deemed equivalent to a legislative declaration that, despite existing facilities, public convenience and necessity required the establishment by Buck of the auto stage line between Seattle and Portland. Thus, the provision of the Washington statute is a regulation, not of the use of its own highways, but of interstate commerce. Its effect upon such commerce is not merely to burden but to obstruct it. Such state action is forbidden by the Commerce Clause. It also defeats the purpose of Congress expressed in the legislation giving federal aid for the construction of interstate highways.

2. The Motor Carrier Act of 1980

The Motor Carrier Act of 1980 was signed into law by President Jimmy Carter on July 1, 1980.[31] This event was the culmination of a long and controversial effort to reform economic regulation (e.g., regulation of entry, prices and quality of service) of the interstate for-hire motor trucking industry. It was the first substantial change in the federal regulatory system for motor trucking since the enactment of the Motor Carrier Act of 1935, which instituted federal economic regulation.

From its inception in 1935, there was criticism of federal economic regulation of motor trucking, principally on the grounds that the industry (1) was comprised of a large number of relatively small carriers, (2) was basically "competitive," and (3) had none of the characteristics of "public utility"-type industries that were usually deemed proper candidates for economic regulation.[32] However, the ICC, which was given the task of carrying out the regulatory system established by Congress, proceeded to establish and develop an elaborate system of regulation.

Efforts to reform the system began to show life in the early 1970s, when the U.S. Department of Transportation (DOT) and the President demonstrated serious interest in general transportation regulatory reform (not just in motor trucking), and ultimately, important members of Congress joined the movement. In the meantime, the ICC, with strong support from the Carter administration, substantially reinterpreted the law in favor of reduced regulation.[33] The bill that was signed by President Carter in July 1980 was the result of a three-year legislative battle.

Contributing to the eventual success of the reform movement, in addition to the support of the executive branch and the personal support of the President and the support of the ICC, were (1) the alleged connection between economic regulation of motor trucking and energy use inefficiency and inflation; (2) the strength of the consumer movement, which was anti-transportation regulation (but pro-regulation of consumer safety and other consumer matters); (3) prior success in enacting airline regulatory reform; and (4) the anti-government, anti-regulation sentiment in the country.

Beginning with the Ford administration and continuing through the Carter regime, inflation became the principal concern of the American political economy.[34] Increased competition was considered to be a weapon to use against the inflationary forces surrounding us. Regulated industries could pass on increased costs of equipment, fuel and labor by going to the appropriate regulatory agency and gaining permission to increase rates.

Increased competition, however, could act as a brake on these automatic cost pass-throughs. Trucking, with relatively low entry costs, seemed to be a good place to introduce more competition. New, lean operations should have less fixed costs than the established truckers.

There was a decided move within the ICC toward liberalizing entry for motor carriers. Frivolous objections by protestants went unheeded; the Commission began to take a more liberal view about the need for a proposed service. It may have been that ICC commissioners, seeing the handwriting on the wall, moved in the direction of liberalizing entry before Congress abolished the whole works.

What emerged from the Congress was not a deregulation bill, but a law which provided new standards, not termination, for the ICC. The congressional finding section states that, in some cases, existing regulation has been counterproductive, that the ICC should be given explicit direction and well-defined parameters for regulation of the motor carrier industry and that the ICC should not attempt to go beyond the power vested in it by the Interstate Commerce Act.[35] The Act is not a new departure, but a codification of much of what the ICC had done in the past decade. Politically, it was a product of a compromise between advocates of deregulation and those who favored reregulation.

The new Act adds to the National Transportation Policy the promotion of competitive and efficient transportation service in order to (1) meet the needs of shippers, receivers and consumers; (2) allow a variety of price and service options; (3) allow the most productive use of equipment and energy resources; (4) allow adequate profits and fair wages; (5) provide and maintain a privately owned motor carrier system; (7) promote minority participation; and (8) promote intermodal transportation.[36]

The Motor Carrier Act of 1980 substantially leaves the ICC intact. It gives new guidance to that agency and exempts a number of areas for service. It makes entry easier and makes it more difficult for certificated carriers to protect their market share. It may make some operating rights worthless. But it does not abolish the common carrier principle or the binding effects of tariff. It keeps, in modified form, the test of public convenience and necessity and preserves the necessary oversight function of the ICC.

3. The Household Goods Transportation Act of 1980

A sidelight after the massive deregulation effort of 1980 with regard to motor carriers was passage of the Household Goods Transportation Act of 1980.[37,38] The dynamics of moving van companies are different from those of carriers of general freight. The shipper is not a business entity, but often an individual householder. Since he only uses the service of moving vans two or three times, on the average, he is usually inexperienced in dealing with such companies.

The moving concerns are geared to hauling government shipments (often for relocating personnel changing posts in the military) or handling large moves by corporations. Here, the company or government agency has a certain amount of power to wield in steering traffic to or from another moving company. There is some equality of bargaining power here, and the companies are more conscientious about dealing with these large institutional accounts.

The companies, such as Allied, Mayflower and North American, are actually only loosely affiliated with the local agents and often have not been quick to respond to abuses by such agents. The main consumer complaint has been "low-balling," by which an agent would quote an unreasonably low price in order to gain traffic. Once the shipper signed with the moving company, the tariff principle was strictly applied; no deviation from the tariff was possible, there could be no rebates, and payment must be in cash, cashier's check, or certified check. Otherwise, the furniture would be carted off to a warehouse, where storage fees would accrue. The customer had no choice but the chase around a strange town for his money.

Since house moving affected members of the public at large, the ICC received an enormous number of complaints about movers. The ICC tried to meet the situation through rule making. The rules which emerged required the shipper to pay an amount more or less equivalent to the estimate and gave him time to get up the rest of the cash. But the Commission was unwilling to do away with the tariff principle, and further legislation was necessary to deal with the problem.

The Household Goods Transportation Act is a clarification of ICC authority in home moving. It establishes the authority of the ICC to permit carriers to establish rates which are based upon binding estimates and guaranteed pick-up and delivery times.[39] This simple, matter-of-fact statement restores the principle of estoppel to transportation law. The mover can quote an estimate of price and schedule, and the company will be bound by it.

The new law establishes the responsibility of the nation-wide moving van lines for the acts of their agents. It requires that agents be fit and establishes a tighter control of the arrangements between the agents and the national companies. To this extent, it now confers antitrust immunity on certain discussions between agents and the moving companies.[40] Reaffirming the ICC authority to protect consumers, it establishes statutory guidelines for a dispute settlement program involving shippers and carriers. Previously, the ICC had balked at the idea of becoming a "small claims court."

The philosophy of the Household Goods Act is the opposite of that of the Motor Carrier Act. Here, Congress felt that competition should be coupled by increased oversight. Congress also declared that the function of the ICC was to protect the homeowner and the small shipper. Evidently, the disparity in bargaining position between the shipper and carrier is responsible for the different concern toward moving vans. It also should be remembered that Congress attempted to meet a major criticism that was voiced about the regulatory scheme of the Motor Carrier Act and enacted a specific consumer-oriented regulatory law.

4. The Bus Regulatory Reform Act of 1982

After the substantial rollback in regulation of trains, trucks and airplanes, and with barge traffic being largely in the exempt sector, the intercity bus industry remained the only common carrier which had not been substantially deregulated.

Buses provide a low-cost, energy-efficient passenger system which serves more stations than any other carrier.[41] Of the major passenger carriers, the intercity bus caters to the least-affluent travelers, who have few other options and are the least likely to protect themselves.

For this and other reasons, Congress was slow to deregulate intercity bus carriers. Until 1982, they operated under the Motor Carrier Act of 1935. On September 20, 1982, President Reagan signed into law the Bus Regulatory Reform Act of 1982, giving bus companies substantial new freedoms of entry, exit and rate making.

Bus companies providing contract, charter and special operations service now need only prove their fitness in order to operate in new markets or serve towns that have lost other passenger service.

The ICC must grant an application for new regular-route bus service unless a competing carrier can prove that the new service is inconsistent with the public interest (including the effect on small communities, and whether a grant would harm a competitor's ability to provide its own regular-route service).

The new law effectively deregulates the passenger tour-broker industry and automatically removes restrictions on bus-operating authorities. The ICC is also required to remove closed-door restrictions unless allowing local service to an intercity carrier would put a commuter bus line out of business.

The 1982 Act eliminates the ICC's investigation and suspension power over special and charter service rates, while giving bus companies an expanded zone of rate-making freedom. Since 1985, the ICC has been prohibited from suspending or investigating any rates unless they are collectively established or deemed predatory or discriminatory. Single-line rate-making immunity ended on January 1, 1983, and joint-line antitrust immunity ended on January 1, 1984.

The ICC may also preempt state rulings on intrastate bus rates if the involved carrier has asked for state action and the state fails to act on its proposal within four months. States may no longer take action against intrastate schedule changes or rate reductions that are part of interstate routes. But the preemption provision does not apply to rates of solely intrastate carriers, or with respect to carriers that are owned or controlled by a state or local government.

State decisions to prevent a carrier from leaving an intrastate market may also be preempted by the ICC. A bus company may apply to the agency to discontinue serving intrastate portions of an interstate route if the state denies the carrier's request for discontinuance or fails to act within 120 days. The public has no corresponding right of appeal.

If ICC authority has been issued to a bus company prior to August 1, the ICC must allow the carrier to discontinue intrastate service unless a protestant can prove public harm or that the involved service is not an "unreasonable burden on interstate commerce."[42]

C. Origins of Air Regulation

The legislative history of the Civil Aeronautics Act of 1938, the predecessor of the Federal Aviation Act of 1958, reveals that Congress recognized the air transport industry to be in its infancy, and believed that the existing competitive environment could, in the absence of regulation, inhibit or impede its sound development.[43] The existing air mail legislation was believed to have imposed certain undesirable influences upon the industry. Moreover, in order to avoid the deleterious consequences of "cutthroat" competition and the economic "chaos" which had plagued the rail and motor carrier industries, Congress sought to establish a regulatory structure similar to that which had been devised for those industries which had also been perceived as "public utility" types of enterprises. Such a system, it was believed, would enhance economic stability and thereby contribute to the sound economic growth and development of air transportation. It would ensure service to small communities and the protection of smaller carriers. It would not be a system of regulated competition which might prohibit the entry of new carriers. The regulatory scheme would assure adherence to the highest standards of safety and would satisfy the needs of commerce, the public interest and the national defense.

The air transportation industry was perceived by Congress to be in its infancy[44] and, potentially, of such fundamental importance to the national economy as to require regulation for its orderly development and economic growth.[45] The Senate Commerce Committee expressed serious concern with the "intensive," "extreme," and "destructive" competition in which all transport modes were engaged; such an economic environment was having injurious effects upon the industry and its ability adequately to provide the service required to satisfy the needs of commerce, the public interest and the national defense. By establishing a system for the orderly development of air transportation analogous to that employed in the regulation of public utilities and other modes of transportation, it was believed that these deleterious consequences could be avoided.

Among the differences faced by air carriers prior to 1938 was an inability to attract sufficient investment capital. It was argued that the order and stability ensured by public regulation would create a situation in which this inability would be diminished. Indeed, government regulation was viewed as fundamental to the creation of an economic environment of sufficient order and stability to ensure the attraction of capital sufficient to maintain the requisite growth of the aviation industry.

Among the difficulties which the pending legislation sought to alleviate were those arising under the existing structure of air mail legislation. In 1918, air mail service was inaugurated by the Army. The Kelly Act (Air Mail Act of 1925) established economically feasible commercial air transportation autonomous from the military by permitting the Postmaster General to award contracts to private air lines for the movement of mail. The Air Commerce Act of 1926 vested jurisdiction over safety and the maintenance of airways and navigation facilities in the Secretary of Commerce. The McNary-Waters Act of 1930 established a formula for air mail payments based upon the amount of mail transported. Congressional discontent with the administration of this legislation by the Postmaster General led to an investigation by a Senate Special Committee chaired by Senator Hugo Black. The outrageous activities revealed by this investigation led President Roosevelt to respond by terminating all existing air mail contracts on the grounds that there had been collusion between air carriers and the Post Office Department in route and rate establishment.

The legislative history also reveals a concern that the past unfortunate economic experience of surface carriers might be repeated in the air transport industry. The Great Depression was an era of economic upheaval and uncertainty during which the fatality level of business was accentuated. Certain industries were deemed so fundamental to the existence of a sound national economy that the federal government intervened to regulate competition, restore order and diminish the uncertainty which prevailed. Among those industries perceived as essential to recovery and therefore entitled to the benefits of "public utility" regulation was that of transportation. In 1935, Congress promulgated the Motor Carrier Act, which established federal regulation of motor carrier entry and rates and placed such jurisdiction in the ICC (which already held extensive regulatory authority over rail carriers).[46]

A representative of the National Association of Railroad and Utilities Commissioners testified:

Any important public-utility industry requires regulation in the public interest and will be regulated sooner or later. . . . The full purpose of regulation can be accomplished only by regulation from the beginning of the development of the industry. . . .

Congress must establish such conditions that there may be an encouraged development of the aircraft business . . . and create conditions—and this is of paramount importance—which will avoid the wastes and losses which will be inevitable if the business is left to struggle to establish itself in open competition.[47]

In light of the economically catastrophic experience of other transport modes, it was believed that regulation might ensure that such consequences might be avoided for the air transport industry. A system of economic regulation was envisioned which would avoid the consequences of excessive competition. In fact, the legislative history repeatedly reveals that destructive competition was among the injurious activities to which the Act was addressed.

The Federal Aviation Commission, which was established by the Black-McKellar Act of 1934, contended that the orderly development of air transportation required two fundamental ingredients. First, in the interest of safety, certain minimum standards of equipment, operating methods and personnel qualifications should be maintained. Second, "there should be a check in development of any irresponsible, unfair, or excessive competition such as has sometimes hampered the progress of other forms of transport." However, it was never maintained that competition among carriers should be prohibited.

Congressman Randolph contended that "unbridled and unregulated competition is a public menace," citing as examples that the air transportation industry was then subjected to such unfortunate economic conditions as "rate wars, cutthroat devices, and destructive and wasteful practices." Other congressmen emphasized that the legislation was intended to inhibit or prohibit monopolization in the industry.

Legislation deregulating domestic all-cargo service was introduced in March 1977 in the form of H.B. 6010, which was signed into law on November 9, 1977, as Public Law 95–163.[48] The significant features of the bill were those dealing with air freight service added to the bill by the Senate. This law eliminated Civil Aeronautics Board (CAB) authority over all-cargo service and sharply reduced the Board's power to control air freight rates.

With the passage of the air freight deregulation bill, a free market began in the 48 contiguous states, with one year's head start for the grandfathered carriers. The air freight industry now has no restrictions on entry, route or rates. Many new carriers have entered the air freight business. There is no lack of competition. The number of flights and carriers have increased, but so have prices. Trends in the air freight industry show a weakening of the principle of common carrier liability for shipments and an abandonment of the tariff principle. The air freight industry is no longer considered an infant needing protection, but the consumer has no protection against high costs of shipment. Nor has the small businessman any right to equal treatment with the large shipper who is a major customer of the cargo airline.

The Airline Deregulation Act of 1978 not only amends, but virtually replaces the economic regulation provisions of the Federal Aviation Act of 1958 in what is surely the most comprehensive overhaul of a government regulatory scheme in history. The preamble states that the purpose of the Act is to foster an air transportation system which relies on minimally restricted competition to determine the quality, variety, and cost of air services. In fact, the Act is intended to remove to the greatest possible extent the government control of air carriers.[49]

Not only does the act call for relaxation of regulation of entry and tariff restrictions, but it also mandates that the authority of the CAB shall be transferred to other agencies or done away with altogether.

The Airline Deregulation Act of 1978[50] is a unique piece of legislation in that in its efforts to deregulate the air transport industry, the Act also provides for the suspension of jurisdiction of the CAB in some areas and the eventual dismantling of the CAB by 1985. These provisions are codified under the section titled "Termination of Civil Aeronautics Board and transfer of certain 'functions,' "[51] but they are more commonly referred to as the "Sunset Provisions."

Under these "Sunset Provisions," the Board's authority to issue certificates on the basis of consistency with the public convenience or necessity for interstate, overseas and foreign air transportation ended on December 31, 1981. Certificated carriers with the above-mentioned certificates will be able to enter the charter business at this time, and exit restrictions, except for those involving "essential services," have been dropped. Virtually all the Board's rate-making authority terminated on January 1, 1983.

Other "Sunset Provisions" touch the area of transferring CAB authority to other departments and the preparation of a review study concerning the effects of the new Act.

Certain elements of the Board's authority is to be carried on by other Federal departments beginning January 1, 1985. The Department of Transportation will handle foreign transportation (in consultation with the Department of State) and compensation for providing essential air transportation.[52]

The first law closing down a major independent regulatory agency scheduled the CAB to self-destruct according to the following timetable:

1. Regulation over certificates for carriers ended on December 31, 1981.
2. Regulation of rates ended on January 1, 1983.
3. On January 1, 1985, the following functions were transferred to the Department of Transportation:
   A. Regulation of foreign air transportation.
   B. Compensation to carriers for essential air transportation to small communities.
   C. Mergers and cooperative working arrangements.[53]

Among the governmental responsibilities which remain after regulation leaves the skies is antitrust. One section of the Act narrows the class of transactions which must be approved by the CAB:

Where formerly any consolidation, merger, or acquisition involving a person engaged in "any phase of aeronautics" was prohibited unless approved by the Board after notice and hearing, the new Act replaces this broadly interpreted phrase with a narrower class of "persons substantially engaged in the business of aeronautics."[54]

D. Water Carrier Regulation

1. Maritime Law

The industry which carries goods and people by sea was the first to enjoy a special body of law administered by a specialized tribunal.[55] In England, for centuries, there were special courts to determine cases involving "a thing done upon the sea," and by the time of the American Revolution, a body of maritime or admiralty law had developed. Article III of the Constitution extended the judicial power of the United States to "all cases of admiralty and maritime jurisdiction." Thus, admiralty law became federal law, and the federal courts deciding admiralty cases adopted from the beginning the generally prevailing maritime law.

This body of maritime law was, and remains to a considerable extent, law developed by tribunals deciding particular cases and is based in large part on long-standing custom and usage. Various congressional enactments and international conventions and treaties have also contributed to and altered this customary law. For example, disputes over the extent to which carriers could exculpate themselves in their bills of lading from liability for loss or damage to goods led to the enactment of the Harter Act in 1893[56] and later to the adoption, internationally, of the Hague Convention, which the United States implemented by the passage, in 1936, of the Carriage of Goods by Sea Act.[57] Other enactments, respecting recovery by seamen for injuries and recovery for wrongful death, are the Jones Act[58] and the Death on the High Seas Act,[59] both dating from 1920.

The type of maritime law just discussed might loosely be described as the private law of shipping. The ocean shipping industry is also subject to a large body of public law, the guiding purpose of which is to promote and protect an industry deemed vital to national security. From the beginning of history, nations have set about to ensure that they would have the means to move men and material in times of war. For insular countries, such as Great Britain and the United States, the existence of a healthy merchant marine has been of particular significance.

Government intervention in the industry in the United States was limited during the early years of the nation's existence, when this country's ship-building and shipping industries were essentially in good health. Governmental assistance was limited at first (in 1789) to a discriminatory tax on foreign vessels in the coasting trade. In 1817, Congress prohibited coastwise trade entirely to foreign ships, a prohibition which has lasted to the present.

During the first part of the nineteenth century and the era of the Yankee clipper, American shipping had its heyday and dominated trade between the United States and other countries. The advent of the steamship, however, shifted the competitive advantages by mid-century to British shipping and shipbuilding, as a consequence of which the American industry steadily declined. Large numbers of American ships were transferred to the British flag during the Civil War, and by 1900, the American merchant marine was utterly insignificant. This deadline, however, was apparently not regarded by Congress as a matter having any serious consequences for national defense: in any case, Congress took no significant measures during this period to restore health, or at least physical capacity, to the industry.

World War I deprived the United States of much of the foreign tonnage it had been relying on and brought about enactment of the Shipping Act of 1916, under which a regulatory board, the U.S. Shipping Board, was created and a public corporation, the Shipping Board Emergency Fleet Corporation, was set up to build, buy, charter and operate merchant vessels. In the period after the war, various direct and indirect subsidies were largely substituted for direct government operation of shipping.

In 1926, with the passage of the Merchant Marine Act,[60] a pattern of governmental policy was established which was continued to the present. The Act created the U.S. Maritime Commission to form and implement overall shipping policy. General policy was set forth in the Act itself:

It is necessary for the national defense and development of its foreign and domestic commerce that the United States shall have merchant marine (a) sufficient to carry its domestic water-borne commerce and a substantial portion of the water-borne export and import foreign commerce of the United States and to provide shipping service on all routes essential for maintaining the flow of such domestic and foreign water-borne commerce at all times, (b) capable of serving as a naval and military auxiliary in time of war or national emergency, (c) owned and operated under the United States flag by citizens of the United States in so far as may be practicable, and (d) composed of the best-equipped, safest, and most suitable types of vessels, constructed in the United States and manned with a trained and efficient citizen personnel. It is hereby declared to be the policy of the United States to foster the development and encourage the maintenance of such a merchant marine.

As a result of a series of governmental reorganizations, the original commission no longer exists. Its regulatory functions are vested in a Maritime Commission independent of the Department of Commerce, while subsidy functions are in a Maritime Administration, headed by an Assistant Secretary of Commerce for Maritime Affairs. (The Maritime Administration was transferred to the Department of Transportation in 1981.)

The 1936 Act established two kinds of subsidy programs. One, the "construction-differential subsidy," was intended to overcome the competitive disadvantage of the American shipbuilding industry resulting from high construction costs; the other, as "operating-differential subsidy," was intended to overcome the competitive disadvantages of U.S. American crews. Amendments of the Act passed in 1970 significantly altered some of the details but not the overall structure and plan of the 1936 Act.

In the regulation of rates and trade practices, the Shipping Act of 1916 exempted rates established by conferences of steamship lines from the antitrust laws and prohibited various types of "unfair" competition, particularly rebates and discrimination. The Maritime Commission now administers these provisions.

In summary, a special body of private law for the ocean-going transportation industry developed in response to the importance in that industry of

trade practices and customs peculiar to it and because of its highly international flavor; if commerce among nations was to thrive, it had to be governed by a set of rules that were fairly uniform throughout the world. The
public law of subsidization and trade regulation, on the other hand, came
about with the emergence of the United States as a world power at a time
when American shipping and shipbuilding were chronically unable to furnish
a sufficient supply of merchant vessels to satisfy military and strategic needs.

2. Vessel Conferences

A steamship conference is a voluntary agreement between ocean common
carriers "formed so that the members may agree upon rates and certain other
competitive practices."[61] Private conference agreements arose in the late
1800s when ocean carriers came to realize that survival under a purely
competitive environment was far too demanding to be further tolerated. To
eliminate such competition, conference members not only agreed upon rates,
but also frequently allocated sailing times and, on occasion, even pooled
earnings. The agreements permitted the conference members to dominate
the relevant trade, control, if not eliminate, competition and ensure that
each member received a reasonable profit on its operations.

Although blatantly anticompetitive, conference proponents did and do
argue that the conferences benefit the immediate consumer, the importer/
exporter who ships goods on the member lines. Because demand for tonnage
can vary, but the supply of that tonnage in the short term is relatively fixed,
conferences were considered necessary to eliminate "cutthroat competition."
During periods of slack demand, unrestrained competition destroys weaker
lines, thereby creating a shortage of supply when demand later picks up.
This continuing boom-to-bust cycle subjects shippers to widely varying rates
and unpredictable sailing schedules, injuring a shipper's efforts to maintain
predictable, stable business relationships with his customers overseas. Although many observers have criticized this economic model justifying the
conference monopoly, Congress, at least, has accepted it.

Congress did not, however, accept the anticompetitive abuses which resulted from the unrestrained use of the private conference system. In its
review of the conference system in 1914, Congress' Alexander Committee
cited and condemned such conference abuses as discriminatory pricing between shippers, "deferred rebate: plans designed to force shippers to use
conference lines exclusively" and "fighting-ships"—a conference-subsidized
"loss-leader" whose function was to eliminate nonconference competition by
charging abnormally low rates on the nonconference line's routes. These
abuses presented Congress with a dilemma: Should the antitrust laws be
applied with full vigor to the conferences? Banning the conferences from
U.S. foreign commerce would eliminate the abuses, but presumably, the
benefits of stability in the maritime industry would be eliminated as well.

Seeking the best of both worlds, Congress passed the Shipping Act of

1916[62] in order to grant antitrust immunity to the ocean conference system as well as to subject the conferences to a regulatory scheme that would eliminate anticompetitive conference abuses. Through Section 15 of the Shipping Act, an agreement between carriers approved by the Federal Maritime Commission would not be subject to antitrust attack.[63] Such immunity, however, was granted upon the condition that cited abuses would be properly controlled. The principal purpose of the Shipping Act was not to immunize the ocean carrier industry from the antitrust laws, but rather to create a mechanism whereby antitrust policies could be practically applied to what Congress considered to be the unique economic circumstances of the maritime industry. The Act requires the Federal Maritime Commission to enforce antitrust purposes and thereby, in effect, creates a partnership between the Commission and the courts for the purpose of subjecting the conferences to appropriate anti-trust restrictions.

3. Inland Waterway Transportation

Barge operations, which consist primarily of multiple-barge tows pushed by a power units, constitute the most significant segment of domestic water carriage; they account for approximately 11 percent of intercity freight ton mileage.[64] More than 1,250 companies provide services on a for-hire basis. Of these, approximately 70 regular-route common carriers and fewer than 50 contract carriers are regulated by the ICC. The remaining 1,100 companies operate as exempt carriers and engage in the unregulated movement of bulk and liquid commodities.

The second major component of domestic water carriage operations consists of movements on the Great Lakes. Five percent of intercity freight ton mileage moves on the Great Lakes by freighter or ferry services. About 70 commercial harbors exist on the lakes, and the traffic flow consists primarily of ore and grain movements. Opening of the St. Lawrence Seaway has provided lake ports with access to service by all but the largest oceangoing vessels and has stimulated the growth of import-export traffic.

The third component of the domestic water system is coastal (along either the Pacific coast or the Atlantic coast, or between Atlantic and Gulf Coast ports) and inter-coastal (connecting East and West Coast ports through the Panama Canal or around South America). Historically, the federal government has restricted such services to vessels that are built, owned and operated by U.S. citizens. Such stipulations, both here and abroad, are generally referred to as cabotage laws. The related guidelines that cover the U.S. situation are contained in the Jones Act (also known as the Merchant Marine Act), which was passed in 1920.

A considerable volume of coastal traffic moves by barge, with the remainder moving by regular cargo ship. Prior to World War II, 19 companies offered package and volume service on intercoastal movements. These services were interrupted by the war, and the business never really recovered.

Contributing to its decline was increasing rate and service competition from railroads, oil pipelines and motor carriers. Traffic volume moving over the intercoastal routes has dwindled, and the number of companies serving the routes has similarly contracted.

In regulating domestic water carriage, the ICC classifies carriers into three groups, based on annual gross operating revenues. Class A carriers are those with annual operating revenues in excess of $500,000; class B carriers generate operating revenues between $100,000 and $500,000; class C carriers generate annual operating revenues of less than $100,000. Commission reports indicate that in recent years the number of class A and B carriers has remained relatively constant, and that the aggregate freight revenues of these two classes have annually averaged more than $600 million.

Responsibility for the economic regulation of domestic water carriage was given to the ICC by the Transportation Act of 1940. A regulatory pattern was adopted which was quite similar to that which had been applied to the railroads. Major provisions of the act stipulate regulation of the following aspects of the industry: entry into common and contract carriage, common carrier rate making (contract carriers must publish minimum rates only) and carrier mergers.

However, a significant difference exists between the regulation of railroads and water carriage in that all water carriers of bulk commodities are exempt from regulation provided that not more than three commodities are carried in the same vessel or tow. Liquid cargo movements are similarly exempt from regulation. The combined effect of these exemptions and the existence of private carriage is that only 8 percent of domestic water carriage traffic is subject to ICC regulation. In 1978, in an action which was quite consistent with its movement toward administrative deregulation, the ICC proposed almost complete elimination of its regulation of the inland water carrier industry. Shortly after this ICC announcement, the DOT formally suggested elimination of such regulation to Congress. While the Commission took no immediate steps to bring about this change, the proposal prompted considerable debate and raised many questions concerning the likelihood of the continuation of such regulations in the 1980s.

The U.S. Coast Guard, now a component of the federal Department of Transportation, enforces federal maritime safety regulations and is charged with provision of navigational aids. It is also responsible for enforcing the antipollution laws that apply to the waterway system.

E. Pipeline Regulation

In 1906, the Hepburn Act had placed oil pipelines in interstate commerce under the ICC.[65] This policy was adopted because Congress had been distressed at the stranglehold which the major oil companies had over the pipeline business. The major companies would buy oil from the independents and transport it in their pipelines, leaving the independent operator relatively helpless in dealing with the pipeline owners. Congress believed that requiring pipeline operators to charge just and reasonable rates would balance the market dominance of the pipeline operators. ICC regulation of the nation's pipeline system seemed a sensible parallel to that agency's regulation of rail, river and highway transport of oil.

Pipelines are a mode of transportation: a substance is physically transported from one place to another on a fixed right of way owned by the operator. Because pipelines have many characteristics of a natural monopoly, high capital expenses and decreasing unit costs, a single operator of a pipeline is often the most efficient way of carrying on the business. Petroleum producers built pipelines as adjuncts to their principal business of producing and selling petroleum products. Once the high initial cost of building a pipeline was incurred, there was little point in building another line because the pipeline could handle most of the petroleum produced by the oil company. Demand for regulation arose from independent oil companies who felt that the Standard Oil Company's dominance of the oil pipeline business was ruinous to their financial health or existence. But because of the nature of this transportation position, pipelines remained in a monopoly position, despite the fact that permission from the ICC was unnecessary for the construction of such a line.

The ICC had never sought its regulatory power, never possessed the requisite expertise over pipeline operation and devoted a small proportion of its time to such regulation. With the formation of the Energy Department, the decision was made to concentrate most regulatory functions in one cohesive department. The Federal Energy Regulatory Commission within the Department of Energy controls rate and valuation of pipelines, gas and electricity.

Some residual jurisdiction over pipelines still remains in the ICC. Through section 10501 of the Interstate Commerce Act, the ICC still has jurisdiction over coal slurry pipelines and their rates, charges and valuation. Other commodities which may in the future utilize pipelines will come under the jurisdiction of the ICC.

The switch to the Department of Energy was the work of a Congress which had finally decided to treat oil pipelines as an energy problem rather than as a transportation problem. The ICC, as a transportation agency, was unsuited for handling the problems of an integrated industry and chose instead to treat the pipelines as carriers similar to railroads or truck lines. Given the mandate received from Congress in 1906, it would have been difficult to do otherwise. The problem of control of the pipelines has never been effectively faced, and the Federal Energy Regulatory Commission is simply charged with following the same type of regulation that the ICC has handled. It may be that economies of scale have made pipelines a natural monopoly best run by the producers of oil products. But recognition of this economic state of affairs seems to have been made by default, as there has never been any legislative mandate to break up the industry or to approve of its present form.

1. Coal Slurry Pipelines

Energy and transportation have long been interdependent. Transport services cannot be provided without fuel; and energy resources located in remote regions of the planet could not be consumed without transportation to bring them to market.[66] Both energy and transportation are industries which have been rigidly regulated by government for some time; both are now entering a new era in which the governmental presence appears to be in a state of flux, subsiding in some areas and increasing in others.

The future of our national energy policy rests on a foundation of coal— the United States has enough coal to last 600 years at current consumption levels.[67] Among the problems which must be resolved for the increased utilization of this abundant fuel are those of the environment and those of transportation.

Although more than 70 percent of this nation's coal reserves lies east of the Mississippi, western coal is viewed as particularly attractive because of its low sulfur content and its proximity to the surface.[68] The mining of these reserves is perceived as a promising opportunity for rail carriers, which presently transport two-thirds of all coal movements. Coal is the single most important commodity to rail transportation, representing almost 30 percent of its traffic volume and 13 percent of rail revenues.[69] The ICC has identified more than 1,000 miles of potential new rail sites in Montana, Utah, Wyoming and New Mexico alone.[70]

But the least expensive and most efficient means of transporting large quantities of coal over long distances is to first mix pulverized coal with water to form a slurry and then pump the slurry through pipelines to its destination. Pipelines have traditionally carried the "lion's share" of our nation's crude oil; but more recently, they have made important inroads into the refined petroleum market and threaten to take a significant portion of the coal market from rail. Pipelines are more attractive than rail for the simple reason that the pipelines have lower unit costs for high-volume movements. These lower costs are attributable to the fact that (1) pipelines are particularly well suited for unidirectional movements, while rail transport must include movement of rail equipment, and the shipper frequently must bear the cost of a return movement of empty equipment back to the point of origin; (2) the technology of pipelines makes them ideally suited for automation (during 1976, pipeline transportation represented more than two-thirds as many ton miles as rail but with only one-thirteenth the number of employees); and (3) once constructed, pipeline costs are relatively fixed, making them highly resistant to inflation and an attractive long-term investment.

Two coal slurry pipelines have been constructed in the United States. The first was built in 1957 and ran from Cadiz, Ohio, to a point on Lake Erie. It was deactivated in 1963 because of the introduction of unit coal trains and sharply reduced rail rates. The second has been operating since 1970 (between a mine in Arizona and a power plant in Nevada) but transports only 5 million tons a year, or less than 1 percent of total domestic production.

Several new coal slurry pipelines have been proposed, but rail carriers have blocked construction by refusing to sell pipelines access across rail right-of-ways. However, slurry investors have already obtained the support of a number of state legislatures in the acquisition of access by means of eminent domain.

The rail industry has opposed coal slurry pipeline construction because of the importance coal would otherwise play in relieving rail's contemporary unfavorable financial posture. In 1977, all class I railroads earned only 1.26 percent rate of return on an average net investment in rail plant of $28 billion. Net ordinary income totaled $283.5 million, and return on net worth was only 1.8 percent. It has been argued that "slurry pipeline development could have a devastating effect on the marginal segments of the railroad industry"[71]

One proposed slurry pipeline promised the movement of 25 million tons of Wyoming coal a year to power plants in Arkansas, Louisiana and Mississippi, if governmental approval was conferred.[72] This single pipeline would have transported the equivalent of 225,000 rail carloads and could have diverted a quarter of a billion dollars annually away from rail transport.[73]

Environmental opposition also stands as a significant hurdle to coal slurry growth. Current technology requires one ton of water for every ton of coal, and many of the western states have limited supplies and sources of water. Many coal development areas are already predicted to suffer water deficits beyond existing legal limits of supply, even without slurry development. For example, Gillette, Wyoming, predicts a deficit of more than 100,000 acre-feet per year by the end of the century—this, even assuming no slurry consumption.[74] At the discharge end of the slurry system, pollution problems arise under the Federal Water Pollution Control Act surrounding reuse and discharge of waste waters which may be acidic and substandard, if not toxic.[75] Considerations of federal energy policy also require an analysis of the competition for scarce western water supplies in the development of alternative western energy resources.

F. The Federal Role In The Transportation Infrastructure

The national transportation bill—the total cost of all private and government (excluding military) spending for transportation equipment and services—amounts to about $500 U.S. 'billion' per year.[76] The National Transportation Policy Study Commission has estimated that total private and government spending on transportation from 1975 through 2000 will exceed

$14 *trillion*. The federal government alone spent about $24 *billion* in 1981 on transportation-related agencies and programs, excluding its own purchases of transportation goods and services. These cost estimates actually understate the impact of transportation on our society, since they exclude the indirect social and environmental costs of accidental deaths and injuries, environmental pollution, urban sprawl, reduced mobility for the elderly and handicapped and dependence on foreign energy sources.

Federal, state and local governments have many responsibilities regarding transportation. Federal responsibilities include:

—Promoting the development of an efficient and accessible national transportation system.

—Encouraging fair competition and protecting the public from abuse of monopoly power.

—Protecting the safety of travelers and cargo.

—Balancing environmental, social and energy goals with transportation needs.

The cost of mass transit has grown dramatically in recent years, while farebox revenues have not kept pace and productivity has declined. Increasing levels of federal, state and local government assistance have been needed to sustain transit operations during this period. Indications are that the amount of federal assistance for mass transit will not be increased and may decline. Major issues continue to face mass transit.

—Controlling transit cost.

—Improving transit productivity.

—Increasing transit revenues.

—Minimizing the cost impacts of federal requirements.

—Adopting less costly public transportation alternatives than traditional scheduled fixed-route service.

—Funding mass transit operating deficits.

Although most transit systems are no longer losing riders and many have shown ridership gains, the cost of providing mass transit service has increased substantially. So have operating deficits, which exceeded $3 billion in 1980 and are expected to continue to increase.

During the late 1970s, concerns over energy problems generated proposals to expand mass transit capacities so that more commuters could travel by transit during peak hours. However, the expansion may add to transit operating deficits and increase the need for government subsidies. In response to increasing deficits, the transit industry is being challenged to be more productive and effective and to recover a greater portion of their costs from the farebox. Increasing transit productivity, efficiency and farebox revenues is complicated by many factors: (1) increasing transit fares could negatively affect transit ridership, which the transit industry has been encouraged to increase; (2) poor transit productivity is often the result of inefficient labor practices called for in union contracts, which are difficult to change because of federally mandated labor protection requirements; and (3) federal requirements for full accessibility to transit systems for the elderly and the handicapped and specifications for mass transit vehicles add to the cost of mass transit, making it difficult for transit operators to control costs. Thus, what to finance is an important issue in mass transit. Another issue is the appropriate roles and functions of federal, state and local governments in funding, managing and regulating mass transit.

After almost a decade of direct federal financial intervention, brought about initially by the financial collapse of the Penn Central and six other northeastern railroads in 1970, railroading remains a troubled industry. Two of the country's largest railroads, the Milwaukee and the Rock Island, have gone bankrupt. The Rock Island has ceased operations, and the Milwaukee is being reorganized and greatly reduced. The rate of return for the industry, as a whole, has been extremely low for many years, and even the most profitable railroads do not consistently earn rates of return comparable to other industries. The federal government has spent more than $5 billion to acquire the properties of bankrupt railroads in the Northeast to operate and improve the region's rail service under the Consolidated Rail Corporation (Conrail).

The fundamental problems that brought the railroads to this present state are unchanged, except in the regulatory area. The Staggers Rail Act of 1980 made many changes in federal regulation of railroads' rates and services, but it is too early to tell how much the railroads will benefit from these changes. Meanwhile, the railroads continue to face the problems of obsolete and deteriorated track, facilities and equipment caused by inadequate earnings. This problem in turn results in poor service to shippers, encouraging them to seek other modes of transportation, which further reduces railroad earnings. The recession of the early 1980s further exacerbated the railroads' economic problems.

Regardless of their problems, the railroads remain an indispensable part of our transportation system, and their importance may grow as an efficient system for moving bulk commodities, such as grain and coal. In addition, the railroads seem to be the best way to carry hazardous materials, such as chlorine and liquefied natural gas.

Americans' love affair with the automobile has provided our society with a lifestyle and freedom of movement enjoyed nowhere else in the world. The private automobile remains the mainstay in the movement of people. Automobiles and buses provide the overwhelming majority of passenger transportation. Motor vehicles, from the small pickup truck and van to the huge, heavy-duty 18-wheeler, also carry a large portion of freight. The U.S.

automobile industry is a major sector of the nation's economy, and many industries support the manufacture, sale, operation and maintenance of motor vehicles. Approximately one-fifth of all U.S. workers are employed by motor vehicle-related industries.

While providing social benefits, motor vehicles also impose substantial burdens and costs on individual owners and society as a whole. For example, purchase and maintenance costs are major items in the family budget. Inadequate and faulty automobile repair is a major consumer problem. Traffic accidents kill and maim thousands and account for a multibillion-dollar national repair bill annually. Huge quantities of gasoline are consumed each day, necessitating greater reliance on foreign oil, with devastating consequences to the nation's international trade balance. Finally, tons of pollutants from engine emissions are spewed into the atmosphere each year. Consequently, these detrimental side effects of motor vehicles is vitally important to all Americans and is of continuing concern to the Congress.

A number of federal programs deal with these detrimental side effects. DOT has the authority and responsibility to (1) improve safety on the nation's highways, (2) improve automotive fuel economy, and (3) promote cost savings in owning and operating motor vehicles. The Environmental Protection Agency, under its responsibility to reduce air pollution, has the authority to regulate exhaust emissions from motor vehicles. The Federal Trade Commission (FTC), under its broad investigative and enforcement powers to stop unfair and deceptive acts and practices, addresses consumer complaints about automobile repair problems.

Americans have paid a high price for their highways. Since the 1920s, federal, state and local governments, which share the responsibility for building, maintaining and operating these highways, have spent more than $600 billion. Although sizable, this investment is small when compared with the cost of replacing the network—estimated to be from $1 trillion to $3 trillion. State and local governments have the primary responsibility for these highways, but the federal government provides aid for certain highways, called federal-aid highways, the best known of which is the Interstate Highway System. These highways constitute about one-fifth of the national highway mileage but account for nearly 80 percent of the vehicle miles traveled.

Spending for construction and maintenance of these roads has increased dramatically, but because of decreasing capital investment, inflation and increased usage, these highways are wearing out faster than they are being repaired. In addition to declining highway conditions, the nation is faced with the ever-increasing cost of completing the Interstate Highway System.

The Federal Aviation Administration (FAA) is primarily responsible for promoting and developing a safe and efficient aviation system. To accomplish this, FAA conducts research; promulgates equipment and personnel standards; inspects and certifies airports, aircraft and pilots; and operates a national air traffic control and navigation system for the orderly, safe and efficient movement of passengers. It also offers assistance for airport planning and construction and partly finances air traffic and navigation facilities and equipment from aviation trust fund revenues received from taxes on passenger fares, freight bills and fuel.

Efficient and effective federal management in the aviation system and careful coordination of federal economic and safety responsibilities for aviation present difficult and complex problems.

Most of the airports in the United States have a comfortable surplus of capacity. However, there is an airport capacity problem in areas of high population density. Years ago, airports were considered good neighbors, and the solution would have been simple—build new ones or expand existing ones. Because of the use of land for other purposes and opposition from an environmental standpoint, additional airport capacity is now hard to come by in the areas in which it is most needed.

Like many other businesses, airlines continue to be plagued by rising costs, primarily labor and fuel. Many of FAA's safety and noise standards and regulations require equipment additions or modifications to the carriers' fleets, changes which can be costly. Delays encountered in the air traffic system are also costly to the airlines—more than $800 million in 1977 plus 700 million gallons of fuel. Without appropriate increases in the capacity of the major airports, delays are expected to increase substantially. It is anticipated that motor vehicles will continue to be the dominant mode of urban transportation for the remainder of this century. Accordingly, the number of highway passenger miles and motor vehicles can be expected to increase. Moreover, the expected reductions in vehicle size and weight to save energy will also produce vehicles which are more susceptible to severe damage in accidents. The Congress is concerned about the apparent lack of coordination among federal programs for automobile fuel conservation, safety and air pollution emission control.

Highways are and will continue to be an important element of the nation's total transportation system. Nearly 90 percent of the intercity passenger miles traveled occurs on highways—more than eight times the volume of aviation, the next most frequently used mode. More than one-fourth of the ton miles of intercity freight is shipped on the nation's highways. Between 1970 and 1978, automobile and truck travel increased 31 and 62 percent, respectively.

More than half of all public transit passenger miles are by bus. DOT data show that there are about 500,000 buses nationally and that the number will probably increase. Even in urban areas having subways or elevated trains, buses provide passenger access to rail transit systems.

The Airport and Airway System Development Act of 1970 was the beginning of significant federal efforts intended to establish a nationwide system of public airports adequate to meet present and future civil aviation needs. Obligational authority for this program expired September 30, 1980. After

10 years and $3 billion spent under the program, traffic delays at airports are still costing airlines and passengers more than $500 million a year. Seventy-five percent of these delays occur at the 26 busiest airports.

In enacting the October 1970 Rail Passenger Service Act, the Congress hoped to halt the decline of intercity passenger train routes. The resulting intercity rail passenger service operated by the quasi-public National Railroad Passenger Corporation (Amtrak) recently celebrated its 15th anniversary, but its prospects for future anniversaries are cloudy.

The federal government has spent about $7 billion on Amtrak, including purchasing and improving the Northeast Corridor, and seems to have achieved many of the improvements originally intended. But Amtrak's annual subsidy needs have grown enormously, and the Congress reluctantly has recognized that, contrary to its original goal, Amtrak will never earn a profit.

Because transportation is so dependent on energy, and because the transport sector is such a major user of energy resources, transportation will be a primary target of future national efforts to conserve energy. The U.S. transportation system is one of the nation's largest energy consumers, accounting for 33 percent of end-use energy consumption and 70 percent of distributed petroleum products consumption. The automobile alone accounts for approximately 40 percent of U.S. petroleum consumption, and reducing automobile energy consumption is a major goal of federal energy conservation plans. Future energy conservation efforts are likely to place particular emphasis on increased use of energy-efficient transportation modes—mass transit, railroads and inland waterways—and more efficient use of existing modes, such as vanpooling and carpooling.

Transportation also plays a vital role in distribution energy materials throughout the economy. Railroads, highways, inland waterways, supertankers and liquid gas and slurry pipelines form a complex transportation network through which coal, petroleum and natural gas are distributed to refineries, industries, utilities and consumers. Economic inefficiencies in the energy transportation network are reflected in the delivered price of energy materials, and thus in the price of energy as a factor of production. The future productivity of the U.S. economy will be strongly influenced by the efficiency with which we plan and operate the energy transportation network.

Toward the end of the 1980s, we expect that increased fuel costs will cause preferences for single-passenger, long-distance commuting by private automobile to change. Greater reliance on carpools, a shift toward shorter commuting trips and increased commuting by public transit seem likely. Also likely is a change in the preferred location of middle-income residential areas from the outer suburbs to the inner suburbs and central city. Improved financial viability for public transit systems may also result as fuel costs make private automobile travel less attractive.

A second important factor in shaping the future U.S. transportation system will be the quality of the physical environment. The interaction and air quality will continue to present difficult and possibly insoluble conflicts. Historically, automobile emissions have been a major contributing factor to air pollution. Modifications in automobile technology have substantially reduced the emissions from individual vehicles, but aggregate emissions from all vehicles continue to present a serious problem.

The federal government is involved in many programs which affect the U.S. transportation system. Some of the most important federal transportation programs are administered by the Department of Transportation. However, many other federal agencies also conduct transportation-related programs, ranging from the aviation and marine weather services of the Commerce Department's National Oceanic and Atmospheric Administration to the inland waterway development projects of the Army Corps of Engineers. Federal and federally supported agencies which administer transportation-related programs include:

Federal Agencies	Mode(s)
Congressional Budget Office	All
Congressional Research Service	All
Council on Environmental Quality	All
Department of Agriculture:	
Forest Service	Highway
Department of Commerce:	
National Oceanic and Atmospheric Administration	Air and water
Department of Defense:	
Military Research and Development	Air and water
U.S. Army Corps of Engineers	Water
Panama Canal Company	Water
Department of Energy:	
Federal Energy Regulatory Commission	All
Department of Housing and Urban Development	Air, highway and transit
Department of the Interior:	
Bureau of Indian Affairs	Highway
Bureau of Land Management	Highway and pipeline
National Park Service	Highway
Department of State	All
Department of Transportation:	
Office of the Secretary	All
U.S. Coast Guard	Water
Federal Aviation Administration	Air
Federal Highway Administration	Highway and transit
Federal Railroad Administration	Rail and transit
National Highway Traffic Safety Administration	Highway and transit

Research and Special Programs Administration	All
St. Lawrence Seaway Development Corporation	Water
Urban Mass Transportation Administration	Transit
Department of the Treasury	All
Environmental Protection Agency	All
Federal Maritime Commission	Water
Interstate Commerce Commission	All except air
National Aeronautics and Space Administration	Air
Office of Technology Assessment	All
National Transportation Safety Board	All
Tennessee Valley Authority	Water
U.S. Railway Association	Rail
National Railroad Passenger Corporation	Rail
Consolidated Rail Corporation	Rail
Washington Metropolitan Area Transit Authority	Transit

NOTES

1. This section is adapted from Dempsey, *Rate Regulation and Antitrust Immunity in Transportation: The Genesis and Evolution of This Endangered Species*, 32 Am. U.L. Rev. 335 (1983).

2. This section is adapted from National Association of Manufacturers, Economic Principles Commission, The American Individual Enterprise System 531 (1946).

3. This section is adapted from Dempsey, *Rate Regulation and Antitrust Immunity in Transportation: The Genesis and Evolution of This Endangered Species*, 32 Am. U.L. Rev. 335 (1983).

4. Harris, *Introduction* 31 Geo. Wash. L. Rev. 1 (1962); D. Bowersox, P. Calabro & G. Wagenheim, Introduction to Transportation 164 (1981).

5. Harris, *Introduction* 31 Geo. Wash. L. Rev. (1962).

6. Harris, *Introduction* 31 Geo. Wash. L. Rev. (1962). By the 1880s, some 15 states and territories had promulgated legislation seeking to constrict monopoly activity. R. Current, A. Deconde & H. Dante, United States History 419 (1967).

7. 94 U.S. 113 (1876).

8. *Id.* at 126. Although *Munn* did not directly involve rail carriers, subsequent decisions applied this principle to such carriers. *See e.g.*, Chicago, B. + O.R.R. v. Iowa, 94 U.S. 155, 163 (1876); Peik v. Chicago & N.W. Ry., 94 U.S. 164 (1876), Winona & St. P. Ry. v. Blake, 94 U.S. 180 (1876).

9. Munn, *supra*, 94 U.S. at 135.

10. Wabash, St. L. & R. Ry. v. Illinois, 118 U.S. 557 (1886).

11. *Id.* at 527–75.

12. The jurisdiction of the ICC has been expanded several times since the initial promulgation of rail-oriented legislation. The Hepburn Act of 1906 extended the Commission's jurisdiction to encompass steamship, express and sleeping car companies. In 1910, the Congress added telephone and telegraph companies to the

regulatory scheme. Motor carriers were brought under the regulatory umbrella with the promulgation of the Motor Carrier Act of 1935. And the Transportation Act of 1940 brought freight forwarders and domestic water carriers within the Commission's jurisdiction.

13. Adapted from Department of Transportation, *A Prospectus for Change in the Freight Railroad Industry* 114–18 (1978).

14. United States v. Trans-Missouri Freight Assoc., 166 U.S. 290 (1897); and United States v. Joint Traffic Assoc., 171 U.S. 505 (1898).

15. *See* Chicago, Milwaukee, St. P. & P. R.R. v. Illinois, 335 U.S. 421 (1958). In the *Illinois* case, for example, the court held: "We do not think that the deficit from a single operation can fairly be adjudged to work an undue discrimination against the Milwaukee Road's intrastate operations without findings which take the deficit into account in the light of the carrier's other intrastate revenues" 335 U.S. at 307–30. This finding requires the ICC to study a company's total intrastate operation before finding a given rate unreasonable.

16. This section is adapted from Webb, *Legislative and Regulatory History of Entry Controls on Motor Carriers of Passengers*, 8 Transp. L.J. 91 (1976).

17. Pub. L. No. 255, 49 Stat. 543 (1935).

18. 267 U.S. 307 (1925).

19. *Hearings on § 1629, § 1632, and § 1635 Before the Senate Committee on Interstate Commerce*, 74th Cong., 1st Sess. 78 (1935).

20. Section 309 of the Act, added by the Transportation Act of 1940, provides that "no common carrier by water shall engage in transportation subject to this part unless it holds a certificate of public convenience and necessity issued by the Commission."

21. 182 I.C.C. 263 (1932).

22. *Id.* at 379.

23. 140 I.C.C. 685, 702 (1928).

24. This section is adapted from Baker & Greene, Jr., *Commercial Zones and Terminal Areas: History, Development, Expansion, Deregulation*, 10 Transp. L.J. 171 (1978).

25. 79 Cong. Rec. at 5651 (1935).

26. *Id.* at 5650.

27. *Id.*

28. 79 Cong. Rec. 12,204 (1935).

29. *Id.* at 12,205.

30. *Id.* at 12,205.

31. This section is adapted from Harper, *Entry Control and the Federal Motor Carrier Act of 1980*, 12 Transp. L.J. 51 (1980).

32. Early criticism of economic regulation of motor trucking may be found in Nelson, *New Concepts in Transportation Regulation*, in Transportation and National Policy 197 (Natural Resources Planning Board 1942) (printed by U.S. Gov't Printing Office), and Pegrum, *The Economic Basis of Public Policy for Motor Transport*, 28 Land Econ. 244 (1952).

33. An excellent discussion of the administration of the 1935 Motor Carrier Act before and after 1977 through 1979 can be forced in Kahn, *Motor Carrier Regulatory Reform—Fait Accompli*, 19 Transp. J. 5 (1979). Recent statutory and administrative changes in federal air and motor truck economic regulation and their impact through

1979 are described in Dempsey, *Erosion of the Regulatory Process in Transportation—The Winds of Change*, 47 I.C.C. Prac. J. 303 (1980).

34. Adapted from W. Thoms, Deregulation: The Motor Carrier Experience, North Dakota State University, Fargo, N.D.

35. Motor Carrier Act of 1980, § 3, Pub. L. No. 96–296, 96 Stat. 793 (1980).

36. 49 U.S.C. § 10101 (b) (1980).

37. This section is adapted from W. Thoms, Deregulation: The Motor Carrier Experience 66–69 (1981).

38. Pub. L. No. 96–454, 94 Stat. 2011 (Oct. 15, 1980).

39. Pub. L. No. 96–454, 94 Stat. 2011, § 4, enacting 49 U.S.C. § 10734 (1980).

40. 49 U.S.C. § 10934 (1980).

41. Webb, *Legislative and Regulatory Controls on Motor Carriers of Passengers*, 8 Transp. L.J. 91, 105 (1976).

42. Traffic World, Sept. 27, 1982, at 89.

43. This section is adapted from Dempsey, *The Rise and Fall of the Civil Aeronautics Board—Opening Wide the Floodgates of Entry*, 11 Transp. L.J. 91, 95–108 (1979).

44. *Regulation of Interstate Transportation of Passengers, Mail and Property by Aircraft, Hearings in S. 3178 by the Senate Comm. on Commerce*, 73rd Cong., 2nd Sess. 1 (1934). See Dempsey, *The International Rate & Route Revolution in North Atlantic Passenger Transportation*, 17 Colum. J. Transnat' l L. 393, 413 (1978).

45. Among the primary proponents of air transport regulation, and the author of the original bills, was Senator Patrick McCarren, who emphasized the significance of the pending legislation by stating that "there was never anything before this country more vital from the standpoint of national development, particularly at this hour of the world's history, and at this hour in our national history, than the legislation which is now pending before this subcommittee, because we are dealing with an infant industry, and we are dealing with it from the standpoint of what it can do for this country commercially, industrially, and as an arm of national defense." *Civil Aviation and Air Transport Hearings on § 3659 Before a Subcommittee on Interstate Commerce*, 75th Cong., 3rd Sess. 7 (1938).

46. The Motor Carrier Act was subsequently scattered throughout the provisions of the Interstate Commerce Act, 49 U.S.C. §§ 10101–11916 (1979).

47. *House Hearings on H.R. 5234 & H.R. 4652, supra note 11, at 163. Aviation: Hearings on H.R. 5234 & H.R. 462 Before the House Committee on Interstate and Foreign Commerce*, 75th Cong., 1st Sess. 53 (1937).

48. This section is adapted from W. Thoms, Deregulation: The Airline Experience 38–39, 58–59, 75–78 (1981).

49. Dubuc, *Significant Legislative Developments in the Field of Aviation Law*, 45 J. Air L. 1, 21 (1979).

50. 1978 Pub. L. 95–504 (Oct. 24, 1970), *amending* 49 U.S.C. §§ 1301–1551 (1980).

51. 49 U.S.C. § 1551 (1980).

52. Sandell, *supra*, at 820–21.

53. 49 U.S.C. §1551 (1980).

54. Dubuc, *Significant Legislative Developments in the Field of Aviation Law*, 45 J. Air L. 1, 21 (1979).

55. This section is adapted from J. Hardman, Transportation Law: An Introductory Study (1978).

56. 46 U.S.C. §§ 190–196.

57. 46 U.S.C. §§ 1300–1315.

58. 46 U.S.C. § 688.

59. 46 U.S.C. §§ 761–768.

60. 46 U.S.C. § 1101 *et seq.*

61. This section is adapted from Pansius, *Plotting the Return of Isbrandsten: The Illegality of Interconference Rate Agreements*, 9 Transp. L.J. 337 (1978).

62. Ch. 451, 39 Stat. 728 (1916).

63. 46 U.S.C. § 814 (1970).

64. This section is adapted from Robert C. Lies, Transportation: The Domestic System 85–87 (2d ed. 1981).

65. This section is adapted from W. Thoms, Regulation of Oil Pipelines by the ICC 1–3, 12–13 (1979).

66. A reflection of this principle exists in the vertical integration of energy corporations of extraction, transportation, refinement and marketing of petroleum. Many such corporations own private fleets of trucks, inland barges, oil and gas pipelines and ocean vessels (including supertankers). Compare Hart, *The Antitrust Aspects of Oil Company Ownership of Deepwater Ports*, 10 Transp. L.J. 67 (1978).

67. *What Must Be Done*, Newsweek, July 16, 1979, at 31.

68. *U.S. Dep't. of Transportation, A Prospectus for Change in the Freight Railroad Industry* 109 (1978).

69. *Id.* at 110.

70. *Interstate Commerce Commission, Annual Report* 26 (1977) [hereinafter cited as *ICC Annual Report*].

71. Lorentzen, *Coal Slurry Pipelines: A Railroad Perspective*, 10 Transp. L.J. 153, 165 (1978) [hereinafter cited as Lorentzen].

72. *Slurry Pipeline Expected to be Completed by 1984*, Denver Post, August 26, 1979, at 36, col. 3–4. This project is the Energy Transportation Systems, Inc. It spent six years in court in 65 separate cases to obtain the rights of way under rail tracks.

73. Lorentzen, *supra*, at 159. In addition, technological improvements in the efficiency of the long-distance transmission of electricity have resulted in a large growth in mine-mouth power-generating plants. During the late 1960s and early 1970s, the coal tonnage by such plants more than tripled, so that by 1976, one out of every nine tons was consumed at the mine.

74. The Wyoming Framework Water Plan, State of Wyoming, State Engineers Office, Laramie, Wyo. (1973).

75. Office of Technology Assessment, Congress of U.S., A Technology Assessment of Coal Slurry Pipelines 105 (1978). *See* Dempsey, *Oil Shale and Water Quality: The Colorado Prospectus Under Federal, State and International Law*, 58 Den. L.J. 715, 720–33 (1981).

76. This section is adapted from U.S. General Accounting Office, Transportation: Evolving Issues for Analysis (1982).

2

Entry, Exit and Adequacy of Service

The Interstate Commerce Commission (ICC) is this nation's largest and oldest independent regulatory agency.[1] In 1887, Congress promulgated the Act to Regulate Commerce,[2] which created the ICC and afforded it primary jurisdiction over the prevention and correction of rate discriminations by railroads. Since then, a number of other modes of transportation have been brought within the jurisdiction of the ICC. The Motor Carrier Act of 1935[3] brought both motor carriers and brokers within the ambit of ICC regulation. The Transportation Act of 1940[4] added domestic water carriers; two years later, freight forwarders were brought within the Commission's regulatory scheme.[5]

Operating authority is required before a carrier may lawfully perform nonexempt for-hire transport operations in interstate or foreign commerce. The ICC has the responsibility for determining whether a carrier which applies for such authority will or will not be permitted to perform the transport operations. The performance of this licensing function is commonly referred to as the "regulation of entry" or "entry control" because no carrier may lawfully enter the field of transportation without acquiring properly certified or licensed operating rights.

The statutory language governing entry control of those transport modes subject to ICC regulation is couched in rather vague and ambiguous terminology. Entry in each mode is governed by one of two concepts: (1) the public convenience and necessity, or (2) the public interest and the national transportation policy. To obtain authority to perform lawful for-hire transportation in interstate or foreign commerce subject to the regulation of the ICC, an applicant must satisfy one of these two statutory concepts. Yet the former concept is not statutorily defined, and as to the latter, only the national transportation policy has been articulated.

The failure of Congress to define specifically the concepts of the "public

convenience and necessity" and the "public interest" has inevitably afforded
the ICC wide latitude in the performance of its regulatory responsibilities.
The ICC has given meaning to these ambiguous concepts and has developed
a rational scheme of entry control and economic regulation of the various
modes of transportation subject to its regulation.

I. RAIL CARRIAGE

A. Rail Entry

Section 10901 of the Interstate Commerce Act[6, 7] provides that no rail
carrier shall extend its lines, construct new lines or acquire existing rail lines
unless it first obtains a certificate from the ICC demonstrating that the
proposal is required by the public convenience and necessity. This statutory
provision was designed primarily to eradicate the excessive depletion of the
capital of rail carriers resulting from the construction or acquisition of unnecessary lines. These lines often offered little promise of profitable operation and were frequently acquired or constructed merely for the pecuniary
rewards arising from the disposition of securities, a situation contrary to the
public interest. The underlying purposes of such legislation have been characterized as (1) the prevention of improvident and unnecessary expenditures
for the operation or construction of rail lines not required for the maintenance
of reasonably adequate transportation services; (2) the protection of interstate
rail carriers from the deleterious consequences arising from the construction
and operation of superfluous lines; (3) the protection of such carriers from
the injurious operation of a competing line not required by public interest;
and (4) the preservation of balanced competition.[8] However, the term "public
convenience and necessity" is not statutorily defined, and therefore, courts
have given the ICC wide latitude in delineating its meaning.

In determining whether a particular rail line proposal will satisfy the public
convenience and necessity, consideration is ordinarily given to the interest
of particular shippers, the creation of new markets, and the existence of rate
advantages. In addition, the ICC has recognized that no carrier holds an
exclusive right to occupy a particular territory. With respect to the adequacy
of existing services, it has been stated:

> To find that construction of a line of railroad is required by the public convenience
> and necessity, it is necessary to consider whether adequate service to the public will
> otherwise be provided. The building of surplus lines of railroads is wasteful in that
> it creates an oversupply of transportation facilities and entails unnecessary expend-
> iture of funds. Where existing railroad facilities are physically available, the addition
> of competitive or duplicating facilities is unwarranted unless it is shown that the use
> of such existing facilities would not provide adequate service or would be
> uneconomical.[9]

The financial aspect of a proposal for the construction or acquisition of rail facilities has become increasingly important in the determination of whether the proposed operations are or will be consistent with the present or future public convenience and necessity. Thus, in *Central of Georgia Railway—Operation in Russell County, Alabama*,[10] the Commission recognized that the

expenditures of . . . large sums of money, together with the substantial length of the track becomes of immediate national concern and, as a direct consequence, of Commission concern, regardless of the financial capability of the involved carrier. Are such expenditures necessary to insure adequate service? Will the carrier be protected from weakening itself through such an expenditure? Will a reasonable return be made on such an investment? And, will the competition to result between the involved carriers in this particular proceeding result in harm to the public? The purpose of these questions is as valid today as in 1920, and it complements the present transportation policy of requiring this Commission to promote safe, adequate, economical, and efficient service, and to foster sound economical conditions in transportation. It is easy to see that where such large expenditures are made for construction purposes the aforesaid questions and requirements strike at the very essence of a need for consideration at a national level of whether or not public convenience and necessity require the construction. A fundamental regulatory process involving the entire areas served by the railroad is concerned. It can no longer be confined to local policy.[11]

The ICC may issue a certificate authorizing a proposed extension of a rail line where it is demonstrated that the involved expansion either presently is or in the near future will be self-sustaining so as not to unduly burden interstate commerce.[12] However, the ICC must be convinced that institution of the proposal will not so significantly deplete the rail carrier's capital resources that the performance of its public service obligations will be impeded to the ultimate detriment of the public through diminished services and increased rates.[13]

Section 10903 of the Interstate Commerce Act also requires, as a condition precedent to the abandonment of rail facilities, a certificate of public convenience and necessity. In order to avoid a discontinuance of transportation services, however, the ICC permits a concurrent filing of an application by a competing rail carrier for the acquisition of the rail facilities proposed to be abandoned.

1. New Rail Lines

A railroad company must have a certificate of public convenience and necessity[14] before building a line or taking over and operating an existing line.[15] In addition, if a railroad which is already in operation desires to extend its current line, it must seek a certificate for the extension. Proof of the adequacy of existing service, traffic to be generated and support of the shipper are necessary for a certificate to be granted. An extension certificate is not required, however, when the line to be built is a mere spur or industrial track. Determining what is a spur and what is an extension has taken up a good deal of the ICC's time. Until passage of the Staggers Act, it was considered to be an extension if a line tapped territory that was currently served by a competitive railroad.

The reason behind such a restriction is to prevent the construction of "nuisance" railroads serving the same area as a parallel line. A good example of such a line was the West Shore Railroad, built parallel to the New York Central from New York City to Buffalo for the very purpose of embarrassing the Vanderbilt interests and persuading them to buy out investors of the competing line. There might be enough traffic in a certain area for one or two railroads but no more. The oversupply would be a waste of resources. Worse, the traffic might be so diluted that no railroad could make money and all might be abandoned. The newest line to be constructed in this country is the Powder Basin line in Wyoming, built by the Burlington Northern in connection with the Chicago & North Western.[16] Otherwise, this section of the Act has seen little use since the 1970s.

* * *

49 U.S.C. § 10901. AUTHORIZING CONSTRUCTION AND OPERATION OF RAILROAD LINES

(a) A rail carrier providing transportation subject to the jurisdiction of the Interstate Commerce Commission under subchapter I of chapter 105 of this title may—

(1) construct an extension to any of its railroad lines;

(2) construct an additional railroad line;

(3) acquire or operate an extended or additional railroad line; or

(4) provide transportation over, or by means of, an extended or additional railroad line;

only if the Commission finds that the present or future public convenience and necessity require or permit the construction or acquisition (or both) and operation of the railroad line.

* * *

49 U.S.C. § 10907. EXCEPTIONS

(b) The Commission does not have authority under sections 10901–10906 of this title over—

(1) the construction, acquisition, operation, abandonment, or discontinuance of spur, industrial, team, switching, or side tracks if the tracks are located, or intended to be located entirely in one State; or

(2) a street, suburban, or interurban electric railway that is not operated as part of a general system of rail transportation.

* * *

2. The Industrial Track Exemption

TEXAS & PACIFIC RY. CO. V.
GULF, COLORADO & SANTA FE RY. CO.

270 U.S. 266 (1925)

[Both the Texas and Pacific Railway (plaintiff) and the Gulf, Colorado and Sante Fe
Railway (defendant) served Dallas, but only the plaintiff served the "Industrial District," located several miles to the west. The district included a number of industrial
facilities which generated a healthy amount of freight. Defendant maintained trackage
only 3 1/4 miles from the district and proposed to construct a new line linking such
trackage with the Industrial District and to construct 7 1/2 miles of trackage through
the district.]

BRANDEIS, J.

Plaintiff seeks to enjoin the Gulf, Colorado & Santa Fe Railway Company from
constructing wholly within the State projected trackage, sometimes called the Hale-
Cement Line. The bill alleges that the line is, within the meaning of the above
provision, an extension of the defendant's railroad; that operation of the line will
result in irreparable injury to the plaintiff, because it will divert to the Santa Fe
traffic which would otherwise be enjoyed by the Texas & Pacific. By answer the
defendant insisted that the line is merely an industrial track.

A guide to the meaning of the terms extension and industrial track, as used in
sections 10901(a) and 10907(b)(1), is furnished by the context and by the relation of
the specific provisions here in question to the railroad policy introduced by Transportation Act, 1920. By that measure, Congress undertook to develop and maintain,
for the people of the United States, an adequate railway system. It recognized that
preservation of the earning capacity, and conservation of the financial resources, of
individual carriers is a matter of national concern; that the property employed must
be permitted to earn a reasonable return; that the building of unnecessary lines
involves a waste of resources and that the burden of this waste may fall upon the
public; that competition between carriers may result in harm to the public as well
as in benefit; and that when a railroad inflicts injury upon its rival, it may be the
public which ultimately bears the loss. The Act sought, among other things, to avert
such losses.

When the clauses in sections 10901(a) and 10907(b)(1) are read in the light of this
congressional policy, the meaning and scope of the terms extension and industrial
track become clear. The carrier was authorized by Congress to construct, without
authority from the Commission, "spur, industrial, team, switching or side tracks to
be located wholly within one State." Tracks of that character are commonly constructed either to improve the facilities required by shippers already served by the
carrier or to supply the facilities to others, who being within the same territory and
similarly situated are entitled to like service from the carrier. The question whether
the construction should be allowed or compelled depends largely upon local conditions which the state regulating body is peculiarly fitted to appreciate. Moreover,
the expenditure involved is ordinarily small. But where the proposed trackage extends into territory not theretofore served by another carrier, its purpose and effect

are, under the new policy of Congress, of national concern. For invasion through new construction of territory adequately served by another carrier, like the establishment of excessively low rates in order to secure traffic enjoyed by another, may be inimical to the national interest. If the purpose and effect of the new trackage is to extend substantially the line of a carrier into new territory, the proposed trackage constitutes an extension of the railroad within the meaning of section 10901(a), although the line be short and although the character of the service contemplated be that commonly rendered to industries by means of spurs or industrial tracks. Being an extension, it cannot be built unless the federal commission issues its certificate that public necessity and convenience require its construction. The Hale-Cement Line is clearly an extension within this rule.

3. Public Convenience and Necessity

CHESAPEAKE & OHIO RY. CO. V.
UNITED STATES

283 U.S. 35 (1931)

[Both the Chesapeake & Ohio and the Norfolk & Western Railways provided service in conjunction with the Virginian and Western Railway, transporting coal from West Virginia mines served solely by the Virginian. The Norfolk carried the bulk of this traffic (80%), while the Chesapeake carried the remainder (20%). The carriers filed applications for certificates of public convenience and necessity to construct lines linking with the Virginian at less circuitous interchange points. The ICC granted certificates to the Virginian to construct a line that shortened its through route between Ittman and Gilbert, West Virginia with the Chesapeake, and to the Norfolk to construct a line between Gilbert and Wharncliff, West Virginia, that shortened its through route with the Virginian. The Chesapeake (appellant) brought suit in federal court to set aside the ICC decision to grant a certificate to the Norfolk.]

BUTLER, J.

The appellant seeks reversal upon the claim that neither the findings of the Commission nor the evidence affords any support for the order and that the record shows the construction of the proposed line between Gilbert and Wharncliff to be contrary to the public interest and to have been authorized under an erroneous theory of the applicable law. It says that the only finding of the Commission that supports the order is that the construction of the line will enable the Norfolk to compete with the Chesapeake for west-bound traffic moving over the Virginian from the Guyandot valley and will assure the coal operators on the Virginian competitive service to the west. And it maintains that the Commission is not authorized by the Act to grant a certificate of public convenience and necessity for new construction upon a naked finding that competition between carriers and competitive service to shippers will result.

The construction of the line of the Virginian from the upper Guyandot to a connection with the Chesapeake at Gilbert would immensely improve the position of the latter in respect of the westbound movement of coal originating on the Virginian. It is also plain, indeed so obvious as scarcely to require statement, that the construction of the Gilbert-Wharncliff connection is necessary in order to enable the

Norfolk to continue, on conditions that are tolerable, to compete with the Chesapeake for that traffic. The construction of that connection cannot reasonably be regarded as an intrusion by the Norfolk into territory already being well-served by the Chesapeake. On the contrary the Norfolk already hauls about four-fifths of the Virginian's westbound coal. By this relatively short connection, it will be able to give a better outlet for that traffic, to make substantial saving in the cost of handling, and to remain in position, at relatively slight disadvantage, to compete for traffic in which it long has had a large share. And shippers will have the benefit of such competitive service.

There is no specification in the Act of the considerations by which the Commission is to be guided in determining whether the public convenience and necessity require the proposed construction. Under the Act it was the duty of the Commission to find the facts and, in the exercise of a reasonable judgment, to determine that question.

Undoubtedly the purpose of these provisions is to enable the Commission in the interest of the public, to prevent improvident and unnecessary expenditures for the construction and operation of lines not needed to insure adequate service. In the absence of a plain declaration to that effect, it would be unreasonable to hold that Congress did not intend to empower the Commission to authorize construction of new lines to provide for shippers such competing service as it should find to be convenient or necessary in the public interest.

AUTO-TRAIN CORP., OPERATION OF RAIL PASSENGER AND AUTOMOBILE TRANSPORT SERVICE, BETWEEN ALEXANDRIA, VA., AND SANFORD, FLA.

354 I.C.C. 707 (1977)

Under its certificates, Auto-Train could provide combined rail passenger-automobile transport service, but only if the owner or driver of the automobile was a passenger on the same train. Auto-Train filed a petition for modification of its certificates to permit Auto-Train to transport automobiles unaccompanied by their drivers, but only pursuant to a joint booking agreement with Eastern Airlines. By the agreement, Auto-Train would transport the automobile, and Eastern Airlines would transport the passenger.

We will first consider the merits of Auto-Train's petition. Auto-Train has shown that there are people who would use the proposed service if offered. Without a promotion campaign, tentative reservations for the combined Auto-Train Service have been made by more than 70 parties. We agree with applicant that presenting a large volume of "supporting" statements from individuals who are potential users of the proposed service would have been of little help to us in our considerations. Auto-Train has substituted in the place of such statements comments by travel agents and statements by individuals associated with Auto-Train attesting to the interest people have shown in the proposed service. These statements considered together with the evidence of tentative reservations, lead us to conclude that there is public need for the service.

The proposed service is different from any service now offered, including the services of protestants. Furthermore, neither protestant has shown that the proposed service would divert any significant traffic that it now handles or that it could handle. Furthermore, any diversion that would occur could be attributed to an individual's preference for a different type of service. Driveaway and truckaway services represent competing modes of transportation for Auto-Train's present and proposed service.

Each mode has advantages and disadvantages peculiar to it. The public has the right to choose from among these modes the means by which they will ship their automobiles and the means by which they themselves will travel. By offering good service, the protesting carriers and Auto-Train can all continue to serve the different needs of different people.

We must, however, fulfill our statutory duty and consider the effect of the proposed new service on Amtrak. The Amtrak Improvement Act of 1973 requires that the Commission find that a proposed service by a person primarily engaged in auto-ferry service (a) will not impair the ability of Amtrak to reduce its losses or to increase its revenues, and (b) is required to meet the demands of the public. Such finding was not required of Auto-Train's initial Alexandria-Sanford route authorization because of a statutory exemption. This division, in approving Auto-Train's service between Louisville and Sanford in 1974, specifically made the requisite findings. We must now consider the impact of this petition upon Amtrak.

Amtrak has not protested Auto-Train's petition. While this factor alone is not controlling, it is worth noting since apparently Amtrak does not anticipate any "impairment of its ability to reduce its losses or increase its revenues." We also find the division's "no harm to Amtrak" finding in 1974 to be helpful since in that case the services to be provided by Auto-Train were identical to auto-ferry service being considered by Amtrak over a similar route. In the instant situation, the proposed service is less like that offered by Amtrak because of the cooperative agreement between Auto-Train and Eastern on air passenger service for individuals whose cars will be transported by Auto-Train.

In light of these factors and because we have no basis to believe that Amtrak would be harmed, we find that the proposed joint auto-ferry/air passenger transportation service will not impair Amtrak's ability to reduce its losses or to increase its revenues. As stated earlier, we also find that the proposed service is required to meet the demands of the public.

* * *

NOTE: Amtrak

The Rail Passenger Service Act of 1970, although specifying that Amtrak is a rail common carrier, nevertheless exempts its operations from ICC regulation over rail rate making, and abandonment and extension of operations.[17] Amtrak is free to expand its operations, without ICC scrutiny, where it "determines that experimental or expanded service would be justified, if consistent with prudent management." Moreover, upon application by Amtrak, the ICC may insist that a rail carrier make its tracks and facilities available for rail passenger service by Amtrak. Where a local governmental entity offers to subsidize additional rail passenger service beyond the Amtrak system in the amount of "50 percent of solely related costs and associated capital costs of such service," Amtrak may inaugurate such new service where it is assured that adequate passenger demand exists.

Amtrak represents an experiment in a national passenger transportation system.[18] In its original declaration of purpose in the 1970 Rail Passenger Service Act, Congress stated that "modern, efficient, intercity railroad passenger service is a necessary part of a balanced transportation system." It found that the public convenience and necessity required the improvement of such service and that federal financial assistance, as well as private investment capital, was needed to establish a national rail passenger system. 45 U.S.C. § 501. The act provided that Amtrak "shall be a for profit corporation, the purpose of which shall be to provide intercity rail passenger service, employing innovative operating and marketing concepts so as to fully develop the potential of modern rail service in meeting the Nation's intercity passenger transportation requirement." 45 U.S.C. § 541. Amtrak was deemed a common carrier subject to all provisions of the Interstate Commerce Act, except, among others, those pertaining to the regulation of rates, fares and charges.

In the 1978 Amtrak Improvement Act, Congress modified this exemption to permit the ICC to hear unfair pricing complaints. That act also amended the provision establishing Amtrak to require that Amtrak, instead of being a for profit corporation shall "be operated and managed as a for profit corporation." The conference explanation of this amendment is unenlightening, but seemingly the change was intended to reflect the perception that Amtrak, without federal subsidy, could not break even.

In the Amtrak Reorganization Act of 1979, Congress added the finding that "rail passenger service offers significant benefits in public transportation for the safe movement of passengers with minimum energy expenditure and represents a significant national transportation asset in time of national emergency or energy shortage." Congress further found that inadequately defined goals for Amtrak had denied its directors an effective role in guiding Amtrak. Congress established certain goals for Amtrak, including improvement of Amtrak's time and average speed performance and coverage of at least 44 percent of operating expenses, excluding depreciation, from revenues by the end of fiscal year 1982 and 50 percent by the end of fiscal year 1985.

Most recently, in the Amtrak Improvement Act of 1981, Public Law 97–35, Congress modified its earlier findings and established new goals for Amtrak. Foremost among these goals were:

1. Exercise of the corporation's best business judgment in taking actions to minimize federal subsidies, including increasing revenues from the carriage of mail and express, reducing losses on food service, improving its contracts with operating railroads, reducing management costs and increasing employee productivity.

2. Encouragement of state, regional and local governments and the private sector to share the costs of operating rail passenger service, including the costs of operating stations and other facilities, in order to minimize federal subsidies.

3. Amtrak's maximization of the use of its resources, including the most cost-effective use of employees, facilities and real estate. Amtrak is encouraged to enter into agreements with the private sector and undertake initiatives which are consistent with good business judgment and designed to maximize its revenues and minimize federal subsidies.[19]

The Amtrak Improvement Act of 1981 also provided that beginning in fiscal year 1982, Amtrak shall recover "an amount sufficient that the ratio of its revenues, including contributions from States, agencies, and other persons, to costs, excluding capital costs, shall be at least 50 percent."[20] This act also clarified the methods for reducing costs and the standards for discontinuing service.

NOTE: The Staggers Rail Act of 1980

The statutory criteria in section 10901 of the Interstate Commerce Act have been amended by the Staggers Rail Act of 1980 to alter the standard of proving public convenience and necessity [PC&N]. A rail applicant need no longer demonstrate that the PC&N "will be enhanced by" the extension; it need now prove only that the PC&N "permit the construction or acquisition." The purposes of the amendment are to make the standard less stringent and to make the rail entry standard comport with the abandonment standard.

B. Rail Abandonments

Railroads have played a major part in the growth of this nation.[21] However, the railroads' prestige and strength have fallen dramatically since the 1930s. Although the demise of passenger service has been a highly visible development, the rail industry's freight transportation has also faltered.

One primary problem for the railroads has been the maintenance of excessive trackage and facilities. Two-thirds of all the rail traffic today moves over only 20 percent of the rail system, while 10 percent of the total trackage accounts for only one-half of 1 percent of the traffic. There are various reasons for such inefficient use of track. Among these reasons is the fact that in the past, rail lines were often built on speculation in anticipation of traffic that failed to materialize. The railroads also frequently built alongside existing lines of competitors in a particular area. Light traffic over a line would result from a cyclical process; less profitable lines were not maintained in good condition, which in turn resulted in a reduction in demand for service. Redundant trackage has also resulted from frequent mergers within the industry.

Railroads have sought to divest themselves of these unprofitable or redundant lines through abandonment proceedings.

To abandon a line prior to the promulgation of the Staggers Act of 1980,[22] a railroad had the burden of proving that the "present or future public convenience and necessity" required or permitted the abandonment or discontinuance.[23] While the economic condition of the line was not a factor in this determination, the Commission was required to consider the "serious, adverse impact on rural and community development."[24] The Commission used a "weighing" or "balancing" approach to determine whether any particular abandonment would be consistent with the present or future public convenience and necessity. Using this method, the Commission compared the burden to the carrier of continued service with the adverse effects on shippers and local communities. Some of the considerations in such a determination were "the population of the territory serviced, the use by the public of the service sought to be discontinued, other available transportation in the area, the general financial condition of the carrier involved and the losses it suffered in providing the service."[25]

In addition to proving public convenience and necessity, the petitioning railroad was required to fulfill a complex and lengthy set of procedural requirements. A carrier submitted its application at least 60 days in advance of the proposed abandonment effective date.[26] If the application was opposed, a certificate could be issued only if the line was described on a diagram showing lines for which the carrier plans abandonment filed with the Commission at least four months prior to the date of the application.[27] After an application for abandonment was filed, the Commission could order an investigation and postpone the abandonment "for a reasonable period of time."[28] Even if the Commission found that a certificate should issue, it could postpone issuance for another six months if it found that a "financially responsible person" had offered assistance equal to the difference between the revenues attributable to the line and the "avoidable cost"[29] of providing service, plus a reasonable rate of return on the value of the line.[30]

49 U.S.C. § 10903. AUTHORIZING ABANDONMENT AND DISCONTINUANCE OF RAILROAD LINES AND RAIL TRANSPORTATION

(a) A rail carrier providing transportation subject to the jurisdiction of the Interstate Commerce Commission under subchapter I of chapter 105 of this title may—

(1) abandon any part of its railroad lines; or

(2) discontinue the operation of all rail transportation over any part of its railroad lines;

only if the Commission finds that the present or future public convenience and necessity require or permit the abandonment or discontinuance. In making the finding, the Commission shall consider whether the abandonment or discontinuance will have a serious, adverse impact on rural and community development.

(b)(1) Subject to sections 10904–10906 of this title, if the Commission—

(A) finds public convenience and necessity, it shall—

(i) approve the application as filed; or

(ii) approve the application with modifications and require compliance with conditions that the Commission finds are required by public convenience and necessity; or

(B) fails to find public convenience and necessity, it shall deny the application.

(2) On approval, the Commission shall issue to the rail carrier a certificate describing the abandonment or discontinuance approved by the Commission. Each certificate shall also contain provisions to protect the interests of employees.

* * *

1. Intrastate Abandonments

COLORADO v. UNITED STATES

271 U.S. 153 (1926)

BRANDEIS, J.

This suit was brought by Colorado against the United States to set aside, in part, an order of the Interstate Commerce Commission permitting the abandonment by the Colorado & Southern Railway Company of a branch line located wholly in that State. The railroad company owns and operates in interstate and intrastate commerce a railroad system located partly in Colorado and partly in other states.

The main contention of the State is that the Commission lacks power to authorize the Company to abandon, as respects intrastate traffic, a part of its line lying wholly within the State. The argument is this. While a railroad cannot, in the absence of express statutory provision or contract, be compelled by a State to continue operating its lines at a loss when there is no reasonable prospect of future profit, and may, therefore, without such consent, abandon all lines within the State, it has no right to abandon part of the lines, merely because operation will be attended by pecuniary loss, and still continue to enjoy the privilege of operating other parts within the State.

Prejudice to interstate commerce may be effected in many ways. One way is by excessive expenditures from the common fund in the local interest, thereby lessening the ability of the carrier properly to serve interstate commerce. Expenditures in the local interest may be so large as to compel the carrier to raise reasonable interstate rates, or to abstain from making an appropriate reduction of such rates, or to curtail interstate service, or to forego facilities needed in interstate commerce. Likewise, excessive local expenditures may so weaken the financial condition of the carrier as to raise the cost of securing capital required for providing transportation facilities used in the service, and thus compel an increase of rates. Such depletion of the common resources in the local interest may conceivably be effected by continued operation of an intrastate branch in intrastate commerce at a large loss.

The sole objective of Sections 10903–10906 of the Interstate Commerce Act is the regulation of interstate commerce. Control is exerted over intrastate commerce only because such control is a necessary incident of freeing interstate commerce from the unreasonable burdens, obstruction or unjust discrimination which are found to result from operating a branch at a large loss. Congress has power to authorize abandonment, because the State's power to regulate and promote intrastate commerce may not be exercised in such a way to prejudice interstate commerce. The exertion of the federal power to prevent prejudice to interstate commerce so arising from the operation of a branch in intrastate commerce is similar to that exerted when a state establishes intrastate rates so low that intrastate traffic does not bear its fair share of the cost of the service, or when the state authorities seek to compel the erection of a union station so expensive as unduly to deplete the financial resources of the carriers, or when one railroad seeks to construct an intrastate branch line, which will deplete its own financial resources or those of another interstate carrier. The jurisdiction exercised by the Commission in these cases is in essence a power to prevent unjust preference to particular intrastate commerce. But there is a broader basis for federal control.

This railroad, like most others, was chartered to engage in both intrastate and interstate commerce. The same instrumentality serves both. The two services are inextricably intertwined. The extent and manner in which one is performed, necessarily affects the performance of the other. Efficient performance of either is dependent upon the efficient performance of the transportation system as a whole. Congress did not, in the respect here under consideration, assume exclusive regulation of the common instrumentality, as it did in respect to safety coupling devices. It expressly excluded from federal control that part of the railroad which consists of "spur, industrial, team, switching or side tracks located . . . wholly within one State." But as to the rest of every railroad line used in interstate commerce, Congress reserved the full authority to determine whether, and to what extent, public convenience and necessity permit abandonment.

The exercise of federal power in authorizing abandonment is not an invasion of a field reserved to the State. The obligation assumed by the corporation under its charter of providing intrastate service on every part of its line within the State is subordinate to the performance by it of its federal duty, also assumed, efficiently to render transportation services in interstate commerce. There is no contention here that the railroad by its charter agreed in terms to continue to operate this branch regardless of loss. Because the same instrumentality serves both, Congress has power to assume not only some control, but paramount control, insofar as interstate commerce is involved. It may determine to what extent and in what manner intrastate service must be subordinated in order that interstate service may be adequately rendered. The power to make the determination inheres in the United States as an incident of its power over interstate commerce. The making of this determination involves an exercise of judgment upon the facts and to exercise thereon the judgment whether abandonment is consistent with public convenience and necessity. Congress conferred such powers upon the Commission.

While the constitutional basis of authority to issue the certificate of abandonment is the power of Congress to regulate interstate commerce, the Act does not make issuance of the certificate conditional upon a finding that continued operation will result in discrimination against interstate commerce, or that it will result in a denial of just compensation for the use in intrastate commerce of the property of the carrier within the State, or that it will result in a denial of such compensation for the property within the State used in commerce intrastate and interstate. The sole test prescribed is that abandonment be consistent with public necessity and convenience. In determining whether it is, the Commission must have regard to the needs of both intrastate and interstate commerce. For it was a purpose of Transportation Act, 1920, to establish and maintain adequate service for both. The benefit to one of the abandonment must be weighed against the inconvenience and loss to which the other will thereby be subjected. Conversely, the benefits to particular communities and commerce of continued operation must be weighed against the burden thereby imposed upon other commerce. The result of this weighing—

the judgment of the Commission—is expressed by its order granting or denying the certificate.

[The determination by the ICC that the abandonment application should be approved was affirmed.]

2. Conditional Abandonments

SEABOARD COAST LINE RAILROAD CO.—ABANDONMENT BE-TWEEN ARCADIA AND PORT BOCA GRANDE, DESOTO, SARA-SOTA, CHARLOTTE AND LEE COUNTIES, FLORIDA
360 I.C.C. 257 (1979)

Commissioner Stafford:

On September 21, 1977, Seaboard Coast Line Railroad Company (SCL) filed an application to abandon its rail line between Arcadia, FL, and Port Boca Grande, FL. In an initial decision served February 12, 1979, the Administrative Law Judge approved the proposed abandonment subject to certain conditions.

Protestants marshal three basic arguments in support of their contention that the abandonment is not warranted by public convenience and necessity. They argue that: (1) there is no adequate alternative service; (2) the abandonment will have a major adverse community impact; and (3) SCL's estimates of Boca Grande rehabilitation costs were inflated and unreliable. We do not believe the evidence of record supports these arguments.

In his initial decision, the Administrative Law Judge carefully weighed the conflicting evidence concerning "adequate alternative service." While noting that alternative Tampa Range facilities[31] would be burdened by normal growth and the diversion of Boca Grande traffic to those facilities, the Administative Law Judge went on to conclude that the Rockport improvement condition would remedy this congestion at Tampa Range and thus insure the availability of adequate alternative facilities to shippers after SCL's abandonment of Boca Grande.

Virtually all abandonments involve some reduction in service. The question of whether a particular abandonment should be granted or denied necessarily involves a balancing process. The adequacy of alternative service is a factor in that balancing process. The basic question is whether the loss of certain rail service—with its attendant negative consequences on shippers and localities, as well as its attendant positive consequences on the applicant railroad—is offset by reasonably adequate alternative service. Here, after full consideration of the record, the Administrative Law Judge found that imposition of the Rockport improvement condition would insure the existence of adequate alternative service. Being based as it was upon substantial evidence, we see no justification for reversing the Administrative Law Judge's conclusion.

Rockport improvement condition. SCL contends that the imposition of the Rockport improvement condition was unsupported by the record.[32] We disagree. The facts of this case clearly warrant imposition of the Rockport condition.

The need for the Rockport improvement condition stems from the following circumstances. At present, phosphate rail traffic from Bone Valley, FL, can move to one of two alternative transloading regions in southwest Florida: Port Boca Grande in the south or the Tampa Range ports in the north. If Port Boca Grande is abandoned as SCL proposes, the volume of phosphate rail traffic to the Tampa Range ports will increase. Rockport (a Tampa Range port owned by SCL) will bear a substantial proportion of this increased volume since most of the other Tampa Range ports are privately owned by phosphate shippers' competitors. The Administrative Law Judge found that unless Rockport's facilities are improved, the abandonment of Boca Grande will leave phosphate shippers without adequate alternative service.

In order to offset these serious adverse consequences, the Administrative Law Judge found it essential that SCL make the improvements at Rockport contemplated by the Rockport condition. As the Administrative Law Judge concluded, the harm resulting from the abandonment could only be offset by a condition such as the Rockport condition. Without the Rockport condition, the abandonment would not be permitted by the public convenience and necessity. Far from being unsupported by the evidence, we believe the Administrative Law Judge's conclusion was amply justified for the following reasons.

First, we reject SCL's argument that, since there are several ports in Tampa Range besides Rockport, the Administrative Law Judge erred in focusing on Rockport's capacity problems. As the evidence shows, most of the other transloading facilities in Tampa Range are owned by phosphate shippers' competitors, and the only port under civic ownership (Manatee) suffers from such problems as car shortages. Thus, given Rockport's role as a prominent transloading facility for phosphate shippers in Tampa Range, the Administrative Law Judge correctly focused on the congestion problems predicted for Rockport. Indeed, the evidence shows that congestion at Rockport is already being experienced by phosphate shippers . . . and that only limited weight can be given to SCL's argument that any overcrowding at Rockport is simply due to poor shipper scheduling. In view of this congestion situation, the Rockport improvement condition was an appropriate qualification on the abandonment.

Further, we believe the Administrative Law Judge's selection of the $5.5 million figure was justified by the record. This figure was not chosen arbitrarily, but rather is the figure which SCL's own cost studies justified as the proper level of expenditure at Rockport. Moreover, it is the level of expenditure which SCL apparently led shippers to believe it would invest at Rockport. Thus, the Administrative Law Judge did not require SCL to expend any more funds at Rockport than it had earlier proposed to spend there itself.

If we granted SCL's request to remove the Rockport condition the abandonment would have to be denied since the evidence shows there would be inadequate alternative facilities. However, by letting the Rockport condition stand, we leave to SCL the business judgment of determining whether the benefits of the abandonment offset its costs (e.g., the cost of constructing the improvements at Rockport which will become necessary if the abandonment occurs).

SCL can always avoid the Rockport condition by simply not abandoning its Arcadia/Boca Grande line. In any event, we should note that removal of the Rockport condition would not only reduce SCL's options, but also be unfair to shippers who have a clear need for adequate alternative facilities and who were led to perceive SCL as being prepared to improve Rockport on its own initiative.

It should also be noted that the required investment at Rockport will not unreasonably burden SCL. Besides being the amount SCL was planning to commit in improving its Rockport facility, it is consistent with savings which SCL will realize from the abandonment and with the increased income from additional business made possible by the expansion of handling capacity at Rockport.

Section 10903(b)(1)(A) of the Interstate Commerce Act (49 U.S.C. § 10903(b)(1)(A)) gives the Commission power to approve an abandonment application "with modifications and require compliance with conditions that the Commission finds are required by public convenience and necessity." The Supreme Court has defined the phrase "public convenience and necessity" broadly, saying that it must be given "a scope consistent with the broad purpose" of the act.

As previously noted, the Rockport improvement condition is vital to making the proposed abandonment consistent with the public convenience and necessity. Following the guidance of *Colorado v. United States*, 271 U.S. 153, 168 (1926), the Administrative Law Judge balanced the costs and benefits of the abandonment and concluded that the Rockport condition would sufficiently offset the abandonment's adverse consequences upon localities and shippers to make the abandonment permissible. Imposition of the Rockport condition, having been found to be required by the public convenience and necessity, was clearly within our authority under 19 U.S.C. § 10903(b)(1)(A).

We are not persuaded by applicant's arguments that the Rockport condition runs afoul of the so-called *Purcell Doctrine* against wasteful conditions. See *Purcell v. United States*, 315 U.S. 318 (1942).

In *Purcell*, the Commission had authorized an abandonment but refused to require as a condition to the abandonment the relocation of the line (even though it would have been at government expense), concluding that the cost of relocation and the increased cost of operating the relocated line were not justified by the public convenience and necessity. The Supreme Court sustained the Commission's order, noting that the legislative intent behind the Transportation Act of 1920 and 1940 included the avoidance of waste, the promotion of adequate, economical and efficient service, and the fostering of sound economic conditions in the transportation system and among the several carriers. Thus, as the court put it:

> When materials and labor are devoted to the building of a line in an amount that cannot be justified in terms of the reasonably predictable revenues, there is ample ground to support a conclusion that the expenditures are wasteful whoever foots the bill. [*Purcell, supra*, 315 U.S. at 385]

Unlike *Purcell*, the improvements contemplated by the Rockport condition would not entail a waste of transportation assets because those improvements can—to cite *Purcell*—be "justified in terms of the reasonably predictable revenues." As the Administrative Law Judge noted, the record contains persuasive evidence of continued traffic through Rockport at least through the end of this century. . . . This is in marked contrast to the bleak traffic prospects which existed in *Purcell*. Thus, we conclude that the Rockport condition does not fall within the *Purcell Doctrine's* prohibition against wasteful conditions.

SCL may avoid the Rockport condition altogether by simply not abandoning its Arcadia/Boca Grande line. We do not see how the Rockport condition can be an abuse of discretion when it plays such a crucial part in making the proposed abandonment consistent with the public convenience and necessity, and especially in light of SCL's intimation to shippers at the outset of this abandonment proceeding that it was considering investing $5.5 million to improve storage facilities at Rockport.

Thus, for all these reasons, we reject protestants' contention that the Administrative Law Judge erred in finding public convenience and necessity.

3. *The Staggers Rail Act of 1980*

The Staggers Rail Act[33] amends section 10904 of the Interstate Commerce Act to impose stringent time deadlines on the disposition of abandonment applicants. Moreover, if the application is unopposed, the ICC must approve the abandonment or discontinuance within 30 days.

If the ICC concludes that the public convenience and necessity requires or permits an abandonment, such findings must be published in the *Federal Register*. Within 10 days thereafter, any person may offer to pay the carrier a subsidy for continuance of such service, or to pay the costs of purchasing the line. The ICC is obligated to postpone issuance of a certificate authorizing discontinuance or abandonment where (1) a financially responsible person has offered financial assistance, and (2) it is likely that such assistance will be equal to (a) the difference between revenues attributable to the line and the avoidable cost of providing such service (plus a reasonable return on the line), *or* (b) the acquisition cost of the line. If the parties fail to agree on the amount of the compensation, they may submit the question to the ICC for resolution.

C. Discontinuance of Service

49 U.S.C. § 10909. DISCONTINUING OR CHANGING TRAIN OR FERRY TRANSPORTATION IN ONE STATE

(a) When a carrier providing transportation subject to the jurisdiction of the Interstate Commerce Commission under subchapter I of chapter 105 of this title has proposed a discontinuance or change of any part of the transportation of a train or ferry operated by it entirely in one State and—

(1) the law of the State prohibits the discontinuance or change;

(2) the carrier has requested the State authority having jurisdiction over the discontinuance or change for permission to discontinue or change the transportation and the request has been denied; or

(3) the State authority has not acted finally by the 120th day after the carrier made the request;

the carrier may petition the Commission for permission to discontinue or change the transportation.

(b) The Commission may grant permission to the carrier to discontinue or change any part of the transportation if the commission finds that—

(1) the present or future public convenience and necessity require or permit the discontinuance or change to be authorized by the Commission; and

(2) continuing the transportation, without the proposed discontinuance or change, will constitute an unreasonable burden on the interstate operations of the carrier or on interstate commerce.

1. The Principal Cases

SOUTHERN RY. CO. V. NORTH CAROLINA

376 U.S. 93 (1964)

STEWART, J.

In 1959 appellant Southern Railway Company filed a petition with the North Carolina Utilities Commission for an order permitting it to discontinue operation of two intrastate passenger trains between Greensboro and Goldsboro, North Carolina, a distance of about 130 miles. The trains in question are No. 16, which operates eastbound in the morning, and No. 13, which operates westbound in the late afternoon. Since 1958 these two trains have provided the last remaining railway passenger service between the two communities. The State Commission denied the petition, and its decision was upheld by the North Carolina Supreme Court.

The railway company then filed a petition with the ICC pursuant to Section 10909 of the Interstate Commerce Act, seeking authority to discontinue operation of the trains. The Commission ordered discontinuance of the trains. It found that the trains, which in 1948 had carried 56,739 passengers, carried only 14,776 passengers in 1960; that the direct expenses of operating the trains during the latter year were over three times the total revenue; that the discontinuance of the trains would result in savings of at least $90,589 per year; that the need shown for these trains was relatively insubstantial when viewed in light of the density of the population of the area served; that the existing alternate transportation service by rail, bus, airline, and other means was reasonably adequate; and that the discontinuance of the passenger train service would not seriously affect the industrial growth of the area. Against the background of these findings, the Commission considered, but gave little or no weight to the overall prosperity of the carrier.

Protestants then instituted an action in District Court seeking to set aside the order of the Commission. The court held that it was erroneous as a matter of law for the Commission to order discontinuance of the trains without first determining whether the profits, including those obtained from freight operations of the particular segment of the railway involved, are contributing a fair share to the overall company operations; that taking into account total operation of this line, there is a profit not a loss; that passenger traffic had slightly increased during the first five months of 1961; that the carrier had done little to promote use of the passenger trains; that continued existence of the alternative of railway passenger service might be considered a necessity under such circumstances as airline strikes or bad weather; and that, in light of the overall prosperity of the Southern Railway Company, the effect of the losses incurred by passenger service on this segment was inconsequential to the railroad. The court held that the conclusions of the ICC were arbitrary and capricious and set aside the Commission's order, perpetually enjoining the carrier from discontinuing the Greensboro-Goldsboro passenger trains. The United States, the ICC and the carrier appealed.

The legislative history clearly indicates that Congress in enacting Section 10909 was addressing itself to a problem quite distinct from that reflected by overall unprofitable operation of an entire segment of railroad line. The Commission already had authority prior to 1958, under Section 10903, to authorize discontinuance of all services on any given intrastate line where continuance of such service would impose an undue burden on interstate commerce. However, the Commission totally lacked power to discontinue particular trains or services while leaving the remaining services in operation. It was precisely this gap which Section 10909 was intended to fill. As both the House and Senate Committee Reports make clear, Congress was primarily concerned with the problems posed by passenger services for which significant public demand no longer existed and which were consistently deficit-producing, thus forcing the carriers to subsidize their operation out of freight profits.

All that need properly be considered under this standard is what effect the discontinuance of the specific train or service in question will have upon the public convenience and necessity and upon interstate operations or commerce.

This Court has long recognized that the Commission may properly give varying weights to the overall prosperity of the carrier in differing situations. Thus, in *Colorado v. United States*, 271 U.S. 153, which also involved a situation in which the Commission was required to balance public convenience and necessity against undue burdens on interstate commerce, it was specifically noted that "In many cases, it is clear that the extent of the whole traffic, the degree of dependence of the communities directly affected upon the particular means of transportation, and other attendant conditions, are such that the carrier may not justly be required to continue to bear the financial loss necessarily entailed by operation. In some cases the question is whether abandonment may justly be permitted, in view of the fact that it would subject the communities directly affected to serious injury while continued operation would impose a relatively light burden upon a prosperous carrier." 271 U.S., at 168–169. In cases falling within the latter category, such as those involving vital commuter services in large metropolitan areas where the demands of public convenience and necessity are large, it is of course obvious that the Commission would err if it did not give great weight to the ability of the carrier to absorb even large deficits resulting from such services. But where, as here, the Commission's findings make clear that the demands of public convenience and necessity are slight and that the situation is, therefore, one falling within the first category delineated in *Colorado*, it is equally proper for the Commission, in determining the existence of the burden on interstate commerce, to give little weight to the factor of the carrier's overall prosperity.

Goldberg, J. dissenting.

This case involves more than the fate of the 6:10 between Greensboro and Goldsboro, North Carolina. It is the first litigation to reach this Court concerning the criteria to be applied by the Interstate Commerce Commission in proceedings seeking discontinuance of intrastate passenger trains under Section 10909 of the Interstate Commerce Act. The Court sustains the ICC in interpreting this provision to mean that, in determining whether an unprofitable intrastate passenger train shall be discontinued, the Commission need give: (1) "little or no weight" to the overall prosperity of the carrier, and (2) no consideration whatsoever to the profitability of "the interstate operations of the carrier as a whole, or any particular segment thereof." In my view the standards employed by the Commission were not the proper ones.

Since "[p]assenger deficits have become chronic in the railroad industry," the Court's decision will allow the Commission to authorize the Nation's railroads to discontinue virtually all intrastate passenger service—including most commuter services. It is difficult to conceive of a situation in this era of widespread bus, airline and automobile transportation in which the Commission cannot find that alternative services are more or less available to handle the diminished railroad passenger traffic. Such a finding coupled with a "net loss" on the passenger trains will meet the discontinuance standard approved by the Court. The Court concludes that this result has been mandated by Congress.

The case turns upon the language and purpose of Section 10909 of the Interstate Commerce Act. This section was first enacted as part of the Transportation Act of 1958 as section 13(a). It is true, as the Court points out, that this legislation reflects concern with "the worsening railroad situation." But it is far from accurate to conclude that Congress was oblivious of the needs of the passenger public and of the primary responsibility of state commissions for the regulation of purely intrastate service. Under Section 10909 a railroad seeking to discontinue an interstate passenger train, as distinguished from an interstate operation, must first apply to the appropriate state commission. Only after the state commission has been given the opportunity and has failed or refused to act is the ICC authorized to intervene. The Comission may reverse the decision of the state agency only upon findings, supported by substantial evidence, that the service is not required by public convenience and necessity *and* that its continuance will constitute "an unjust and undue burden . . . upon interstate commerce."

In this case the State of North Carolina points out that between 1951 and 1956, of 44 requests for discontinuance of intrastate passenger trains, some emanating from appellant Southern Railway, 42 were approved by the State. Indeed, on the line between Greensboro and Goldsboro, Southern operated three pairs of passenger trains until September 1954. The State, on Southern's application, authorized discontinuance of one pair of trains in 1954 and another pair in 1958.

The two trains in question, No. 13 and No. 16, are the last remaining pair of east-west passenger trains between the two communities. They are the only interconnecting service at Greensboro for passengers from Goldsboro and intermediate points with north-south trains on Southern's main line. For such passengers, they furnish a convenient overnight pullman service to Washington, New York and other east coast cities and conserve working time for the traveler having business at the north or south terminal cities. Trains 13 and 16 run on tracks leased by Southern from the state-owned North Carolina Railroad Company. The lease clearly contemplates both passenger and freight service. Furthermore, as the Court recites in its opinion, while during the relevant year Southern sustained a loss on its passenger service on the line of approximately $90,000, it made a profit of over $600,000 on freight on the same leased line and an overall profit on its entire system in excess of $36,000,000. While passenger traffic on this line has declined in recent years, the traffic is still substantial—14,776 passengers used the two trains in 1960, an increase of more than 500 over the previous year—and the area served has been growing in population and industrial importance. On these facts, the state agency denied Southern's request to discontinue the two trains. In overruling the decision of the State, the ICC, as already stated, gave "little or no weight" to Southern's overall prosperity and no consideration whatsoever to its freight profits on the line. In my view, the Commission wrongfully ignored these factors and the Court errs in approving this action of the Commission.

I read the Act and its history to require the Commission to take into account all material factors established by evidence presented by the parties and bearing on the issues of public need and burden on interstate commerce. The three-judge District

Court properly observed that these issues are "not susceptible of scientific measurement or exact formulae but are questions of degree and involve the balancing of conflicting interests." I cannot comprehend how the Commission can achieve a proper balance without fully considering the railroad's relevant profit data. The issues—whether the public need will allow discontinuance of the passenger service and whether continued operation will unduly burden interstate commerce—are interrelated. Under any commonsense view of the statute, the amount of the railroad's financial loss on the two intrastate passenger trains cannot be considered in isolation from its freight profits on that line, its intrastate profits, or its overall prosperity. The words "unjust" and "undue" clearly indicate that Congress intended that the mere fact that a particular passenger train is operating at a loss—i.e., is a burden—would not in itself justify discontinuance of that train. The burden must be "unjust" and "undue," and whether this is so cannot be determined except in light of the total circumstances. The final determination must be made by balancing all the relevant factors. . . .

The requirement that the Commission consider such factors certainly does not mean that it is precluded from authorizing the abandonment of an uneconomic passenger train because the remainder of the railroad's intrastate or overall operations are profitable. It means only that in making its determination the Commission shall give appropriate consideration to all relevant factors. One factor or a combination may prove controlling, but all must be considered in making the statutory determination. This the Commission refused to do and, therefore, its isolated finding that public convenience and necessity would permit a discontinuance was insufficient, absent an appropriate consideration of the burden on commerce, to sustain its conclusion.

CHICAGO, SOUTH SHORE AND SOUTH BEND R.R. DISCONTINUANCE OF ALL PASSENGER TRAIN SERVICE

354 I.C.C. 307 (1977)

Division 3, Commissioners Brown, Macfarland and Clapp

By the Division:

Pursuant to the provisions of section 10909 of the Interstate Commerce Act, the Chicago South Shore and South Bend Railroad, hereinafter referred to as the "South Shore," proposed to discontinue all passenger service between Chicago, Ill., and South Bend, Ind., including all intermediate points, on December 8, 1976.

Simultaneously, South Shore filed an application, in docket No. AB–136, seeking a certificate authorizing the abandonment of its trackage rights over the line of the Illinois Central Gulf Railroad between Randolph Street and 115th Street (Kensington) in Chicago, a distance of approximately 14.2 miles. These trackage rights are for the operation of electrically propelled passenger service only and were approved in *Chicago S.S. & S. B. R. Trackage Rights, Cook County, Ill.*, 307 I.C.C. 329 (1959). The application for abandonment is supplementary to and incidental to the discontinuance application and was consolidated with the discontinuance application.

Upon consideration of numerous protests, complaints, and requests for an investigation, by order served December 3, 1976, we instituted an investigation of the proposed discontinuance of service and directed continued operation of the trains for a period not to exceed 4 months—the maximum allowed by the Act—beyond the effective date of the notice.

The South Shore is an electrically powered common carrier of both freight and passengers, and the last of its kind remaining in the country. It operates its passenger service between Chicago and South Bend, a distance of approximately 88 miles. The South Shore basically provides a commuter and other short-haul passenger service. It operates between Randolph Street and 115th Street, Chicago, a distance of approximately 14 miles, over the track of the Illinois Central Gulf Railroad under a trackage leasing agreement. Between Kensington and the Illinois-Indiana State line, the carrier operates under a perpetual lease of tracks owned by the Kensington and Eastern Railroad.

Between the Illinois-Indiana State line and South Bend, operations are conducted over its own track via Hammond, Gary, Michigan City, and South Bend, serving 28 stations, many of which are flag stops. Between Gary and South Bend the line of the South Shore is single track. Most of the passengers transported by the railroad are commuters who are moved over the segment between Gary and Randolph Street during the morning and evening rush hours.

South Shore owns and operates in its passenger service a total of 49 passenger cars, consisting of 43 electrically propelled motorcars and six trailers. Five additional cars are out of service with major structural defects. The cars vary in seating capacity from 48 to 80 seats. The cars are approximately 50 years old, having been purchased between 1926 and 1929, and during cold or wet freezing weather the number of cars out of service or involved in breakdowns reduces the total available seating capacity drastically. The equipment is operable in multiple units, and the carrier's trains can be composed of any number of cars to a maximum of eight.

The South Shore proposes to eliminate its entire passenger service. It points to the condition of its car fleet which has long since reached the end of its physical life and is "bordering on unsafe." It argues that its financial resources are utterly inadequate to finance new equipment. Patronage has declined from 6,163,789 revenue passengers in 1946 to 1,816,957 in 1975. This decline parallels the overall decrease nationwide in passenger transit ridership. South Shore states that the public has deserted its trains for many reasons including increased affluence, the private automobile, construction of toll roads such as the Indiana Toll Road, and freeway I–94. Other reasons include the growth of Chicago suburbs in Indiana away from the industrialized corridor in which the South Shore operates, and the "increased emphasis placed by the political community on development away from the corridor."

South Shore states that its passenger deficits have grown steadily, reaching an alleged $1,523,035 in 1974, $1,740,262 in 1975, and $1,766,889 for the first 9 months of 1976 after crediting Illinois grants. South Shore contends that it should no longer be required to cross-subsidize these enormous passenger deficits from its freight revenues. It also argues that despite years of effort it has been unable to stimulate any meaningful response from the public officials and agencies of Indiana to the problems engendered by its antiquated fleet and its recurring, ballooning passenger deficits. South Shore asserts that in spite of the existence of plans, planning agencies and statements of political leaders in Indiana, there has been no realistic action, other than publicity, toward providing public financial assistance to procure new cars and to meet the operating loss generated by the service currently operated.

In *Atchison, T. & S.F. Ry.Co. Discontinuance of Trains*, 344 I.C.C. 735, 745 (1969), the Commission stated:

> The fundamental question for resolution in proceedings under section 13a(1)*** is "***what effect the discontinuance of the specific train or

service in question will have upon the public convenience and necessity and upon interstate operations or commerce." *Southern R. Co. v. North Carolina*, 376 U.S. 93, 104 (1964). Among the factors this Commission considers in making such a determination are the population of the territory serviced, the use by the public of the service sought to be discontinued, other available transportation in the area, the general financial condition of the carrier involved, and the losses it suffers in providing the service. No one factor is, standing alone, dispositive. Thus, the fact that these trains are operating at a deficit is significant. By the same token, public use of, and reliance upon, this rail service, is also an important consideration. *Missiouri Pac. R. Co. Discontinuance of Passenger Trains*, 320 I.C.C. 1. The short of the matter is: we must balance public convenience and necessity against undue burdens on interstate commerce. Cf. *Southern Pac. Co. Discontinuance of Trains*, 334 I.C.C. 159, and *Colorado v. United States*, 271 U.S. 153 (1926).

The Commission also must consider what impact, if any, the proposed discontinuance would have upon the environment, and the probable effects upon employees.

Because the South Shore operates the last commuter service in a large and heavily industrialized metropolitan area, any cessation of service will be subject to the strictest scrutiny. See *Southern R. Co. v. North Carolina*, 376 U.S. 93, 105 (1963). Another newer factor to be weighed is the importance which the involved States accord to the service as demonstrated by their activities in applying for available Federal subsidies for mass transit. Speaking generally, commuter rail service has been a deficit producing operation for many years. Many State and regional agencies, such as the Commuter Operating Agency of New Jersey, the Southeastern Pennsylvania Transportation Authority, the Massachusetts Bay Transportation Authority, as well as the Illinois Regional Transportation Authority are providing subsidies to the railroads in order to offset revenue losses incurred from commuter operations. The Congress passed legislation to assist mass transit in 1964 and by amendments in 1970 and 1974 has enlarged the involvement and financial assistance of the Federal Government.

The South Shore is used by approximately 6,000 daily commuters to get to their jobs in Chicago. Without this service these passengers would have no comparable means of mass transit available. With discontinuance, passengers from western Lake County could possibly use the Illinois Central Gulf, the Chicago and Calumet District Transit Co., or the South Suburban Safeway Lines, but their use of these alternative modes of transportation would involve some degree of hardship because of the location of the bus stops and the distance to the ICG stations. In addition, the buses are presently overcrowded and are considerably slower than the South Shore. For commuters located east of Gary, the only alternative would be the private automobile. The automobile is not a common carrier and merits little consideration as an alternative service. *Atchison, T. & S.F. Ry. Co. Discontinuance of Trains*, 333 I.C.C. 497 (1968).

We have a great concern regarding the adverse environmental impacts, especially to the area's air quality, which might result from a discontinuance of this operation. The area along the south rim of Lake Michigan is highly industrialized. While some success has been achieved in recent years to improve air quality, we think any action which will worsen conditions in this area should be avoided if possible.

We are also concerned with the continued financial health of the South Shore. After a careful examination of the railroad's figures we have found that the South Shore is losing heavily on its passenger service. (Almost no railroad in the United States is performing commuter rail service at a profit.) The South Shore is profitable overall, in part due to its affiliation with the Chesapeake & Ohio Railroad. The public feels betrayed because Chesapeake & Ohio officials stated in 1966 that they would continue the passenger operation and because between 1966 and February 1973, officials of the South Shore stated unequivocally that the Chesapeake & Ohio would stand behind the South Shore's payment of the 20-percent local match for an urban mass transit grant for new cars. Neither of these promises has been kept. While the South Shore appears financially sound at this date, we have some reservations since the carrier's rather substantial increase in profitability over the last few years appears to have slowed down. While we find the South Shore is able to sustain these losses now, we do not know how long this situation will continue. In any event, without new equipment and a firm commitment by the State of Indiana and the local communities for a continuation of the service and financial backing that entails, the problem of the South Shore will continue.

In brief many of the participants have cited numerous Commission cases for discussion of the various elements to be considered in a passenger continuance proceeding. One element not previously considered in any of these cases is the existence of the Federal policy on mass transit. This policy is reflected in the Urban Mass Transportation Assistance Act of 1964, as amended in 1970 and later in 1974. In this statute Congress found that Federal financial assistance for the development of efficient and coordinated mass transportation systems is essential to the solution of urban problems. As administered by the Federal Mass Transit Administration, which is part of the Department of Transportation, the Federal Government can provide 80 percent of the cost of new equipment and other capital items and 50 percent of the railroad's operating deficits. Under the statute, the difference is to be made up by either the State or local communities involved. The carrier cannot be expected to supply these funds, nor did it have that as its intention when it passed the legislation. The problem before us is a problem for the States of Indiana and Illinois. The State of Illinois has made its position clear but the State of Indiana has not, even though most of the people who will be affected are residents of that State. We recognize the high level of concern of many people in northwest Indiana and their attempts to get action from their elected representatives. Because we are convinced that South Shore's service should be continued if at all possible, we will order the railroad to continue the operation of service for 10 months from the date of service of our order. We expect that this will be sufficient time for the State of Indiana to take steps to save the service. If this does not occur, we think it highly likely that there is no future for the South Shore's passenger operations.

Protestant labor unions have requested that labor conditions be imposed both as to the discontinuance and the abandonment. In this connection, we note that the Commission is without authority to impose conditions for the protection of employees in train discontinuance proceedings.

While the South Shore would be required to file another notice of discontinuance at the end of the 10-month period, this Commission has the ultimate responsibility to decide whether or not an investigation is required. One important consideration will be what the governmental authorities have done. We also wish to make it clear that the South Shore is under an obligation to negotiate in good faith to reach an agreement. Any indication that this has not happened will, likewise, be considered if this Commission is required to pass on this matter again. We doubt that it would be in the interest of any party to have this matter returned to the Commission. We think that a satisfactory resolution of the problem posed by the threatened discontinuance more likely can be avoided if both sides are aware that we view the matter as one involving mutual obligations and responsibilities.

* * *

NOTE: Aftermath of the Chicago & South Shore Decision

The decision of the ICC in *Chicago and South Shore* prompted the Indiana legislature to act to save its last private commuter railroad. It established the Northern Indiana Commuter Transportation District, which began to funnel operating subsidies into the line in 1978. A \$40 million contract for 36 electrified cars for the system was awarded during 1980 to Japan's Sumitomo Corporation. The cars are 85-foot-long stainless steel electrified carriages capable of seating 97 passengers. Other capital improvements of the South Shore include increasing the power supply of the electric line system and modernizing and expanding passenger stations and surrounding parking lots.

NOTE: Governmental Support for Urban Mass Transportation

As the *Chicago and South Shore* case indicates, the federal government provides operational and equipment subsidies through the Urban Mass Transit Administration of the Department of Transportation. Although the federal government has been providing such subsidies for highway construction since 1916, and established the Highway Trust Fund in 1956, urban mass transportation received no significant financial support until 1965. Today, fewer than 18 percent of working Americans use public transportation. Yet urban mass transit is by far more desirable, from both an environmental and an energy perspective, than is the automobile.

2. Intercity Trains

During the 12 years of ICC jurisdiction over train-offs, from 1958 to 1970, the number of passenger trains in operation declined 60 percent (a loss of more than 1,000 trains) and 13 railroads discontinued all passenger service.[34] Then the Rail Passenger Service Act (the "Amtrak law") imposed a moratorium on ICC train-off petitions. From this act was created the National Railroad Passenger Corporation, which, when it started service on May 1, 1971, effected the largest train discontinuance of all time.

The Commission's jurisdiction over passenger trains stemmed from Section 13a of the Transportation Act of 1958, which did not mention the word "passenger." (This provision was subsequently recodified as 49 U.S.C. § 10909.)

Before October 30, 1970, the ICC had exclusive jursidiction over interstate passenger trains as well as concurrent jurisdiction with state regulatory commissions over intrastate trains. With the passage of the Amtrak law, railroads were prohibited from discontinuing any intercity trains until May 1, 1971, and nonparticipating lines were barred from pulling off trains until January 1, 1975.

Because the 1970 law did not apply to commuter trains, Section 13a has been used only a few times. But in the first of the post-Amtrak cases, the ICC determined that the Penn Central Boston-Providence trains, although operating between major cities, were in fact commuter operations and could be discontinued with approval by the Commission. The ICC outlined a number of criteria which it uses to determine whether a service is "commuter," notably the issuance of multiple-ride tickets, type of equipment used, and schedules.

The nation's commuter fleet has in general remained stable and even increased in frequency. Dicta emerging from ICC decisions indicate that the Commission will not look favorably on mass-scale discontinuances of commuter service in crowded metropolitan areas. In August 1975, however, the Commission did allow Chicago & North Western to trim its commuter runs from Lake Geneva, Wisconsin, to Richmond, Illinois. The physical condition of the branch-line track allows a maximum speed of only 15 miles per hour, and Wisconsin did not subsidize the line.

3. Amtrak

Upon a railroad's contracting with Amtrak to provide service, the carrier was relieved of the responsibility for operating its own passenger trains.[35,36] But if a railroad did not contract with Amtrak at its inception, it could not discontinue service until 1975.[37] Most carriers were quick to take advantage of this provision, although some hung on for quite a while.[38] Even Amtrak was subject to the ICC if it wanted to eliminate trains in the "basic system," but that provision was later removed by amendment of the Amtrak law. Presently, the ICC has no role in Amtrak, and the passenger corporation is limited only by its own internal criteria (and whims of Congress) in discontinuing service.[39] As far as exit from the market is concerned, Amtrak is a deregulator's dream. The route structure of the system is deregulated, and Amtrak can (theoretically) spend its resources as it sees fit.

Congress has not been content to let Amtrak pick and choose routes. Several times it has intervened to protect or institute certain politically sensitive routes. Congressmen are reluctant to let a service which benefits their district disappear. The only substantial cuts to date have been those which were implemented by congressional directive in 1979 and 1981. The secretary of transportation was mandated to draw up a revised system, which is the slimmed-down Amtrak network that is operated today.[40] Even then,

Congress set some standards to incorporate "regional balance" into the criteria for discontinuance.

4. Independent Passenger Trains

Because Amtrak and most commuter services are beyond the scope of the ICC's jurisdiction, Section 10908 (formerly 13a) of the Interstate Commerce Act has been little used. The Southern Railway managed to discontinue its remaining passenger trains, with ICC approval, in 1979, on the condition that the *Southern Crescent* be operated by Amtrak.[41]

The Denver & Rio Grande Railroad was the last independent operator of interstate passenger trains. In 1979, the ICC denied the railroad's petition to drop the *Rio Grande Zephyr* west of Grand Junction, Colorado, since patronage had remained steady or increased, alternative transportation was insufficient, and the record indicated "a complete lack of promotion of the Zephyr by the Rio Grande. While there has been no affirmative effort by DRGW to discourage patronage by downgrading the on-board services, there clearly has been a lack of affirmative effort to encourage patronage. Such promotion must be an indispensable part of any serious program to maximize revenues."[42] The Rio Grande was ultimately given the opportunity to terminate its passenger service in 1983. Amtrak stepped in to fill the void, rerouting its Chicago-San Francisco line over the Rio Grande–Denver–Salt Lake City segment and, consequently, abandoning the parallel Wyoming corridor Amtrak had traditionally served.

In another case involving the Rio Grande, the Commission authorized the acquisition and operation by a new carrier of a Rio Grande narrow-gauge line then operated solely for passenger service. On acquisition by the new company, the Rio Grande was relieved of the operation responsibility for the passenger trains.[43]

Under Section 10505 of the Act, the Commission has the discretion to exempt an operation from ICC regulation if it has negligible impact on interstate commerce. In 1981, the Soo Line petitioned the Commission to exempt its mixed train service in Wisconsin and Michigan from the requirements of a formal discontinuance hearing. On January 13, 1982, the ICC denied Soo's request.

VIA Rail Canada, the Canadian government-owned passenger operation, was able to exempt the section of its Montreal-Halifax line which crosses Maine from regulatory approval when it shut down much of the system because of a Parlimentary directive in November 1981.

Because most passenger operations run by virtue of subsidy, continuation of these trains depends on the willingness of legislatures and communities to support the trains, rather than on the decisions of regulatory agencies to allow them to live or die. The ICC's only responsibilities concerning Amtrak, for example, are to complete and publish an annual report to Congress on the state of rail passenger service.

D. Adequacy of Service

WINNEBAGO FARMERS ELEVATOR CO. v. CHICAGO AND NORTH WESTERN TRANSP. CO.

354 I.C.C. 859 (1978)

By the Commission:

The Chicago and North Western Transportation Company (North Western or defendant) operates a rail line from Lake Crystal to Winnebago, Minnesota, a distance of 24.6 miles. In a prior Proceeding, the ICC had denied North Western authority to abandon this line. Winnebago Farmers Elevator Company (WFEC or complainant) contends that since 1971 North Western has failed and refused to provide reasonable and adequate transportation service to it and has failed and refused to furnish safe and adequate car service. Specifically, WFEC states that North Western refused to tender railcars upon reasonable request when there was not general car shortage and that North Western never furnished WFEC with covered hopper cars for carriage of grain. Complainant states that the covered hopper car is the most economical method of transporting grain by rail and is available to WFEC's competitor, Frank Brothers, Inc. of Winnebago which is served by the Chicago, Milwaukee, St. Paul and Pacific Railroad Company (Milwaukee). The Milwaukee's line at Winnebago has apparently been upgraded to Federal Railroad Administration (FRA) class III track standards (49 CFR 213), thus making it capable of handling covered hopper cars. Because of the availability of this service, WFEC believes that it is severely handicapped when competing with Frank Brothers.

WFEC states that North Western has spent a small amount for maintenance of the line and that it has allowed the line to fall into such disrepair as to be inadequate to accommodate covered hopper car service, or for that matter adequate rail service in any respect. Derailments and closures for extended periods of time occur with frequency. As a result of this disrepair, the line is subject to a speed restriction which prevents North Western from operating covered hopper cars over the line.

WFEC also states that it constructed an additional storage facility with a capacity of 600,000 bushels in 1977, in reliance on the Commission's denial of the North Western abandonment. Since 1971 WFEC has shipped in excess of 1 million bushels of grain annually, by motor carrier and rail combined. It asserts that if North Western would provide reasonable and adequate car service, it would ship at least 90 percent of its grain by rail.

In its complaint WFEC charges that sections 11101(a) and 11121(a) of the Interstate Commerce Act (act) have been violated. Complainant requests injunctive relief and that the Commission order North Western to repair, refurbish, and provide reasonable and adequate rail transportation including, without limitation, covered hopper car service for the carriage of grain. Damages are also sought.

Defendant argues that the Commission lacks jurisdiction to enforce section 11101(a) of the act, which provides that "it shall be the duty of every common carrier to provide and furnish transportation upon reasonable request therefor."

We find that section 11702 of the act, which provides that "the Commission is hereby authorized and required to execute and enforce the provisions of Part I of the act," furnishes the Commission with ample authority to enforce the section 11101(a) duty to provide adequate service.

The relief asked in the instant case does not tend to erode managerial prerogative. Complainant specifically states that it would not require defendant "to purchase additional equipment or use eqipment not now owned by defendant and rail carriers in general." Moreover, an express delegation of power is not necessary in a case such as this.

If the act provides the right to pursue one's remedy before the Commission, it follows that it must also give the Commission jurisdiction to hear the complaint. Lastly, we note that there is no express prohibition against enforcement of section 11101(a) by the Commission.

We believe that in most cases involving the duty to provide adequate service the Commission should have primary jurisdiction. In the interest of uniformity and in order to obtain the benefit of the Commission's administrative expertise, referral to the Commission should be made when the defendant has elected to pursue its remedy in the courts. Because in nearly every case relating to service arising under section 11101(a) there are administrative questions concerning what level of service is adequate and whether a request for service is reasonable, we believe that the doctrine of primary jurisdiction requires that these cases be referred to the Commission.

We recognize that in finding that the Commission has jurisdiction to enforce the duty to provide adequate service under section 11101(a) of the act, that we are in effect overruling long-standing Commission precedent. But an administrative agency is not inextricably bound by its past decisions or policies since this would deter necessary flexibility.

In light of the preceding discussion we conclude that the Commission has jurisdiction to enforce the carrier's duty under section 11101(a) of the act "to provide and furnish transportation upon reasonable request therefor."

Levels of Service

Complainant alleges that sections 11101(a) and 11121(a) of the act have been violated. It is imperative to our analysis of the issues in this proceeding that we differentiate between the subject matter of the two sections. Section 11101(a) requires that common carriers provide adequate "transportation" upon reasonable request. In turn, section 10102(24) defines "transportation" broadly, to include:

> locomotives, cars and other vehicles, vessels, and all instrumentalities and facilities of shipment or carriage, irrespective of ownership or of any contract, express or implied, for the use thereof, and all services in connection with the receipt, delivery, elevation, and transfer in transit, ventilation, refrigeration or icing, storage, and handling of property transported.

Section 11121 requires that safe and adequate "car service" be furnished. Section 10102(3) defines "car service" as including:

> the use, control, supply, movement, distribution, exchange, interchange, and return of locomotives, cars, and other vehicles used in the transportation of property, including special types of equipment, and the supply of trains, by any carrier by railroad subject to this part.

While "transportation" is a broadly defined term, "car service" has been found to relate only to "the use to which the vehicles of transportation are put; not the transportation service rendered by means of them." *Peoria Ry. Co. v. United States*, 263 U.S. 528, 533 (1924). Section 11121(a) deals not with the transportation itself, but with the vehicle by which transportation is accomplished. Thus, in *Houston Belt & T. Ry. Co. v. Texas & N. O. R. Co.*, 298 I.C.C. 221 (1956), the Commission found it had no jurisdiction under section 11121(a) to require a carrier to deliver freight. Similarly, it was found in *Louisiana Grocer Co-Operative v. Illinois C. G. R.*, 353 I.C.C. 606, 608 (1977), that switching was not within the scope of section 11121(a). It seems clear that the duty to provide safe and adequate "car service" under section 11121(a) involves the vehicles which are used, but not the transportation provided by means of them. Thus, in this proceeding only the request that we make the use of 100-ton covered hopper cars feasible comes within the scope of section 11121(a). In no other respect does complainant allege that the vehicles themselves are deficient, but only that the regularity of their transportation is inadequate.

The limited duty under section 11121(a) can be contrasted with the duty to provide "transportation" under section 11101(a). The latter duty includes not only transportation services provided and vehicles used, but also "all instrumentalities and facilities," such as tracks. Thus, section 11101(a) is broad enough to encompass the entire subject matter of the complaint.

Turning first to whether the cars provided have been safe and adequate under both sections 11101(a) and 11121(a), we note that there are no facts alleged from which we could conclude that the cars now used are unsafe. We also note that WFEC has asked that we order North Western to upgrade the track to such a level that service could be offered by means of hopper cars. This would require that the load limitation be raised from 251,000 to 263,000 pounds. WFEC states that this is the only way it can compete with the Frank Brothers elevator, which is also located in Winnebago, but on a different rail line.

We reject this argument. Such upgrading would require a virtual reconstruction of the line. As North Western notes, the line was not intended to carry hopper cars when built. North Western submitted evidence of the estimated cost of upgrading the 24.6-mile line to FRA class I standards, suitable for handling 263,000-pound loads. This would allow operation of jumbo hopper cars over the line. Through service interruptions would continue in the winter months because of inability to plow snow at a speed of 10 m.p.h. The cost is estimated at $2,051,400. Estimated annual maintenance of the upgraded line would be $78,565.

We find that these costs illustrate that the cost of upgrading the 24.6-mile line to handle 263,000 pounds of load is excessive, and thus not warranted on this record. We also note that if North Western was required to upgrade all the branch lines in its system so that covered hopper cars could be used, that an expenditure of $200 million would be required. This is an expenditure which even the most financially successful railroad would find onerous, and one which the North Western could find impossible. Nor does the mere fact that a competing elevator has access to superior facilities automatically require that we find that sections 11101(a) and 11121(a) of the act require that that level of service must be produced in all other situations. Expense and physical limitations of the Lake Crystal-Winnebago line are controlling in such a situation. Thus, we find that there is no violation of section 11121(a) and no violation of section 11101(a) as it applies to use of covered hopper cars. Suitability of the track for movement of box cars is sufficient.

Even though we find that upgrading the track so that 100-ton hopper cars can be used is not required, the question of whether the transportation provided by means of the cars now is adequate under section 11101(a) of the act still remains.

The occurrence of derailments requiring closure of the line and North Western's admission that it maintains the line at a level below the Federal minimum level, as well as the necessity of dumping grain when transportation was not available, all support WFEC's claim that the transportation provided by North Western was not adequate. We, therefore, find that the transportation provided was not adequate within the meaning of section 11101(a) of the act.

For the Lake Crystal–Winnebago line adequate service is: (1) track maintained to FRA class I standards, (2) service commensurate with this level of maintenance, and (3) reasonable availability of equipment that can be accommodated on track maintained at FRA class I level (boxcars). Maintenance, service, and equipment at levels in excess of this for branch line operations is a matter within the managerial discretion of the carrier. Thus, the financial condition and management philosophy of the carrier determines what place branch lines have in its system, provided the minimums required in this proceeding are maintained by North Western.

In finding that North Western must upgrade its track to the class I level in order to provide adequate transportation and car service, we are not unmindful of the fact that the Commission has found that deferred maintenance is a legitimate carrier policy, and does not constitute deliberate downgrading of service, except in certain situations. However, where deferred maintenance is of such degree that a line requires upgrading to meet FRA class I standards, as in this proceeding, it may violate the railroad's duties as a common carrier.

Though we are allowing North Western to maintain service upon an "as needed" basis, we expect that if North Western upgrades the line and commits funds to the projects, that it will try to keep the level of service adequate. Upgrading of the line to minimum FRA class I standards would improve the overall level of service, and would probably reduce the expenses associated with the frequent derailments and stopgap measures North Western has had to undertake, such as examination of the line prior to an actual train movement. However, we reserve the right to order a minimum number of trips in the future if the situation were to warrant it.

The pending abandonment proceeding raises an additional problem: should the Commission stay the effectiveness of our order to upgrade the Lake Crystal-Winnebago line until this abandonment proceeding is finally decided, or should our order requiring upgrading be issued while the abandonment is still pending?

We believe that within the factual context of this proceeding, an order requiring upgrading should be issued regardless. To do otherwise would be to render a nullity the remedy enunciated in this proceeding.

From an examination of this chronology it is apparent that North Western never intended to upgrade service on the line as a result of the denial of its prior abandonment application, but merely intended to file another abandonment application. It should be noted that in [the pending abandonment application] applicant relies on the same arguments used in the prior application, except that it now maintains that the cost of upgrading the line to the minimum standards required by Federal law has increased due to inflation and North Western's noncompliance with 49 CFR 213. The line itself continues to operate at a small loss. In such a situation the carrier's arguments that declining traffic, increasing losses and rehabilitation costs making abandonment necessary become self-fulfilling prophecies. One abandonment application is followed by a second, and the arguments for abandonment are then strengthened because applicant has not made the repairs necessary to upgrade the line to minimum FRA standards.

If damages are to be awarded for failure to provide adequate service, such damages must be fully and precisely documented and be directly related to the carrier's failure to render the level of service which we require. Damages must originate in the carrier's failure to supply appropriate equipment, or the carrier's maintenance of the line below FRA class I standards.

WFEC has not proven damages. Its request for damages is deficient in two significant respects. First, WFEC has not given sufficient supporting detail to establish the amount of damage suffered.

The second major deficiency in the request for damages is the inconsistency of the figures upon which they are based.

We emphasize that damages must be traced directly to the carrier's failure to maintain the line at FRA class I levels, and that the failure to provide service and equipment and the resulting transportation by motor carrier must be related to an analysis of the precise comparisons of motor carrier and rail rates to determine if additional costs were, in fact, incurred as a result of the railroad's refusal to provide such service and equipment.

NOTE: Safety Regulation by the Federal Railroad Administration

The Federal Railroad Administration, a component of the Department of Transportation, establishes minimum track standards for rail carriers, as indicated by the preceding decision. Its first such regulations were promulgated in 1973 in response to its finding that track defects, equipment defects and human error were responsible for approximately 41 percent, 20 percent, and 20 percent, respectively, of all rail accidents.

II. MOTOR CARRIAGE

A. The Exempt Sector

The motor carrier industry and its federal regulation has recently undergone the most intensive period of legislative and regulatory scrutiny in its history.[44] Few industries are as important to the nation's well-being as the trucking industry. As Senator Howard Cannon has acknowledged, "There is virtually nothing worn, eaten, or used by the American public that has not at one time or another been transported in a truck. It is no exaggeration to say that the trucking industry is critical to the growth and prosperity of the nation's economy."[45] Similarly, Senator Russell Long presented data describing the magnitude of the industry:

In 1978, there were over 28 million vehicles registered as trucks in the United States. Of this number, over 1 million are engaged in for-hire operations and over 16,000 trucking companies are regulated by the Interstate Commerce Commission (ICC). The trucking industry serves over 60,000 communities in the United States, many of which rely on trucking as the sole mode of transportation of freight. In 1978, the trucking industry had revenues in excess of $35 billion and this figure represented over 50 percent of the total revenues from intercity freight carried by the various transportation modes. There are over 9 million individuals engaged in the trucking industry accounting for over $100 billion in wages each year. The trucking industry is truly a multibillion-dollar business. Clearly, the trucking industry plays a major role in our economy and our society.[46]

In this section the principal unregulated sectors of the motor carrier industry are explored. Many of the statutorily based exemptions have recently been extended by the ICC in its effort to constrict the jurisdiction of the agency. Many of these regulatory efforts have recently been affirmed and expanded by the Congress in its promulgation of the Motor Carrier Act of 1980.

1. The Statutory Exemptions: An Overview

The Interstate Commerce Act exempts several areas of the motor carrier industry from regulation. Thus, although for-hire transportation is regulated, private carriage is not.[47] Although interstate and foreign commerce movements fall within the jursidiction of the ICC,[48] intrastate movements do not.[49] The Act also provides exemptions for various types of agricultural interests, including farmers' vehicles,[50] livestock and agricultural commodities[51] and agricultural cooperatives.[52] Four exemptions are territorial, including those involving incidental-to-air movements[53] and transportation within a terminal area,[54] within a commercial zone[55] and within a single state.[56] Finally, several additional statutory provisions exempt peripheral movements, including the transportation of newspapers[57] and wrecked vehicles[58]; the performance of nonhousehold goods brokerage services[59]; schoolchildren, taxicab and hotel service[60]; and casual, occasional or reciprocal transportation.[61] Beyond these significant statutory exemptions from regulation (which the ICC has generously expanded), the Commission has itself effectively deregulated major aspects of transportation, perhaps the most significant of which involve the movement of waste products[62] and the performance of nonhousehold goods brokerage services.[63]

Private Carriage. The most significant of the statutory exemptions involve private carriage. Of the 24.5 million trucks on the highway in 1975, 23.5 million were operated by private carriers.[64] Even among the largest vehicles, private carriers operate almost as many as regulated, for-hire carriers.[65] And in 1977, although 16,600 for-hire motor carriers were subject to ICC regulation, approximately 113,000 to 150,000 interstate private carriers were not.[66]

When a shipper operates its own vehicles in the furtherance of its primary nontransportation business, such operations ordinarily fall clearly within the statutory exemption for private carriage.[67] But when a shipper chooses to

secure vehicles from other entities, an issue arises as to whether such operations are for-hire, and thereby subject to the jurisdiction of the ICC.[68]

Corporate conglomerations have been involved in a number of proceedings
before the ICC dealing with transportation services performed by one corporate affiliate for another. The issue in such proceedings is whether the
movements are for-hire (and therefore subject to ICC jurisdiction) or whether
they are proprietary (and thus exempt from regulation). Such a determination
traditionally rested on the "primary business test," initially developed in
L.A. Woitishek Common Carrier Application[69] and *Lenior Chair Co. Contract Carrier Application.*[70] Generally, a legal entity was precluded from
furnishing transportation for compensation on behalf of an affiliated, but
separate, legal entity. The ICC has rarely refused to pierce the corporate
veil among commonly owned corporations so as to find transportation services performed for compensation between affiliated firms to fall within the
exemption.[71]

The Commission has indicated that a business corporation might bring its
operations within the private carriage exemption by (a) merging with the
affiliate to become a single legal person, (b) becoming a bona fide distributor,
wholesaler or dealer of the involved commodities, or (c) providing gratuitous
carriage.[72] Otherwise, it must file an application for motor carrier operating
authority with the ICC.[73]

The Commission has recently proposed to liberalize its traditional policies
on intercorporate hauling, to permit the performance of such services without the requirement for the acquisition of operating authority.[74] And in *Toto
Purchasing & Supply Co., Inc,*[75] the ICC announced that private carriers
could be issued for-hire operating authority to serve nonaffiliated firms.[76]
Section 10524 of the new Act expands the exemption for private carriage to
include for-hire intercorporate transportation services under circumstances
in which the parent owns 100 percent of the participating subsidiaries.[77] The
legislative intent of this provision is to "contribute towards reducing empty
backhauls and, thus, contribute to further energy conservation."[78]

Intrastate Commerce. Both the Commission and the courts have long
recognized that the Interstate Commerce Act confers no authority for federal
regulation of intrastate movement,[79] although the ICC clearly holds jurisdiction over interstate and foreign commerce.[80] However, the Commission
will not permit intrastate routing of shipments as a subterfuge to avoid the
agency's jurisdiction when the movements in question are actually interstate.[81]

The issue of whether a particular movement is intrastate, interstate or
foreign has traditionally turned on the essential character of the commerce.[82]
More specifically, the Commission has evaluated the "fixed and persisting
transportation intent of the shipper at the shipment"[83] and concluded that
such character is retained throughout the movement in the absence in the
interruption of its continuity.[84] In *Petroleum Products Transported Within
a Single State,*[85] the Commission delineated the principal factors to be ex-

amined in evaluating whether such a fixed and persisting intent exists, as follows:

As applied to the type of traffic here involved, the major manifestations of this intent, or absence thereof, may be found in the following: (1) at the time of shipment, there is no specific order being filled for a specific quantity of a given product to be moved through to a specific destination beyond the terminal storage, (2) the terminal storage is a distribution point or local marketing facility from which specific amounts of the product are sold or allocated, and (3) transportation in the furtherance of the distribution within the single State is specifically arranged only after sale or allocation from storage. These things, it is believed, are basically sufficient to establish that the continuity of transportation has been broken, that the initial shipments have come to rest, and that the interstate journey has ceased.[86]

2. The Territorial Exemptions

The Commercial Zone–Terminal Area Exemptions. Section 10526(b) of the Interstate Commerce Act[87] provides a partial exemption from regulation for:

(1) transportation provided in contiguous municipalities, and commercially a part of, the municipality or municipalities,(A) or shipment to or from a place outside the municipality, or municipalities, or zone.

This exemption permits local movements within a municipality and its surrounding commercial zone to be free from regulation. To avail itself of the commercial zone exemption, a motor carrier must (1) perform transportation wholly within a single municipality or between contiguous municipalities or within a zone adjacent to and commercially a part of such municipality or municipalities, and (2) must not perform transportation under a common control, management or arrangement for a continuous carriage to or from a point located outside such municipality, municipalities or zones. The first criterion requires a geographic evaluation of the proximity of the points between which the traffic is moving.[88] The latter requires evaluation of the relationships between the carriers performing the through movement—transportation which may involve more than a single mode of carriage.

This exemption is closely related to the terminal area exemption of section 10523[89] of the Act. This provision exempts motor carrier operations which involve "transfer, collection, or delivery" within a terminal area. Thus, when a carrier holds authority to serve a particular municipality as a terminal point, such operating rights shall be construed as authorizing service at all points within the terminal area of said municipality, an area which is coextensive with the commercial zone of that municipality as defined by the Commission.[90] The terminal area exemption extends only to operations in intracity or intraterminal transportation performed in the picking up and gathering together at origin, or in the distribution at destination, of shipments prior or subsequent to such an intercity or intercommunity movement and as an incident thereof.[91] For example, a carrier holding Salt Lake City-Denver authority could lawfully deliver freight within its Denver terminal area which had originated in Salt Lake City, but only as an incident of its line-haul movement over the interstate route. In contrast, the commercial zone exemption would permit the transportation of commodities which both originate in and are destined to points within said commercial zone.

Congress failed to define physically either exemption; thus the practical interpretation and implementation of their geographic perimeters were left to the ICC. In 1978, the ICC significantly expanded the geographic scope of these exemptions as follows:

Population	From (miles)	To (miles)[92]
Less than 2,500	2	3
2,500–24,999	3	4
25,000–99,999	4	6
100,000–199,999	5	8
200,000–499,999	5	10
500,000–999,999	5	15
1,000,000 and up	5	20

The Commission has subsequently expanded the commercial zones and terminal areas of particular municipalities beyond these generous radii on an *ad hoc* basis.[93]

Section 10526(a)(8) of the Interstate Commerce Act[94] establishes a limited exemption from economic regulation by the ICC of the motor carrier transportation performed "incidental to transportation by aircraft." For purposes of this discussion, it shall hereinafter be referred to as the "air terminal area exemption."

Prior to 1964, the ICC examined each situation on a case-by-case basis, scrutinizing (a) whether the movement in question was continuous and on a through bill of lading, (b) whether it had an immediately prior or subsequent movement by aircraft, (c) whether it constituted a bona fide collection, delivery, or transfer service performed within the air carrier's terminal area as set forth in its published tariffs filed with the CAB, and (d) the geographic scope of the service performed. In 1964, the ICC and the Civil Aeronautics Board (CAB) both published complementary regulations designed to define precisely the scope of the air terminal area. The CAB established a 25-mile "rule of thumb"; air carriers seeking to file tariffs embracing a movement beyond the 25-mile radius were required to file an application under part 222 of the Board's regulations.[95] The ICC's regulations incorporated many of the criteria it had developed on a case-by-case basis. Although it established no geographic limits to the exempt zone for the movement of property, it tended to follow the CAB's 25-mile rule of thumb, allowing the CAB to make the initial determination as to the propriety of the service proposed and generally deferring to that agency's judgment.[96] Basically, the CAB held jurisdiction within the zone, and the ICC held jurisdiction without.

The Motor Carrier Act of 1980 effectively deregulates all surface transportation of passengers or property having a prior or subsequent movement by air.[97] Apparently, there are now no geographic limits on the air terminal area exemption.

The combined effect of the commercial zone exemption of Section 10526(b) and the terminal area exemption of Section 10523 of the Interstate Commerce Act is partially to exempt from regulation local motor carrier movements performed in interstate or foreign commerce within a municipality and its immediately adjacent commercial zone or terminal area.[98] Before 1979, however, the surface transportation between points located within the comercial zone of a port city of commodities having a prior or subsequent movement by water was not held to fall within either the commercial zone or the terminal area exemptions. Indeed, local motor pickup and delivery services performed in connection with Federal Maritime Commission (FMC)-regulated carriers were not deemed to be exempt from economic regulation even though such transportation took place wholly within a single commercial zone or terminal area.[99]

The terminal area exemption of Section 10523 of the Act[100] exempts from regulation motor carrier collection, delivery and transfer services performed for and within the terminal area of railroads, motor carriers, water carriers and freight forwarders which fall within the jurisdiction of the ICC. Ocean carriers operating in foreign commerce, although subject to regulation by the FMC,[101] are not water carriers within the Interstate Commerce Act and could not, therefore, avail themselves of the benefits of the aforementioned exemptions. Thus, the surface transportation of commodities between points in the commercial zone of a port city as part of a continuous foreign commerce movement in connection with ocean transportation was, prior to 1979, deemed to require certified authority issued by the ICC.[102]

Let us take as an example the movement of Italian sandals from Venice to warehousing facilities located within the commercial zone of Boston. Their movement across the North Atlantic would ostensibly be subject to the jurisdiction of the FMC. However, their subsequent for-hire motor carrier movement from the port facilities of Boston to the consignee's inland warehouse facilities, located within the commercial zone of Boston, would require licensed authority and would fall neither within the commercial zone exemption nor within the terminal area exemption, although the local cartage movement was controlled by the FMC ocean carrier.[103]

In 1979, the Commission promulgated regulations which significantly simplified the certification procedure for motor carriers that seek to handle ex-water traffic within the commercial zone of a port city.[104] Essentially, the ICC made a general finding that the transportation by motor carriers of such commodities is required by the public convenience and necessity.

The Single-State Exemption. Section 10525 of the Act[105] exempts interstate motor carrier operations performed wholly within the geographic perimeters of a single state under circumstances in which the Commission concludes that "the nature or quantity of transportation provided . . . does not substantially affect or impair uniform regulation by the Commission of motor carrier transportation."[106] In order to fall within the statutory exemption, carriers performing interstate or foreign commerce movements within a single state must secure from the ICC an appropriate Certificate of Registration prior to the commencement of such operations.[107]

3. Agricultural Exemptions

Agricultural and Horticultural Commodities. Section 10526(a)(6) of the Act[108] has traditionally exempted from economic regulation the transportation of unprocessed agricultural and horticultural commodities. Certain commodities have been statutorily included[109] and excluded[110] from this exemption. In determining whether a particular commodity falls within the argicultural exemption, the Commission has followed the "continuing substantial identity" test, established by the U.S. Supreme Court in *East Texas Lines v. Frozen Food Express.*[111] Under this analysis, the Commission focuses on the congressional intent to exempt only those agricultural products which are in their raw state or, if not generally marketable in their raw state, have been processed solely for the purpose of making them marketable. To that point, a commodity retains its continuing substantial identity as an unmanufactured agricultural commodity.[112]

Criticism of regulated trucking has generally focused on three principal areas relative to the agricultural exemption: fuel consumption, the cost of regulation, and the absurdity of ICC interpretation. Thus, Congresswoman Millicent Fenwick testified:

Mr. Chairman, I must marvel as must the American people at the bureaucratic manpower that is certainly necessary to establish the various guidelines and criteria that the ICC uses to currently distinguish between exempt and nonexempt products.

The ICC has 36 categories of exempt and nonexempt products listed under the heading of "Milk and Cream." Buttermilk is exempt, but butterfat and buttermilk with condensed cream are regulated. Concentrated, skim milk, and powdered are exempt, but condensed and evaporated are not.

And, believe it or not, Mr. Chairman, manure in its natural state is an exempt commodity but manure, fermented, with additives such as yeast and molds, producing a rich liquor which in water solution is used for soil enrichment is not.[113]

The Motor Carrier Act of 1980 expands the exemption to alleviate the empty-backhaul problem by permitting an unregulated carrier to transport certain farm supply commodities (i.e., livestock and poultry feed and certain seeds and plants) back to the areas of agricultural production.[114] It is also anticipated that the Act's other liberalized entry provisions will enable owner-operators to secure operating authority for the movement of processed foods and agricultural fertilizers in order to enhance their operating economies and efficiencies and conserve fuel.[115]

Agricultural Cooperatives. Section 10526(a)(5) of the Act[116] establishes an exemption for motor carriage in vehicles owned and operated by cooperative associations.[117] Agricultural cooperatives were traditionally free to conduct interstate operations for non-farm commodities for nonmembers so long as such activities did not exceed 15 percent of the operations of the cooperatives.[118] The Motor Carrier Act of 1980 amends this figure to permit nonmember traffic in the amount of 25 percent of the cooperative's total operations, measured by tonnage.[119]

Farmers' Vehicles. Section 10526(a)(4) of the Act[120] exempts from economic regulation motor vehicles controlled and operated by a farmer transporting his own agricultural products and supplies. Even if this specific statutory exemption did not exist, most such movements would fall within the exemption for private carriage, discussed earlier.[121]

4. Miscellaneous Exemptions

The remaining statutory exemptions are of little relative importance. They involve the transportation of wrecked vehicles,[122] newspapers,[123] and schoolchildren[124]; taxicab and hotel service[125]; casual, occasional or reciprocal transportation[126] and movements within national parks.[127]

Beyond the specific statutory exemptions created by Congress and significantly expanded by the ICC, the Commission itself has, through rule making and the establishment of quasi-judicial precedent, restricted its jurisdiction by creating new areas that are virtually free from economic regulation. Three of these are explored here: waste products, incidental movements, and brokerage of motor carrier services.

Waste Products. The Commission, in 1971, inaugurated a rule-making proceeding whose purpose was to encourage the movement of recyclable commodities on behalf of pollution control programs by effectively deregulating most existing entry barriers.[128] Although beset by procedural irregularities and remanded by a federal district court,[129] the ICC ultimately succeeded in promulgating such regulations.

In order to transport waste products, a carrier need only file a sworn statement and notarized request essentially setting forth its tariff under which such operations will be performed, a description of the relevant pollution control program it will be serving and a description of its fitness to perform the proposed operations. Eligible carriers are notified by letter.

Incidental Movements. The ICC has exempted certain incidental types of movements, in that such transportation is incidental to the carriage of regulated commodities for which appropriate operating authority is held. Thus, operating authority is not required for the return movement of commodities which have been rejected by consignees because they were damaged in transit, or for any other reason.[130] In addition, no operating authority is required for the movement of component parts or accessories of an authorized commodity when shipped in conjunction with and at the same time as such commodity.[131] Similarly, commodities used in the installation of the carriers' authorized commodities may be transported at the same time as and incidental to such basic commodities without specific authorization.[132] No specific authority is required for the movement of advertising materials when moving incidental to, at the same time as and in conjunction with the basic commodity for which operating authority is held.

The movement of shipper-owned equipment incidental to the movement of an authorized commodity requires no operating authority when transported with said authorized commodity.[133] The Commission recently reversed a long line of precedent to conclude that the movement of used empty intermodal cargo containers no longer requires operating authority,[134] and that such containers will henceforth be deemed instrumentalities of commerce rather than regulated commodities.[135] Congress, in promulgating the Motor Carrier Act of 1980, affirmed Commission precedent in this area by specifically exempting from economic regulation the movement of "used pallets, used empty containers (including intermodal cargo containers), and other used shipping devices."[136]

Brokers. A "broker" is defined by statute as a person[137] who sells, or offers to sell, transportation by motor carriages[138] or who holds himself out to perform such services.[139] Prior to the promulgation of the Motor Carrier Act of 1980, Section 10924 of the Act[140] required issuance of a broker's license to any qualified applicant who convincingly demonstrated (1) that he was fit, willing and able properly to perform the proposed service and to conform to the provisions of the Act and the Commission's rules and regulations thereunder; and (2) that the proposed service was consistent with the public interest and the national transportation policy.[141] The achievement of these requirements was not deemed as burdensome as the "public convenience and necessity" criteria imposed in the issuance of authority to operate as a motor common carrier.[142]

The ICC has interpreted these statutory provisions to require that an applicant seeking authority to operate as a broker demonstrate that his services will fulfill a useful public function and will contribute something of value or be of benefit to carriers or the public.[143] The applicant must also establish that the proposed operations will not needlessly duplicate existing services.[144] The proposed services must fulfill a public need which is not already being adequately satisfied.[145] This determination, of course, requires an examination of existing transportation services.[146] It is inconclusive, however, that existing brokers are not entitled to exclusivity in the markets they serve.[147] Thus, entry for a broker applicant may not be denied merely because the tour services of existing brokers are available.

Consideration of an applicant's fitness to perform properly licensed brokerage operations is also a significant requirement of Section 10924 of the Act. Indeed, the legislative history of this statutory provision clearly demonstrates that the primary purpose of Congress in promulgating legislation regulating entry in this field was to protect the shipping and traveling public against dishonesty and financially unstable middlemen in the transportation industry.[148] The criteria which the ICC ordinarily used to determine an applicant's fitness were (1) his good character, (2) his ability to conduct the proposed operations in an appropriate and satisfactory manner, (3) his willingness to comport with the established regulatory requirements, and (4) his ability to satisfy his bonding obligations.[149]

The ICC, in Ex Parte MC–96, *Entry Control of Brokers*,[150] recently promulgated regulations significantly relaxing barriers to entry for brokers, except brokers of household goods, by creating streamlined procedures for the uncomplicated acquisition of brokerage authority.[151] The traditional entry requirements for household goods brokerage have been maintained.[152] And although entry for household goods brokerage is quite liberal, the Commission nevertheless appears to scrutinize carefully such applications in order to protect consumers from the difficulties inherent in household goods transportation.[153]

The Motor Carrier Act of 1980 effectively codifies the ICC's attempts to deregulate brokerage of commodities other than household goods by eliminating all entry barriers except those involving fitness.[154] Passenger brokers were exempted from ICC regulation by the Bus Regulatory Reform Act of 1982.

B. The Motor Carrier Act of 1980: Expanding the Exemptions

As indicated earlier, in promulgating the Motor Carrier Act of 1980, Congress has affirmed or expanded the statutory exemptions involving agricultural cooperatives.[155] Further, the new legislation affirms the Commission's effective deregulation of incidental transportation and brokerage services. Besides these changes, the Motor Carrier Act of 1980 adds decorative rock and wood chips to the list of exempt commodities[156] and liberalizes the rule involving mixed loads of regulated and unregulated commodities.[157]

The new legislation also permits the Commission to issue operating authority in certain sectors of the industry without making a public convenience and necessity determination (i.e., the applicant need merely demonstrate its fitness to perform the proposed operations): (a) when a community is not regularly served by a certificated motor carrier;[158] (b) when a community suffers a loss of rail service through abandonment;[159] (c) for movements of U.S. government property (except household goods, hazardous or secret materials, weapons and munitions);[160] (d) for shipments weighing less than 100 pounds;[161] and (e) for movements by owner-operators of food and fertilizer.[162] The ICC can be relied on to effectively deregulate these sectors of the motor carrier industry rather promptly.

The liberalized entry and rate provisions of the Motor Carrier Act of 1980, as interpreted by the current Commission, may well result in the de facto deregulation of additional sectors of the industry. As to entry, once an applicant demonstrates that it is fit and that its proposed operations "will serve a useful public purpose, responsive to public demand or need,"[163] the burden of proof shifts to an opponent of new entry to prove that the proposed operations are "inconsistent with the public convenience and necessity."[164] The potential for diversion of revenue from incumbents is specifically designated by the statute not to be controlling in such proceedings and the ability of existing certificated carriers to oppose an application is similarly constrained.[166] Further, the Commission is now empowered to expand the authority of licensed carriers by (a) broadening the commodities they hold authority to transport; (b) permitting them to serve intermediate points and provide round trip service; and (c) eliminating territorial restrictions and "any other unreasonable restriction that the Commission deems to be wasteful of fuel, inefficient, or contrary to the public interest."[167]

C. Common Carriage

In the summer of 1980, President Carter signed into law one of the most significant pieces of legislation in almost fifty years of surface transport regulation—the Motor Carrier Act of 1980.[168, 169] In many respects, this new law affirms the quasi-judicial relaxation of regulatory standards begun three years before the majority of recent presidential appointees to the ICC, the nation's oldest independent regulatory agency.[170] This liberalization had already begun to swing the pendulum away from protection of established carriers from the deleterious effects of excessive competition toward a philosophy which had prompted a previous Congress to promulgate the Motor Carrier Act of 1935,[171] which first established ICC jurisdiction over the motor carrier industry, to an ideology which espoused enhanced competition and free market economics. In other respects, the legislation reflects a belief that Congress should specify the parameters within which the ICC may exercise its discretion, and that the flexibility of the ICC to become excessively liberal in its regulatory approach should be constricted.[172] In any event, the 1980 legislation constitutes the culmination of one of the most intensive inquiries ever undertaken by the relevant congressional committees.[173]

Both the statute and its legislative history emphasize that the ICC is to exercise its discretion only within the confines of the powers specifically conferred by the new law.

Most of the proceedings before the ICC involve motor carriers, which numerically compose the most substantial single mode of transport subject to ICC regulation.[174] Federal regulation of motor carriers was initiated with the promulgation of the Motor Carrier Act of 1935. Among the purposes of this legislation were the prevention of destructive competition among motor carriers and the protection of motor and rail carriers from each other.[175]

Prior to the promulgation of the Motor Carrier Act of 1980, an applicant seeking authority to operate as a motor common carrier was required to demonstrate that the proposed operation would be required by the present or future "public convenience and necessity."[176] Because Congress failed to define public convenience and necessity,[177] it was the Commission's responsibility to devise quasi-judicial standards to breathe life into this ambiguous statutory terminology.

In *Pan-American Bus Lines Operation*,[178] one of its earliest and most frequently cited decisions, the ICC established three quasi-judicial "common law" considerations to be weighed in determining whether proposed operations satisfied this ambiguous statutory criterion: (1) whether the proposed service would "serve a useful public purpose, responsive to a public demand or need"; (2) whether that purpose could "be served as well by existing lines or carriers"; and (3) whether the applicant could satisfy that purpose "without endangering or impairing the operations of existing carriers contrary to the public interest."[179] However, *Pan-American* did not stand for the proposition that competition should be stifled. The decision acknowledged that "public regulation can enforce what may be called reasonable standards of safe, continuous, and adequate service, but it can hardly be expected to take the initiative in experimentation and the development of new types of service. . . . Competition is the best known spur to such endeavor."[180]

Subsequent decisions condensed the *Pan-American* considerations into a single question: whether the advantages to those members of the shipping public who would use the involved motor carrier service would outweigh the actual or potential disadvantages to existing carriers which might result from the institution of the proposed operations.[181] It was within this broad policy framework that the ICC evaluated applications for motor carrier operating authority.[182]

The first criterion of *Pan-American*—whether the proposed operations would serve a useful purpose responsive to a public demand or need—could only be established by evidence of either an existing contemporary need or a reasonably foreseeable future one.[183] Even in the absence of opposition, a carrier seeking operating authority was required to prove by substantial and competent evidence a public need for the proposed operations.[184] More specifically, in order to establish a prima facie case of public need for the proposed operations, an applicant seeking motor carrier authority was obligated to comply with the requirements set forth in the ICC's decision in *John Novak Contract Carrier Application*[185]:

Those supporting the application should state with specificity the transportation service which they believed to be required.

The shippers and consignees supporting applications for authority to transport property should identify clearly the commodities they ship or receive, the points to or from which their traffic moves, the volume of freight they would tender to applicant, the transportation services now used for moving their traffic, and any deficiencies in existing services.

Those supporting an application for authority to transport passengers should indicate the frequency with which they would use the proposed service and should identify any transportation services now available and the inadequacies believed to exist in such services.[186]

Under the traditional approach, the cumulative burdens of proof established by *Pan-American* and *Novak* fell most heavily on applicants, while the corresponding burdens on protestants remained relatively low. The tripartite test of *Pan-American* demanded consideration of the services and operations of existing carriers and the ultimate effect of a grant of operating authority on the total quantity and quality of service provided to the shipping, receiving and consuming public.[187] The inadequacy of existing services was frequently deemed to be a fundamental ingredient in the evaluation of what constituted the public convenience and necessity.[188] To protect certificated common carriers providing adequate and dependable service, the applicant was frequently required to demonstrate affirmatively that the proposed transportation was such that available existing carriers either could not or would not perform it in a reasonably satisfactory manner.[189]

Finally, the ICC generally held that between competing carriers of the same mode, the level of rates was not a matter which could be considered in determining whether a proposed service was in the public interest, unless the existing rates were so unreasonably high as to constitute, in effect, an embargo.[190] The inherent advantages of one mode of transportation over another, however, is a factor which the ICC is required to consider in evaluating whether operating authority should be issued.[191]

Thus, the traditional approach has been a conservative one. The Commission heavily loaded the scales in favor of protestants by regularly suggesting, despite reprimands from the judiciary, that among the evidentiary obligations imposed on applicants was a demonstration that the services of existing carriers, including protestants, were inadequate in some material respect. The protection of existing carriers from the deleterious effects of excessive competition seemed to become the policy of the agency.[192]

5. The ICC's Liberalization of Entry Standards (1977–1980)

It was President Gerald Ford who first began to press for significant legislative reform of the traditional regulatory environment. Failing to obtain congressional approval of his legislative initiatives, he began to appoint individuals to the Commission who were firmly dedicated to regulatory reform. This effort was expanded and intensified under the Carter administration.

Curiously, a misinterpretation of a 1974 U.S. Supreme Court decision gave the new Commission the requisite springboard from which to launch a reversal of the ICC's traditional approach, described previously.

In *Bowman Transportation v. Arkansas-Best Freight System, Inc.*,[193] the Supreme Court concluded that it was well within the Commission's lawful realm of discretion to find "that the benefits of competitive service to consumers might outweigh the discomforts existing certificated carriers could feel as a result of new entry."[194] Nothing in the Supreme Court's opinion suggests that the ICC *must* evaluate the benefits of enhanced competition in determining whether proposed operations are consistent with the public convenience and necessity. The Court merely held that on the basis of the facts before it, "the Commission's conclusion that consumer benefits outweighed any adverse impact upon the existing carriers reflects the kind of judgement that is entrusted to it, a power to weigh the competing interests and arrive at a balance that is deemed 'the public convenience and necessity.' "[195]

The District of Columbia Circuit, in the 1977 decision of *P.C. White Truck Line, Inc. v. ICC*[196] (a per curiam opinion that relied heavily on *Bowman*), established the notion that Commission consideration of the benefits of competition was an indispensable prerequisite to the Commission's evaluation of the public convenience and necessity. As many federal courts had previously done, the District of Columbia Circuit reprimanded the ICC for giving excessive weight to the issue of inadequacy of existing service.[197] But the court then went far beyond the principles previously established by the other courts, emphasizing that:

The Commission ignored almost entirely the possible benefit to the public from increased competition which a grant of the application likely will foster. . . .

Because the Commission failed to exercise its "power to weigh the competing interests," the orders under review must be reversed and the case remanded to the Commission for consideration of the contribution that increased competition might make to the public weal.[198]

On remand, the ICC maintained that it was compelled to consider the competition arising from a grant of operating authority in arriving at an appropriate balance of competitive interests.[199] The Commission took the court's mandate one step further, however, by imposing additional burdens on protestants seeking to have an application for operating authority denied.

On the basis of the facts before the Commission, it was clear that the protestants would lose revenue as a result of the inauguration of new operations and would thereby suffer injury because of the increased competition.[200] However, the ICC held that a pecuniary loss would not be sufficient to warrant a denial of operating authority if the protestant had failed to demonstrate that such a loss would be so significant as to jeopardize its operations in a manner contrary to the public interest.[201] The Commission insisted that protestants must demonstrate a nexus between their potential loss of revenue and adverse effects on their operations, at least when such loss of revenue does not constitute a substantial portion of their aggregate income.[202]

The significance of this decision lies in the fact that it constitutes the first major step ever taken to place significant evidentiary burdens on protestants. Prior to *P.C. White*, in the *Pan-American* and *Novak* line of cases, the focus had been on the evidentiary obligations of the applicant.

In *Liberty Trucking Co. Extension—General Commodities*,[203] the Commission took the crusade for increased competition two steps further. It defined the competitive interests that must be balanced as the benefits which might be realized by the shipping and consuming public as a result of new competition and the "destructive impact a new service might have on existing carriers."[204] But the Commission then went on to insist that the protestant "establish an interest worthy of regulatory protection from competition"[205] and to suggest that even when the inauguration of new service would materially jeopardize existing carriers' ability to serve the public (and, conceivably, throw the protestant into bankruptcy),[206] such injury might be outweighed by the benefits of new competition.[207] *Liberty* expanded the obligations created in *P.C. White* by insisting that in order to establish an interest worthy of regulatory protection, protestants must prove (a) that authorization of a competitive service will lead to substantial traffic diversion and material revenue loss; (b) that loss of traffic and revenue will affect their ability to serve the public; and (c) that such injury is not outweighed by the benefits to be derived as a result of heightened competition. The ICC indicated that with respect to the potential for injury of existing carriers as a result of new entry, it would "not deny the public the benefits of an improved service or heightened competition merely to protect the inefficient or to insulate existing carriers from more vigorous competition."[208]

Just as prior Commissions had loaded the scales heavily in favor of protestants in order to shield them from the deleterious effects of excessive competition, the Commission of the late 1970s began to load the scales heavily in favor of applicants in order to allow them and the public to enjoy the fruits of new competition. The presumption that enhanced competition was clearly in the public interest became so significant that it was likely that protestants would only rarely be able to shoulder the onerous evidentiary burdens placed on them.[209] By 1979, as a result of this liberalized approach to entry, the ICC was granting 98 percent of the motor carrier operating authority applications filed.

Expanding its new devotion to the attributes of enhanced competition beyond *Liberty*, the Commission, in 1979, developed a policy that encouraged applicants to submit evidence that they would offer lower rates to shippers if the application was granted.[210] This, of course, reversed a long line of cases which had prohibited consideration of the issue of rates except when an embargo existed or when the issue was relevant to the determination of the inherent advantages of alternative modes of transportation.[211]

6. The Congressional Recodification of Entry Standards: The Motor Carrier Act of 1980

Prior to the enactment of the Motor Carrier Act of 1980, the Interstate Commerce Act required that an applicant seeking motor common carrier authority demonstrate (a) that it was fit, willing and able to provide the proposed service and to conform to the provisions of the Act and the Commission's rules and regulations promulgated thereunder, and (b) that the proposed operation "[was] or [would] be required by the present or future public convenience and necessity."[212] For motor carriers of *property*, while retaining the fitness requirement set forth above, the 1980 Act requires only that the applicant prove that the proposed operations "will serve a useful public purpose, responsive to a public demand or need,"[213] in effect codifying the first *Pan-American* criterion. Further, the Motor Carrier Act of 1980 imposes a novel statutory burden on protestants. It is no longer the applicant's burden to prove that the proposed operations are consistent with the public convenience and necessity; the burden has now been shifted to protestants to demonstrate that such operations are "inconsistent with the public convenience and necessity."[214] Protestants are not left totally out in the cold, however, for the Commission is directed to make findings in entry proceedings of "the effect of issuance of the certificate on existing carriers."[215] But the statute proceeds to direct the ICC not to conclude that the burden on protestants has been satisfied solely by proof of diversion of traffic or loss of revenue resulting from new entry.[216] In addition, existing common carriers may not submit a protest unless they hold at least a portion of the proposed service and either (a) have provided service within the scope of the application within the preceding 12 months (or have actively solicited such traffic); (b) have pending before the ICC a previously filed application in which they are seeking operating authority substantially duplicative of the authority sought; or (c) are granted leave to intervene by the ICC.[217]

The other major provision in the Act is Section 10101, the congressional expression of the National Transportation Policy.[218] This policy statement guides all of the Commission's regulatory activities, but Congress felt it necessary to emphasize the importance of this policy in entry proceedings by expressly requiring that the ICC make findings in such proceedings with respect to the policy.[219] The 1980 legislation also adds a new subsection addressing motor carriers of property, for which the ICC must now

promote competitive and efficient transportation services in order to (A) meet the needs of shippers, receivers, and consumers; (B) allow a variety of quality and price options to meet changing market demands and the diverse requirements of the shipping public; (C) allow the most productive use of equipment and energy resources; (D) enable efficient and well-managed carriers to earn adequate profits, attract capital, and maintain fair wages and working conditions; (E) provide and maintain service to small communities and small shippers; (F) improve and maintain a sound, safe, and competitive privately-owned motor carrier system; (G) promote greater participation by minorities in the motor carrier system; and (H) promote intermodal transportation.[220]

Two overriding conclusions can be drawn from the provisions of the 1980 Act. First, by reversing the burden of proof on the public convenience and necessity issue, Congress clearly intended to make entry more liberal than it had been during the protectionist era (1935–1977) under the prior statute. Second, by retaining the concept of public convenience and necessity, Congress clearly did not intend that entry be unlimited. Indeed, although it expanded the list of motor carrier activities which would be exempt from the public convenience and necessity requirement, Congress expressly prohibited the ICC from making across-the-board findings of general consistency with the public convenience and necessity, so as to thwart the Commission's attempts to accomplish wholesale deregulation of specific sectors of the industry under the "Master Certificate" approach.[221]

7. The ICC's Expansion of the Legislation

The Motor Carrier Act of 1980: A Statute of First Impression. The first major decision by the ICC interpreting the new entry standards was *Art Pape Transfer, Inc., Extension—Commodities in End Dump Vehicles.*[222] In *Art Pape*, the Commission announced that for cases pending at the time the Motor Carrier Act of 1980 was enacted, where evidence had been submitted under the standards of the prior law, the ICC would examine that evidence under the entry standards prior to the new Act.[223] If the application would have been denied under those standards, the ICC would then examine the evidence under the criteria established by the Motor Carrier Act of 1980.[224]

The Protestant's Extraordinary Public Convenience and Necessity Burden. *La Bar's, Inc., Extension—Mountaintop Insulation*[225] was the first major decision which comprehensively described the Commission's interpretation of the protestants' burden under the 1980 legislation. In *La Bar's*, the ICC noted that "the Motor Carrier Act of 1980 significantly altered the decisional framework in motor carrier licensing cases, placing increased importance on the role of competition in the national trucking industry."[226] The Commission further asserted that adequacy of existing services is now irrelevant in the determination of public convenience and necessity.[227] But the Commission cited nothing in the statute or its legislative history to support this statement. Even the federal courts, which over the years have admonished the ICC not to view the element of inadequacy of existing service as effectively synonymous with public convenience and necessity, have stated that inadequacy of existing service remains one of the elements to be considered, along with other factors, including "the desirability of competition, the desirability of different kinds of service, and the desirability of improved service."[228]

Presumably, the Commission interprets the effective elimination of the second *Pan-American* criterion, coupled with the codification of the first and third criteria, as reflective of a congressional intention that the ICC should no longer give any weight to the issue of whether existing services are inadequate.[229]

On the facts before the Commission in *La Bar's*, the protestant strongly contended that its future was "dependent upon the outcome of this application. Granting the application will undoubtedly cause [protestant's] financial ruin."[230] Nevertheless, in a five-step analysis, the ICC found that the protestant had failed to meet its burden and that, therefore, the application should be granted. First, the Commission found the fact that the supporting shipper had come to rely increasingly on the applicant's services performed under temporary authority demonstrated not only that the applicant's services must be different from the protestant's, but also that benefits would be derived from increased competition.[231]

Focusing on the financial plight of the protestant in *La Bar's*, the Commission noted that the applicant had also recently suffered a financial loss. "Considering financial health alone, one could just as easily argue that the application should be granted because a denial would prevent applicant from offering an expanded service in an attempt to improve its financial plight," declared the Commission.[232] But this analysis cannot be passed over without closer scrutiny. The protestant in *La Bar's* already operated in the involved territory, and it may already have made a significant investment in terminals and equipment, all of which might be lost in bankruptcy with the applicant's new entry. The applicant, on the other hand, had not made such an investment to serve the territory.

The Commission in *La Bar's* went on to elaborate the criteria that protestants must prove if they are to prevail. According to the Commission, protestants must not only demonstrate a financial loss, but they must also present "evidence conclusively demonstrating (1) that the loss was attributable to the applicant's operations, (2) that the losses were certain to continue beyond the year in question, and improtantly [*sic*], (3) that there were no economy or marketing measures that the protestant could have taken to eliminate the loss."[233] Further, the protestant "must not only show harm from additional competition, it must show that its ability to serve the public will be jeopardized."[234] In *La Bar's*, the Commission said that with the promise of the shipper that he would "continue to tender large amounts of traffic to the protestant . . . the protestant [had] failed to demonstrate that granting the application [would] foreclose it from adapting its operation to handle this reduced but still substantial volume of traffic."[235] In essence, the protestant had failed to show that the new competition would drive it into bankruptcy.[236]

Even if it had, the Commission's decision in *La Bar's* suggests that this would not be enough to warrant a denial of the application. Citing *Liberty* and *Arrow*, the ICC insisted "that the protestant must show that injury to it involves some harm to the public interest. After all, injury to existing carriers through competition becomes relevant only when there is a corresponding injury to the public."[237] Even the forced bankruptcy of an existing carrier would not warrant a denial of an application for motor common carrier authority:

Confronting the protestant with more vigorous competition—indeed, even competition which forces an existing carrier out of business—does not automatically cause harm to any aspect of the public interests. Congress, after all, requires us to foster efficiency in motor carrier transportation and there may be situations in which, considering the transportation industry as a whole, it is preferable to replace an inefficient operator with a more efficient one and promote the introduction of innovative services or prices.[238]

Nothing in the evidence suggested that the protestant in *La Bar's* was an "inefficient operator" (unless, of course, the pecuniary losses sustained by the protestant as a result of the applicant's operations are interpreted as demonstrative of inefficiency), that the applicant was more efficient than the protestant or that the applicant proposed to introduce innovative prices or services. Nevertheless, the Commission concluded that "the connection between harm to carriers and the public harm must be made explicit, and certainly no connection is evident here."[239]

The Applicant's De Minimis Public Need Burden. Having made the protestants' burden so onerous, the Commission began to make the applicant's burden exceedingly light. It must be remembered that the Motor Carrier Act of 1980 imposed on applicants the evidentiary burden of proving that the proposed service "will serve a useful public purpose, responsive to a public demand or need."[240] This was, in essence, a codification of the first *Pan-American* criterion. It could, therefore, be argued that Congress intended that the ICC follow the precedent established under the first *Pan-American* criterion, including the applicant's prima facie obligations enunciated in *Novak*.

The ICC first described the applicant's post–1980 Act burden in *Art Pape*, in which it acknowledged that "the applicant must still come forward with some evidence of the utility of the proposed service."[241] The Commission, however, seemed to feel that less evidence should be required of an applicant and that a broader scope of operating authority, from both a commodity and a territorial perspective, should be granted to an applicant than had been the case prior to the promulgation of the 1980 legislation. Although the administrative law judge had granted a certificate to transport only the 14 specified commodities for which a public need had been demonstrated, the Commission in *Art Pape* expanded the commodity description to authorize the transportation of "*commodities, in bulk in dump vehicles.*"[242] The ICC felt that the judge's approach was "unduly restrictive and results in an impractical and ineffective fragmentation of applicant's operating abilities. It also fails to accord sufficient weight to the apparent need for comprehensive motor carrier service to enable users . . . to expand their operations."[243] Thus, it appears that the Commission wanted to give a sufficiently broad grant of operating authority so that the applicant would not need to come back to the agency at some future date to request that its authority be expanded. A broad grant at the outset would, in the ICC's estimation, allow users to expand their operations.[244]

The ICC further elaborated on its desire to grant broad authority in terms of the territory in which the applicant would be authorized to operate:

Similarly, when an applicant for a certificate seeks new authority to provide transportation to many localities in a large geographic area, we have not traditionally required that it demonstrate a specific need and benefit be gathered for every village and hamlet in the area of proposed operations before a certificate of such encompassing scope be awarded. All that is required is that the applicant submit evidence which is sufficiently representative of the transportation needs of the shipping public in the relevant market to enable us to make an informed determination of the public interest in a given case.[245]

In support of this approach, the Commission noted that Congress had conferred on it the authority to remove restrictions and broaden authorities on motor carrier certificates.[246] Further, the ICC stated its belief that Congress intended that all new grants include "reasonably broad commodity and territorial descriptions as well."[247]

The Commission has extended this policy of expansion of territorial and commodity descriptions in two major proceedings. In Ex Parte No. MC–142 (Sub-No. 43A), *Removal of Restrictions From Authorities of Motor Carriers of Property*,[248] the Commission established procedural rules for the generous expansion of existing operating authorities. In Ex Parte No. 55 (Sub-No. 43A), *Acceptable Forms of Requests for Operating Authority (Motor Carriers and Brokers of Property)*,[249] it proceeded to issue a parallel set of standards in the form of a policy statement applicable to the commodity and territorial descriptions encompassed in new motor carrier operating authority applications. Both of these actions were purportedly based on the 1980 Act, which requires the Commission to

implement, by regulation, procedures to process expeditiously applications of individual motor carriers of property seeking removal of operating restrictions in order
to—

> (i) *reasonably* broaden the categories of property authorized by the carrier's
> certificate or permit; . . .
> (iv) eliminate *unreasonable* or *excessively narrow* territorial limitations; or
> (v) eliminate any other *unreasonable* restriction that the Commission deems
> to be wasteful of fuel, inefficient, or contrary to the public interest.[250]

Thus, the essential issue is whether the Commission acted reasonably in
these two proceedings.

The most salient provisions of the first proceeding, the *Restriction Removal*
decision, provide that broad, generic commodity descriptions, no less comprehensive than those in the Standard Transportation Commodities Code,[251]
may be substituted for any narrower commodity description presently contained in a certificate.[252] Further, all restrictions traditionally imposed on a
general commodity authority have now been deemed by the Commission
to be unreasonably narrow, except those involving explosives.[253] Finally,
any territorial description smaller in scope than a county is deemed to be
excessively narrow.[254]

These standards have been generally extended in the latter proceeding,
the *Future Policy* statement, as a general policy prospectively governing the
filing of applications for new operating authority. As to commodity descriptions, the Commission noted:

We expect applicants to employ commodity descriptions which are at least as broad
as the [STCC]. Our Employee Boards will screen applications to ensure that broad
commodity descriptions are being used. . . . Carriers are to be able to perform as
complete a service as possible for shippers, with competition—not narrowly limited
authority—defining the boundaries of service.[255]

If a carrier is to receive nationwide general commodities authority, how
is it to respond to a request for the bulk transportation of granite between
Seattle and Boston, or for the transportation of frozen foods between Baltimore and Denver, when it operates neither dump nor refrigerated vehicles
and is not prepared to serve those parts of the country? Will it not violate
its common carrier responsibilities if it fails to meet these requests for service?
This scenario could pose significant pragmatic difficulties for the Commission
in its efforts to initiate such an ambitious policy of certificate authorization.
In its *Future Policy* decision, the ICC announced that it did "not believe
that the common carrier obligation present [*sic*] a problem."[256]

A little more than one month later, the ICC apparently regained its senses
and realized that the common carrier obligation does present a problem.
Rather than solving the problem by issuing authority commensurate with

the public need for service, as intended by Congress, the Commission launched Ex Parte No. MC–77 (Sub–3), *Elimination of Certificates as the Measure of "Holding Out,"*[257] a proceeding which seeks to dilute the common carrier obligation.[258] As had been indicated, Congress clearly intended that the common carrier obligation should not be diluted.

This rule making, the *Common Carrier Obligation* proceeding, begins with an interesting interpretation of the new legislation: "The traditional Commission responsibility for the careful administration of competitive relationships has been changed [by the Motor Carrier Act of 1980] to place a greater emphasis on competition and potential competition as a principal regulatory device."[259] This interpretation is somewhat spurious. The Motor Carrier Act of 1980 preserved the Commission's responsibility for the careful administration of competitive relationships by insisting on a case-by-case adjudication of entry proceedings, by requiring a careful balancing of the effects of competition on both applicants and protestants and, with respect to the latter, by insisting on a specific finding as to "the effect of issuance of the certificate on existing carriers."[260] Moreover, the new legislation does not mandate that competition must become the principal regulatory device. The National Transportation Policy speaks only in terms of promoting "competitive and efficient transportation" in order to effectuate the other objectives specified therein.[261]

The ICC, in the *Common Carrier Obligation* rule making, acknowledged that its *Future Policy* decision would

have the effect of broadening commodity and territorial descriptions in certificated authorities, and prohibiting many restrictions in certificated authorities. Under the framework of Ex Parte No. 55 (Sub-No. 43A) motor common carriers of property will receive grants of authority generally broader in scope than those which have been issued in the past.

The new grants often will exceed the authority which the carrier actually needs to perform a particular transportation operation. It will clearly be much more common in the future than in the past to find carriers who lack the capacity to provide more than a portion of the services they are authorized to provide. This is the natural result of reliance on a policy of potential competition, eased entry, and broader grants of authority.[262]

Hence, the Commission acknowledges that its new policies will result in the issuance of operating authorities broader in scope than that for which a public need has been shown. However, the Commission goes on to note the severe problems which may arise as a result of this approach:

If our approach were to remain unchanged, and if failure to provide service coextensive with certificate authority were still seen to give rise to a potential violation of the carrier's obligations, then the issuance of certificates intentionally broader in scope than immediately proposed operations would be a "Catch 22" of unusual proportions. We are certain, however, that Congress intended no such result in enacting section 10922(h) to broaden certificate grants. It remains then only to disconnect the issue of holding out from the issuance of certificate authority, which requires foremost the designation of an acceptable substitute for the certificate.[263]

The ICC then proceeds to suggest that whatever the common carrier obligation is, it should be wholly divorced from the operating authority the carrier holds itself out as possessing by virtue of the commodities and territory embraced in its certificate of public convenience and necessity.

Finally, in *Pre-Fab Transit Co. Extension—Nationwide General Commodities*,[264] the Commission effectively destroyed the traditional notion of the applicant's burden of proving public need by eradicating the *Novak* evidentiary guidelines.

The U.S. Court of Appeals for the Fifth Circuit recently addressed the issue of whether the Commission's major actions implementing the Motor Carrier Act of 1980 "are within the wide discretion imparted to it by the statute, or whether, on the other hand, they exceed or transgress the congressional mandate."[265] Significantly, the court held that both the Commission's *Restriction Removal* and *Future Policy* decisions are "improper because they exceed the statutory direction to *reasonably* broaden existing certificates" and are "invalid as beyond the Commission's authority."[266] The court acknowledged that the new legislation liberalized the entry criteria by shifting the burden of proving inconsistency with the public convenience and necessity to protestants.[267] Nevertheless, said the court, Congress did not diminish the dual burdens on applicants to demonstrate both that they are fit, willing and able to provide the proposed service and that there is a public need for the proposed service.[268] "Presumably aware that such a presumption went beyond either business reality or its statutory powers,"[269] the court said, the ICC nevertheless promulgated rules insisting that carriers accept certificates embracing excessively broad commodity and territorial descriptions, even when such operating authority exceeded that which the applicants sought.[270] The court emphasized that it was "unable to find support in the statutory language for the Commission's conclusion that it was required, or even authorized, to implement the policies of the Motor Carrier Act by granting to new applicant the very broad authority it prescribes."[271]

The Commission had proffered three rationales in support of its issuance of broad authority, saying that narrowly defined authority (1) increases fuel use, (2) dulls competition, and (3) increases the likelihood of unnecessary regulation and corresponding economic loss. To this, the court responded: "[The Commission's] objectives may be laudable. They would be served even better by the complete removal of all licensing requirements. Congress did not, however, see fit to deregulate motor carriage. Indeed, it explicitly forbade the Commission to go beyond the powers vested in it by statute."[272]

The Bus Act. A new provision of the law provides that a carrier seeking to discontinue intrastate passenger service may petition the ICC if the state has not acted within 120 days of its petition to state authority. Or if the state has denied the bus carrier's request, the carrier may appeal to the ICC. The public has no such appeal if the state agency grants the request for discontinuance. This procedure is similar to that found in old Section 13a(2) of the Interstate Commerce Act, now 49 U.S.C. § 10909, pertaining to discontinuance of intrastate passenger trains. In addition, the Commission is authorized to preempt state authority if it finds that there is discriminatory state regulation of rates and practices.

The major provisions of the new bus law provide for greater freedom to enter markets, flexibility in setting fares, increased ability to exit markets if the service burdens interstate commerce, preemption of certain state regulatory controls and the elimination of antitrust immunity in the discussion of rates.

The law also provides for labor protection similar to that afforded in the rail and airline industries. Laid-off bus drivers and other employees are put on a preferential hiring list. No substantial displacement allowances are scheduled to be paid to the former employees, however. Congress apparently felt badly stung by the labor protection costs of the Conrail legislation. Nonetheless, some labor protection provisions were necessary to ensure against labor's opposition to the deregulation bill. As it was, opposition came mostly from legislators from rural states, who rightly feared loss of services to places which had already lost regular-route trucking, railroad branch lines, passenger service and commercial aviation.

Bus service had not been dealt with in the Motor Carrier Act of 1980 because of such community fears. It was also thought that the bus industry, a duopoly dealing with individual passengers and small shippers, was not conducive to a deregulated environment. Despite the specter of failures in the airline industry, the spirit of deregulation had continued to roll on, and now buses will have a go at something approaching a free market. Apparently, if a little deregulation is good, more must be better.

D. Contract Carriage

A motor contract carrier of commodities is one who provides for-hire transportation under agreement(s) with one or more shippers by (a) assigning vehicles to the shipper's exclusive use or (b) satisfying the distinct needs of said shipper.[273] A permit authorizing such operations shall be issued to a contract carrier if the ICC concludes that (a) the applicant is fit, willing and able to provide the proposed operations and to comport with the applicable provisions of the Interstate Commerce Act and the ICC's rules and regulations promulgated thereunder, and (b) the proposed operations will be "consistent with the public interest and the transportation policy of section

10101" of the Interstate Commerce Act.[274] Further, the Commission must consider the following four criteria:

(A) the nature of the transportation proposed to be provided;

(B) the effect that granting the permit would have on the protesting carriers if such grant would endanger or impair their operations to an extent contrary to the public interest;

(C) the effect that denying the permit would have on the person applying for the permit, its shippers, or both; and

(D) the changing character of the requirements of those shippers.[275]

Since promulgation of the Motor Carrier Act of 1980, the Commission has concluded that it will no longer limit such carriers to serving a limited number of shippers, or that anything less than nationwide operating authority will be issued to successful applicants, thereby effectively blurring the traditional distinctions between contract and common carriage.

As to the first criterion regarding the nature of the involved service, the U.S. Supreme Court, in *ICC v. J.T. Transport*,[276] concluded that consideration must be given to the specialized transportation requirements of the supporting shipper, the manner in which the applicant proposes to satisfy them and whether they may be satisfied equally as well by the protestant.[277]

In considering the second and third criteria, the Supreme Court, in *J.T. Transport*, observed:

The adequacy of existing services is a criterion to be considered by the Commission, as it is instructed to consider "the effect which granting the permit would have upon the services of the protesting carriers," as well as the effect of a denial upon the shippers. Or to put the matter otherwise, the question of the need of the shipping public for the proposed service necessarily includes the question whether the extent, nature, character, and suitability of existing, available service makes the proposed service out of line with the requirements of the national transportation policy. . . . The "distinct need" of shippers for the new contract carrier service must be weighed against the adequacy of existing services.[278]

The Court emphasized that the matter of rates is one factor to be evaluated in determining the public need for the proposed operations.[279]

The final criterion is ordinarily of little moment in determining whether the proposed operations will satisfy the public interest and the national transportation policy. Generally, little evidence is adduced regarding the changing character of a shipper's transportation requirements.

E. Other Entry Principles

Among the concomitant elements which the ICC ordinarily examines to determine whether proposed operations satisfy the statutorily imposed requirement of public convenience and necessity are those involving the operational feasibility of the proposed service and the operating economies and efficiencies to be realized as a result of the institution of those services.[280] Although these considerations do not ordinarily dominate application proceedings, they could tip the scales in certain cases.

Operational feasibility involves an evidentiary presentation by an applicant that, for example, a grant of the proposed authority will enable it to balance its inbound and outbound operations. The applicant may already have authority to operate in the involved territory, and it may therefore maintain equipment and terminal facilities which could efficiently serve the supporting shipper. The applicant's acquisition of the shipper's traffic may eliminate the necessity of "deadheading," an empty one-way movement of the carrier's equipment. For example, assume that an applicant is already transporting commodities from points in Pennsylvania to points in Texas but does not yet hold operating authority to transport commodities from points in Texas to points in Pennsylvania. Unless it can acquire exempt traffic[281] or can lease its vehicles to a carrier holding appropriate authority,[282] its return movements to Pennsylvania will be empty, or in the terminology of the transportation industry, its vehicles will be deadheaded back to the point of origin.

Suppose, however, that the applicant finds a shipper domiciled in Texas who requires the transportation of commodities to points in Pennsylvania. That shipper may support the carrier for appropriate operating authority, the acquisition of which will relieve this imbalance between inbound and outbound operations. In the application proceeding, the prudent applicant will, as an ancillary issue, emphasize the operational feasibility of the proposed services and the operational economies and efficiencies to be derived from the institution of those operations. The National Transportation Policy, as expressed by Congress, requires the promotion of safe, adequate, economical and efficient transportation services. The operating economies and efficiencies theoretically arising from the institution of proposed motor carrier operations are therefore significant considerations in any application proceeding.

The ICC attempts to foster efficient and economical operations among carriers subject to its regulation.[283] This policy is dynamically depicted in the ICC's regulations providing for the elimination of gateways[284] and those involving superhighway rules.[285] These rule-making proceedings had the promotion of fuel conservation and the elimination of excessively circuitous routes as objectives.[286] The former proceeding involved the promulgation of regulations whereby, under certain specified circumstances, a carrier holding two separate segments of operating authority need not observe their common point in performing a "through" transportation service from origin to destination. For example, if a carrier holds authority to transport widgets from point A to point B and holds a separate segment of operating authority (which may have been acquired at a later time) to transport these commodities from point B to point C, by "tacking" these two separate segments of operating authority, the carrier could provide a through transportation service of widgets from point A to point C, provided he observed the gateway of point B. The carrier's vehicles would, at some stage of the movement, have to pass through B despite the existence of a shorter route from A to C. The gateway elimination regulations established procedures whereby a carrier could, under certain circumstances, transport commodities from their origin to their ultimate destination without traversing the gateway. Thus, in our example, the carrier could transport widgets from A to C, using the shorter route, without passing through the gateway of B. In addition, the superhighway rules were promulgated to enable carriers holding authority to traverse a particular route which parallels an interstate highway to use the freeway under specified circumstances. Both sets of regulations promote efficient and economical motor carrier services.

Similarly, a regular-route carrier seeking alternate-route authority may predicate his application exclusively on proof of the improved operating economies and efficiencies to be derived from the institution of the proposed service. To obtain a grant of authority on this basis, the carrier, in addition to establishing operating economy and efficiency, must satisfy three criteria: (1) that it currently operates between the involved terminals over a practical and feasible route; (2) that it effectively competes for traffic moving between the aforesaid points because it handles a substantial volume of traffic; and (3) that a grant of the proposed authority would not cause a material improvement of its competitive position to the detriment of existing carriers.[287]

The ICC has expressed an official policy in support of efficient and economical two-way motor carrier operations.[288] For example, the Commission has taken a somewhat liberal approach in the authorization of backhaul operations to enhance the free flow of commerce and, simultaneously, foster balanced, economical and efficient motor carrier operations.[289]

Sacrificing both the economy and the efficiency of operations, the deadheading of equipment substantially increases the cost of transportation.[290] Such operations also aggravate the nation's energy shortages and are thus inconsistent with the public interest. Therefore, the decisions have recognized that an existing carrier should not be required to absorb higher operational costs as the result of deadheading when an applicant can supply equipment to a supporting shipper from a nearby terminal facility without deadheading.[291] Likewise, in multiple application proceedings, the ICC has recognized the inherent advantages of carriers who maintain operations and terminal facilities near prospective origins and destinations, so as to ensure balanced and efficient services.[292]

ICC decisions[293] indicate that operating economies and efficiencies are significant factors in evaluating whether an applicant's proposed single-line operations will be authorized in lieu of existing joint-line services. One such decision, *Kroblin Refrigerated Xpress, Inc., Extension,* emphasized that it is fundamental that public convenience and necessity may be found in operating economies and in those things which contribute to expedition and efficiency because, while they may most obviously benefit the carrier and shipper, they also contribute indirectly to more reliable, expeditious, and less costly transportation—the advantages of which are realized ultimately by the consuming public.[294]

The Commission's policy has been to discourage inefficient motor carrier operations whenever possible.[295] The ICC has frequently emphasized the promotion of efficient and economical motor carrier operations which benefit both the shipper and the carrier.[296] New methods of distribution which assist the transportation industry and the national economy should be encouraged, for the pecuniary savings inure to the benefit of the carrier, the shipper and, ultimately, the consumer.[297]

In *Transport, Inc., of South Dakota Extension—Sanborn LPG,* [298] the ICC exhibited far greater receptivity to the issue of potentially realizable operating economies and efficiencies in application proceedings seeking substitution of direct service for existing interline operations. In that decision, the current policy concerning the weight to be accorded such evidence was expressed as follows:

While a denial would, for all practical purposes, have no effect on the amount of service available—albeit by interlining—to the public, a grant would improve the quality of existing service by eliminating circuity and generally enhancing the efficiency of applicant's operations. Along with a decrease in the number of miles traveled, savings in fuel consumption and time in transit will be realized. Such savings and economies of operation have been actively encouraged by this Commission . . . . The instant application represents just such an effort to eliminate circuity, and while empty mileage on backhaul may not necessarily be decreased, it will be no greater than it is under the present interline operation. A complete denial of this application would result in an unwarranted maintenance of the status quo at the expense of efficiency, economy and fuel savings.[299]

SCHAFFER TRANSP. CO. v. UNITED STATES
355 U.S. 83 (1957)

WARREN, C.J.

The issue in this case is whether the Interstate Commerce Commission adequately and correctly applied the standards of the National Transportation Policy in denying a motor carrier's application to provide service between points now served exclusively by rail. The applicant, A. W. Schaffer, a common carrier by motor doing business as Schaffer Transportation Co., holds a certificate of public convenience and necessity authorizing him to transport granite from Grant County, South Dakota, to points in 15 States. In the present application he sought additional authority under Section 10922 of the Interstate Commerce Act to transport granite from Grant County to various new points in Vermont to several States in the Midwest and South. From all that appears in the Commission's report, rail service is currently the only mode of transportation available to shippers of granite between the points sought to be served by Schaffer.

The evidence adduced to demonstrate the need for Schaffer's service came from three shippers, six receivers and an association composed primarily of Vermont manufacturers of finished granite products. Their evidence disclosed the following advantages to be gained from motor carrier service.

> They all agree that existing rail service, in the main, is satisfactory for the transportation of carload shipments but entirely inadequate for the transportation of less-than-carload shipments, not only from the standpoint of cost, but also and primarily from a service standpoint. In this respect, the record shows that on movements of small shipments the supporting witnesses have experienced delays, damage to their merchandise, and have been hampered to some degree by the lack of insufficiency of rail sidings. In many instances, they have been asked by customers to furnish delivery by motor carrier but because of the lack of such service they have been unable to comply with these requests. Moreover, and no less important from a business point of view, the shippers are faced with the competitive disadvantage of having to compete with producers of granite at other locations which have truck delivery available. Then, too, the lack of truck service has impeded shippers' ability to increase their sales and expand their markets in this area. By use of the proposed service, certain other benefits also would accrue to the shippers or dealers. For example, the latter would be able to maintain lower inventories, receive their freight faster and more frequently, and thus, be able better to meet erection deadlines, especially during the peak seasons. Furthermore, the amount of crating now necessary would be reduced with resultant savings in time and money.

The Commission denied Schaffer's application on the following basis:

> Less-than-carload rail service, while not as expeditious as the proposed service, is fairly good, but because of the higher rate involved this service is seldom used by the supporting witnesses. The testimony of the South Dakota shipper also indicates that its support of the application is largely motivated by anticipated cheaper transportation.
>
> We have carefully considered applicant's arguments to the contrary, but are forced to conclude that the service presently available is reasonably adequate. The evidence indicates that the witnesses' main purpose in supporting the application is to obtain lower rates rather than improved service. It is well established that this is not a proper basis for a grant of authority, and the application, therefore, must be denied.

Viewing these conclusions in light of the National Transportation Policy [49 U.S.C. § 10101] we find at the outset that there has been no evaluation made of the "inherent advantages" of the motor service proposed by the applicant. That policy requires the Commission to administer the Act so as to "recognize and preserve the inherent advantages" of each mode of transportation. When a motor carrier seeks to offer service where only rail transportation is presently authorized, the inherent advantages of the proposed service are a critical factor which the Commission must assess.

How significant these advantages are in a given factual context and what need exists for a service that can supply these advantages are considerations for the Commission.

Rather than evaluate the benefit that Schaffer's proposed motor service might bring to the public, the Commission cast its first principal conclusion in terms of the adequacy of existing rail service, finding that service to be "reasonably adequate." Yet the Commission itself has previously stated: "That a particular point has adequate rail service is not a sufficient reason for denial of a certificate [to a motor carrier]." Of course, adequacy of rail service is a relevant consideration, but as the Commission recognized in *Metler Extension—Crude Sulphur*, 62 M.C.C. 143, 148, "relative or comparative adequacy" of the existing service is the significant consideration when the interests of competition are being reconciled with the policy of maintaining a sound transportation system. The record here does not disclose the factors the Commission compared in concluding that existing rail service is "reasonably adequate." For example, the Commission has not determined whether there are benefits that motor service would provide which are not now being provided by the rail carriers, whether certification of a motor carrier would be "unduly prejudicial" to the existing carriers, and whether on balance the public interest would be better served by additional competitive service. To reject a motor carrier's application on the bare conclusion that existing rail service can move the available traffic, without regard to the inherent advantages to the proposed service, would give one mode of transportation unwarranted protection from competition from others.

The Commission's second basic conclusion was that the main purpose of the witnesses in supporting the application was the prospect of obtaining lower rates. For this reason the Commission discounted the testimony of these witnesses, apparently without even evaluating the claimed advantages of the proposed service other than reduced rates. We think this approach runs counter to the National Transportation Policy. The ability of one mode of transportation to operate with a rate lower than competing types of transportation is precisely the sort of "inherent advantage" that the congressional policy requires the Commission to recognize. In these circumstances a rate benefit attributable to differences between the two modes of transportation is an "inherent advantage" of the competing type of carrier and cannot be ignored by the Commission.

Since the Commission has failed to evaluate the benefits that Schaffer's proposed service would provide the public, including whatever benefit may be determined to exist from the standpoint of rates, and since the findings as to the adequacy of rail service do not provide this Court with a basis for determining whether the Commission's decision comports with the National Transportation Policy, that decision must be set aside, and the Commission must proceed further in light of what we have said.

We do not minimize the complexity of the task the Commission faces in evaluating and balancing the numerous considerations that collectively determine where the public interest lies in a particular situation. And we do not suggest that the National Transportation Policy is a set of self-executing principles that inevitably point the way to a clear result in each case. On the contrary, those principles overlap and may conflict, and, where this occurs, resolution is the task of the agency that is expert in the field. But there is here no indication in the Commission's findings of a conflict of policies.

For the foregoing reasons, the judgment is reversed and the cause is remanded to the District Court with directions to set aside the Commission's order and remand the cause to the Commission for further proceedings in conformity with this opinion.

NOTE: Postscript to the Schaffer Decision

Letter from Donald A. Morken to Paul Stephen Dempsey (May 21, 1982).

I represented Schaffer filing the application in 1951. Mr. Schaffer was a farm boy from Revillo, SD. He had some limited authority to haul granite from Milbank to some midwest states plus Ohio, Pennsylvania, and New York, from which he usually returned empty. He operated four tractor-trailer units. Schaffer proposed a new service to several eastern states, but the real purpose was to get authority from the quarries in the Barre, Vermont area back to the midwest for a two-way movement. At that time, all of Vermont granite moved by rail. The manufacturers in Barre had a shipper's pool where they jointly loaded pool-car shipments. These pool cars came to Minneapolis–St. Paul with some frequency but rarely to smaller towns. As a result, most of the monument dealers within three to four hundred miles of Minneapolis drove in with their own trucks to pick up their pooled shipments. They did this to avoid LCL [less-than-carload] service, which was expensive and slow. Damage to LCL traffic was very heavy. With proper shipper-receiver support, I knew we could put on a very strong case. Since no motor carrier held authority from Vermont, our only problem could be rail service. Longhaul traffic was generally considered rail traffic. At this time, '51 and '52, the ICC was granting a substantial majority of new applications. I think between 80 and 90 percent of them.

The Hearing Examiner recommended a grant in February of 1953. Exceptions were filed and it was not until May of 1954 that Division 5, in a two-to-one decision, recommended that the authority be granted. It was at this point in time that this case became a ploy in a political game.

President Eisenhower had been elected in 1952, taking office in January of 1953. One of the last things Harry Truman did was appoint two new Commissioners, Kelso Elliott and Anthony Arpaia at the end of 1952. President Eisenhower appointed four new Commissioners in 1953, and the railroads set up a program to educate the Commissioners. In 1954, once every week, a President of a railroad would make a personal call on each one of the new Commissioners. The message told by each President was about the same. The theme was that there were so many new motor carriers being authorized that even the Commission itself did not know how many carriers were operating between any two points.

The railroad's efforts were not without success. By the end of 1954 and early in the year 1955, the grant-to-denial ratio on new applications had dropped to where only 10 to 15% were being granted. It was at this time that the Schaffer case came before the full Commission on Petitions for Reconsideration of the Division 5 grant. In an Order served February 7, 1955, 63 MCC 247, the full Commission, in a six-to-four decision, denied the Schaffer application on the grounds that the railroad service was reasonably adequate. While the railroads were protesting substantially all new motor carrier applications, their activity, if anything, increased until the Supreme Court decision. When the Schaffer case was appealed to the Supreme Court, 57 railroads intervened as defendants. After the Supreme Court decision, there was a substantial change at the Commission level; and the pendulum swung back so that again, motor carrier applications were determined on the merits. If a reasonably good case had been put on by the applicant, he could be assured of getting a grant in whole or in part of the authority sought.

As an interesting aside to the above, during the summer of 1955 after the full Commission denied Petition for Reconsideration by Schaffer and the American Trucking Association appeal was filed on behalf of Schaffer before a three-judge special Court in Sioux Falls, SD, Mr. Schaffer fell on a serious personal misfortune. He lost the use of his right hand and right arm while trying to clean out a corn picker on his farm. Not too long after that, he developed leukemia that in those days could be treated with transfusions but not cured.

The favorable Supreme Court Decision was quite a boon to Mr. Schaffer. He was able to work out an arrangement with another carrier, that this office did not represent at the time, to sell his business. Probably the most valuable asset in the sale was the fact the Vermont authority would be granted by the Commission on remand. A substantial portion of a good sale price was contingent on the authority being granted, which eventually it was, to Anderson Trucking Service, Inc. of St. Cloud, MN. Fortunately for myself, Anderson Trucking became my client and still is today. Anderson has become the largest carrier in the United States of granite, marble, slate, and stone. Mr. Schaffer lived to see the authority he had sought for over six years granted to Anderson; but not too long after, he lost his life to his leukemia condition.

F. Fitness

Both Section 10921(b)(1) and Section 10923(a)(1) of the Interstate Commerce Act provide that a certificate and a permit, respectively, shall be issued to a qualified applicant who affirmatively demonstrates, inter alia, that he is fit, willing and able to perform properly the proposed service and to comply with the provisions of the Interstate Commerce Act and the Commission's rules and regulations promulgated under the Act.[300, 301] Therefore, a finding of fitness by the ICC is a statutorily imposed condition precedent to the issuance of motor carrier operating authority.

These statutory provisions protect the shipping, receiving and consuming public from those carriers whose conduct demonstrates an inability or unwillingness to perform their motor carrier operations in a lawful manner.[302] If the evidence convincingly demonstrates a pattern of serious or continuing violations by the involved carrier, that carrier has the burden of refuting the import of its prior behavior to establish its fitness to receive additional motor carrier operating authority.[303]

In *Associated Transport, Inc., Extension—TVA Plant*,[304] the Commission succinctly set forth the criteria it ordinarily uses to determine a carrier's fitness:

The fitness of a carrier encompasses (a) its financial ability to perform the service it seeks to provide, (b) its willingness to adhere to the rules and regulations established pursuant to the Interstate Commerce Act, and (c) its ability to properly and safely perform the proposed service. Cf. Eagle Motor Lines, Inc., Invest. & Revoca. of Certif., 117 M.C.C. 30, 35 (1972).

There is of course, no inflexible rule by which an applicant's fitness can be determined. It is well settled, however, that in determining whether an applicant has satisfied its statutory burden of proof in establishing its fitness, consideration must ordinarily be given to (1) the nature and extent of past violations, (2) the mitigating or extenuating circumstances surrounding the violations, (3) whether the carrier's conduct represents a flagrant and persistent disregard of this Commission's rules and regulations, (4) whether it has made sincere efforts to correct its past mistakes, and (5) whether applicant is willing and able to comport in the future with the statute and the applicable rules and regulations thereunder.[305]

However, each proceeding must be independently evaluated on the basis of its unique evidentiary situation.[306]

The National Transportation Policy and the satisfaction of the statutory criteria of public convenience and necessity or the public interest on the one hand and the carrier's fitness, willingness and ability to perform the proposed operations on the other are independent questions. One may not be resolved on the basis of the other.[307] A failure to demonstrate a public need for the proposed service will ordinarily preclude an examination of the issue of fitness.[308] Findings regarding a carrier's fitness should be based solely on evidence regarding the applicant's conduct and should not be predicated on the strength of the case made by the other parties in an operating rights proceeding.[309] Thus, an applicant may not be found fit exclusively because the supporting shippers may require a proposed transportation service and the protestants have presented limited evidence regarding their individual or collective ability to provide the involved service.[310]

In denying an application because the applicant has failed affirmatively and convincingly to demonstrate its fitness, the ICC is not unsympathetic to the supporting shipper's transportation requirements. Indeed, the shipper may well be able to obtain relief elsewhere. It may immediately support an application for temporary authority to provide the required operations.[311] It also may support another carrier for permanent operating authority duplicative of that denied by the Commission on the issue of fitness. Moreover, existing carriers may independently or collectively be able to satisfy a significant portion, if not all, of the supporting shipper's transportation needs.[312]

A prerequisite to continued operation as a licensed motor carrier is lawful compliance with the established rules and regulations governing its performance. A carrier which contumaciously disregards these rules, regulations and interpretations will not be granted additional authority to engage in interstate operations.[313] The denial of an application based on a finding of unfitness is not intended as a punitive sanction against past reprehensible conduct, but reflects a determination that the applicant is deficient in either its willingness or its ability to perform motor carrier operations in a lawful manner.[314]

SAMMONS TRUCKING EXTENSION—ABERDEEN, S. DAK.

124 M.C.C. 373 (1976).

Murphy, Commissioner:

The application although uncontested relative to the issue of the public convenience and necessity for the proposed service, is opposed by the Bureau of Enforcement and by intervener Popelka, appearing for the purpose of contesting the fitness of authority.

Sammons Trucking, appearing in these consolidated proceedings as both an applicant and protestant, is substantially involved, or otherwise implicated, in a series of actions or reported occurrences of utmost concern to this Commission. In a report and recommended order by Hearing Examiner (now Administrative Law Judge) John P. Dodge served May 24, 1971, in No. MC-F.10958, Sammons Trucking—Purchase—Henry Lambert Trucking Co., Inc., it was recommended that the application be denied for the reason that Sammons failed to demonstrate that it was fit to acquire Lambert because of enumerated violations of the Interstate Commerce Act and regulations thereunder. By order served May 18, 1973, the Commission, Division 3, Acting as an Appellate Division, ultimately affirmed the recommended order in the purchase proceeding. Subsequently, in October and November 1973, four Commission investigators performed an audit of Sammons' operations in order to determine the extent of compliance with Commission rules and regulations undertaken by the carrier. Specific unlawful activities were discovered which included instances of unauthorized transportation, unlawful extensions of credit, tariff violations, and failures to comply with prescribed lease and interchange regulations. Enforcement actions which were based upon the findings of the compliance survey resulted in a permanent injunction issued by the United States District Court, District of Montana, adjoining defendant Sammons from engaging in specified unlawful activities and a payment by Sammons of $7,000 in settlement of civil forfeiture claims against the carrier.

By application filed January 7, 1974, Sammons applied for the authority involved in the instant Sub-No. 130 proceeding. In August 1974, the Bureau informed applicant as to the matters of fact and law upon which it intended to rely in contesting the fitness of applicant to receive the authority it sought. During the course of the oral hearing in the Sub-No. 130 proceeding, the Bureau presented evidence pertaining basically to the prior noncompliance record of Sammons and such factors would bear upon the fitness of applicant in its ability to comport itself within the regulatory framework. Extensive testimony, moreover, was offered in support of the Bureau's allegation that the executive vice president of Sammons, Mr. Richard Bebel, had on at least two occasions threatened to cause bodily harm to Administrative Law Judge Dodge with the explicit intent to intimidate him into changing his decision in the above-mentioned Lambert Purchase case. The evidence shows that, with regard to the alleged threat, Mr. Bebel appeared at the hearing in support of the purchase application and during the course of the proceeding he became acquainted with Administrative Law Judge Dodge. A short time after the report was served, Mr. Bebel initiated a visit with the Administrative Law Judge at his office in Washington, D.C. According to Administrative Law Judge Dodge's testimony, Richard Bebel, who was very upset because the report recommended that the application be denied, explained that there was a risk that he (Bebel) would lose his investment of $25,000 in the transaction and that they must work to change the decision to a grant rather than a denial. Mr. Bebel was reported to have stated that if the result was not changed, "I have got my gun and I am coming gunning for you." Subsequently, on or about April 19, 1972, Mr. Bebel again visited the Administrative Law Judge at his office and, while appearing much less upset, the Sammons official allegedly stated that the denial just cannot stand and if it does "I am coming gunning for you." The Administrative Law Judge did not report the incidents to law enforcement officials since, in his view, to do so might have aggravated the situation. Although Administrative Law Judge Dodge has stated that he had some doubt as to whether Bebel's threats should be considered serious, he was sufficiently concerned to take precautions to see that the alleged threats would not be carried out. Thus, subsequent to Bebel's first visit to his office, Administrative Law Judge Dodge undertook the following steps to protect himself: (a) he apprised himself as to when the Commission would serve any orders or reports relative to the Lambert Purchase proceeding, (b) he locked his office door during business hours from the time a Commission order was cleared for service, (c) he brought a pistol from his residence, keeping it in his desk during that period and subsequently taking it to his residence, and (d) at one of Bebel's visits to his office and upon Bebel's temporary absence therefrom, he searched the coat and briefcase of Bebel for the presence of a firearm and found none. While initially "terribly concerned" about Bebel's statements, Administrative Law Judge Dodge is currently of the view, after a period of several years and approximately five visits from Bebel, that the threat upon his life was not intended to be carried out to fruition.

Another incident involving a high official of Sammons Trucking occurred during the same period of time. In the latter half of 1971, Mr. Gerry Rawles, transportation manager for the Lumber, Plywood, and Door Division of St. Regis Paper Company, filed periodic performance reports with the Interstate Commerce Commission's Region 6 Field Office at Billings, Mont., with respect to the quality of service provided by authorized carriers, including Sammons, for his company's Libby, Mont., plant. Inasmuch as these reports reflected negatively upon Sammons' service, they became the basis of an inquiry into the carrier's fitness in its Sub-No. 84 application proceeding and the Bureau of Enforcement intervened therein. Oral hearing in Sammons' Sub-No. 84 proceeding was held on August 7, 1972, in Missoula, Mont. While Rawles was scheduled to appear in person as a witness at this hearing, counsel for Sammons offered into evidence an affidavit executed by Rawles in Missoula on August 4, 1972, which asserted that the difficulties St. Regis experienced with Sammons were only "occasional," occurring during peak shipping periods, that the service had improved substantially during 1972, and that St. Regis desired to have this service continued. In reliance upon this affidavit, the Administrative Law Judge in the Sub-No. 84 proceeding recommended that Sammons be found fit to conduct the proposed service.

During the course of the hearings held in Popelka's Sub-Nos. 51 and 63 application proceedings embraced herein, applicant presented evidence which it alleged would show protestant Sammons to be "unfit" and also reflect adversely upon the credibility of Sammons' operating witnesses. Counsel for Popelka related that in April 1972, 4 months prior to Sammons' Sub-No. 84 fitness hearing Gerry Rawles received a telephone call from Myron (Pete) Sammons, the then president and principal stockholder of Sammons Trucking, threatening Rawles' life if he did not withdraw his service complaints against Sammons. On applicant's cross-examination, witness William Grimshaw, a Sammons' vice president, testified that immediately after receiving the threatening call from Myron (Pete) Sammons, Rawles telephoned witness Grimshaw at his home and related it to him. Although Grimshaw stated at the hearing that this threat was nothing more than "an irresponsible remark made by a man under the influence of alcohol," he "acknowledged that Rawles was a little upset" by the call. In its reply to applicant Popelka's January 21, 1974, request for review of the Administrative Law Judge's evidentiary rulings, Sammons' counsel acknowledges that the Rawles incident occurred and does not dispute its substance as shown in the record. Thus, it is admitted:

> What started out as some letters to the District Supervisor from a shipper (coinciding noticeably with a temporary authority application) ultimately resulted in the granting of a temporary authority to a carrier that is not a party to this proceeding. They became the thorn in the side of protestant Sammons which at a crucial unfortunate time became unbearable to the then president of the company. This in turn precipitated an act which will undoubtedly haunt Sammons Trucking for years.

A third matter which tends to implicate Sammons in unlawful or otherwise culpable activities occurred during the first half of 1973. On April 18, 1973, Mrs. Alice Williams, a former employee of Popelka whose duties included work on logs and leases, received a telephone call at her home in Livingston, Mont., from a person whose voice she recognized and who identified himself as Jim Tripp. She was offered $1,000 to provide information which, it was hoped, might be damaging to Popelka in the Sub-Nos. 51 and 63 applications. Specifically, she was requested to supply logs and leases which might show unlawful operations, and a key to the accounting office. On May 30, 1973, Alice Williams was again contacted by the same voice and asked to meet with the caller at a named location in Bozeman, Mont. At Bozeman she met with two men as instructed and was told that Sammons Trucking was financing the matter and that three Popelka employees were already receiving payments from Sammons. Alice Williams was next contacted by telephone on June 13, 1973, when a man who did not identify himself told her that she was not safe where she was living because she had informed applicant's president, Mr. Wayne Waggoner, about the contacts they had had with her and because the Popelka hearings were not going well. Frightened for her life, Alice Williams immediately telephoned Mr. Waggoner who was attending the hearing on the involved application at Missoula. Applicant's counsel then advised her that she should bring the matter, including the threat, out in the open by coming to Missoula and testifying about it at the hearing. She appeared at the hearing and testified as to the substance of the telephone calls and the meeting.

The records in the proceedings consolidated herein establish that Sammons Trucking has a history of successive investigations of its fitness and that recently the carrier, through its ranking officials, engaged, or is implicated, in a series of instances involving highly improper conduct of significant import to this Commission and its interest in enforcing regulations and procedures which are not tainted by duress, threats, or other forms of illegality. Sammons generally responds that since its inception in 1962, the expansion and vigor characteristic of its enterprise has brought upon it the substantial enmity of its competitors. According to Sammons, this hostility by others has led to serious unsubstantiated accusations which in turn have provoked the intervention of this Commission's Bureau of Enforcement. While we join with Sammons in the view that the accusations are grave, we are also of the opinion that they are corroborated by the ample record developed in these proceedings.

The testimony is uncontroverted that subsequent to Administrative Law Judge Dodge's initial decision in Lambert Purchase, supra, which found Sammons unfit to acquire the rights of the vendor, Sammons' executive vice president, Richard Bebel, came to the Washington, D.C. office of the Administrative Law Judge Dodge and spoke words to the effect that "I am coming gunning for you" or "I am going to get my gun."

A Sammons official, Richard Bebel, did in fact use language directed to the Administrative Law Judge which reasonably could be construed as a threat to do serious bodily harm. A specific finding to this effect has been made in the initial decision with regard to Sammons' fitness to conduct the service proposed in No. MC–124692 (Sub-No. 130). We view with similar gravity the threat to Gerry Rawles made by Myron (Pete) Sammons, the then president and principal stockholder of Sammons Trucking, which the carrier does not deny, but rather has admitted. In this regard, the record shows that Rawles, a division transportation manager for St. Regis Paper Company, received a telephone call from Myron Sammons threatening Rawles' life if he did not withdraw his service complaints against Sammons Trucking. The Alice Williams matter, moreover, is an additional incident implicating the carrier in clearly improper activities, albeit controverted by Sammons insofar as its knowing direction is concerned, which culminated in yet another attempt at duress and a threat upon the life of an individual or participant in regulatory proceedings before this Commission for the purpose of unlawfully affecting the outcome of such proceedings.

In regard to the Bebel threat, Sammons' explanation that the relationship between Bebel and the involved Administrative Law Judge was cordial and that the purpose of meetings initiated by Bebel was to "solicit information of an extraordinary nature that might be helpful," does not excuse the extreme, coercive words spoken and, in fact, tends to substantiate the proclivity on Sammons' part to go beyond the bounds of propriety to influence decisions. The explanation that Rawles' service complaints levied against Sammons constituted "the thorn in the side of protestant Sammons which at a crucial unfortunate time became unbearable" and that the subsequent threat upon Rawles' life was "an irresponsible remark made by a man under the influence of alcohol," cannot in good conscience be accepted in mitigation of this incident. Even if we were not to consider the incident involving Alice Williams, the gravity and similarity of the prior threats by Sammons' officials demonstrate a disturbing tendency on Sammons' part all too freely to resort to the menace of threatened bodily violence in order to influence the disposition of proceedings in which its interests are involved. Thus, Sammons has manifested, as a general pattern of conduct established through its actions, that it will engage in illegal activities with hoped for impunity in an attempt to corrupt the regulatory process for its own devices. We conclude, therefore, that Sammons purposely and willfully engaged in the described conduct in order to improperly affect proceedings before this Commission; that Sammons' conduct exemplifies the carrier's abhorrence of due process and its obvious disregard of the law; and that on the record before us we are precluded from finding that Sammons is fit and willing to operate in accordance with the Interstate Commerce Act and the Commission's regulations thereunder.

A review of Sammons' past record shows no likely promise that it would comply with the law and our regulatory procedures if it were granted a limited 3-year certificate as recommended. The issuance of such a certificate would not appear to be sufficient incentive for it to comply with the law, particularly when one considers the gravity and repetition in the carrier's conduct. Therefore, in finding Sammons unfit, no authority can be issued in those of its applications now pending before the Commission, including the proceedings in which a need for the proposed service was found but which were held open pending the determination of applicant's fitness herein. Nationwide Carrier, Inc. Ext.—Foodstuffs, 120 M.C.C. 353 (1974). These matters are now being separately considered by us. We deem it unnecessary, however, as recommended by the Administrative Law Judge in the Popelka proceedings, to at this time reopen Sammons' fitness action in No. MC–124692 (Sub-No. 84), or institute a separate investigation and revocation of certificate proceedings against Sammons. We believe that our decision in this regard is consistent with our objective not to punish for past wrongdoing, but rather to ensure the willingness and ability of the carrier to conduct its future operations in a lawful manner and, in accordance with this policy, we believe that Sammons should not be subjected to harsher measures than those imposed against it herein. It should be emphasized, however, that any continued unlawful activities or operations will necessarily lead to the institution of a proceeding looking toward the imposition of appropriate sanctions, including the possible revocation of existing authority. See Metler Hauling & Rigging Ext.—Laudon County, Tenn., 117 M.C.C. 557, 561 (1972).

Commissioner Clapp, concurring in part:

I believe that the majority has been too lenient in dealing with Sammons. Considering the serious nature of Sammons' offenses and the evidence indicating that it obtained a finding of fitness in its Sub-No. 84 proceeding through fraudulent means, I would, in addition to the action taken by the majority, institute an investigation proceeding against Sammons under section 10925 of the act in order to determine whether its outstanding authority should be revoked. Surely a higher standard of behavior than that evidenced by Sammons and its officers must be demanded by this Commission. Obviously, death threats cannot be tolerated under any circumstances.

Except as indicated herein, I agree with the decision of the majority.

G. Entry Controls of Intercity Bus Operations

Buses provide a low-cost, energy-efficient passenger system which serves more stations than any other carrier. Of the major passenger carriers, the intercity bus caters to the least affluent travelers, who have few other options and are the least likely to protect themselves.

There have been some disturbing trends in the bus industry. Patterns of decline in traffic have been observed which are similar to those of rail passenger service in the 1950s. There is a good deal of cross-subsidization within the system. The profitable routes cross-subsidize a lot of local service, and charter and package express revenues support much of the regular-route system.

The Bus Regulatory Reform Act of 1982 amended the entry provisions of the Interstate Commerce Act to provide that a regular-route passenger certificate would be issued to an applicant which demonstrates that it is fit, willing and able to provide the proposed operations and to comply with the Act and the Commission's rules and regulations promulgated thereunder, unless the ICC concludes, on the basis of evidence adduced by the protestant, that the issuance of such authority would not be in the public interest. In determining whether the proposed operations would be consistent with the public interest, the Commission must consider (a) the National Transportation Policy of Section 10101 of the Act, (b) the value of competition, (c) the effect of a grant of operating authority on small communities, and (d) whether a grant of authority would impair the ability of another carrier to provide a substantial portion of its regular-route service over its entire system. Again, the burden of proof on the public interest issue is placed on protestants. Furthermore, diversion of revenue of traffic, standing alone, is not sufficient to satisfy this burden.

Applicants seeking authority to perform special or charter operations, or to engage in contract carrier service, need merely demonstrate their fitness. Fitness is defined by the new legislation to include two criteria: safety fitness and proof of minimum financial responsibility.

The 1982 Act also gives the Commission new jurisdiction over intrastate bus service. The ICC must issue intrastate operating authority to a passenger carrier which holds commensurate interstate authority on proof of carrier fitness, unless such service would have a significant adverse effect on a commuter bus operation. Strict time limitations are imposed on states to decide intrastate discontinuance applications. Adverse determinations must be approved by the Commission unless it concludes that approval would be inconsistent with the public interest or that continuing such intrastate operations would not impose an unreasonable burden on interstate commerce. As to operating authority acquired after August 1, 1982, discontinuance of interstate operations may be granted unless the ICC concludes that continuation of such service would not impose an unreasonable burden on interstate commerce.

III. WATER CARRIAGE

A. Common Carriage

An applicant seeking authority to operate as a common carrier by water must, pursuant to Section 10922(a) of the Act,[315] demonstrate that the proposed service is or will be required by the present or future public convenience and necessity, and that applicant is fit, willing and able to perform such operations in a lawful manner.[316] In a number of proceedings the principle has been expressed that the word "necessity" must not be taken so literally as to impose the prerequisite of a transportation crisis of significant proportions before the ICC will grant an application.[317] Such an interpretation would effectively render the word "convenience" meaningless.[318]

Not an absolute prerequisite to a grant of water carrier authority, the inadequacy of existing operations represents only a single factor which should ordinarily be evaluated in the broader determination of whether the proposed service satisfies the public convenience and necessity. Other significant factors include (a) the public's requirement for additional water carrier competition; (b) the shipper's need for different kinds, types or modes of transportation; and (c) the demonstrated necessity for an improved transportation service.[319]

The ICC has traditionally recognized the existence of certain inherent advantages in water carriage; among them the primary attribute, from a shipper's perspective, is the diminished cost of transportation. In water carrier application proceedings, when a shipper's support is primarily predicated on the expectancy of lower transport charges, the ICC has frequently concluded that the shipping public is entitled to the benefits of water carriage, including inherently lower rates.[320] In applications involving other modes of transportation, the ICC has usually decided that the potential acquisition of lower rates is not a factor to be considered, except when an "embargo" is convincingly shown to exist.[321] As in the case of motor carrier operating authority application proceedings, the desire for lower rates, standing alone, will not ordinarily justify a grant of operating authority. The ICC has recognized, however, that a shipper's anticipation of diminished transportation expenditures should be considered when the proposed service is to be performed by a water carrier, because the mode of carriage has traditionally offered lower rates.[322]

As to the opposition of applications for water carrier authority by existing rail carriers, it has frequently been held that the availability of rail service does not preclude the ICC from granting the application when the applicant seeks authority territorially duplicative of that held by protestants. Because of the inherent attributes of the aquatic mode of transport, including lower transportation costs, the shipping public is frequently deemed entitled to both modes of transportation.[323]

B. Contract Carriage

Section 10923(a) of the Act[324] authorizes the issuance of contract carrier authority to water carriers which demonstrate (1) that they are fit, willing and able to perform the proposed operations and to conform to the provisions of the Act and the Commission's rules and regulations thereunder, and (2) that the proposed operations "will be consistent with the public interest and the national transportation policy." These are essentially the same criteria governing entry control of contract carriage in the motor carrier mode of transportation.

Applications for authority to operate as a contract carrier by water have been denied when the services of existing water, motor and rail carriers have not been demonstrated to be inadequate or unsatisfactory.[325] Again, as in motor carrier application proceedings, the ICC has recognized the principle that "existing carriers are entitled to transport all of the traffic which they can handle adequately, efficiently and economically without the competition of a new service in the considered territory."[326]

Shipper-controlled water carriers have been granted authority to expand their transportation services in the interest of operating economies and efficiencies.[327] In addition, such authority has been issued when the applicant's equipment is specially adapted to satisfy the shipper's distinct transportation requirements.[328] Although a shipper's desire for lower rates does not ordinarily warrant a grant of water carrier operating authority when an existing carrier demonstrates its willingness to transport the involved commodities at its published tariffs,[329] the ability of a proposed service to provide low-cost transportation is a factor supporting a grant of such authority.[330]

IV. FREIGHT FORWARDING

Freight forwarding is, in many respects, a unique mode of transportation.[331] It is the only mode subject to the jurisdiction of each of the three federal transport regulatory agencies. Surface freight forwarders are regulated by the ICC. Airfreight forwarders (indirect air carriers) and non–vessel-operating common carriers by water—the counterparts to ICC-regulated surface freight forwarders—are subject to the jurisdiction of the DOT and the FMC, respectively.[332] The performance of forwarding operations thus frequently entails interagency jurisdictional considerations. Moreover, because forwarders do not actually perform the underlying transportation movement, they must enlist the assistance of motor, rail, water or air carriers to move goods. Thus, freight forwarding is inevitably an intermodal operation.

Freight forwarding usually is defined as the aggregation of numerous small shipments of individual consignors into a single consolidated shipment tendered to a carrier for subsequent movement.[333] From the carrier's perspective, the service is analogous to that performed by a shipper of its own commodities. The term "freight forwarder" is defined by Section 10102(8) of the ICA[334] as any person, other than a carrier subject to parts I, II and III of the Interstate Commerce Act, who purports to provide transportation for compensation and who (a) assembles and consolidates shipments and performs break-bulk and distribution operations with respect to such consolidated shipments; (b) assumes liability for the transportation thereof from the point of origin to the point of destination; and (c) employs a carrier subject to parts I, II or III of the Interstate Commerce Act for the performance of any portion of such underlying transportation. Each of these requirements must be fulfilled before freight-forwarding status will be ascribed.[335] They may be summarized into five separate requirements: (1) holding oneself out to the general public as a common carrier (other than one subject to the other provisions of the Act) to transport or provide transportation of property, for compensation, in interstate commerce; (2) assembly and consolidation or provision therefor; (3) performance of break-bulk and distribution, or provision therefor; (4) assumption of responsibilty for the transportation from point of receipt to point of destination; and (5) utilization of the services of a carrier subject to the Act.[336]

The absence of any of these requirements may preclude freight-forwarding status.[337] Yet each of these component elements of Section 10102(8) need not exist on every shipment handled, nor need such movements be performed solely within the territorial confines of the United States.[338]

Section 10923 of the Interstate Commerce Act [339] provides that a permit to operate as a freight forwarder shall be granted if the applicant demonstrates that it is fit, able and willing to perform the proposed service and that operations will be consistent with the public interest and the National Transportation Policy. A permit may not be denied solely because it would authorize operations in competition with existing services.[340] The "public interest and National Transportation Policy" criteria used in the licensing of freight-forwarding operations are not as stringent as the "public convenience and necessity" test used in motor common carrier operating authority application proceedings, but involve a consideration of factors other than those relating to the adequacy or inadequacy of existing operations.[341]

V. AIR CARRIAGE

A. Public Convenience and Necessity

1. Traditional Entry Criteria

As originally promulgated, the Federal Aviation Act authorized the issuance of operating authority to any applicant who was "fit, willing, and able," under circumstances in which the transportation in question was "required by the public convenience and necessity."[342, 343] In performing such responsibilities, the CAB was obligated by the Act to "foster sound economic conditions" in transportation; to promote "adequate, economical and efficient service by air carriers at reasonable 'charges"[344]; to promote "competition to the extent necessary to assure the sound development of an air transportation system"[345]; and to avoid "destructive competitive practices."[346]

In interpreting the statutory concept of public convenience and necessity, the Board traditionally weighed and balanced a number of criteria.[347] Most such proceedings involved essentially a two-step process: (1) determining the number of carriers the market in question could reasonably and profitably support; and (2) selecting from among the various applicants which carrier(s) should be designated to receive (a) certificate(s) of public convenience and necessity.

In the *Miami–Los Angeles Competitive Nonstop Case*,[348] the Board enumerated ten factors it weighed in determining which, among multiple applicants, should or should not receive certificated authority to serve a particular market:

(1) route integration as evidenced by the ability to convenience beyond segment traffic;

(2) frequencies to be operated over the involved segment;

(3) the type of equipment to be employed;

(4) the fares to be charged;

(5) the identity of the involved points;

(6) the historic participation in the involved traffic;

(7) efforts to promote and develop the involved market;

(8) the need of the applicant for route strengthening;

(9) the profitability of the route for the applicants and the existing carriers; and

(10) the potential of diversion of traffic from existing carriers.[349]

Only the first four criteria have as their objective the protection of the consumer interests. Most relate to how a regulated carrier's operations might become more profitable by diminishing the potential adverse influence of competition.

The CAB traditionally sought to improve the competitive posture of smaller carriers vis-à-vis the larger incumbents, and reduce industry concentration, by favoring the issuance of operating authority to the small carriers.[350] This policy of route strengthening "was intended to combat excessive concentration and to maintain a balance of competitive opportunities within the industry by strengthening the smaller carriers who were at a disadvantage because of their route system."[351]

Enhancing the competitive posture of smaller carriers by issuing segments of potentially lucrative route authority was viewed as being "of great importance in perfecting the route structure of the nation."[352] Thus, the Board frequently scrutinized the competitive positions of various applicants and their relative requirements for route strengthening.[353] By enhancing the competitive posture of smaller carriers, the Board could bring a concomitant reduction in their subsidy requirements, which in itself became another important criterion of carrier selection.[354]

In other cases, the Board concluded that the potential service benefits offered by larger carriers outweighed the need of smaller carriers for subsidy reduction. For example, in the *Fort Myers–Atlanta Case*,[355] the Board recognized that a carrier "having access to the largest volume support traffic will be in the best position to provide the greatest frequency and capacity and flow the maximum number of passengers over the . . . segment and thereby convenience the largest number of beyond-segment passengers."[356] Similarly, the ease with which a proposed segment integrated with a carrier's existing route structure was frequently perceived as a factor weighing in favor of the carrier, for such a coherent structure might enable it to convenience a larger segment of the traveling public.

The relative beyond-segment capabilities of the applicants frequently was perceived as an important criterion of carrier selection.[357] For example, the Board, in the *Memphis–Twin Cities/Milwaukee Case*,[358] recognized that

flow traffic is important in developing a thin market because it helps support the frequencies necessary to permit service levels sufficient to attract and hold new customers. In addition, it generates systemwide profits and benefits passengers by increasing single-plane and single-carrier alternatives. Because beyond traffic contributes significant benefits to carriers and passengers it has become an important element in selecting a carrier to serve this sort of market.[359]

The Board also tried, from time to time, to strengthen the financial posture of even large carriers facing financial difficulties through the issuance of lucrative segments of operating authority.[360] Concern with the financial strength of carriers subject to its regulation frequently led the Board to view the potential diversion of traffic from incumbent carriers and consequential revenue loss as a factor militating against the issuance of operating authority to a new entrant.[361] Similarly, the Board scrutinized route proposals to determine whether the inauguration of service pursuant thereto might cause financial injury to the applicant or, as the Board has stated, "whether the proposed operation would result in a revenue deficiency that would weaken the carrier and impair its ability to properly serve its route."[362]

Congressional scrutiny of arguments for deregulating the airline industry began with a series of hearings in 1975 under a Senate subcommittee chaired by Edward Kennedy. Such congressional analysis was subsequently expanded by Senator Howard Cannon, Chairman of the Senate Commerce Committee, who held a parallel series of hearings. Together, these two senators are largely responsible for the legislation which ultimately resulted.

Whether their conclusions were accurate or inaccurate is an issue which must be left to future commentators. The significance of the instant summarization lies not in the accuracy of these allegations; but right or wrong, this summary represents the perspective from which Congress viewed the airline industry and CAB regulation, and the foundation on which Congress acted.

The legislative history of the 1938 Act reveals that Congress intended that the Board implement a cautious, yet moderately liberal approach to entry, permitting new enterprises to compete as the air transportion market expanded. Yet entry into the industry has been effectively prohibited by the restrictive regulatory policies of the CAB. Between 1950 and 1974, the CAB received 79 applications from firms seeking to obtain operating authority to provide scheduled domestic service. None was granted.[363] Moreover, between 1969 and 1974, the CAB imposed a "route moratorium," a general policy of refusing to grant or even hear any applications to serve new routes.[364] As a result of these policies, the big four in 1938—United, American, Eastern, and TWA—were the big four today, thirty years later. In 1938, United controlled 22.9 percent of the market; in 1975, it accounted for 22.0 percent.[365]

Actually, not a single new domestic trunkline carrier was authorized. Although 16 such carriers were "grandfathered" in 1938, only 10 such carriers existed in 1978. The CAB had not permitted a single bankruptcy. The 16 domestic trunkline carriers of 1938 merged into the 10 which existed three decades later; the 19 local service carriers licensed shortly after World War II merged into the nine which existed in 1975.[366]

2. The Entry Provisions of the Airline Deregulation Act

In introducing the Airline Deregulation Act to the full Senate, Commerce Committee Chariman Howard Cannon, one of the Bill's chief architects, described the legislation as follows:

Mr. President, I bring to the Senate today one of the most significant pieces of legislation in the past several decades. Important not so much by itself, but because it represents one of the only opportunities this body has had in recent years to vote for less government regulation and more free enterprise for a major U. S. industry.[367]

The new legislation substitutes increased reliance on competition for classical price, profit and entry regulation.[368] It reflects the modern economic view that increased competition in the airline industry will force prices down and eliminate excess capacity; if firms were free to set prices and enter markets without regulatory constraints, they would experiment in offering different combinations of price and service. Thus, the underlying theory of this legislation is that liberalized entry and pricing will force carriers to adhere to the competitive pressures of the marketplace to provide the range of price and service options desired by the public.

3. The New Policy Declaration

The statutory criteria governing all modes of transportation has traditionally been couched in inherently vague, if not vacuous, terminology. Congress recognized that it had neither the expertise nor the time to fulfill properly its obligations under Article 1, Section 8, of the Constitution, to regulate commerce between and among the several states. Therefore, it created regulatory bodies to develop the requisite expertise and gave them rather wide discretion to regulate the industry as they best perceived the fulfillment of the congressional intent. Furthermore, Congress recognized that the needs of the public would not remain static, but that the optimum regulatory structure would evolve to meet the dynamic growth and maturity of our nation's commerce.

Hence, such statutory criteria as "public convenience and necessity," standing alone, have virtually no inherent meaning. Nevertheless, Congress set forth its Declaration of Policy in Section 102 of the Act to indicate more specifically its interest as to precisely how transportation should be regulated, to give the agency some indication of the congressional purpose and the ultimate objectives for which the agency should strive and to thereby breathe life into what might otherwise be virtually vacuous statutory phraseology.

The Airline Deregulation Act amended the Federal Aviation Act to establish a new declaration of policy for interstate and overseas transportation.[369] The declaration includes 10 subsections which specify the criteria deemed by the Board to be consistent with the public interest and the public convenience and necessity.

The first two subsections stress the importance of safety, emphasizing that it shall be a policy objective of the highest priority[370] and that the Board shall prevent any deterioration in establishing safety procedures.[371] There can be no doubt that Congress intended that there be no diminution in the Board's safety evaluation.

Two of these provisions also deal with the role to be accorded competition as a policy objective. Prior to the 1978 amendments, this section's only reference to competition was that the CAB should promote "competition to the extent necessary to assure sound development of the air transportation system." Today, competitive market forces (including actual and potential competition) are to be used "to provide the needed air transportation system . . . to encourage efficient and well managed carriers to earn adequate profits and to attract capital,"[372] and "to provide efficiency, innovation and low prices and to determine the variety, quality and price of air transportation services."[373] The Senate has emphasized that

The new declaration of policy . . . is designed to give the Board a clear and firm mandate to regulate in a manner which places primary reliance on competition. The Board is instructed to make every effort to utilize competition and market forces to achieve regulation goals, such as low-cost efficient air transportation. And, the policy statement designates a competitive industry as a goal in itself.[374]

Low fares are to be encouraged, as is the adequacy, economy and efficiency of service, but "without unjust discriminations, undue preferences or advantages, or unjust or deceptive practices."[375] Similarly, the Board must guard against "unfair, deceptive, predatory, or anticompetitive practices" and avoid "unreasonable industry concentration, excessive market domination" and similar occurrences which might enable "carriers unreasonably to increase prices, reduce services, or exclude competition."[376]

In addition to promoting rate competition, as a policy objective the Board is directed to encourage new entry and route expansion by existing air carriers. The Board is also obliged to strengthen smaller carriers so as to assure a more competitive and effective industry.[377] Curiously, the Conference Report indicates that the CAB is not to interpret this language "to mean that the Board must engage in carrier selection in its route proceedings to preclude large carriers from new routes."[378] Instead, the Board is to "continue providing opportunities for small carriers in as many ways possible and not restrict them solely because they have historically had operations limited in area or extent."[379]

Three other subsections promote the prompt procedural disposition of regulatory proceedings,[380] encourage use of satellite airports in urban areas[381] and attempt to ensure that reasonably adequate service is provided to small communities, with federal subsidies when appropriate.[382]

4. Public Convenience and Necessity and the Burden of Proof

Entry in air transportation by domestic carriers has traditionally been governed by two statutory criteria: (1) that the proposed service is required by the public convenience and necessity; and (2) that the applicant is fit, willing and able.[383] The burden of proof in application proceedings was, under Section 556(d) of the Administrative Procedure Act,[384] on the applicant.

The 1978 Act left these provisions unchanged for carriers seeking to serve international routes.[385] However, it significantly amended the entry criteria for domestic and overseas transportation (between points located within the territories and possessions of the United States, albeit over international waters) by requiring the issuance of a certificate when the proposed service is consistent with the public convenience and necessity.[386] The fitness standard remains unchanged.[387] The burden of proof was shifted to an opponent (typically an incumbent carrier), however, who was required to demonstrate that the proposed operations were not consistent with the public convenience and necessity.[388] In order to deny an application for operating authority, the CAB was required to conclude "based upon a preponderance of the evidence that such transportation is not consistent with the public convenience and necessity."[389] The burden of proof on the fitness issue remains unchanged.[390]

5. Automatic Market Entry

During the first month of 1979, 1980, and 1981, each certified passenger carrier was free to apply for nonstop route authority between any one pair of points (which had not been protected) by filing a notice.[391] It was not required to demonstrate consistency with the public convenience and necessity.[392]

Each carrier could also protect from automatic entry one pair of points between which it already holds nonstop authority.[393] The Act also included an escape clause enabling the Board to modify the program if it caused substantial harm to the national transportation industry or a substantial reduction in service to small and medium-sized communities.[394]

6. Dormant Authority

A certificate authorizing transportation between two points was considered dormant when the certificated carrier had not provided at least five round trips a week for 13 weeks during the preceding 26-week period.[395] The Board awarded the dormant route within 60 days to the first carrier submitting an application which demonstrated that it had satisfied FAA regulations and was able to comply with the Board's regulations,[396] unless the Board concluded that the issuance of such a certificate was not consistent with the public convenience and necessity.[397] However, there was a rebuttable presumption that the authority sought was consistent with the public convenience and necessity. If no more than a single carrier served the route, the Board suspended the dormant incumbent's authority for 26 weeks, unless it concluded that such suspension was unnecessary to encourage continued service by the newly authorized carrier.[399]

7. Experimental Certificates

If the CAB concluded that a test period is required to evaluate proposed new operations, it could issue a certificate for a temporary period.[400] If such a certificate was issued on the basis that the carrier would provide innovative or low-cost transportation, and the carrier failed to provide such service, the Board could modify, suspend or revoke the authority.[401]

8. Other Entry Provisions

Carriers could carry domestic fill-up traffic on flights in foreign transportation. This privilege was limited to one round trip daily.[402]

Carriers operating aircraft seating fewer than 56 passengers or with cargo service of 18,000 pounds or less were exempted from the certificate requirements of Section 401.[403] The Board's regulations had previously limited the commuter carrier exemption to aircraft seating 30 or fewer passengers.

On December 31, 1981, the CAB terminated its licensing function insofar as it determined consistency with the public convenience and necessity.[404] It continued to make fitness determinations until it went out of existence on January 1, 1985,[405] at which time these responsibilities were transferred to the U.S. Department of Transportation.

B. Fitness

1. Traditional Fitness Criteria

Pursuant to section 401(d) act the Act,[406] the CAB [now DOT] is directed to issue certificated operating authority when it concludes, inter alia, that the applicant is "fit, willing and able" properly to perform the proposed air transportation services[407] and to conform to the provisions of the Act and the Board's rules, regulations and requirements promulgated thereunder.[408] Although the Act does not define the terms "fit, willing and able," the Board traditionally evaluated these primary factors in its analysis of the applicant's operations: (1) the existence of a proper organizational basis for the conduct of air transportation; (2) the presence of a plan for the conduct of the service made by personnel shown to be competent in such matters; and (3) the availability of adequate financial resources.[409]

In applications seeking operating authority to perform interim supplemental air transport services, the Board has frequently held that

in order for an applicant to meet the statutory tests of fitness, willingness and ability, it must demonstrate to the Board's satisfaction that it is operationally fit to perform properly supplemental air services with due regard to the convenience and needs of the traveling public; that it possesses the requisite disposition and ability to comply with the Act and the Board's rules and regulations thereunder; and that it has the necessary ability and disposition to comply with the rules and regulations pertaining to safety.[410]

The issues of fitness, willingness and ability to perform certain air transport operations was not a matter of degree. Either a carrier was deemed "fit, willing and able" to perform proposed air transportation services or it was not. There was no weighing and balancing between competing applicants to ascertain which carrier was most or least "fit, willing and able."[411] Indeed, once the Board determined that, for some reason, a particular carrier did not satisfy this statutory criterion, the Board was not compelled to evaluate whether the carrier might otherwise be more fit, willing and able than are other applicants.[412]

The fitness, willingness and ability of an applicant to perform proposed certificated operations required a consideration of the applicant's competence to operate the transport services for which authority was sought and its financial capacity to do so.[413] As was emphasized by the Federal Court of Appeals for the District of Columbia, in *Western Air Lines, Inc. v. Civil Aeronautics Board*:[414]

Before the Board may issue a certificate authorizing air transportation to any carrier it must find that the carrier is "fit, willing and able properly to perform" the transportation authorized. The Board has given content to this language through its decisions, focusing mainly on the adequacy of (1) technical and managerial resources and (2) resources available to the carrier.[415]

In *Pan Am. Airways Company (of Delaware)—Certificate of Public Convenience and Necessity*,[416] the Board expressed the following policy in the evaluation of application for certificated operating authority:

Title IV of the act is concerned primarily with air carrier economic regulation, and accordingly the findings of the Board as to the applicant's fitness, willingness and ability to perform the transportation covered by the application, to conform to the provisions of the Act and the rules, regulations and requirements of the Board thereunder . . . is primarily concerned with the economic aspects of the questions involved.[417]

Consequently, the financial posture of an applicant seeking authority to perform either supplemental or scheduled air carrier service was of paramount importance in the evaluation of its fitness, willingness and ability.[418] Thus, in *United States Overseas Airlines Inc., Interim Certificate Proceeding*,[419] the Board stated:

The meaning of the phrase "(fit, willing and able)" . . . must be determined in the context of the problems Congress saw and the objectives it intended to accomplish. Looking at the pattern of the supplemental legislation and its legislative history, we are convinced that Congress viewed the financial fitness of supplemental carriers as having a direct bearing on safety of operations and fair treatment of the public; that it contemplated that such carriers should have and maintain a minimum financial strength and stability sufficient to protect the public from risk and abuse; and that it intended for the Board to eliminate from the supplemental field carriers who did not meet such minimum standards before financial weakness could translate itself into injury to the public rather than withholding action until after the financial unfitness had evolved into damage or injury to the public.[420]

Congress intended that only those carriers which could convincingly demonstrate minimum financial strength and sufficient stability to protect the public from abuse or risk should be authorized to perform air transport operations.[421] In general, the Board evaluated an applicant's financial history and current and future resources in order to determine its potential benefits to commerce and for sustained operations, and to operate efficiently without exposing the public to financial risk or unsafe operations.[422]

As recently as 1977, the Board interpreted its primary responsibility on fitness requirements to ensure that carriers have "the wherewithal and willingness to operate properly and in accordance with the law, and to protect the public from undue risk."[423] Although the Board recognized that the criteria for measuring these requirements could not be determined with mathematical precision, financial posture, experience, operating plans and compliance disposition have historically proved to be among the most important factors considered.

As important traditionally as the evaluation of an applicant's financial posture has been the determination of whether an applicant is operationally fit. Both the applicant's experience and its operating proposal have been deemed relevant to this issue.[424] Among the multitude of factors which have been evaluated by the Board in its determination of whether an appplicant is operationally fit were those expressed in *American Flyers Airline Corp., Interim Certificate*,[425] in which a finding of operational fitness was predicated, inter alia on the following factors: (a) the applicant's financial position was relatively secure and it appeared able to satisfy its obligations as they matured; (b) it possessed a substantial fleet of insured flight equipment; (c) it had established a satisfactory maintenance program; (d) its management held extensive experience in airline operations; and (e) it had satisfactorily demonstrated a willingness and ability to provide the proposed operations with due regard for the protection of the traveling and shipping public (by maintaining sufficient liability and property insurance and by expressing a willingness to adhere to the Board's regulations involving reasonable guarantees to the public.[426] In *Eugene Horbach Acquisition of Modern Air Transport, Inc.*,[427] the acquiring party was not a carrier already in operation, and Modern had ceased operations for some time. The Board based its determination of operational fitness on the factors that the applicant had "submitted a reasonably defined plan for future operations"[428] that it intended and felt that it could implement the plan and that there was a reasonable possibility that the operations of the type proposed could be profitable.

When an applicant fails to submit a reasonably defined plan for its proposed operations, has not demonstrated that said operations would eventually be profitable, and has not proved that its financial condition is of sufficient strength to sustain those services then, even assuming that the public convenience and necessity requires their institution, the authority has ordinarily been denied.[429]

An applicant seeking operating authority was also traditionally required to establish its compliance disposition or its willingness and ability to comport with the requirements of the Act and the Board's rules and regulations promulgated thereunder. In the *Large Irregular Air Carrier Investigation*,[430] the Board expressed the following attitude regarding a carrier's compliance disposition:

Evidence of wrongdoing is not appropriate for consideration . . . for any purposes of punishment. Rather, such evidence has been evaluated solely from the viewpoint of its indications concerning the respective applicant's qualification to engage in air transportation in the future. Particularly, it has been concluded that the Board desires an appraisal as to whether each applicant can and will comply with the provisions of the Act and the Board's regulations. In such an appraisal, a negative conclusion on qualification would not follow from the finding of relative unimportant, isolated violations. Failure to qualify on account of violations has been found only in situations where the evidence shows that the violater whose disregard of the Act and the Board's regulations, considered in conjuction with all other evidence, shows that it can be expected to violate the Act and the regulations if given the authority covered herein.[431]

The failure of an applicant to adhere to its responsibilities under the Act and the Board's rules and regulations thereunder does not constitute a legal prohibition to future certification, but it is a factor of importance to be evaluated in determining whether the applicant should receive the authority.[432] A determination that a particular carrier has not satisfied the statutory criteria of fitness, willingness and ability properly to provide the proposed operations has not been imposed for punitive reasons, for that is not the purpose of Section 401. In so concluding, the Board has merely evaluated the fitness of the applicant pursuant to the statutory standard and the prospects for its reliability in the future in comporting with the Act and the regulations.[433]

In evaluating fitness issues on currently operating certificated carriers, the Board has recognized that a carrier's record of successful existing service, as well as its sound financial condition, may be sufficient to establish its fitness, willingness and ability to perform proposed operations.[434] The Board has frequently recognized that, in evaluating the fitness and ability of an applicant, an existing carrier is on a different footing than an applicant seeking entrance into the air transport industry.[435] With respect to the former, the Board has appraised the carrier's balance sheet and operational experience.[436] When the applicant is an uncertificated entity seeking its initial segment of operating authority, the Board has been inclined to scrutinize its financial condition more closely.[437] Such an applicant traditionally was required to

shoulder a substantial burden in establishing that it is fit to be entrusted with a certificate of public convenience and necessity. The fact that certain of the deficiencies in their showings might not be disqualifying for a going concern which has demonstrated through continuous operations its ability to cope successfully with the ups and downs of financial fortune, does not warrant a finding that they too are fit.[438]

When an existing carrier seeks a renewal or extension of a segment of its route system, the Board has held that the "continued performance of operations is convincing if not conclusive proof of the ability to operate satisfactorily, in the absence of proof to the contrary."[439] The Board, in the *West Coast Case*,[440] expressed the following sentiments regarding existing vis-à-vis noncertificated carriers in application proceedings:

In passing upon the fitness, willingness and ability of an applicant the Board has required it to show adequate financial resources. It is clear, however, that the position of an existing carrier operating pursuant to certificates of public convenience and necessity authorizing the carriage of persons, property, and mail differs from that of a new company seeking entrance into the air transportation industry. Route extensions, if they are not too great in relation to the carrier's other operations, can usually be added to existing operations of a carrier and successfully operated despite the fact that the carrier has not shown that it intends or is able to obtain new capital financing.[441]

2. Fitness in the Post Airline Deregulation Act Environment: Erosion of the Traditional Standards

As has been indicated, the Airline Deregulation Act did not diminish the fitness issue as a potential barrier to entry in any way. The burden of proving fitness remains with the applicant.[442] and the CAB was obligated to continue its fitness scrutiny until the U.S. Department of Transportation assumed those functions in 1985.[443] The first two subsections of the new Declaration of Policy strengthen and emphasize the overriding importance of safety as a regulatory obligation of the highest priority.[444]

One would have assumed, then, that Congress intended that the Board continue, if not make more stringent, its quasi–judicial interpretation of its fitness responsibilities. Incredibly, the Board did precisely the opposite.

The first important regulatory diminution of the fitness standards came in the *Chicago–Midway Low-Fare Route Proceeding*.[445] In *Chicago–Midway*, the Board acknowledged an interrelationship between fitness and safety. Although it argued that operational safety was principally the obligation of the FAA, it admitted that passengers could reasonably assume that the issuance of operating authority by the CAB represented a determination by the Board that the carrier had the requisite personnel, compliance disposition and financial ability to operate properly.[446] Nevertheless, the Board felt compelled to relax the traditional fitness standards so that they would be compatible with the thrust of multiple permissive entry[447] and "would not unnecessarily discourage new entry into the industry in the name of consumer protection."[448]

As a result, the Board, in *Chicago–Midway*, designed a simplified, streamlined test whereby a carrier could easily establish its fitness. The CAB required that an applicant adduce evidence that it

1. will, before inaugurating its operations, have the requisite managerial skills and technical ability to operate safely;

2. if not internally financed, has a plan for financing which, if implemented, will generate resources sufficient to commence operations without undue risk to consumers;

3. has a proposal for operations reasonably satisfactory to meet a part of the demand for service in the city-pair markets embraced in its application; and

4. will comply with the Act and the rules and regulations promulgated thereunder.[449]

In the *Transcontinental Low-Fare Route Proceeding*,[450] the Board further expanded the second criterion of *Chicago–Midway*. Although the Board, as recently as 1977, had required a new operator to demonstrate that it possessed "resources commensurate with the nature and scope of its undertaking" sufficient to enable it to operate safely (i.e., that the firm possessed either sufficient capital to operate the proposed service or commitments from investors or lending institutions to provide the requisite capital,[451] the Board, in *Transcontinental*, believed that this requirement, "could impose a serious barrier to entry. . . ."[452] It therefore eliminated the obligation that a carrier demonstrate its ability to obtain the requisite capital to commence reasonably safe operations. An applicant for operating authority now need merely proffer a financial plan which, if implemented, will generate sufficient financial resources to commence operations.[453]

VI. PIPELINE TRANSPORTATION

The Federal Energy Regulatory Commission (FERC), within the Department of Energy, has jurisdiction over the transportation of oil and petroleum products and natural gas through pipelines. Coal slurry pipelines fall under the jurisdiction of the ICC, and water pipelines are regulated by local authorities, it at all.

No entry controls exist for construction of oil or coal slurry pipelines. The constraining factor in building these systems seems to be eminent domain powers. Without condemnation powers, pipeline operators would find it virtually impossible to cross rights-of-way owned by railroads and other recalcitrant firms.

Natural gas is subject to the Natural Gas Act of 1938, which declares that the business of transporting and selling natural gas for ultimate distribution to the public is affected with a public interest, and that federal regulation of interstate commerce in natural gas is necessary for the public interest. Thus, utility-type regulation by FERC applies to natural gas pipelines, as the FERC has assumed the powers once held by the former Federal Power Commission (FPC).

Under the Natural Gas Act, a person is required to obtain a certificate of public convenience and necessity as a prerequisite to the transportation or sale of natural gas subject to FERC jurisdiction, or prior to the construction, extension, operation or acquisition of any facilities for the transportation or sale of natural gas.

FERC's certification power includes the power to impose conditions on a certificate. The applicant cannot be forced to accept the conditions; if he refuses to accept them, or if the FERC thinks that no permissible terms or conditions will be adequate, the Commission may veto the issuance of such certificate.

To obtain a certificate, the applicant must be able and willing to perform the services proposed and conform to the provisions of the Natural Gas Act and the regulations promulgated by the FERC. The applicant must be willing to enter into long-term contracts and to have an adequate supply of natural gas, the facilities for construction and the financial resources to complete the project. There must be a market for the gas, and the applicant must have a firm commitment from suppliers for the gas.

The FERC is free to promote competition and may take into account the effect on national defense and other suppliers the competition of the new pipeline will provide.

Section 7 of the Natural Gas Act refers to public convenience and necessity and applies these familiar criteria from transportation law to gas pipeline operation. The FERC is authorized under subsections (c) and (e) of Section 7 to impose conditions precedent to the issuance of a certificate. The extent of these powers have not yet been judicially determined; FERC believes that its authority is as broad as the public interest; that is, if public convenience and necessity requires the imposition of conditions, the Commission may do so. The alternative is for the Commission to veto the entire application. Conditions have included certain accounting procedures, rate structures, changes in contractual agreements and specific directions as to routes followed and customers to be served.

Jurisdiction over pipeline construction permits is limited to natural gas pipelines, but synthetic gas mixed with natural gas still partakes of the characteristics of natural gas for regulatory purposes.

NOTES

1. This section is adapted from Dempsey, *Entry Control Under the Interstate Commerce Act: A Comparative Analysis of the Statutory Criteria Governing Entry in Transportation*, 13 Wake Forest L. Rev. 729 (1977).

2. 49 U.S.C. §§ 1–27 (1970).

3. 49 U.S.C. §§ 301–327 (1970).

4. 49 U.S.C. §§ 901–923 (1970).

5. Id. §§1001–1022

6. This section is adapted from Dempsey, *Entry Control Under the Interstate Commerce Act: A Comparative Analysis of the Statutory Criteria Governing Entry in Transportation*, 13 Wake Forest L. Rev. 729 (1977).

7. 49 U.S.C. § 1(18) (1970). This provision was amended by the Railroad Revitalization and Regulatory Reform Act of 1976, Pub. L. 94–210, 90 Stat. 125, at 59 U.S.C.§ 10901 (1980).

8. Union Pac. R.R. v. Denver & Rio Grande W. R.R., 198 F.2d 854, 858 (10th Cir. 1952). These principles are entirely consistent with the national rail transport policy as formulated by Congress, which requires (1) the development and maintenance of an adequate railway system, (2) the preservation of the earning capacity and conservation of the financial resources of individual rail carriers, (3) the insurance of a reasonable rate of return on property used for transport purposes, (4) the avoidance of pecuniary losses resulting from constructing unnecessary lines, and (5) the prevention of destructive competition among carriers. Georgia R. Constr. & Operation, 320 I.C.C. 25, 28 (1963).

9. Cambria & I.R.R. Constr. & Acquisition, 317 I.C.C. 685, 688–89 (1963).

10. 336 I.C.C. 623 (1970).

11. *Id.* at 634.

12. Illinois C.R.R. v. Norfolk & W.R.R., 385 U.S. 57, 66 (1966).

13. *Id.* at 67.

14. This section is adapted from Thoms, *Clear Track for Deregulation*, 12 Transp. L.J. 183 (1982).

15. 49 U.S.C. § 10901 (1980).

16. This line opened in 1980 and is the longest new trackage since the 1920s.

17. Portions of this note are adapted from Greyhound Lines, Inc. v. National Railroad Passenger Corp., 365 I.C.C. 399 (1981).

18. *See e.g.*, G. Hilton, Amtrak: The National Railroad Passenger Corporation (The American Enterprise Institute for Public Policy Research, 1980).

19. Pub.L. 97–35 1172.

20. Pub.L. 97–35 1183.

21. This section is adapted from Note, *Proposed Regulatory Reform in the Area of Railroad Abandonment*, 11 Transp. L.J. 213, 213–17 (1979) (footnotes omitted) authored by D.U. law student Linda Burlington.

22. 49 U.S.C. §§ 10101–11999 (1979).

23. 49 U.S.C. § 10904(b) (1979).

24. 49 U.S.C. § 10903(a) (1979).

25. *Atchison, T. & S.F. Ry. Co. Discontinuance of Trains, Proposed Regulatory Reform in the Area of Railroad Abandonment*, 11 Transp. L.J. 213, 215–217 (1979) (footnotes omitted).

26. 49 U.S.C. § 10904(a)(1) (1979).

27. 49 U.S.C. § 10904(d) (1979).

28. 49 U.S.C. § 10904(c)(2) (1979).

29. 49 U.S.C. § 10905(a)(1) (1979) defines "avoidable cost" as all expenses incurred over that line that would not be incurred if the line were abandoned.

30. 49 U.S.C. § 10905(b) (1979).

31. Phosphate rail traffic from Bone Valley, Fla., presently can move to two alternative port facilities in southwest Florida: Port Boca Grande in the south and Tampa Range in the north.

32. The "Rockport improvement" condition requires that as a condition precedent to its receiving an abandonment certificate covering its Arcadia/Boca Grande line, SCL submit a proposal describing its plans to commit $5.5 million to improving its Rockport transloading facility at Tampa Range, Fla.

33. 49 U.S.C.§§ 10903–06, 10910 (1981).

34. This section is adapted from Thoms, *The Return of Section 13A*, Trains, Jan. 1976, at 13.

35. This section is adapted from Thoms, *Clear Track for Deregulation*, 12 Transp. L.J. 183, 199 (1982).

36. 45 U.S.C. § 561 (1976).

37. 45 U.S.C. § 564(a) (1976).

38. The Rock Island lasted until 1978, the Southern, until 1979, and the Rio Grande, until 1983. These railroads, when they did discontinue service, were subject to ICC jurisdiction.

39. 45 U.S.C. § 564(b)(c) (1980).

40. 45 U.S.C. § 564(b)(c) (1980).

41. Southern Ry. Co.—Disc. of Trains, 354 I.C.C. 630 (1978). *See also* Consolidated Rail Corporation—Disc., 360 I.C.C. 324 (1979), in which Conrail was ordered

to keep its remaining Chicago commuter trains running until an Amtrak takeover could be arranged.

42. Denver & R.G.W.R. Co.—Disc. of Pass. Trains, 360 I.C.C. 216 at 134 (1979).

43. Durango & S.N.G.R. Co.—Acquisition & Operations, 363 I.C.C. 292 (1979).

44. This section is adapted from Dempsey, *The Experience of Deregulation: Erosion of the Commission Carrier System*, 13 Transp. L. Inst. 121 (1980).

45. *Economic Regulation of the Trucking Industry: Hearings Before the Senate Comm. on Commerce, Science, and Transportation*, 96th Cong., 1st Sess. 1 (1979) (testimony of Sen. Howard Cannon) [hereinafter cited as *Senate Hearings*].

46. *Id.* at 3 (testimony of Sen. Russell Long).

47. *See* 49 U.S.C. §§ 10102 (13), 10524 (1979).

48. *See* 49 U.S.C. § 10521(a) (1979).

49. *See* 49 U.S.C. § 10501(b) (1979).

50. *See* 49 U.S.C. § 10526(a)(4) (1979).

51. *See* 49 U.S.C. § 10526(a)(6) (1979).

52. *See* 49 U.S.C. § 10526(a)(5) (1979).

53. *See* 49 U.S.C. § 10526(a)(8) (1979).

54. *See* 49 U.S.C. § 10523 (1979).

55. *See* 49 U.S.C. § 10526(b)(1) (1979).

56. *See* 49 U.S.C. § 10525 (1979).

57. *See* 49 U.S.C. § 10526(a)(7) (1979).

58. *See* 49 U.S.C. § 10526(b)(3) (1979).

59. 49 U.S.C. § 10526(a)(9) (1979).

60. *See* 49 U.S.C. § 10526(a)(1)(2)(3) (1979).

61. *See* 49 U.S.C. § 10526(b)(2) (1979).

62. 49 C.F.R. Part 1026 (1978).

63. *See* Entry Control of Brokers, 126 M.C.C. 476 (1977).

64. Borghesani, *Motor Carrier Regulatory Reform and Its Impact on Private Carriers*, 10 Transp. L.J. 389, 392 (1978).

65. *Id.*

66. *Id.*

67. *See* 49 U.S.C. §§ 10102(13), 10524 (1979).

68. All Points, Inc., Angelo J. Picciolo, and Tempo Drivers, Inc.—Investigation of Operations, 123 M.C.C. 242 (1975).

69. 42 M.C.C. 193 (1943).

70. 51 M.C.C. 65 (1949), *aff'd sub nom.*, Brooks Transp. Co. v. United States, 93 F. Supp. 517 (E.D. Va. 1950), *aff'd per curiam*, 340 U.S. 925 (1951). *See* Hansen—Investigation of Operations, 113 M.C.C. 362 (1971); Whitehurst Paving Co.—Investigation of Operations, 113 M.C.C. 390 (1971).

71. Petition for Declaratory Order Regarding Intercorporate Parent-Subsidiary Transportation, 123 M.C.C. 768 (1975). *See* Snyder's Wholesale Liquors, Inc., Petition, 113 M.C.C. 528, (1971); Boyd Brothers Transportation Co., Inc., Extension—Farm Equipment and Gypsum, 129 M.C.C. 528, 532 (1978).

72. Status of Certain Church Transp., 112 M.C.C. 59, 62 (1970).

73. Dempsey, *Entry Control Under the Interstate Commerce Act: A Comparative Analysis of the Statutory Criteria Governing Entry in Transportation*, 13 Wake Forest L. Rev. 729, 755 n.122 (1977).

74. Ex Parte No. MC-122, Intercorporate Hauling, 44 Fed. Reg. 42838 (1979).

75. 128 M.C.C. 873 (1978).

76. *See* Grant of Motor Carrier Operating Authority to an Applicant Who Intends to Use It As an Incident to the Carriage of Its Own Goods and Its Own Non-Transportation Business, 43 Fed. Reg. 55051 (1979).

77. 49 U.S.C. § 10524(b) (1980). A perfunctory notice provision must, however, be observed. *See id.*

78. Motor Carrier Act of 1980: Report of the House Committee on Public Works and Transportation, H.R. Rep. No. 96–1069, 96th Cong., 2d Sess. 22 (1980) (hereinafter cited as House Report).

79. *See e.g.*, ICC v. Columbus & Greenville Ry., 153 F.2d 194 (5th Cir. 1946). This exemption is set forth in 49 U.S.C. § 10501(b) (1978).

80. *See* 49 U.S.C. § 10521(a) (1978).

81. *See* Pennsylvania P.U.C. v. Arrow Carrier Corp., 113 M.C.C. 213 (1971).

82. Atlantic Coast Line R.R. Co. v. Standard Oil of Kentucky, 275 U.S. 268 (1927).

83. United States v. Majure, 162 F. Supp. 594, 598 (S.D. Miss. 1957). *See* Dallum v. Farmers Co-Operative Trucking Ass'n, 46 F. Supp. 785 (D. Minn. 1942).

84. Melburn Truck Lines (Toronto) Co., Ltd., Comm. Car., 124 M.C.C. 39, 48 (1975).

85. 71 M.C.C. 17 (1957).

86. *Quoted in* Petition for Declaratory Order—Transportation of Empty Intermodal Cargo Containers, 131 M.C.C. 269, 279–80 (1979).

87. 49 U.S.C. § 10526(b) (1979).

88. The ICC has emphasized that it does not affirmatively create a particular commercial zone, but that it recognizes the existence thereof surrounding and embracing each municipality as an economic entity born by reason of trade practice, the uses to which the region is part, and by political or geographical considerations. Washington, D.C., Commercial Zone, 103 M.C.C. 256, 259 (1966). Commercial Zones and Terminal Areas, 46 M.C.C. 665, 672 (1946).

89. 49 U.S.C. § 10523 (1979).

90. Commercial Zones and Terminal Areas, 54 M.C.C. 21 (1952).

91. Joint Northeastern Motor Carrier Assn., Inc. v. Creger, 91 M.C.C. 494 (1962); United Truck Lines, Inc., Ext. Malaga Reduction Plant, 64 M.C.C. 535, 539 (1955).

92. *See* Commercial Zones and Terminal Areas, 128 M.C.C. 422 (1976), *aff'd sub. nom.* Short Haul Survival Committee v. United States, 572 F.2d 240 (9th Cir. 1978). 49 C.F.R. §§ 1041, 1048, 1049 (1980).

93. *See e.g.*, Washington, D.C., Commercial Zone, 132 M.C.C. 38 (1980); Tacoma, Wash., Commercial Zone, 132 M.C.C. 132 (1980).

94. 49 U.S.C. § 10526(a) (8) (1978). This section was inserted into the Interstate Commerce Act by the Civil Aeronautics Act of 1938, ch. 601, § 1107(j), 52 Stat. 1029. This latter statute was subsequently replaced by the Federal Aviation Act of 1958, Pub. L. No. 85–726, 72 Stat. 731.

95. 14 C.F.R. § 222.2 (1978).

96. 49 C.F.R. § 1047.40 (1976). The ICC presumed that the CAB would reject tariff publications that might result in an unreasonable geographic enlargement of the terminal area. Air Cargo Terminals, Inc.,—San Bernardino, Calif., 88 M.C.C. 468, 469 (1961); Panther Cartage Co. Ext—Air Freight, 88 M.C.C. 37, 40 (1961).

In Panther Cartage, the ICC concluded that traffic tendered by an air freight forwarder (a CAB indirect air carrier) under its own bill of lading would fall within the
air terminal area exemption if the motor carrier segment of the intermodal through
movement was performed within those points specified in the air freight forwarder's
tariff and within the terminal area established by the air carrier that performs the
air segment of the involved transportation. See 88 M.C.C. at 40–41. See Wycoff Co.,
Ext.—Airfreight, 89 M.C.C. 369, 371 (1961). In Motor Transp., 95 M.C.C. at 88–
89, however, this holding was modified somewhat, for it was held that the question
whether the commodities moved under the billing of a direct air carrier or an air
freight forwarder was irrelevant for purposes of the Section 10526(a)(8) exemption.
See Airline Freight, Inc., Ext.—Philadelphia Air Terminal Area, 108 M.C.C. 197,200
(1968).

97. 49 U.S.C. § 10526(8)(A)(B) (1980). The legislative history of this section
provides: "This section also expands the statute's current exemption for motor carrier
transportation which is incidental to air transportation. The current exemption has
been interpreted by the Commission and the courts to be limited to transportation
of air freight which constitutes bona fide collection, delivery, or transfer service. It
does not include line-haul transportation by motor carriers. In addition, the exemption has been limited under Commission regulations to geographical areas surrounding airports and cities adjacent to those airports. The bill eliminates the distinction
between exempt pick-up, delivery, or transfer operations and regulated line-haul
transportation. Further, the bill does away with the geographical limitations imposed
by the Commission. The Committee's purpose in expanding the existing exemption
is to bring it into line with what the Congress has done on air cargo movements.
Since the transportation of air cargo now is exempt from Federal economic regulation,
the Committee believes that it makes sense to exempt the entire movement, including the motor carrier transportation portion. Further, extending the exemption
will allow maximum flexibility in dealing with air cargo which generally requires
specialized and expedited handling." House Report, supra, at 19. This provision also
exempts emergency substitution of motor carriage for air transportation. 49 U.S.C.
§ 10526(8)(C) (1980).

98. Commercial Zones, 46 M.C.C. at 669. Cf. Washington, D.C., Commercial
Zone, 103 M.C.C. 256, 259 (1966) (noting the purpose of Section 203(b)(8). In Bartz
Cartage Co., Common Carrier Applic., 107 M.C.C. 378, 381–82 (1968), the statutory
exemptions were summarized as follows: "In summary, then, if property is transported wholly within a municipality and its 'commerical zone,' such transportation
is exempt from economic regulation pursuant to section 203(b)(8) if it is not performed
under a common control, management, or arrangement for a through movement to
or from a point without the municipality or zone, and is exempt from direct economic
regulation pursuant to section 202(c)(2) if the incidental transfer, collection or delivery
service is performed as an agent of, or under a contractual arrangement with, a line-
haul common carrier for a through movement to or from a point without the line-
haul carrier's terminal area. This latter section does not, however, permit the local
carrier, as a participant in a through rate, to perform a through service with line-
haul carriers. Such service must be performed by the local carrier for the line-haul
carrier under the latter's tariff rather than under through rates published by the local
and line-haul carrier." See also United States v. Motor Freight Express, 60 F. Supp.
288, 293 (D.N.J. 1945).

Perhaps the most significant decision in this area of the law in the past several decades is the ICC decision in Triangle Trucking Co., Inc., Contract Carrier Applic. 128 M.C.C. 386 (1977), in which a motor carrier sought contract carrier authority to transport Coca-Cola between points in the Baltimore commercial zone. A segment of the involved traffic had its ultimate destination in Europe, while another district segment was ultimately destined for Latin America. With respect to the European traffic, the local motor carrier movement was arranged and controlled by the transatlantic FMC ocean carrier. Because this segment was under a common control, management or arrangement between the two carriers participating in the through international movement, it was held to fall within the commercial zone exemption of Section 10526(b) of the Act. *Id.* at 392. In addition, it was found that inasmuch as the European traffic was performed on behalf of the maritime carrier not subject to the Act, the terminal area exemption of Section 10523 was also inapplicable. *Id.* at 393. Thus, operating authority was clearly required for the European traffic. The local cartage movement (within Baltimore) of the Latin-American traffic, however, was arranged and controlled by the local consignor (*i.e.*, Coca-Cola). With respect to this segment of the involved traffic, the ICC concluded that no operating authority was required by virtue of the commercial zone exemption. *Id.*

99. *See* Triangle Trucking Co., Inc., Contract Carrier Applic., 128 M.C.C. 386 (1977); and Dempsey, *Foreign Commerce Regulation Under the Interstate Commerce Act*, 5 Syracuse J. Int'l L. & Com. 53 (1977).

100. 49 U.S.C. § 10523 (1979).

101. The Federal Maritime Commission regulates ocean transportation in domestic-offshore or foreign commerce by vessel operators, non-vessel operators and independent ocean freight forwarders. Shipping Act of 1916, 46 U.S.C. §§ 801–42 (1970) & Supp. V 1975); Intercoastal Shipping Act of 1933, 46 U.S.C. §§ 843–48 (1970 & Supp. V 1975).

102. Drive Away Auto Transp., Inc., Comon Carrier Applic., 99 M.C.C. 75, 79 (1965); Trans-Caribbean Motor Transp., 66 M.C.C. at 597; Oregon Draymen & Warehousemen's Ass'n v. Sellwood Transfer Co., 61 M.C.C. 384, 386 (1941).

103. See AAA Transfer, Inc., 120 M.C.C. at 821; Consolidated Freightways, Inc.,—Ext.—Seattle, Wash., 74 M.C.C. 593, 594–97 (1958).

104. Ex Parte No. MC–105, Ex-Water Traffic, 44 Fed. Reg. 7965 (1979).

105. 49 U.S.C. § 10525 (1978).

106. *Id.*

107. 49 C.F.R. § 1047.10 (1978).

108. 49 U.S.C. § 10526(a)(6) (1978).

109. Included are "cooked or uncooked fish, whether breaded or not, or frozen or fresh shellfish, other than fish or shellfish that have been treated for preserving, such as canned, smoked, pickled, spiced, corned, or kippered products"; *id.* § 10526(a)(6)(D), and commodities incorporated on the Commissions's list of March 19, 1958. *Id* § 10526(a)(6)(C).

110. Commodities specifically excluded from the exemption are "frozen fruits, frozen berries, frozen vegetables, cocoa beans, coffee beans, tea, bananas, or hemp, or wood imported from a foreign country, wool tops or noils, or wool waste (carded, spun, woven, or knitted)." *Id* § 10526(a)(6)(C).

111. 351 U.S. 49 (1956).

112. Exempt Status of Precooked and Cooked Poultry, 113 M.C.C. 225 (1971). See Gleason Transportation Co., Inc.—Petition for Declaratory Order, 126 M.C.C. 301 (1976).

113. Hearings on the Motor Carrier Reform Act of 1980, Senate Comm. on Commerce, Science and Transp., S. Rep. No. 96–641, 96th Cong. 2d Sess. 424 (1980) (testimony of Congresswoman Millicent Fenwick). This view was affirmed by the Senate Commerce Committee, which concluded that "the current law results in many arbitrary decisions as to what is or is not unprocessed food. The record abounds with countless examples of feed items that are exempt in one form but regulated in another form." Motor Carrier Reform Act of 1980: Report of the Senate Comm. on Commerce, Science and Transp. S. Rep. No. 96–941, 96th Cong., 2d Sess. 8 (1980).

114. 49 U.S.C. § 10526(a)(6)(E) (1980). It also exempts fish by-products not fit for human consumption. Id. § 10526(a)(6)(D).

115. House Report, supra.

116. 49 U.S.C. § 10526(a)(5) (1978).

117. See 12 U.S.C. § 1141(a) (1975). For an exellent review of this area of the law, see Erenberg, The History and General Scope of Part II of the Interstate Commerce Act, in Transp. L. Inst. 26–33 (1975).

118. Agricultural Services Assn., Inc.—Investigation of Operations and Practices, 131 M.C.C. 666, 667–68 (1979). See Sunkist Growers, Inc., Petition for Declaratory Order—"Member Transportation," 121 M.C.C. 448 (1975); and Agricultural Services Assn., Inc.—Investigation of Operations and Practices, 131 M.C.C. 1 (1978).

119. 49 U.S.C. § 10526(a)(A)(ii) (1980).

120. 49 U.S.C. § 10526(a)(4) (1978).

121. "Farmer-owned and commercial for-hire trucks now haul 73 percent of all fresh fruits and vegetables, 99 percent of the cattle and calves, 100 percent of the hogs, and 98 percent of the sheep and lambs that go to market." Senate Hearings, supra, at 130 (statement of M. Kent Hafen).

122. 49 U.S.C. § 10526(b)(3) (1978).

123. 49 U.S.C. § 10526(a)(7) (1978).

124. 49 U.S.C. § 10526(a)(1) (1978).

125. 49 U.S.C. § 10526(a)(2)(3) (1978).

126. 49 U.S.C. § 10526(b)(2) (1978).

127. 49 U.S.C. § 10526(a)(9) (1978).

128. Transportation of "Waste Products for Reuse and Recycling," 114 M.C.C. 92 (1971).

129. Chemical Leaman Tank Lines, Inc. v. United States, 368 F. Supp. 925 (D. Del. 1973).

130. National Refrigerated Transport, Inc., Extension—Tampa, Fla., 129 M.C.C. 12 (1978); Western Auto Transports, Inc., Ext.—Hydraulic Hammers, 72 M.C.C. 249, 252 (1957); Fox-Smythe Transp. Co., Ext.—Oklahoma, 106 M.C.C. 1, 35 (1967); National Trailer Convoy, Inc., Ext.—Portable Buildings, 91 M.C.C. 301, 305 (1962); Whitehouse Common Carrier Applic., 47 M.C.C. 529, 535 (1947); 49 C.F.R. § 1041.10 (1978).

131. Warren Transport, Inc., Ext.—Lodi, N.J., 119 M.C.C. 107, 116–17 (1973); Pre-Fab Transit Co., Ext.—International Falls, 112 M.C.C. 664, 692, 693, 694 (1970); Fox-Smythe Transp. Co., Ext.—Okla., 106 M.C.C. 1, 36 (1976).

132. James F. Black, Extension of Operations—Prefabricated Houses, 48 M.C.C. 695, 703 (1948).

133. Dealers Transit, Inc., Ext.—Missiles, 86 M.C.C. 327 (1961).

134. Brown Transport Corp., Ext.—Containers, 126 M.C.C. 684 (1977); Berry Transport, Inc., Ext.—Containers, 124 M.C.C. 328 (1976); Monkem Co., Inc., Petition for Interpretation of Certificate and Issuance of Declaratory Order—"Containers," 130 M.C.C. 874 (1978); Petition for Declaratory Order—Transportation of Empty Intermodal Cargo Containers, 131 M.C.C. (1979). See Dempsey, Foreign Commerce Regulation Under the Interstate Commerce Act, 5 Syracuse J. Int'l L. & Com. 53, 61–65 (1977).

135. Petition for Declaratory Order—Transportation of Empty Intermodal Cargo Containers, 132 M.C.C. 30 (1980). See also CF Tank Lines, Inc., et al. v. Ziebel Transport, Inc., 132 M.C.C. 304 (1980).

136. 49 U.S.C. § 10526(a) (10) (1980). The House Report states that "Currently the Commission does not require specific authority for the "return transportation" of these shipping devices. That authority is implied in certificates and permits. This provision goes beyond the Commission's determination by not restricting the exemption to return transportation. The exemption is intended to encourage the use of existing shipping devices by allowing greater flexibility in their shipment. Recently, the Commission determined that used empty intermodal containers are instrumentalities of commerce and therefore are not regulated commodities. This provision confirms that determination." House Report, supra, at 19–20.

137. 49 U.S.C. § 10102(1) (1978).

138. Authority to operate as a broker is not required for persons who arrange transportation subject to provisions of the Interstate Commerce Act other than Part II thereof. See Wisconsin-Mich. Coaches, Inc., 124 M.C.C. 448, 451 (1976).

139. 49 U.S.C. § 10924 (1980); 49 C.F.R. § 1045.2(a) (1976).

140. 49 U.S.C. § 10924.

141. See, e.g., Continuous Movement of Chems. & Petroleum Prod., 353 I.C.C. 301, 311 (1977).

142. Collette Travel Serv., Inc. v. United States, 263 F. Sup. 302, 304 (D.R.I. 1966); Goodman Broker Applic., 125 M.C.C. 223, 229 (1976); Elegante Tours, Inc., Broker Applic., 113 M.C.C. 156, 158 (1971). Compare Gray Line Nat'l Tours Corp., Broker Applic., 114 M.C.C. 914, 920 (1972).

143. See, e.g., Holiday Internat'l, Inc., Broker Applic. 128 M.C.C. 34, 38 (1977).

144. Carla Ticket Ser., Inc., Broker Applic., 94 M.C.C. 579, 582 (1964).

145. See, e.g., Paragon Travel Agency, Inc., Ext.—Warwith, R.I., 120 M.C.C. 61, 65 (1974).

146. Paragon Travel Agency, Inc., Ext.—Mass. & R.I., 100 M.C.C. 641, 644 (1966).

147. Peter Pan World Travel, Inc., Broker Applic., 125 M.C.C. 641, 644 (1976); Paragon Travel Agency, Inc., Ext.—Atlanta, Ga., 120 M.C.C. 1 (1974).

148. Although this was the primary intent of Congress in enacting such legislation, it has been held that it was by no means the sole intent, and that the ICC must therefore also examine the public interest to be served in licensing individual proposed brokerage operations. See Elegante Tours, Inc., Broker Applic., 113 M.C.C. 156, 158 (1971); Carla Ticket Serv., Inc., Broker Applic., 94 M.C.C. 579, 580–81 (1964). Undoubtedly however, the issue of fitness is the most important aspect of

the regulation of brokers by the ICC. *See* Broker Sec. for the Protection of the Pub., 115 M.C.C. 1 (1972).

149. Russel Ricter Cook, Broker Applic., 119 M.C.C. 709, 718–20 (1974).

150. 126 M.C.C. 476 (1977).

151. 49 C.F.R. § 1045A (1977). *But see* National Tour Brokers Ass'n v. United States, 591 F.2d 896 (D.C. Cir. 1978), in which this rule making was remanded for procedural irregularities.

152. Ex Parte MC-96, Entry Control of Brokers, 126 M.C.C. 476, 514–24 (1977). *Cf.* McEvoy, Broker Applic., 124 M.C.C. 32 (1975).

153. The leading case in this area is Exec-Van Systems, Inc., Broker Applic., 128 M.C.C. 669 (1978).

154. 49 U.S.C. § 10922(b) (1980).

155. This section is adapted from Dempsey, *The Experience of Deregulation, Erosion of the Common Carrier System*, 13 Transp. L. Inst. 121 (1980).

156. 49 U.S.C. § 10526(a)(11)(12) (1980).

157. 49 U.S.C. § 10528 (1980). House Report, *supra.*

158. 49 U.S.C. § 10922(b)(4)(A) (1980).

159. 49 U.S.C. § 10922(b)(4)(B) (1980).

160. 49 U.S.C. § 10922(b)(4)(C) (1980).

161. 49 U.S.C. § 10922(b)(4)(D) (1980).

162. 49 U.S.C. § 10922(b)(4)(E) (1980).

163. 49 U.S.C. § 10922(b)(1) (1980).

164. *Id.*

165. 49 U.S.C. § 10922(b)(2) (1980).

166. 49 U.S.C. § 10922(b)(7) (1980).

167. 49 U.S.C. § 10922(h)(1)(B) (1980). Such regulations must be promulgated within 180 days after the enactment of the new legislation. *See* Removal of Restrictions from Authorities of Motor Carriers of Property. 132 M.C.C. 114 (1980).

168. This section is adapted from Dempsey, *Congressional Intent and Agency Discretion—Never the Twain Shall Meet: The Motor Carrier Act of 1980*, 58 Chi. Kent L. Rev. 1 (1981).

169. Pub. L. No. 96-296, 94 Stat. 793 (1980).

170. The Interstate Commerce Commission was created in 1887. The agency will hereinafter be referred to as the ICC or the Commission.

171. In 1935, the Interstate Commerce Act of Feb. 4, 1887, ch. 104, 24 Stat. 379, was amended by the Act of Aug. 9, 1935, ch. 498, 49 Stat. 453. This amendment divided the Interstate Commerce Act into two parts. The original Act was designated "Part I." The Motor Carrier Act of 1935 was then added as "Part II." The Motor Carrier Act of 1980 amends the Motor Carrier Act of 1935.

172. *See* Senate Comm. on Commerce, Science and Transportation, Report on the Motor Carrier Reform Act of 1980, S. Rep. No. 641, 96th Cong., 2d Sess. 2–3 (1980) [hereinafter cited as Senate Report]. There was, perhaps, also some recognition that the ICC should be prevented from becoming the defiant, radical body that its sister agency, the Civil Aeronautics Board, had already become. *See* Dempsey, *The Rise and Fall of the Civil Aeronautics Board—Opening Wide the Floodgates of Entry*, 11 Transp. L.J. 91.

173. *See* Senate Report, *supra*, at 2; House Comm. on Public Works and Transportation, Report on the Motor Carrier Act of 1980, H.R. Rep. No. 1069, 96th Cong.,

2d Sess. (1980) [hereinafter cited as House Report]. The introduction to the House Report provides an insight into the effort Congress devoted to this investigation: "The Motor Carrier Act of 1980 is the product of over 18 months of continuous study of one of the most complex issues ever undertaken by this Committee. In the last 1 1/2 years, 16 days of hearings were conducted, with 215 witnesses presenting the views of nearly every entity in our society touched by this industry. On two of those days, the Committee's hearings were held in Chicago jointly with the Senate Committee on Commerce, Science and Transportation. In addition, thousands of letters from consumers—from beef processors to independent owner-operators—have been received and considered. Through this process, Congress has reaffirmed its role to control and set policy and guidelines for the conduct of interstate commerce." *Id.*

174. *See* 94 I.C.C. Ann. Rep. 99–100 (1980); 93 I.C.C. Ann. Rep. 102–03 (1979); 92 I.C.C. Ann. Rep. 94–96 (1978); 91 I.C.C. Ann. Rep. 101–02 (1977); 90 I.C.C. Ann. Rep. 113–14 (1976).

175. T. Morgan, Economic Regulation of Business 66–67 (1976). Another principal impetus for the promulgation of the Motor Carrier Act of 1935 was the decision of the U.S. Supreme Court in Buck v. Kuykendall, 167 U.S. 307 (1925), which eliminated state regulation of transportation in interstate commerce.

176. 49 U.S.C. § 306(a)(1) (1976) ["public convenience and necessity" will also hereinafter be referred to as PC & N].

177. *See* Trans-American Van Serv., Inc. v. United States, 421 F. Supp. 308, 317 (N.D. Tex. 1976). For a discussion of the statutory evolution of the phrase "public convenience and necessity" and the intention of Congress in using the phrase in the Interstate Commerce Act, *see* I.C.C. v. Parker, 326 U.S. 60 (1945).

178. 1 M.C.C. 190 (1936). This proceeding involved an application seeking authority to transport passengers between New York and Miami.

179. *Id.* at 203. This decision has undoubtedly been the most frequently cited piece of legal literature ever drafted by the ICC.

180. *Id.* at 208. In so holding, the Commission followed the precedent established by the U.S. Supreme Court in Chesapeake & Ohio Ry. v. United States, 283 U.S. 35 (1931), which acknowledged that competition may stimulate better service to the public, and that "reasonable competition may be in the public interest." *Id.* at 43.

181. *See* All Am. Bus Lines, Inc., Common Carrier Applic., 18 M.C.C. 755, 776–77 (1939). *See generally* Chandler, *Convenience and Necessity: Motor Carrier Licensing by the Interstate Commerce Commission*, 28 Ohio St. L.J. 379 (1967); Hutchison & Chandler, *Evidence in Motor Carrier Application Cases*, 11 Vand. L. Rev. 1053 (1958).

182. A motor carrier application typically involves at least three parties: the applicant, the shipper and the protestant. There may, however, be any number of applicants seeking the same operating authority, multiple shipper supporting such applications and numerous protestants opposing its issuance.

183. *See, e.g.*, L.P. Transp., Inc., Ext.— Methane, 126 M.C.C. 427, 431 (1977); Freeport Transp., Inc., Ext.—Insulation, 121 M.C.C. 66, 70 (1975).

184. *See e.g.*, Road Runner Trucking, Inc., Ext.—Meat and Frozen Bakery Products, 124 M.C.C. 245, 248 (1976); Aero Trucking, Inc., Ext.—Iron and Steel Articles, 121 M.C.C. 742, 752 (1975); Coastal Tank Lines, Inc., Ext.—Eufaula, Ala., 110 M.C.C. 217, 220 (1969).

185. 103 M.C.C. 555 (1967). These criteria were not intended as procedural

impediments, but were designed to ensure that the ICC will have sufficient information to determine whether a public need exists. Twin City Freight v. United States, 360 F. Supp. 709, 712–13 (D. Minn. 1972).

186. 103 M.C.C. at 558 app. *See* note 15, *supra*. These requirements were extended to motor common carriers in West Neb. Express, Inc., Ext.—Five States, 118 M.C.C. 423 (1973), and Cloud Common Carrier Applic., 115 M.C.C. 77 (1972). The burden of proof applied in proceedings of regulatory bodies such as the ICC requires that the application be supported by "reliable, probative and substantial evidence." 5 U.S.C. §§ 551–559 (1976), Manufacturers Express, Inc., Ext.—Malt Beverages, 1216 M.C.C. 174, 177 (1977). *See* East Tex. Motor Freight Lines, Inc., Ext.—Off-Route Point, 125 M.C.C. 574, 579–80 (1976). The burden of proof is on the applicant. *See* 5 U.S.C. § 556(d) (1976).

187. Motor Common Carriers of Property, Routes & Serv., 119 M.C.C. 170, 187 (1973).

188. *See, e.g.*, Southern Kan. Greyhound Lines, Inc. v. United States, 134 F. Supp. 502, 510 (W.D. Mo. 1955).

189. *See* Zuzich Truck Line, Inc., Investigation & Revocation of Permit, 83 M.C.C. 625, 637 (1960). The ICC repeatedly held that in the absence of a showing that available motor carrier services were inadequate in some significant respect, it would not be in the public interest to authorize the entry of a competitive newcomer into the field.

190. Roadway Express, Inc., Ext.—Eastern Md. Counties, 120 M.C.C. 578, 584 (1974); Southland Produce Co., Contract Carrier Applic., 81 M.C.C. 625, 628 (1959).

191. Schaffer Transp. Co. v. United States, 355 U.S. 83, 89–90 (1957); Karl Arthur Weber, Ext.,—California, 119 M.C.C. 67, 72–73 (1973). One can only speculate as to the economic injury suffered by rail carriers as a result of the U.S. Supreme Court's decision in *Schaffer*, for shortly thereafter, rail carriers found it futile to participate as protestants in motor carrier operating authority application proceedings.

192. *See* Freeman & Gerson, *Motor Carrier Operating Rights Proceedings—How Do I Lose Thee?*, 11 Transp. L.J. 13, 17–18 (1979) [hereinafter cited as Freeman & Gerson].

193. 419 U.S. 281 (1974).

194. *Id.* at 298.

195. *Id.* at 293 (citing United States v. Pierce Auto Lines, 327 U.S. 515, 535–36 (1949).

196. 551 F.2d 1326 (D.C. Cir. 1977) (per curiam).

197. *See, e.g.*, Trans-American Van Serv., Inc. v. United States, 421 F. Supp. 308, 324–26 (N.D. Tex. 1976); Nashua Motor Express, Inc. v. United States, 230 F. Supp. 646, 653 (D.N.H. 1964).

198. 551 F.2d at 1328–29.

199. P.C. White Truck Line, Inc., Ext.—Atlanta, Ga., 129 M.C.C. 1, 6 (1978).

200. *Id.* at 8.

201. *Id.*

202. The Commission held that "protestants should normally be obligated to introduce more than mere evidence of the revenues they may lose to the applicant, unless it is patently clear that the revenues amount to a significant percentage of the carrier's overall income. The protestants should indicate specifically how the potential

loss of revenue resulting from the applicant's competition will adversely affect their operations." *Id.* at 9.

203. 130 M.C.C. 242 (1978), 131 M.C.C. 573 (1979).

204. 130 M.C.C. at 246.

205. *Id.*

206. *See* Freeman & Gerson, *supra*, at 23.

207. 130 M.C.C. at 246.

208. 131 M.C.C. at 576. The ICC further states: "[C]ompetition is generally presumed to be in the public interest, not contrary to it . . . . Harm to a particular carrier becomes relevant only if there is a corresponding impact upon the public interest." *Id. See also* May Trucking Co. v. United States, 593 F.2d 1349, 1356 (D.C. Cir. 1979).

209. One decision in which protestants satisfied this burden was Colonial Refrig. Transp., Inc., Ext.—Florida to 32 States, 131 M.C.C. 63 (1978).

210. Change of Policy Consideration of Rates in Operating Rights Application Proceedings, 559 I.C.C. 613 (1979). Regarding the hoped for results of this change in policy, the Commission stated: "We hope that this change in policy will stimulate innovative pricing and service options, promote efficient and well-managed operations, and encourage rate competition. Furthermore, by allowing carriers who can operate efficiently to enter the market, we believe that increased efficiency and productivity by all carriers will be encouraged which will help control the cost of transportation and inflation." *Id.* at 616.

211. *See* Schaffer Transp. Co. v. United States, 355 U.S. 83, 91–92 (1957).

212. 49 U.S.C. § 307(a) (1976).

213. *Id.* § 10922(b)(a)(B).

214. 49 U.S.C. § 10922(b)(1) (West Supp. 1981).

215. *Id.* § 10922(b)(2)(B).

216. *Id.* The ICC is further directed to adhere to the congressional statement of the National Transportation Policy set forth in § 10101 of the Act. *Id.* § 10922 (b)(2)(A).

217. 49 U.S.C.A. § 10922(b)(7) (West Supp. 1981). Contract carriers are prohibited from opposing motor common carrier applications. *Id.* § 10922(b)(8). However, opposition by common carriers of contract carrier applications, although restricted, is not prohibited. *See id.* § 10923(b)(4).

218. *Id.* § 10101.

219. *Id.* § 10922(b)(2)(A).

220. *Id.* § 10101(a)(7). *See, generally,* Harper, *Entry Control and the Federal Motor Carrier Act of 1980,* 12 Transp. L.J. 51 (1981).

221. The "Master Certificate" approach involved a general finding by the ICC in rule making that a wide range of applications in a particular area would be consistent with the public interest, without the requirement for case-by-case adjudication of the issue. *See* House Report, *supra,* note 5, at 6; notes 66–68 and accompanying text, *supra.*

222. 132 M.C.C. 84 (1980).

223. *Id.* at 93. "If the application passes under the old law, it will except perhaps in extraordinary circumstances, pass muster under the new law." *Id. See* Ex Parte No. 55 (Sub-No. 43), 45 Fed Reg. 45,534 (1980). *See also* Santini Bros., Inc.— Purchase—Trans-Universal Van Lines, Inc., 127 M.C.C. 281, 283 (1980).

224. 132 M.C.C. at 94. The commission was "hard pressed to imagine circum-

stances in which an application would be granted under the old standards [and] be denied under the new." *Id.* at 94–95.

225. 132 M.C.C. 263 (1980).

226. *Id.* at 267 (footnotes omitted). The ICC here may be ignoring the legislative history and statutory language which indicate that both competition *and* efficiency are equally important considerations in determining whether operating authority should be issued.

227. 132 M.C.C. at 269.

228. Trans-American Van Ser., Inc. v. United States, 421 F. Supp. 308, 320–21 (N.D. Tex. 1976); Nashua Motor Express, Inc. v. United States, 230 F. Supp. 646, 653 (D.N.H. 1964).

229. Alternatively, the Commission might be relying on Ex Parte No. MC-121, which eliminated consideration of the element of adequacy of existing service and with which Congress expressed general approval.

230. 132 M.C.C. at 270.

231. *Id.* at 271.

232. *Id.*

233. 132 M.C.C. at 271. The Commission noted that "[e]ven under the rules of law in effect prior to the enactment of the new Motor Carrier Act, these points had to be shown to indicate a connection between applicant's proposal and protestant's fortunes." *Id.* The Commission cited no authority to sustain this proposition.

234. *Id.* at 271–72. *See* Tiger Transp., Inc., Ext.—Points in Ten Midwestern States, 132 M.C.C. 218, 284 (1980).

235. 132 M.C.C. at 272. In the subsequent decision of Western Gillette, Inc., Ext.—Louisiana, 132 M.C.C. 325 (1980), the Commission elaborated on evidence needed to warrant denial of an application. *Id.* at 343–44. *See also* Continental Contract Carrier Corp., Ext.—Modification of Permit, 132 M.C.C. 141, 147 (1980).

236. 132 M.C.C. at 272.

237. 132 M.C.C. at 272. *See* Continental Contract Carrier Corp., Ext.—Modification of Permit, 132 M.C.C. 141, 144 (1980).

238. 132 M.C.C. at 272.

239. *Id.* Two observations are warranted. First, evidence adduced by the applicant showing public need can be speculative and vague and will still be accepted by the Commission as convincing. In contrast, evidence offered by protestants must be definite, precise and well documented. Second, when the Commission refers to "injury to the public," it apparently does not consider carriers, their owners, or their employees as members of the public. The Commission in *La Bar's* went on to state: "We realize that a grant of this application will cause protestant to lose certain traffic that is [*sic*] now handles. That loss is difficult to assess but may be substantial in the short run if protestant loses still further traffic. However, by altering the size of its fleet to reflect business conditions or any diversion that might occur, or by expanding service to other shippers, protestant has a reasonable chance of adjusting succcessfully to its altered circumstances. A loss to the public has not been shown. The major shipper affected, CertainTeed, obviously finds the potential loss less than the gain from granting the sought authority. The shipper has made the determination that on balance the decreased reliance on existing carriers is a benefit that outweighs any potential losses. There is no specific evidence that other shippers will suffer any loss.

Thus, on balance, we conclude that a grant of the public authority is in the public interest." *Id.* at 272–73.

240. 49 U.S.C. § 10922(b)(1)(B) (West Supp. 1981).

241. 132 M.C.C. at 94. The ICC continued: "Congress no longer intends that we rely exclusively on methods of evidentiary support—notably, shipper statements—which have ordinarily been required in the past. An applicant may present the Commission with statements of public officials, receivers, trade associations, civic associations, consumers, and employee groups, as well as statements by the applicant itself. The Commission, in measuring the sufficiency of these evidentiary submissions, may consider the need for increased competition, minority opportunities, innovative pricing and service, fuel efficiency and improved service for small communities in determining whether a threshold case has been amply set forth." *Id.* at 94.

242. *Id.* at 100 (emphasis in original).

243. *Id.* at 96.

244. *Id.* The ICC specifically states that it "has always sought to act under the general policy of issuing grants of authority with broad commodity and territorial descriptions to enable a carrier to render shippers and the public a complete transportation service. Broad grants of authority also take cognizance of technological modifications, changing industrial patterns, and future needs, and allow carriers to meet the changing needs of shippers and receivers, market demands, and the diverse requirements of the shipping public." *Id.* (citations omitted).

245. *Id.* (citations omitted).

246. *Id. See* 49 U.S.C.A. § 109222(h)(1)(B) (West Sup. 1981).

247. 132 M.C.C. at 96–97. *See also* Green Field Transp. Co. Ext.—General Commodities, United States, 132 M.C.C. 485 (1981); Tri-State Motor Transit Co., Ext.—General Commodities, United States, 132 M.C.C. 504 (1981); Consolidated Freightways, Inc., 132 M.C.C. 320 (1980).

248. 132 M.C.C. 114 (1980), 45 Fed. Reg. 86,747 (1980) (to be codified in 49 C.F.R. §§1002 & 1137 [hereinafter cited as *Restriction Removal*].

249. 45 Fed. Reg. 86,798 (1980) [hereinafter cited as *Future Policy*].

250. 49 U.S.C.A. § 10992(h)(1)(B) (West Supp. 1981) (emphasis added).

251. The current version of the Standard Transportation Commodities Code (STCC), containing 29 categories of commodities, appears in Appendix A of the *Future Policy* statement:

STCC

01—Farm Products
08—Forest Products
10, 14—Ores and Minerals
11, 29—Coal and Coal Products
13, 29—Petroleum, Natural Gas and Their Products
19—Ordinance and Accessories
20—Food and Related Products
21—Tobacco Products
22, 23—Textile Mill Products
24—Lumber and Wood Products
25—Furniture and Fixtures

26—Pulp, Paper and Related Products
27—Printed Matter
28—Chemicals and Related Products
30—Rubber and Plastics Products
31—Leather and Leather Products
32—Clay, Concrete, Glass or Stone Products
33, 34—Metal Products
35, 36—Machinery
37—Transportation Equipment
38—Instruments and Photographic Goods
40—Waste or Scrap Materials Not Intended by Industry Producing
49—Hazardous Materials
　—General Commodities (except Class A and Class B Explosives)
　—Commodities in Bulk
　—Those Commodities Which Because of Their Size or Weight Require the
　Use of Special Handling or Equipment
　—Household Goods
　—Building Materials
　—Mercer Commodities

45 Fed. Reg. at 86,759 (1980) (to be codified in 49 C.F.R. § 1137.21(b)).

252. 45 Fed. Reg. at 86,759 (1980) (to be codified in 49 C.F.R. § 1137.21(b)).

253. *Id.* (to be codified in 49 C.F.R. § 1137.21(a)).

254. *Id.* (to be codified in 49 C.F.R. § 1137.24(a)).

255. *Future Policy, supra,* at 86,799. "[W]e expect applicants to seek authority much more extensive than the minimum. Grants for entire States would tend to obviate recognition problems." *Id.* at 86,803.

256. 46 Fed. Reg. 8,604 (1981) (to be codified in 49 C.F.R. § 1310) [hereinafter cited as *Common Carrier Obligation*].

257. 46 Fed. Reg. 8,604 (1981) (to be codified in 49 C.F.R. S 1310) [hereinafter cited as *Common Carrier Obligation*].

258. Under the common law, anyone who undertook the responsibility to transport, for hire, the property of the general public was deemed to be a common carrier and to be liable as an insurer for loss of or damage to the commodities.

259. *Common Carrier Obligation, supra,* at 8,605.

260. 49 U.S.C.A. § 10922(b)(2)(B) (West Supp. 1981).

261. *Id.* § 10101(a)(7).

262. *Common Carrier Obligation, supra,* at 8,605. The Commission also maintained that several provisions of the Motor Carrier Act of 1980 "effectively shift the emphasis in administering the competitive relationships among carriers to market-place competition and potential competition as principal regulatory devices, subject to continuing Commission jurisdiction. Since the policy proposed in Ex Parte No. 55 (Sub–No. 43A), *Acceptable Forms of Requests for Operating Authority (Motor Carriers and Brokers of Property)*, has been adopted, carrier's authorities will shortly be couched as generic categories rather than as specific commodities. Coupled with the liberalized entry criteria set forth in the Act, and the national transportation policy sought to be achieved, market competition becomes a self-regulating system which ensures the shipping public of needed transportation services." *Id.* at 8,606.

263. *Id.* at 8,605.

264. 132 M.C.C. 409 (1981).

265. American Trucking Ass'ns, Inc. v. ICC, 659 F.2d 452, 459 (5th Cir. 1981). The court properly noted that "[t]he delegation of power to administrative agencies is essential to the implementation of legislative policy in a complex society. Yet Congress knew that governors must themselves be governed and regulators regulated." *Id.* at 462.

266. 659 F.2d at 475 (emphasis in original).

267. "There is no doubt that the Motor Carrier Act, while continuing the policy of industry regulation, was designed to change the Commission's authority and the operating practices of the industry. Congress desired to reduce, but not to eliminate regulation." *Id.* at 459. *See id.* at 470.

268. "In mandating the removal of unreasonable restrictions, the statute does not dispense with the primary requirement that every carrier be 'fit, willing, and able to provide the transportation to be authorized by the certificate.' " *Id.* at 464. "The retention of this standard, tested by forty-five years of interpretation, was deliberate." *Id.* at 469.

269. *Id.* at 465.

270. *See id.* at 471 n.99.

271. *Id.* at 469. *Id.* at 467. "Similarly, as to the ICC's requirement that such carriers also accept authority to transport bulk commodities, the court concluded: '[T]he Commission has exceeded its statutory mandate. . . . Bulk service requires special equipment, such as tank trucks, that many carriers do not have. Moreover . . . most carriers are not fit to provide bulk service because they will not have the proper cleaning facilities for tank trucks and in the case of hazardous bulk materials . . . will not know the appropriate safety regulations for handling bulk items, or have satisfied the special insurance limits pertaining to hazardous materials.' " *Id.* at 473. *See id.* at 465.

As to the Commission's adoption of essentially mandatory STCC commodity descriptions, the court held: "The Commission may not . . . require all applicants, regardless of circumstances to fit Procrustean descriptions, and it may not assume that an applicant fit, willing, and able to carry one commodity in an STCC classification is fit, willing, and able to carry all commodities in that classification." *Id.* at 472. The regulations promulgated by the Commission "[make] it likely that a carrier with authority to transport only one commodity who desires to transport only one additional commodity would be required to seek authority for an entire class of commodities, some of which the carrier may not wish to transport or may lack the ability to transport." *Id.* at 462.

Finally, as to the ICC's refusal to issue nationwide authority to less than all 50 states, the court stated: "[T]he notion that any carrier fit, willing, and able to transport throughout the continental forty-eight states is ipso facto fit, willing, and able, by intermodal service or otherwise, to provide service to Alaska, 2,385 miles by land from the northernmost point of Washington State to Anchorage, and to Hawaii, 2,392 miles by sea or air from San Francisco, defies logic. The Commission's decision obviously rests on the stimulation of competition, a goal that cannot be exalted above all others, for . . . were it the sole objective, there would be no certificates. Accordingly, we hold this automatic authority provision to be invalid." *Id.* at 474.

272. *Id.* at 470. "The House Report reviewed the efforts of the Commission in the recent past to reevaluate its historic approach to entry standards, and then stated, '[b]road policy decisions of this type should be made by the Congress and should not be left to the discretion of the Commission.' " *Id.* at 469.

273. 49 U.S.C. § 10102(13)(B) (1980).

274. *Id.* § 10923(a) (1980).

275. *Id.* § 10923(b)(3) (1980).

276. 368 U.S. 81 (1961).

277. *Id.* at 90. *See* C-Line, Inc., Ext.—New Orleans, 126 M.C.C. 228, 232–33 (1977); Rau Cartage, Inc., Ext.—Tenn., 120 M.C.C. 439, 446 (1974); Interstate Contract Carrier Corp., Ext.—Indianapolis–Paper, 120 Segundo, 105 M.C.C. 524, 530 (1967).

278. 368 U.S. 81 (1961).

279. Id.

280. This section is adapted from Dempsey, *Entry Control Under the Interstate Commerce Act: A Comparative Analysis of the Statutory Criteria Governing Entry in Transportation,* 13 Wake Forest L. Rev. 729 (1977).

281. *See* 49 U.S.C. § 303(b) (1970); 49 C.F.R. §§ 1047.1 to 1049.2 (1976).

282. *See* 49 U.S.C. § 304(e) (1970); 49 C.F.R. § 1057 (1976).

283. *See* Stilwell Canning Co., Common Carrier Applic., 123 M.C.C. 614, 621 (1975). *See also* Rogers Cartage Co., Ext.—Monsanto Liquid Chem., 124 M.C.C. 573, 579–80 (1976); Chickasaw Motor Line, Inc., Ext.—Memphis, Tenn., 121 M.C.C. 476, 479–80 (1975).

284. 49 C.F.R. § 1065 (1976).

285. *Id.* § 1042.

286. *See* Motor Carriers of Prop., Routes & Serv., 119 M.C.C. 530 (1974); Motor Serv. on Interstate Highways—Passengers, 110 M.C.C. 514 (1969); *see also* Enlargement of Operational Circuity Reduction, 121 M.C.C. 685, 699–700 (1975).

287. Consolidated Freightways Corp.—Alternate Routes, 119 M.C.C. 441, 446 (1974); Hayes Freight Lines, Inc., Ext.—Alternate Routes in Mich., 54 M.C.C. 643–50 (1952).

288. *See* Indianahead Truck Line, Inc., Ext.—Methane, 123 M.C.C. 1, 12 (1975). In November 1973, the ICC issued a general policy statement, *see* 38 Fed. Reg. 32,856 (1973), which is also pertinent to the value which the ICC ascribes to the issue of the operating economies and energy efficiencies to be derived from the institution of proposed operations. The statement provides that those seeking motor carrier authority are required to submit evidence in their initial representations regarding the operational feasibility of the proposed service. In fact, it has frequently been recognized that efficient and economically balanced round-trip operations which eliminate the costs inherent in empty vehicular movements benefit both the motor carriers and the shippers and consumers they serve. Mason & Dixon Tank Lines, Inc., Ext.—Florida, Chems., 117 M.C.C. 539, 547 (1972); Maxwell Co., Ext.—Chicago to Cincinnati, 112 M.C.C. 235, 239 (1970); Rogers Cartage Co., A. Corporation—Extension, 110 M.C..C. 139, 147 (1969). Such efficient and economical two-way operations, by eliminating the empty dead-head mileage, will ordinarily reduce the carrier's costs, and such savings may ultimately be passed on to the consumer through reduced transport charges. Moreover, an evaluation of the operational feasibility of a carrier's proposed operations has long been an integral

element in motor carrier entry control. Stone Lines, Inc., Contract Carrier Applic., 54 M.C.C. 310 (1952); Bos Truck Lines, Inc., Ext.—Boston, Mass., 48 M.C.C. 50 (1948); cf. Ace Freigh Line, Inc., Ext.—Canned Goods, 124 M.C.C. 799, 802 (1976).

289. See Samack, Inc., Contract Carrier Applic., Segundo, 105 M.C.C. 524 (1967); Aubrey, Ext.—Milwaukee & New York City, 100 M.C.C. 652 (1966).

290. Marrone, Common Carrier Applic., 117 M.C.C. 680, 682 (1973).

291. Chandler Trailer Convoy, Inc., Ext.—Tenn., 121 M.C.C. 506, 519 (1974). See Suwanee Transfer, Inc., Ext., 126 M.C.C. 326, 374 (1977). See also Sammons Trucking, Ext.—Aberdeen, S.D., 124 M.C.C. 373, 391 (1976).

292. Riss & Co., Ext.—Dakota County, Neb., 102 M.C.C. 336, 342 (1966).

293. Kroblin Refrigerated Xpress, Inc., Ext., 125 M.C.C. 374 (1976); Transport, Inc., Ext.—Sanborn LPG, 124 M.C.C. 435, 439 (1976).

294. 125 M.C.C. at 378–79. The approach in these cases appears inconsistent with that taken in the two prior decisions of Dealers Transit, Inc., Ext.—Wis., 123 M.C.C. 191, 195–96 (1975), and D & L. Transp., Inc., Ext.—Chames, 120 M.C.C. 254, 260 (1974), which also evaluated the weight to be accorded the issue of operating economies and efficiencies to be derived from the institution of direct, single-line services to replace existing interline operations.

In a number of proceedings before the ICC, established carriers which have provided joint-line service of substantial volume and duration, but which are faced with loss of access to an origin point by deterioration or cancellation of interline connections, have been granted authority to serve the point directly. See Transamerican Freight Lines, Inc., Ext.—Dover, Del., 108 M.C.C. 791 (1969); Burnham Van Serv., Inc., Household Goods—Thirteen States, 98 M.C.C. 58, aff'd per curiam sub. nom., United Van Lines, Inc. v. United States, 266 F. Supp. 586 (E.D. Mo. 1967); T.E.K. Van Lines, Inc., Common Carrier Applic., 86 M.C.C. 139, aff'd per curiam sub. nom., Aero-Mayflower Transit Co. v. United States, 208 F. Supp. 303 (S.D. Cal. 1962).

The Commission has, in fact, frequently granted single-line authority to an applicant faced with serious disruption or deterioration of interline connections through no fault of its own. See Tennessee Carolina Transp., Inc., Ext.—Memphis, 113 M.C.C. 711, 721 (1971), and cases cited therein. Such decisions have been founded, to a significant degree, on equitable considerations and seek, in effect, to maintain the status quo in order to prevent the affected motor carrier from suffering serious, if not disastrous, economic consequences arising as a result of the termination of its interline arrangements. Cartwright Van Lines, Inc., Ext.—Cal., 114 M.C.C. 303, 307 (1971), aff'd sub. nom., Cartwright Van Lines, Inc. v. United States, 373 F. Supp. 579 (W.D. Mo. 1973). In such circumstances, authority has been granted because applicants were unable to overcome the adverse effects of deteriorating interline operations by any means other than an authorized extension of single-line service. The foregoing general principles are those which have traditionally governed applications of motor carriers seeking to provide a direct, single-line service in lieu of existing interline operations.

295. Sammons Trucking, Ext.—Aberdeen, S.D., 124 M.C.C. 373, 391 (1976).

296. See Rogers Cartage Co., Ext.—Monsanto Liquid Chem., 124 M.C.C. 573, 580 (1976); Mason & Dixon Tank Lines, Inc., Ext.—Florida Chems., 117 M.C.C. 539, 547 (1972); Rogers Cartage Co., A Corp., Ext.—Liquid Acids & Chems., 110 M.C.C. 139, 147 (1969). In November of 1973, the Commission issued a general

policy statement, *see* 38 Fed. Reg. 32, 856 (1973), which is also directly pertinent to its efforts in promoting energy efficiency in the industry it regulates. The statement requires that those seeking motor carrier operating authority submit in their initial representations evidence regarding the operational feasibility of the proposed service. *See* Lease & Interchange of Vehicles—Contract Carriers, 121 M.C.C. 714, 729 (1975).

297. *Cf.* Maxwell Co., Ext.—Chicago to Cincinnati, 112 M.C.C. 235, 239 (1970).

298. 124 M.C.C. 435 (1976).

299. *Id*, at 439.

300. This section is adapted from Dempsey, *Entry Control Under the Interstate Commerce Act: A Comparative Analysis of the Statutory Criteria Governing Entry in Transportation*, 13 Wake Forest L. Rev. 729 (1977).

301. *See* Carolina Cartage Co., Ext.—Atlanta, 125 M.C.C. 49, 55 (1976). Where the evidence reveals a pattern of serious or continuous unlawful conduct, the burden is on the applicant to refute the evidence and establish its fitness to perform the proposed operations. Sammons Trucking, Ext.—Aberdeen, S.D., 124 M.C.C. 373, 387 (1976), and cases cited therein.

302. E & H Distrib. Co., Contract Carrier Applic., 120 M.C.C. 731, 737 (1974).

303. Kroblin Refrigerated Xpress, Inc. v. United States, 197 F. Supp. 39, 47 (N.D. Iowa 1961); Clarence R.. Berger, Common Carrier Applic., M.C.C. 894, 897 (1974); Fournier's Express Inc., Ext.—Hartford, Conn., 108 M.C.C. 584, 586 (1969).

304. 125 M.C.C. 69 (1976).

305. *Id.* at 73.

306. *Id.*; *see also* Barrett Mobile Home Transp. Inc., Ext.—Bldgs., 126 M.C.C. 73, 82–83 (1976); Shippers Truck Serv., Inc.—19 States, 123 M.C.C. 323, 331 (1976); Johnny Brown's, Inc., Extension—Winchester, Va., 111 M.C.C. 905, 908, 909 (1970).

307. Metler Hauling & Rigging, Inc., Ext.—Loudon County, Tenn., 117 M.C.C. 337, 559–60 (1972).

308. *But see* Pulaski Highway Express, Inc., Ext.—Elkton, 126 M.C.C. 382 (1977), in which the ICC departed from its usual practice and proceeded to consider the issue of applicant's fitness, even though the carrier had failed to demonstrate that the proposed operations were consistent with public convenience and necessity. *Id*, at 388–89.

309. Metler Hauling & Rigging, Inc., Ext.—Loudon County, Tenn., 117 M.C.C. 557, 559–60 (1972).

310. *Id.* at 560; *see also* Nationwide Carriers, Inc., Ext.—Foodstuffs, 120 M.C.C. 353, 358 (1974); Provisioners Frozen Express, Inc., Ext.—Meats, 120 M.C.C. 20, 22–23 (1974).

311. Pre-Fab Transit Co., Ext.—Int'l Falls, Minn., 112 M.C.C. 664, 677 (1970); H.R. Ritter Trucking Co., Ext.—Perryville, Md., 111 M.C.C. 771, 776–77 (1970); *see* Sullivan's Motor Delivery, Inc., Ext.—Small Shipments, 123 M.C.C. 559, 565 (1975); Fore Way Express, Inc., Ext.—Wausau, Wis., 120 M.C.C. 299, 305 (1974); Ewen Bros., Inc., Common Carrier Applic., 117 M.C.C. 101, 104 (1972).

312. *See* 49 U.S.C. § 310a (1970); 49 C.F.R § 1131 (1976).

313. *See* Midwest Energy Freight Sys., Inc.,—Invest & Revoc., 123 M.C.C. 105, 119 (1975); Levitts Freight Ser., Inc., Ext.—Saginaw, Ore., 119 M.C.C. 467, 472 (1972); Metler Hauling & Rigging, Inc., Ext.—Loudon County, Tenn., 117 M.C.C. 557 (1972).

314. Kissick Truck Lines, Inc., Ext.—Iron & Steel, 125 M.C.C. 183, 193 (1976)

315. 49 U.S.C. § 10922(a) (1970). Those water carrier operations in existence prior to the promulgation of the Transportation Act of 1940 were deemed entitled to a "grandfather" certificate. *See* Cornell Steamboat Co. v. United States, 53 F. Supp. 349 (S.D.N.Y.), *aff'd*, 321 U.S. 634 (1943).

316. All material under the heading Water Carriage is adapted from Dempsey, *Entry Control Under the Interstate Commerce Act: A Comparative Analysis of the Statutory Criteria Governing Entry in Transportation*, 13 Wake Forest L. Rev. 729 (1977).

317. Sioux City & New Orleans Barge Lines, Inc., Ext.—Miss. River, 343 I.C.C. 412, 419 (1973). *Cf.* Mascony Transp. & Ferry Serv., Inc., Initial Operators, 353 I.C.C. 60 (1976).

318. *See* Ohio River Co., Ext.—Lower Miss. River, 343 I.C.C. 509, 523 (1973); Hennepin Towing Co., Ext.—Upper Miss. River, 343 I.C.C. 422, 429 (1973).

319. Ohio River Co., Ext.—Lower Miss. River, 343 I.C.C. 509, 523 (1973). *Cf.* Security Barge Line, Ext.—Removal of Restriction, 344 I.C.C. 235, 243 (1973).

320. *See* McAllister Bros., Inc., Ext.—Steel, 335 I.C.C. 52, 55 (1969).

321. *See, e.g.,* Southland Prod. Co., Contract Carrier Applic., 81 M.C.C. 625 (1959).

322. McAllister Bros., Inc., Ext.—Steel, 335 I.C.C. 52, 55 (1969).

323. *See* Hennepin Towing Co., Ext.—Upper Miss. River, 343 I.C.C. 422, 430 (1973); Sioux City & New Orleans Barge, Ext.—Miss. River, 343 I.C.C. 412, 419–20 (1973); A. L. Mechling Barge Lines, Inc., Ext.—Fla., 285 I.C.C. 667, 675 (1955); John I. Hay Co., Ext.—Milwaukee, 285 I.C.C. 472, 478 (1954). This principle has also been followed in the field of water contract carriage. *See, e.g.,* American Coastal Lines, Inc., Ext.—Houston, Tex., 337 I.C.C. 849, 856 (1970).

324. 49 U.S.C. § 10923(a).

325. Sause Bros. Ocean Towing Co., Ext.—General Commodities, 305 I.C.C. 311, 316–17 (1958).

326. Hanson Towing Co., Contract Carrier Applic., 31 I.C.C. 609, 613–14 (1960); Indian Towing Co., Contract Carrier Applic., 309 I.C.C. 473, 478 (1960).

327. *See* Ohio Barge Lines, Inc., Ext.—Pig Tin, 285 I.C.C. 5, 7 (1951). However, a shipper was denied authority to operate a licensed common carrier barge service in Davison Chem. Corp. Applic., 250 I.C.C. 291, 296 (1942).

328. *See* W. L. McGehee, Contract Carrier Applic., 285 I.C.C. 107, 111–12 (1951).

329. Hanson Towing Co., Contract Carrier Applic., 311 I.C.C. 609, 612 (1960).

330. *See* Marine Transp. Lines, Inc., Ext.—Los Angeles, 285 I.C.C. 655, 657 (1955).

331. This section is adapted from Dempsey, *Intermodal and International Transport Regulation Under the Interstate Commerce Act*, 10 Vand. J. Transnat'l L. 505 (1977).

332. In Common Carriers by Water—Status of Express Companies, Truck Lines and Other Non–Vessel Carriers, 6 Dec. Fed. Mar. Comm'n 245 (1961), the FMC concluded that entities that undertake to transport in foreign commerce commodities from one port to another, but which do not operate ocean vessels, are to be treated as common carriers by water and subject to its jurisdiction.

333. *See* Motor Rail Co., Determination of Status, 296 I.C.C. 205, 211 (1955); Barge Service Co., Freight Forwarder App., 285 I.C.C. 104, 106 (1951). For an analysis of the historical development of freight forwarding, *see* Investigation into

Status of Freight Forwarders, 339 I.C.C. 711, 716–29 (1971). *See, generally,* Ahearn, *Freight Forwarders and Common Carriage,* 14 I.C.C. Prac. J. 401 (1947); Coddaire, *Freight Forwarders and Federal Regulations,* 27 I.C.C. Prac. J. 393 (1950); Givan, *Air Freight Forwarding,* 15 I.C.C. Prac. J. 671 (1948); Morrow, *Updating Transportation Law as It Applies to Freight Forwarders,* 11 I.C.C. Prac. J. 171 (1943).

334. 49 U.S.C. § 10102(8) (1980).

335. *See* Central Forwarding, Inc., Ext.—Household Goods, 107 M.C.C. 706, 708 (1968); National Motor Freight Traffic Ass'n v. Pacific Shippers Ass'n, 105 M.C.C. 199, 240 (1966).

336. Japan Line, Ltd. v. United States, 393 F. Supp. 131, 136 (N.D. Cal. 1975).

337. *See* National Motor Freight Traffic Ass'n v. United States, 242 F. Supp. 601, 605 (D.D.C. 1965); Kagarise, Freight Forwarder Applic., 260 I.C.C. 745, 747 (1946).

338. Compass, Nippon & Transmarine—Investigation, 344 I.C.C. 246, 278 (1973), and cases cited therein.

339. 49 U.S.C. § 10923 (1980).

340. 49 U.S.C. § 10101(d) (1970). *See* Acme Fast Freight v. United States, 146 F. Supp. 369, 374 (D. Del. 1956).

341. Aloha Consolidators Int'l v. United States, 395 F. Supp. 1006, 1010 (C.D. Cal. 1975); Florida–Texas Freight, Inc. v. United States, 373 F. Supp. 479, 486 (S.C. Fla. 1973), *aff'd* 416 U.S. 976 (1974); Yellow Forwarding Co. v. I.C.C., 369 F. Supp. 1040, 1045 (D. Kan. 1973); Home-Pack Transp., Applic. for Forwarder Permit, 340 I.C.C. 98, 102 (1971); D. C. Andrews & Co. of Ill. Inc., Ext.—Baltimore, Md., 326 I.C.C. 743, 755 (1966).

342. This section is adapted from Dempsey, *The Rise and Fall of the Civil Aeronautics Board—Opening Wide the Floodgates of Entry,* 11 Transp. L.J. 91 (1979).

343. Former Federal Aviation Act § 401(d)(2), and (d)(3); 49 U.S.C. § 137(a)(1), (d)(2), and (d)(3) (1977).

344. Former Federal Aviation Act § 102; 49 U.S.C. § 1302 (1977).

345. Former Federal Aviation Act § 102(a)(4); 49 U.S.C. § 1302(a)(4) (1977).

346. Former Federal Aviation Act § 102(a)(3); 49 U.S.C. § 1302(a)(3) (1977).

347. Memphis–Tampa/St. Petersburg/Clearwater Subpart N. Proceeding, CAB Order 77–5–66 (1977), at 2–3.

348. CAB Order 76–3–93 (1976).

349. *See id.* at 31.

350. Oklahoma–Denver–Southeast Points Investigation, CAB Order 77-4-146 (1977), at 7; Transpacific Route Investigation, 51 C.A.B. 161, 287 (1986).

351. Oklahoma–Denver–Southeast Points Investigation, CAB Order 77-4-146 (1977), at 15.

352. New York–Chicago Service Case, 22 C.A.B. 973 (1955).

353. Southwest–Northwest Service Case, 22 C.A.B. 52 (1955).

354. Southern Airways Route Realignment Investigation, CAB Order 73-2-90 at 9–16 *aff'd* Southern Airways et al. v. C.A.B. 498 F.2d 66 (D.C. Dir. 1974); Norfolk–New York, Subpart M. Proceeding, CAB Order 70-9-56 (1970). Indianapolis/Dayton–New York Nonstop Subpart M. Case, CAB Order 69-8-130 (1969). See North Central Airlines, Inc. Subpart M., 49 C.A.B. 138, 151, 153 (1968); Northern New England–Great Lakes Service Case, 49 C.A.B. 255, 291 (1968); Ozark Extension to New York/Washington, 50 C.A.B. 305, 317 (1969).

355. CAB Order 75–10–119 (1975).

356. *Id.*

357. *See* Sacramento–Denver Nonstop Case, CAB Order 77-6-27 (1977), at 4–5; Midwest–Atlanta Competitive Service Case, CAB Order 78-4-13 (1978), at 7, 9; *id.* CAB Order 78-7-137 (1978), at 7, 9; Denver–Twin Cities Service Investigation, 50 C.A.B. 423, 445 (1969).

358. CAB Order 78-3-35 (1978).

359. *Id.* at 2. See Memphis–Tampa/St. Petersburg/Clearwater Subpart N. Proceeding, CAB Order 77-5-66 (1977).

360. *See* Oklahoma–Denver–Southeast Points Investigation, CAB Order 77-4-146 (1977), at 16.

361. *See* Memphis–Tampa/St. Petersburg/Clearwater Subpart N. Proceeding, CAB Order 77-5-66 (1977), at 4–5; American Airlines, Palm Springs Restriction, 50 C.A.B. 359, 360 (1969).

362. Continental Air Lines v. CAB, 519 F.2d 944 (D.C. Cir. 1975). In so concluding, the court reviewed the legislative history of the Federal Aviation Act, finding that Congress intended that air transportation be regulated both to protect the public and the industry against the deleterious effects of unrestrained competition and the potential of monopoly. Congress established the regulatory structure to achieve the attributes of competition without the injurious consequences of unrestrained entry or rate wars. *Id.* at 952–55.

363. Kennedy Report, *supra*, at 15.

364. *Id.* at 6. During the late 1960s, Chairman Secor Brown led the CAB to implement the moratorium on the grounds that there was excessive capacity in the industry. As a result, no entry applications were even set for hearing for several years. *Id.* at 7. *See id.* at 84–96. *See, e.g.*, Additional Service to San Diego Case, 64 C.A.B. 634 (1974); Atlanta–Detroit/Cleveland/Cincinnati Investigation, 64 C.A.B. 647 (1974); Mohawk Segments 8 and 9 Renewal, 63 C.A.B. 338 (1973); and Twin Cities–Des Moines–St. Louis, Nonstop Service, 53 C.A.B. 580 (1970).

365. Kennedy Report, *supra*, at 79–80.

366. *Id.* at 6.

367. Cong. Rec. § 5849 (April 19, 1978).

368. The Conference Committee emphasized that the purpose of the Act is "to encourage, develop, and attain an air transportation system which relies on competitive market forces to determine the quality, variety, and price of air services ." Conference Report, Airline Deregulation Act of 1978, Rep. No. 95–1779, 95th Cong., 2d sess. 53 (Oct. 12, 1978) [hereinafter cited as Conference Report].

369. 49 U.S.C. § 1302(a) (1979).

370. 49 U.S.C. § 1302(a)(1) (1979).

371. 49 U.S.C. § 1302(a)(2) (1979). Indeed, the Act further provides that "the Congress intends that the implementation of the Airline Deregulation Act of 1978 result in no diminution of the high standards of safety in transportation attained in the United States at the time of the enactment of this Act." 49 U.S.C. § 1301 (1979).

372. 49 U.S.C. § 1302(a)(4) (1979).

373. 49 U.S.C. § 1302(a)(4) (1979).

374. Conference Report, *supra*, at 55.

375. 49 U.S.C. § 1302(a)(3) (1979). This provision also encourages coordinated air transport operations, as well as "fair wages and equitable working conditions." *Id.*

376. 49 U.S.C. § 1302(a)(7) (1979).

377. Conference Report, *supra*, at 56.

378. Conference Report, *supra*, at 56.

379. *Id.*

380. 49 U.S.C. § 1302(a)(5) (1979).

381. 49 U.S.C. § 1302(a)(6) (1979).

382. 49 U.S.C. § 1302(a)(6) (1979).

383. Former Section 401 of the Federal Aviation Act; former 49 U.S.C. § 1371 (1977).

384. 5 U.S.C. § 556(d) (1979).

385. *See* 49 U.S.C. §§ 1302(c), 1371(d)(1)(B) (1979).

386. 49 U.S.C. § 1371(d)(1)(A) (1979).

387. 49 U.S.C. § 1371(d)(1) (1979).

388. 49 U.S.C. § 1371(d)(9)(B) (1979).

389. 49 U.S.C. § 1371(d)(9)(C) (1979).

390. *See* 49 U.S.C. § 1371(d)(9)(A) (1979).

391. 49 U.S.C. § 1371(d)(7)(A) (1979).

392. *Id.*

393. 49 U.S.C. § 1371(d)(7)(C) (1979).

394. 49 U.S.C. § 1371(d)(7)(D) (1979).

395. 49 U.S.C. § 1371(d)(5)(A)(O) (1979). An exception exists for seasonal markets. 49 U.S.C. § 1371(d)(5)(B)(E) (1979).

396. 49 U.S.C. § 1371(d)(5)(A)(D) (1979).

397. 49 U.S.C. § 1371(d)(5)(F)(i) (1979).

398. 49 U.S.C. § 1371(d)(5)(F)(ii) (1979).

399. 49 U.S.C. § 1371(d)(J) (1979).

400. 49 U.S.C. § 1371(d)(B) (1979).

401. *Id.*

402. 49 U.S.C. § 1371(d)(6) (1979).

403. 49 U.S.C. § 1386(b) (1979).

404. 49 U.S.C. § 1551(a)(1)(A) (1979).

405. Other provisions which are likely to enhance entry opportunities are those providing for elimination of restrictions on certificates, 49 U.S.C. § 1371(d)(7) (1979), and those requiring the establishment of expeditious and simplified procedures for the disposition of operating authority applications. 49 U.S.C. §§ 1371(c)(1)(B), 1371(d)(7)(A)(ii), 1371(e)(7)(B), 1371(p) (1979).

406. 49 U.S.C. § 1371(d) (1979).

407. It has been emphasized that, as a condition precedent to the issuance of operating authority, an applicant must demonstrate that it is fit, willing and able to perform the specific transport services for which the authority is sought. United Air Lines v. Civil Aeronautics Board, 278 F.2d 446, 449 (D.C. Cir. 1960).

408. This statutory language is almost identical for both scheduled and supplemental carriers (compare 49 U.S.C. § 1371(d)(1), (d)(2), and (d)(3) (1979).

409. Braniff Airways v. Civil Aeronautics Board, 147 F.2d 152, 153 (D.C. Cir. 1945); Large Irregular Air Carrier Investigation, 28 C.A.B. 224, 309 (1959); Reopened Latin American Air Freight Case, 19 C.A.B. 225, 260 (1954); South Pacific Air Lines, Inc., Hawaii–Tahiti Service, 17 C.A.B. 762, 769 (1953); United States–Alaska Service Case, 14 C.A.B. 122, 136 (1951); Southeastern States Case, 7 C.A.B. 863, 896 (1947),

North Central Case, 7 C.A.B. 639, 663 (1946); American Export Air., Temporary New York–Foynes Ser., 3 C.A.B. 294, 298 (1941).

410. American Flyers Airline Corp., Interim Certificate, 37 C.A.B. 96, 97 (1962); Johnson Flying Service, Inc., Interim Certificate, 37 C.A.B. 120, 121 (1962); World Airways, Inc., Interim Certificate, 37 C.A.B. 130, 132 (1962); Southern Air Transport, Inc., Interim Certificate, 36 C.A.B. 656, 657–58 (1962). See Santop Air Transport, Inc., Interim Certificate, 37 C.A.B. 12, 13 (1962).

411. The Board may consider the issue of "comparative fitness" as a public interest factor in selecting a carrier to operate over a proposed route. "For example, where there is little or no difference between applicants on economic grounds (e.g., cost, diversion, integration, etc.) the comparative fitness of the applicants may be decisive in the selection of one carrier over another. In weighing these factors, the Board is not passing on the fitness of the applicants—both are deemed to be fit, willing and able within the meaning of the statutory standard—but rather is evaluating their qualifications (financial strength, type, and availability of equipment, management capability) to determine which applicant will best meet the requirements of the public convenience and necessity." New York–Florida Renewal Case, 41 C.A.B. 404, 408–09 (1964).

412. See Continental Southern Lines, Inc., v. Civil Aeronautics Board, 197 F.2d 397, 403 (D.C. Cir. 1952). However, where it is concluded that an applicant is fit, willing and able, the Board may proceed to an evaluation of the public interest. For example, in California Service Investigation, 52 C.A.B. 1 (1969), the Board, in considering the applications of a number of carriers seeking additional operating authority, recognized that each had adequately demonstrated its operational plans to perform the proposed operations and could obtain the requisite capital, personnel and equipment. Considering these factors in conjunction with their experience in providing trunkline air transport services, the Board concluded that each was fit, willing and able to perform the proposed operations. Consequently, it proceeded to evaluate the comparative public interest factors which dominate the issue of which carrier should be selected to provide the service. Id. at 22. However, the failure of an applicant to demonstrate that it possesses sufficient experience, ability or financial resources to perform its proposed services may lead to a finding that the applicant is not fit, willing and able to receive such operating authority. See North Central Case, 7 C.A.B. 639, 672 (1946). The failure of an applicant to prove that it has an appropriate "organizational plan to provide personnel having sufficient transportation experience to conduct satisfactorily the proposed operations, or that it has adequate capital resources to inaugurate such service" may lead to a denial of the application. Southeastern States Case, 7 C.A.B. 863, 897 (1947).

413. Pan American Airways Company (of Nevada), Certificate of Public Convenience and Necessity, 1 C.A.A. 695, 711 (1940).

414. 495 F.2d 145, 154 (D.C. Cir. 1974).

415. Id. at 154. Similarly, among the criteria which have been assessed in the evaluation of the fitness, willingness and ability of an applicant properly to perform proposed supplemental services are its experience, financial posture, compliance disposition and equipment availability. Transatlantic Charter Investigation, 40 C.A.B. 223, 263 (1964).

416. 1 C.A.A. 118 (1939).

417. *Id.* at 120–21. *See also* National Airlines, Inc., et al.—Certificates of Public Convenience and Necessity, 1 C.A.A. 612, 637 (1940).

418. Although a carrier may have experienced financial difficulties, the performance of past unprofitable operations does not preclude the Board from finding that the issuance of additional operating authority, by improving an applicant's financial posture, will enable it to perform reasonably adequate air transportation services, and that the applicant is financially fit to perform the proposed operations. Western Air Lines, Inc. v. Civil Aeronautics Board, 495 F.2d 145, 154–55 (D.C. Cir. 1974). Although carriers have been found to have experienced a net loss in their operations, they may nevertheless be found to be financially fit under circumstances where the payment of stockholder subscriptions will satisfy their existing liabilities and where they have never defaulted on the performance of their existing transportation commitments. Aircadia Ltd., CAB Order 73-4-47 (1973). The issue of a carrier's financial fitness cannot adequately be evaluated exclusively by reference to its financial statement. A carrier which may have an economic deficiency with respect to a particular item under generally accepted standards used in the evaluation of financial statements may be able to demonstrate mitigating circumstances which outweigh the deficiency. United States Overseas Airlines, Inc., Interim Certificate Proceeding, 41 C.A.B. 461, 465 (1964). Moreover, the Board has construed the ability of a carrier to serve and promote a market, despite its financial handicaps, to be a far more valuable indication of the carrier's fitness than its monthly balance sheets. Transatlantic Charter Investigation, 40 C.A.B. 233, 264 (1964).

419. 41 C.A.B. 461 (1964).

420. *Id.* at 463–64.

421. Supplemental Air Service Proceeding, 45 C.A.B. 231, 267 (1966). In evaluating the financial and operating ability of an applicant seeking operating authority to engage in supplemental air transportation, the going-concern status of an air carrier, as evidenced by existing supplemental operations, has traditionally been accorded heavy weight.

422. *See, e.g.*, Pennsylvania–Cent. Air., Youngstown–Erie–Buffalo Op., 1 C.A.A. 811 (1940); United A. L., Red Bluff Operation, 1 C.A.A. 778 (1940). *Id.* at 436–37. Subsequently, this carrier's economic posture deteriorated to a point which required a finding of unfitness, and its application was denied. United States Overseas Airlines, Interim Certificate Amendment, 38 C.A.B. 1114 (1963). *Cf.* Standard Airways, Suspension, 39 C.A.B. 898 (1974), with United States Overseas Airlines, suspension, 41 C.A.B. 750 (1964). Where the applicant could not demonstrate going-concern status as an air carrier, it was required to demonstrate its operational and financial ability by a stronger array of other evidence. Large Irregular Air Carrier Investigation, 28 C.A.B. 224, 310 (1959).

423. *See* Supplemental Renewal Proceeding, CAB Order 77-1-98 (1977), at 34 and Eugene Horbach Acquisition of Modern Air Transport, Inc., CAB Order 77-3-88-89 (1977), at 5.

424. In evaluating the financial and operating ability of an applicant seeking operating authority to engage in air transportation, the going-concern status of the carrier as evidenced by existing operations has traditionally been accorded heavy weight. Thus, in a number of proceedings, the Board concluded that an applicant is fit, willing and able to perform air transport operations where it has a long record of successful operations and a sound financial condition. *See, e.g.*, Supplemental Air

Service Proceeding, 45 C.A.B. 231, 267 (1966), and Pennsylvania–Cent. Air., Youngstown–Erie–Buffalo Op., 1 C.A.A. 811 (1940). Where the applicant could not demonstrate going-concern status as an air carrier, it was required to demonstrate its operational and financial ability by a stronger array of other evidence. Large Irregular Air Carrier Investigation, 28 C.A.B. 224, 310 (1959).

425. 37 C.A.B. 96, 97–99 (1962).

426. *See also* Johnson Flying Service, Inc., Interim Certificate, 37 C.A.B. 120, 121–22 (1962); World Airways, Inc., Interim Certificate, 37 C.A.B. 130, 132–33 (1962); Southern Air Transport, Inc., Interim Certificate, 36 C.A.B. 656, 658–59 (1962). Among the factors which have been evaluated by the Board in its determination of whether an applicant is operationally fit were those expressed in Santop Air Transport, Inc., Interim Certificate, 37 C.A.B. 12 (1962), in which the Board rested its conclusion of fitness on the following considerations: (a) the applicant's financial position was relatively sound and it was able to satisfy its financial obligations as they fell due; (b) the applicant had been engaged in air transportation for a number of years, and it had demonstrated an ability to conduct extensive and continuing transport operations in an efficient and economical manner; and (c) it had exhibited a willingness and ability to perform its operations with due regard for the protection of the traveling and shipping public by carrying adequate insurance and expressing a willingness to provide reasonable performance guarantees to the public. *Id.* at 13–15. *See also* Saturn Airways, Inc., Interim Certificate, 37 C.A.B. 45, 47–49 (1962).

427. CAB Order 77-3-88/89 (1977).

428. Specifically, the Board noted that they "have clearly described the nature and method and manner in which they will operate, and have provided sufficient detail relating to the proposed areas they will serve, the charters they will offer, the equipment they will use, and the traffic they will most likely carry." *Id.*

429. Airline Transport Carriers, Inc., d/b/a California–Hawaiian Airlines, Supplemental Air Services Case, 39 C.A.B. 200, 300-303 (1963).

430. 28 C.A.B. 224 (1969).

431. *Id.* at 310–11 (citation omitted).

432. Transatlantic Cargo Service Case, 21 C.A.B. 671, 689 (1954); see Hawaiian Intraterritorial Service, 10 C.A.B. 62, 67 (1948); Twentieth Century Air Lines, Inc. et al., 21 C.A.B. 133, 159 (1955). The Board has concluded that, despite a carrier's violations of the Act and the rules and regulations promulgated thereunder, operating authority should nevertheless be issued. Such a conclusion is preceded by a weighing and balancing of the factors involved, including the nature of the violation and the requirements of the public convenience and necessity. New York–Florida Case, 24 C.A.B. 94, 110 (1956).

433. New York–Chicago Service Case, 22 C.A.B. 973, 990 (1955). Similarly, where an applicant fails to demonstrate the compliance disposition required for the issuance of supplemental air carrier operating authority, the Board need not proceed to a consideration of the applicant's financial and operational fitness to perform the proposed operations. Paramount Airlines, Inc., Supplemental Air Service Case, 39 C.A.B. 350, 352 (1963).

434. United Air Lines Transport Corporation—Certificate of Public Convenience and Necessity, 1 C.A.A. 778, 790 (1940); Pennsylvania–Central Airlines Corporation—Amendment of Certificate of Public Convenience and Necessity, 1 C.A.A. 811,

821 (1940); Braniff Airways, Inc.—Certificate of Public Convenience and Necessity, 2 C.A.B. 199, 205 (1940).

435. New York–Florida Renewal Case, 38 C.A.B. 680, 730 (1963); Intra-Area Cargo Case, 28 C.A.B. 200, 205 (1959); Large Irregular Air Carrier Investigation, 28 C.A.B. 224, 308–09 (1959); Trans-Pacific Airlines, Ltd., Renewal Case, 21 C.A.B. 253, 257 (1955); Pioneer Air Lines, Inc., Amended Certificate, 18 C.A.B. 11, 12 (1954).

436. Trans-Pacific Airlines, Ltd., Renewal Case, 21 C.A.B. 253, 257 (1955). The existence of financial resources sufficient to ensure inauguration of proposed services and operation thereof for a period sufficient to test their usefulness is an essential ingredient to a finding of fitness, willingness and ability. Samoan Airlines Case, Reopened, 18 C.A.B. 533, 538 (1954).

437. *Cf.* Pioneer Air Lines, Inc., Amended Certificate, 18 C.A.B. 11, 12 (1953) (with respect to the Board's financial evaluation of supplemental carriers); *see, e.g.,* United States Overseas Airlines, Interim Certificate, 38 C.A.B. 1114, 1116 (1963); and Riddle Airlines, Transatlantic Passenger Charters, 38 C.A.B. 1170, 1173 (1963); Airline Transport Carriers, Inc., d/b/a/ California–Hawaiian Airlines, Supplemental Air Service Case, 39 C.A.B. 299, 301 (1963).

438. Supplemental Air Service Proceeding, 45 C.A.B. 231, 267 (1966). Moreover, the discontinuance of existing air carrier operations may reasonably be interpreted as demonstrating a lack of willingness or ability to provide transport services, to operate, or to conform to the Act and the Board's rules and regulations thereunder. However, despite the discontinuation of air services, an applicant might nevertheless demonstrate its fitness, willingness and ability to perform proposed air carrier operations on the basis of other evidence, such as previously successful operations, financial ability, a competent organization and available equipment. Large Irregular Air Carrier Investigation, 28 C.A.B. 224, 310 (1959).

439. Large Irregular Air Carrier Investigaion, 28 C.A.B. 224, 238 (1959); New York–Florida Renewal Case, 38 C.A.B. 680, 730 (1963).

440. 8 C.A.B. 636 (1947).

441. *Id.* at 638–39. Boston–New York–Altanta–New Orleans Case, 9 C.A.B. 38, 57–58 (1948). The existence of financial difficulties may not be an impediment to a finding of fitness where the applicant is a going-concern and where its financial situation is improving. Airlift International, C.A.B. Order 73-3-58 (1973).

442. 49 U.S.C. § 1371(d)(9)(A).

443. The U.S. Department of Transportation assumed the remaining CAB functions on January 1, 1985, under the Civil Aeronautics Board Sunset Act of 1984.

444. 49 U.S.C. § 1301.

445. Chicago–Midway Low-Fare Route Proceeding, CAB Order 78-7-40 (1978), at 50; see Chicago–Midway Expanded Service Proceeding, CAB Order 79-9-55 (1979), at 8–9.

446. CAB Order 79-1-75 (1979).

447. Eugene Horbach, Acquisition of Modern Air Transport, CAB Order 77-3-88 (1977), at 7–9.

448. CAB Order 79-1-75 (1979) at 26.

449. *Id.*

3

Rate Regulation

I. THE INTERSTATE COMMERCE ACT

A. Tariff Filing, Suspension and Investigation

Under the Interstate Commerce Act,[1] carriers initiate rates and include them in tariffs.[2,3] Motor carriers must file the tariffs 30 days prior to the effective date of the rates, unless special permission is granted to file within a shorter period.[4] Rail carriers must file 20 days before the effective date of the tariff, unless special permission is granted.[5] If the Interstate Commerce Commission (ICC) fails to reject the proposed tariff within the applicable notice period, the tariff automatically becomes effective.[6] During these notice periods, the ICC may suspend the tariff either on the motion of an interested party or sua sponte.[7] The Commission currently cannot suspend a rail tariff unless it appears that

1. there is a substantial likelihood that the protestant will prevail on the merits;

2. without suspension, the rate will cause substantial injury to the protestant; and

3. because of peculiar circumstances of the protestant, provisions for subsequent compensation will not adequately protect him.[8]

If the ICC suspends a tariff, it has a designated time period within which to investigate and determine the validity of the proposed rate.

The ICC can investigate a tariff without suspending it. When determining whether to investigate a rail tariff, the ICC must consider several factors: the amount of traffic generating revenues that do not contribute to going concern value, the efforts made to reduce such traffic, the amount of traffic that contributes only marginally to fixed costs and the effect of the proposed rate on national energy objectives and rail transportation policy. In reaching its decision, the ICC must recognize "the railroad's role as a primary source of energy transportation and the need for a sound rail transportation system."[9] If the proposed rate is deemed unlawful, the ICC will cancel it. If the ICC decides not to investigate a rail rate increase, it must set forth its reasons. The courts may not review a no-suspension decision by the Commission resulting from a tariff investigation.[10]

Given that an aggrieved party protesting under Section 10707 or 10708 of the Interstate Commerce Act cannot compel the ICC to suspend a filed tariff, such a party may nevertheless institute a formal complaint under Section 11701 of the Act, thus requiring the ICC to investigate the lawfulness of the filed tariff.[11] In this situation, the Commission's failure to investigate, as well as its decision to approve or disapprove the carrier rates, is subject to judicial review. Generally, the burden of proving the reasonableness of a proposed tariff under Section 10707 or 10708 lies with the carrier that originally filed it.[12] In a Section 11701 proceeding, however, the burden of proof lies with the complaining party, who must establish that the rates are unlawful.[13]

When the ICC concludes that a rate charged is unlawful, it may prescribe the maximum or minimum rate to be charged.[14] In the situations in which the ICC has investigated but not suspended a rail rate, the carrier must refund that portion of the rate determined to be unreasonable, plus interest.[15] If the tariff originally had been suspended and the ICC ultimately determines that some portion is reasonable, the carrier must collect the difference between the actual rate charged and the rate level determined to be reasonable, plus interest.[16]

The U.S. Supreme Court has held that pending investigation of a proposed tariff, the ICC can impose a mandatory condition precedent to nonsuspension of the tariff requiring the carrier to spend the resulting profits for specified purposes.[17] The Court has upheld such action as a legitimate extension of the Commission's explicit suspension powers, necessary to protect the public from unjustified increases in transportation costs, safeguard the community against irreparable losses and establish and maintain reasonable charges and proper rate relationships.[18] In *Trans-Alaska Pipeline Rate Cases*,[19] the Supreme Court expanded the Commission's suspension powers by concluding that the ICC held not only authority to suspend initial tariff schedules, but also auxiliary power to fix maximum interim rates for the suspension period and require that as a condition of nonsuspension, the carriers must refund any amounts collected but ultimately found to be unlawful. The Court reasoned that these auxiliary powers, in conjunction with the suspension powers, allowed the Commission to balance the needs of the public against the needs of the carriers.[20]

B. Rate Regulation as a Means of Prohibiting Discrimination

The Interstate Commerce Act requires that a carrier provide interstate transportation services only at the rate specified in the tariff filed with the

ICC.[21] This rule, which represents congressional intent to prevent unjust discrimination in interstate commerce, has prevailed over theories based on either contract and agency law or estoppel principles. Nevertheless, differences in rates, classifications, rules or practices do not violate the antidiscrimination provisions of the Interstate Commerce Act if they reflect substantive differences in services performed.[22]

The Act establishes several basic standards. A carrier may not charge any person a different rate for a like or contemporaneous service under substantially similar circumstances,[23] nor may a carrier charge a higher rate for transportation over a shorter distance vis-à-vis a longer distance over the same line in the same direction.[24] It is also unlawful for a carrier to confer any undue or unreasonable preference or advantage to any person, region, territory or traffic.[25] Furthermore, a carrier cannot discriminate between interlining carriers in its rates, fares or charges.[26]

C. Just and Reasonable Rates

In addition to preventing discrimination, the Commission is charged with determining the reasonableness of a proposed rate schedule.[27] Reasonableness is principally a question of fact, and thus the Commission has been given considerable deference and discretion in rate making.[28] The ICC's flexibility in determining whether a rate is reasonable is limited by common law and statutory notions of a "zone of reasonableness." Justice Cardozo, in *United States v. Chicago, Milwaukee, St. Paul & Pacific Railroad*,[29] characterized the common law zone as follows: "A zone of reasonableness exists between maxima and minima within which a carrier is ordinarily free to adjust its charges for itself. . . . 'A carrier is entitled to initiate rates and, in this connection, to adopt such policy of rate-making as to it seems best.' "[30] The cost of service has traditionally been deemed to be the point below which rates should not be lowered, and the value of service, the point above which rates should not be raised. Thus, competition itself becomes the determiner of the precise point within this zone at which the rates should be set.

The ICC has used a variety of criteria in determining whether proposal rates are just and reasonable. These include the existence of competition, distance of haul, transportation characteristics of the commodity, anticipated volume of shipments and economic status of the industry served. The ICC has emphasized rate comparisons for similar commodities, territories, distances, revenues per unit, traffic densities and transportation peculiarities affecting costs.[31] The Commission also has considered the economic effect of the proposed rate on consumers of the commodity, as well as the relationship between the rate proposed and variable costs.[32]

The judiciary has upheld rate ceilings imposed by the ICC and set at a carrier's fully allocated costs as being within the common law zone of reasonableness.[33] In addition, the courts have upheld the general notion of differential pricing[34] as being beneficial in achieving the statutory objective of providing adequate revenues for carriers.[35] Nevertheless, the Court of Appeals for the District of Columbia Circuit has found a recent ICC decision, which set unit coal rates 7 percent above fully allocated costs, to be arbitrary and capricious.[36] The court noted that the need to consider the revenue requirements of the carriers and the economics of differential pricing constituted so broad a rationale as to result in a meaningless standard.[37]

D. The Motor Carrier Act of 1980, the Staggers Rail Act and the Zones of Reasonableness

Recent legislation has expanded the common law zone of reasonableness. The Motor Carrier Act of 1980,[38] which amended the Interstate Commerce Act, prohibits the ICC from interfering with a proposed rate on the ground that it is excessively high or low when the rate in question is 10 percent above or below the rate set one year before.[39] Moreover, the Commission may increase the zone by 5 percent during any year in which it concludes that not only is there sufficient competition to regulate the rates adequately, but also the public will benefit from the increased rate flexibility.[40]

The purpose of these amendments is to reduce government regulation and broaden the carriers' opportunities to set transportation rates. Thus, the intent is to spur competition in both service and pricing. These provisions, however, do not interfere with the Commission's powers to police discriminatory or predatory pricing. The Motor Carrier Act of 1980 also permits motor carriers to take into account foreseeable future costs when determining a rate base.[41] For motor carriers of property, the 1980 Act authorizes rate levels that would provide "a flow of net income, plus depreciation, adequate to support prudent capital outlays, assure repayment of debt, permit the raising of equity capital, and cover the effects of inflation."

The Staggers Rail Act,[42] to free the railroads from unnecessary government regulation and to aid market mechanisms in providing adequate revenues for a financially needy industry, adds to the Interstate Commerce Act a new congressional declaration of policy for railroads.[43] Competition is mentioned repeatedly as a policy objective. In order to increase competition, rail carriers must be able to enter and exit the market without being subject to unnecessary federal regulatory barriers. Furthermore, they must be permitted to earn adequate revenues.[44] Nevertheless, the ICC must continue to prohibit discriminatory or predatory pricing,[45] regulating those markets that lack effective competition among carriers.[46]

The Staggers Rail Act, which focuses primarily on rail rate making, narrows the jurisdiction of the ICC and increases the freedom of the rail carriers to raise or lower rates without ICC interference. The ICC's jurisdiction is eliminated with respect to the reasonableness of rate increases unless the carrier has "market dominance."[47] The legislation affirms the concept of market dominance as established by the Railroad Revitalization and Regulatory Reform Act of 1976 (4R Act).[48] When Congress passed the 4R Act, it indicated that market dominance "refers to an absence of effective competition from other carriers or modes of transportation, for the traffic or movement to which a rate applies."[49] The concept was not imposed as a test of the reasonableness of the rate, but was designed as a jurisdictional threshold. Only when the rail carrier had market dominance over the traffic could the ICC address the question of whether the rate was excessively high. Although the definition of market dominance has not been altered, the ICC has adopted a tripartite test to define the concept.[50] In determining the reasonableness of rates, the ICC must recognize that carriers are entitled to earn adequate revenues.

In addition to addressing the issue of rate increases, the Staggers Rail Act eliminates the ICC's jurisdiction over rate decreases unless the rail rates are below a reasonable minimum.[51] Rates contributing to the going concern value will be construed as reasonable, whereas rates not contributing to the going concern value will be presumed unreasonable.[52] Although Congress acknowledged that there may be circumstances in which such rates are reasonable even though they do not contribute to the going concern value, such circumstances are likely to be unusual. In essence, a rate that meets or exceeds the variable costs of providing particular services is "conclusively presumed to contribute to the going concern value" and thus is not below a reasonable minimum. Yet once a party has demonstrated that the rail carrier's rates do not meet this statutory minimum, the burden of establishing that the proposed rates are in fact reasonable shifts to the carrier. On concluding that the rate is too low and that the "carrier is worse off than it would be if the rates were raised," the ICC may order the rate raised to a minimum level benefiting the carrier.

In an attempt to increase a carrier's freedom to adjust its rates, the Staggers Rail Act expands the zone of reasonableness by establishing a zone of rate flexibility. This zone consists of a base rate, which is the rate that was in effect on the date the legislation was enacted,[53] and an adjusted base rate,[54] which is computed quarterly through the use of a "rail cost adjustment factor."[55] A rail carrier is free to adjust its rates to conform to the adjusted base rate at any time without challenge, except when it has received an inflation increase through the general rate increase provisions of Section 10706 or through the inflation rate increase provisions of Section 10712.[56] Therefore, if the rate conforms to the adjusted base rate, the ICC cannot claim that it exceeds a maximum reasonable level.[57] Moreover, certain percentage increases over the adjusted base rate are presumed reasonable as a procedural mechanism to reduce ICC interference with industry rate making.[58] These statutory changes reflect the belief that the marketplace can better regulate rate making than can government.

In addition to the provisions discussed, the Staggers Rail Act authorizes rail carriers to enter into contracts with shippers for transportation services.[59] The contracts must be filed with the ICC,[60] and within 30 days of filing, the ICC may begin reviewing them.[61] Shippers may protest the contract on the grounds that the contract impairs the railroad's duty to fulfill its common carrier obligations, whereas ports may protest on the grounds that they will be discriminated against.[62] Furthermore, the ICC may order carriers transporting agricultural commodities to adhere to rates and services offered in a contract for shippers, not parties, thereto, when the refusal to contract constitutes unreasonable discrimination.[63] If the ICC determines that additional contracts would impair the railroad's ability to fulfill the common carrier obligations, it may limit the right of the carrier to enter into future contracts.[64]

E. Rail Contract Rates

Prior to the promulgation of the Staggers Rail Act of 1980, there was some question as to the legality of contract rate making between rail carriers and the shippers they serve. The ICC attempted to allay such fears with the issuance of a policy statement in 1979, which announced its interpretation of the Interstate Commerce Act that contract rate making was legal, and to encourage consummation of such contracts. Prior to the promulgation of the Staggers Act, only 80 contracts were filed with the ICC.

The Staggers Act explicitly affirmed the propriety of such rates.[65] By the summer of 1982, some 2,200 contracts were on file with the ICC, and they were being filed at the rate of 200 a month. The Commission's Contract Advisory Service has estimated that rail carriers will earn at least 50 percent of their revenues from such contracts by the end of the 1980s.

Under the regulations[66] promulgated by the ICC, a carrier need only file two documents: the confidential contract and a succinct contract summary. Only the latter will be made available to the public. This enables the parties to keep the specific terms of their agreement secret.

F. Regulation of Passenger Fares

Rate regulation by the ICC generally consists of passing on the reasonableness of freight rates. Fares (the rates charged for carriage of passengers) have been largely deregulated in the rail and airline industries, but prior to 1985 the ICC still retained wide jurisdiction over fares charged by bus companies. The Motor Carrier Act of 1980 did not alter regulation of the intercity bus industry.

Interstate bus fares must be just, reasonable and nondiscriminatory. Some promotional fares (such as an unlimited bus travel pass) and special rates for senior citizens, youth, clergy and the military have been upheld. Charter parties, which use the entire bus, pay a flat rate for use of the bus and driver regardless of the number of occupied seats.

Intrastate bus fares are regulated by state public service commissions except in those states that have abolished such regulations. A fare for intrastate travel that constitutes a burden on interstate commerce may be suspended by the ICC. Local transit fares are usually regulated by the governing body supervising operations of the transit authority.

Representatives of the motor bus industry have complained that their industry is the only passenger carrier subject to complete economic regulation. Amtrak fares have been deregulated since 1971, although the ICC may hear a motor carrier complaint that Amtrak is engaging in destructive price competition. Section 10504 of the Interstate Commerce Act exempts from ICC regulation commuter rail traffic provided by a public body whose fares are subject to the approval of the governor of that state. The ICC does have jurisdiction over fares charged by the few existing non-Amtrak interstate passenger railroads.

The Bus Regulatory Reform Act of 1982 established a zone of rate freedom for motor passenger carriers. During 1983, the first year, the Commission could not suspend or investigate proposed single-line or joint-line rates that were 10 percent above or 20 percent below the rate in effect on the date of the Act's promulgation, or the rate in effect one year prior to the effective date of the proposed rate. In both the second year and the third year after the Act's promulgation, the ceiling and the floor of the zone are expanded by 5 percent. In 1985, the Commission lost its jurisdiction to suspend or investigate proposed passenger rates on the grounds that they are excessively high or low. Although the Commission has no authority to suspend or investigate proposed rates, it may find such rates to be unreasonable on complaint or on its own initiative. Moreover, the ICC retains jurisdiction to suspend or investigate proposed rates on the grounds that they are discriminatory or predatory.

G. Household Movers' Rates

The Household Goods Transportation Act of 1980 is a clarification of ICC authority in the moving van industry. It establishes the power of the ICC to permit carriers to establish rates which are based on binding estimates and guaranteed pick-up and delivery times.[67] This simple, matter-of-fact statement restores the principles of estoppel to transportation law. The mover may quote an estimate of price and schedule and will be bound by it.

The new law establishes the responsibility of the nationwide moving van lines for the acts of their agents. It requires that agents be fit and establishes a tighter control of the arrangements between agents and the national van companies. To this extent, it confers antitrust immunity on certain discussions between agents and the van lines. Reaffirming the ICC authority to protect consumers, it establishes statutory guidelines for a dispute-settling program involving shippers and carriers.

Complaints about household goods movers had been the most frequent consumer criticism of the ICC's regulatory role and were highlighted in the Nader Report of 1970. The philosophy of the Household Goods Act is a coupling of competition with increased oversight. Congress declared that the function of the ICC in household moving cases is to protect the home-owner and small shipper whose disparity in bargaining power vis-à-vis the carrier requires continuing supervision of the industry and abandonment of the prohibition on rebates in favor of binding carriers to their written estimates.

II. APPLICATION OF ICC RATE PRINCIPLES

A. Tariffs Filed with the ICC Are the Only Lawful Rates

LOUISVILLE & NASHVILLE RR v. MAXWELL

237 U.S. 95 (1915)

Mr. Justice Hughes delivered the opinion of the court.

This action was brought, before a Justice of the Peace in Tennessee, by the Louisville & Nashville Railroad Company to recover $58.30 as the amount of an alleged undercharge on the sale of railroad tickets. Judgment for the defendant was affirmed by the Court of Civil Appeals and by the Supreme Court of the State. The case comes here on error.

The facts, which were said to be undisputed, were found by the state court to be as follows:

Defendant in error, G. A. Maxwell, after repeated interviews, and correspondence, with the representatives of the Louisville & Nashville Railroad Company in regard to rates on round-trip tickets to Salt Lake City, purchased on or about the first day of June, 1910, "two passenger tickets from Nashville, Tennessee, to Salt Lake City, by way of Chicago, Illinois, Denver, Colorado and routed to return by Denver, Colorado, Amarillo and Fort Worth, Texas, and Memphis, Tennessee, and paid for each ticket the sum of $49.50.

There were at the time, published rates under the provisions of the Interstate Commerce Act by which fares over the route actually traveled, going and coming, aggregated $78.65 each, or $29.15 each more than was charged and collected therefore, making a difference of $58.30 between the amount paid by Mr. Maxwell for the tickets in question, and the amount that should have been charged and collected.

Mr. Maxwell was informed when he first made inquiry about the tickets in January, that there were no special rate tickets at that time, but likely would be by May or June first. He then, and on several occasions thereafter, made known his desire to go to Salt Lake City by one route, and return by another, and was told that he could not be furnished reduced rates except by going and coming over the same route, but after repeated inquiries, and the correspondence referred to, he was informed that he could make the trip on reduced rate one way, and return another; and when he went finally to purchase the two tickets, he stated to the agent that he wanted to go by way of Chicago and Denver and return by way of Stamford, Texas, and was given the tickets routed as hereinbefore noted, at the rates mentioned. At that time, he in fact could have gone to Salt Lake City at the rate which he paid, but over other routes, going and returning through Chicago and Denver, or through St. Louis and Denver, or through Memphis and Denver, or going through St. Louis and Denver and returning through Denver, Amarillo and Memphis.

Mr. Maxwell was in no way at fault in the matter. He did no more than tell the agent the points to which he wished to go and make it known that he did not wish to go and return by the same route. The agent fixed the routing in the tickets and named the fare, and Maxwell paid without further question.

Under the Interstate Commerce Act, the rate of the carrier duly filed is the only lawful charge. Deviation from it is not permitted upon any text. Shippers and travelers are charged with notice of it, and they as well as the carrier must abide by it, unless it is found by the Commission to be unreasonable. Ignorance or misquotation of rates is not an excuse for paying or charging either less or more than the rate filed. This rule is undeniably strict and it obviously may work hardship in some cases, but it embodies the policy which has been adopted by Congress in the regulation of interstate commerce in order to prevent unjust discrimination. The Act . . . provides:

> Nor shall any carrier charge or demand or collect or receive a greater or less or different compensation for such transportation of passengers or property, or for any service in connection therewith, between the points named in such tariffs than the rates, fares, and charges which are specified in the tariff and in effect at that time; nor shall any carrier refund or remit in any manner or by any device any portion of the rates, fares, and charges so specified, nor extend to any shipper or person any privileges or facilities in the transportation of passengers or property, except such as are specified in such tariffs.

In *Texas & Pac. Ry. v. Yugg*, 202 U.S. 242, it appeared that a rate, less than the lawful scheduled rate, had been quoted to the shipper by the agent of the railroad. The shipper had relied upon the quoted rate in making his shipments and sales. But it was held that he was bound to pay the established rate and was not entitled to the delivery of the goods without such payment. This was upon the ground that it was beyond the power of the carrier to depart from the filed rates and that the erroneous quotation of the rate by its agent did not justify it in making a different charge from that which was lawfully applicable to the shipment. As was said in *Kansas Southern Rwy. Co. v. Carl*:

> Neither the intentional nor accidental misstatement of the applicable published rate will bind the carrier or shipper. The lawful rate is that which the carrier must exact and that which the shipper must pay. The shipper's knowledge of the lawful rate is conclusively presumed, and the carrier may not be required to surrender the goods carried upon the payment of the rate paid, if that was less than the lawful rate, until the full legal rate has been paid.

It was "the purpose of the Act to have but one rate, open to all alike and from which there could be no departure." *Boston & Main R.R. v. Hooker*, 233 U.S. 97.

B. Suspension and Investigation

SOUTHERN RY. v. SEABOARD MILLING CORP.

442 U.S. 444 (1979)

Mr. Justice Stevens delivered the opinion of the court.

On September 14, 1977, the Interstate Commerce Commission decided not to exercise its authority under § 10707 of the Interstate Commerce Act ("the Act") to order a hearing to investigate the lawfulness of a seasonal rate increase proposed by a group of railroads. The question presented is whether the Commission's refusal to conduct such an investigation is subject to judicial review.

We now hold that the Commission's "no investigation" decision is not reviewable.

In August of 1977, the Southern Freight Association proposed a 20% increase in the rates for grain and soybeans shipped from the Midwest in railroad-owned cars between September 15 and December 15, 1977. The railroads supported their proposal with statistics describing the high volume of grain shipments in the fall, an explanation of the anticipated effect of the temporary rates on rail car usage, and some cost evidence.

A number of shippers and large users of transported grain (hereinafter "shippers") filed protests claiming the proposed rates were unlawful. They requested that the Commission exercise its authority under 10707 to suspend these rates and to investigate the charges of illegality. On September 14, 1977, a month after the rates were filed, and eight days after receiving the protests, the Commission issued its order declining either to suspend or to investigate the legality of the rates. With respect to the basic question whether to suspend the rates and conduct a formal investigation, the Commission concluded: "Weighing the contentions before us and the clear congressional purpose to permit experimental rate-making, we will permit this temporary adjustment to become effective." It noted, however, that § 11701 of the Interstate Commerce Act, which allows shippers to initiate mandatory post-effective proceedings to inquire into and remedy violations of the Act, would still be available to "protect" persons aggrieved by the rates.

The court of appeals held that the Commission had begun an investigation but had then erroneously terminated it without "adequately investigating the charges" of "patent illegality" and without supporting its decision "with appropriate findings and conclusions." 570 F2d at 1352, 1355, 1356. It directed the Commission to hold hearings to investigate more fully the protestants' charges of patent illegality and, if the investigation revealed that the tariff was unlawful, to make appropriate provisions for refund of increased charges collected under the tariff. Id., at 1356.

We reverse. First, to the extent that the Court of Appeals interpreted the Commission's order as a final decision not now to investigate its lawfulness, it has misconstrued the order. Second, to the extent that its decision transcends this misinterpretation of the Commission's order and suggests that even a "no-investigation" determination would be reviewable, it has misconstrued Congress' intent with respect to 10707.

It is of course true that a decision by the Commission following a § 10707 investigation to approve or disapprove a set of rates is a judicially reviewable final decision. The shippers contend that this rule governs here. In their view, the Commission, by reviewing and then leaving intact rates it knew to be unlawful, effectively approved those rates. But the express language of the Commission's order belies an interpretation of its decision as a ruling on the legality of respondents' seasonal tariff.

The Act leaves the Commission only 30 days to decide on suspension before the rates automatically become effective. The Commission's primary duty, therefore, is to make a prompt appraisal of the probable and general reasonableness and legality of the proposed schedule—which may, as in this case involve thousands of rates for designated commodities and routes—rather than a detailed review of the lawfulness of each individual component of the tariff schedules. In short, the Commission simply has no time to, and did not in this case, finally decide on the lawfulness of the rate schedule or its individual components during the preliminary 30-day period.

Initially it is important to note the extremely limited scope of the administrative decision that we conclude is not judicially reviewable. We are not here concerned with the Commission's rate-suspension authority because, as we shall see, our prior cases have already placed the exercise of that authority beyond the control of the courts. Nor, in fact, are we holding entirely unreviewable the Commission's exercise of its rate-investigation authority. For any shipper may require the Commission to investigate the lawfulness of any rate at any time—and may secure judicial review of any decision not to do so—by filing a § 11701 complaint.

Instead, our sole concern is the Commission's decision not to investigate under § 10707, a decision that has only two final consequences. First, the burden of proof with regard to reasonableness is placed on the shipper under § 11701 rather than on the carrier, who would have borne it in a § 10707 proceeding. (With respect to all other aspects of lawfulness, however, the burden is borne by the shipper in both proceedings.) Second, the shipper's relief, if unlawfulness is proven, is limited under § 11710 to actual damages rather than the full refund of over charges available under § 10707. It is only with regard to these two determinations, neither of which necessarily affects any citizen's ultimate rights, that we conclude—based on the language, structure, and history of the Act as well as the relevant case law—that the agency's exercise of discretion is unreviewable.

With respect to the Commission's investigation power, § 10707 is written in the language of permission and discretion. Under it, "the Commission may, upon the complaint of an interested party or upon its own initiative, order a hearing concerning the lawfulness of a rate which hearing may be conducted without answer or other formal pleading."

The statute is silent on what should guide the Commission's decision.

The structure of the Act also indicates that Congress intended to prohibit judicial review. Congress did not use permissive language such as that found in § 10707 when it wished to create reviewable duties under the Act. Instead, it used mandatory language, and it typically included standards to guide both the Commission in exercising its authority and the courts in reviewing that exercise. In particular § 11701, which plainly authorizes rate-investigation decisions that are reviewable, provides that "if . . . there shall appear to be any reasonable ground for investigating said complaints, it shall be the duty of the Commission to investigate the matter complained of."

The Court of Appeals' interpretation therefore treats § 10707 as if it were written in the mandatory language of § 11701.

Of even greater significance, that interpretation would allow shippers to use the open-ended and ill-defined procedures in § 10707 to render obsolete the carefully designed and detailed procedures in § 11707. For under the court's reading, at least when one of the perhaps thousands of rates in a proposed schedule is "patently illegal," any party could (and, given the burden-of-proof and remedial advantages, many surely would) force the Commission immediately to undertake an investigation under § 10707 and to reach a judicially reviewable decision on the legality of the rates. Nothing would be left for considerations under § 11701. We, of course, are reluctant almost a century after the Act was passed to adopt an interpretation of it that would effectively nullify one of its original and most frequently used provisions.

The disruptive practical consequences of such a determination confirm our view that Congress intended no such result. The Commission reviews over 50,000 rate-schedule filings each year; many, including the one involved here, contain thousands of individual rates. If the Commission, which generally makes its § 10707 investigation decisions within 30 days in order to allow pre-effective suspension, must carefully analyze and explain its actions with regard to each component of each proposed schedule, and if it must increase the number of investigations it conducts, all in order to avoid judicial review and reversal, its workload would increase tremendously.

* * *

There is an additional structural reason why the Commission's investigation decisions are unreviewable. Section 10707 was originally included in the Mann-Elkins Act of 1910, 36 Stat. 552. As adopted, and as it has remained during the ensuing 70 years, the provision has given the Commission the power not only to investigate but also to suspend proposed rates. 49 U.S.C. § 10707. Congress phrased the two powers in precisely the same language and placed the same time limits on the exercise of both. The two powers are inextricably linked because the Commission has no occasion to suspend a rate unless it also intends to investigate it.

In view of this linkage, we need look no further than our previous decisions concluding that the merits of a suspension decision are not reviewable to find a sufficient answer to the question presented in this case.

* * *

The legislative history of the Mann-Elkins amendments to the Interstate Commerce Act also supports nonreviewability. Prior to the enactment of those amendments, the Commission had no authority to suspend rates or to adjudicate their lawfulness in advance either of their becoming effective or of their being challenged by a private party.

In the years immediately preceding the enactment of the amendments, rapidly rising rates encouraged shippers, with some success, to ask the courts to enjoin unlawful rates before they went into effect. As a result of the ensuing judicial intervention in the ratemaking process, the Commission was divested of much of its primary jurisdiction with respect to rates, and the public was subjected to nonuniform rates that depended on whether or not the local District Court had issued an injunction.

In short, the necessary " 'clear and convincing evidence' that Congress meant to prohibit all judicial review" of the Commission's limited decision not to initiate an investigation under § 10707 is provided by the language of the statute, as well as its place within the statutory design of the Interstate Commerce Act, its legislative history, and the light shed on it by our case law concerning analogous statutes.

The judgment of the Court of Appeals is reversed.

The *Southern Railway* decision discussed both the long and short haul and the seasonal rates provisions of the Interstate Commerce Act. Dating from the original Act to Regulate Commerce of 1887, the former prohibits a carrier, except under extraordinary circumstances, from receiving any greater compensation for transportation for a shorter distance than for a longer distance over the same line in the same direction.[68] It exists as part of the general antidiscrimination provisions of the Act.

The seasonal rates provision, which originated in the 4R Act of 1976, required that the ICC establish by rule:

standards and expeditious procedures for the establishment of railroad rates based on seasonal, regional, or peak-period demand for rail services. Such standards and procedures shall be designed to (a) provide sufficient incentive to shippers to reduce peak-period shipments . . . ; (b) generate additional revenues for the railroads; and (c) improve (i) the utilization of the national supply of freight cars, (ii) the movement of goods by rail, (iii) levels of employment by railroads, (iv) levels of employment by railroads, and (v) the financial stability of markets served by railroads.[69]

It was deemed not to have been successful in accomplishing its objectives, and was repealed by the Staggers Rail Act of 1980.

UNITED STATES v. THE CHESAPEAKE & OHIO RY.
426 U.S. 500 (1976)

Mr. Chief Justice Burger delivered the opinion of the Court.

This case is here on direct appeal from an order of the District Court which permanently enjoined the Interstate Commerce Commission from enforcing, against the appellee railway system, an order requiring the application of increased revenues to deferred capital improvements and deferred maintenance as a condition for the nonsuspension of the rate increases.

In April 1974, the Nation's railroads, including the appellees, filed with the Interstate Commerce Commission a joint petition for a general revenue increase "with respect to the revenue needs of all carriers by railroad operating in the United States."[70] The proposed tariffs included a 10% increase in the level of freight rates. The Commission found that the Nation's railroads were "in danger of further deterioration detrimental to the public interest," and recognized that "without the additional revenues to be derived from increased freight rates and charges, the earnings of the nation's railroads would be insufficient to enable them under honest, economical and efficient management to provide adequate and efficient railroad transportation services." The Commission concluded that "the increases proposed would, if permitted to become effective, generate additional revenues sufficient to enable the carriers to prevent further deterioration and improve service." At the same time, it noted that "if the schedules were permitted to become effective as filed and without conditions designed to promote service improvements, the increases proposed would be unjust and unreasonable and contrary to the dictates of the national transportation policy." The Commission, therefore, suspended the operation of the new schedules but authorized the railroads to file new tariffs, subject to conditions providing that revenues generated by the increases "should be expended for capital improvements and deferred maintenance of plant and equipment and the amount needed for increased material and supply cost, other than fuel."

On July 18, 1974, the Commission entered the second pertinent order in this case. This order provided that "up to 3 percentage points of the 10-percent authorization may be applied to increased material and supply costs, excluding fuel, provided such costs have been incurred."

On July 30, appellee Chessie System sought reconsideration of the Commission's order of July 18 "for the reason that under the Commission's definitions of deferred maintenance and delayed capital improvements they will be unable to apply any of the increased revenues (other than those earmarked for increased material and supply costs) to any projects now scheduled or which may be scheduled in the foreseeable future." Chessie alleged it had no such "deferred maintenance" or "delayed capital improvements." Chessie further noted that it had made significant expenditures for capital improvements in the six months prior to the Commission order. It pointed out that these projects did not qualify under the Commission's definition, because the funds had been committed before June 1, 1974, and the projects "had not been deferred because funding or financing was not available." Unless it was permitted to apply these additional revenues to these earlier commitments, contended Chessie, "they will simply lie dormant in a sterile, segregated account which will result in several serious consequences both to Chessie System and the shipping public." Basically, argued Chessie, the consequences of the order were to place Chessie

> at a distinct competitive disadvantage vis-à-vis other railroads, which for one reason or another have deferred maintenance of delayed capital improvements within the meaning of the Commission's order. These lines will be able to use the additional revenues to buy cars and other equipment while Chessie System's money will lie fallow. In effect, the order penalizes Chessie System and other efficient carriers and rewards only those railroads which are inefficient.

Chessie specifically asked the Commission to permit the expenditure of funds generated by the increases for any valid corporate purpose if the railroad had no deferred maintenance or deferred capital improvements as defined by the Commission's order. Chessie, for the first time, also argued that the Commission "exceeded its statutory authority by conditioning the use to which the revenues derived from (the ICC's order) might be applied."

The present suit was commenced by Chessie on August 15, 1974. Chessie sought to set aside the June 3, July 18, and August 9 orders of the Commission. On August 18, a single District Judge issued a temporary restraining order which prohibited the Commission from "enforcing the limiting conditions on the use of plaintiffs' revenues and of certain reporting conditions included in the orders."

On October 3 the Commission concluded that if any railroad was "unable to use the full amount of the funds generated by the increase for deferred maintenance or delayed capital improvements" it might "expend such funds for new and additional capital improvements providing advance approval is obtained from the Commission."

The precise question presented in this case, while one of first impression in this Court, is also a narrow one. In their application before the Commission, the railroads sought to justify the proposed general revenue increase on several grounds, including the need for additional funds for deferred capital and deferred maintenance expenditures. We are confronted with the question of whether the Commission may, as a condition for not suspending and subsequently investigating the lawfulness of a proposed tariff, require the railroads to devote the additional revenues to a need which, they allege, justifies the increase.

The overall statutory mandate of the Commission in railway ratemaking proceedings can, for present purposes, be stated quite simply. The Congress has charged the Commission with the task of determining whether the rates proposed by the carriers are "just and reasonable." In fulfilling this obligation, the Commission must assess the proposed rates not only against the backdrop of the National Transportation Policy, but also with specific reference to the statutory criteria set forth by the Congress to guide the ratesetting process. These provisions, in short, require the Commission to ensure that the rate imposed on the traveling or the shipping public will support both an economically sound and efficient rail transportation system.

Rates, in the first instance, are set by the railroads. The proposed rate is filed with the Commission and notice is given to the public. After 30 days' notice (or a shorter period, if authorized by the ICC), the rate becomes effective. The Commission has the authority, during that 30-day period, to suspend the proposed tariff for a maximum of seven months in order to investigate the lawfulness of the new rates. At the end of the seven-month suspension period, the proposed rate becomes effective, unless the ICC has, prior to the deadline, completed the investigation and found that the rate is unlawful. The proceeding at issue here, was a "general revenue proceeding." The railroads, while not seeking specific authority for an increase in the rate applicable to any particular commodity or group of commodities, proposed to increase the average rates charged.

The power to suspend the proposed rates pending investigation—the regulatory tool at issue here—was added to the Interstate Commerce Act by the Mann-Elkins Act of 1910, 36 Stat. 552. Its purpose was to protect the public from the irreparable harm resulting in unjustified increases in transportation costs by giving the Commission "full opportunity for . . . investigation: before the tariff became effective." It provided a "means . . . for checking at the threshold new adjustments that might subsequently prove to be unreasonable or discriminatory, safeguarding the community against irreparable losses and recognizing more fully that the Commission's essential task is to establish and maintain reasonable charges and proper rate relationships." The Commission's setting of this particular condition precedent to the immediate implementation of the rate increase was directly related to its mandate to assess the reasonableness of the rates and to suspend them pending investigation if there is a question as to their legality. The ICC could have simply suspended the rates originally proposed by the railroads for the full statutory seven-month period. Instead, it pursued a more measured course and offered an alternative tailored far more precisely to the particular circumstances presented. The railroads had made the representation that the increase was justified, at least in part, by the need to take care of deferred maintenance and deferred capital expenditures. If the railroads did, in fact, use the increased revenues for such purposes, the Commission perceived no reason to impose a suspension of the tariff or to undertake a lengthy investigation and consequently, no reason to frustrate the clear congressional intent that "just and reasonable" rates be implemented. Delay through suspension would only have aggravated the already poor condition of some of the railroads. On the other hand, the Commission was cognizant of a history of poor financial planning by the railroads in regard to outlays of this nature. If the revenues derived from the new tariffs, once received, were used for other purposes, an investigation prior to their implementation might indeed be warranted.

In upholding what we find to be a legitimate, reasonable, and direct adjunct to the Commission's explicit statutory power to suspend rates pending investigation, we do not imply that the Commission may involve itself in the financial management of the carriers. The action taken by the Commission here is both conceptually and functionally different from any attempt to require specific managing action, whether it be of a financial or operational nature; it specified no particular projects and it set no priorities. In deciding not to suspend the rates and investigate their lawfulness on the condition that the revenues be used in the broadly defined areas of "delayed capital maintenance," the Commission simply held the railroads to their representation that the increase was justified by needs in these two areas. The railroads were, of course, not required to submit a tariff imposing such a condition on the use of the resulting revenue. They had the option to continue to insist on an unconditional increase, to submit proof of their reasonableness to the Commission, and, if successful, or if the investigation were not completed within the statutory seven-month period, to collect rates based on the new tariffs.

Accordingly, the judgment is reversed, and the case is remanded for further proceedings consistent with this opinion.

Reversed and remanded.

Mr. Justice Powell took no part in the consideration or decision of this case.

Mr. Justice Stevens, with whom Mr. Justice Stewart joins, dissenting:

The question presented is not whether it is desirable for a railroad to spend its money wisely. It clearly is. The question is not whether Congress could authorize the Interstate Commerce Commission to regulate a railroad's expenditure of funds for capital improvements, deferred maintenance, or costs of material. It clearly could. The question is simply whether or to what extent Congress did grant the Commission such authority.

If the power the Commission purports to exercise in the case really exists, it is rather surprising that it has lain dormant for so long and has been disavowed so often. Nowhere in the voluminous statutory language quoted by the Court can I find an authorization to the Commission to impose direct regulatory controls on a railroad's expenditures. Nor is there any precedent for this action in either the Commission's decisions, or in the decisions of this Court. Quite the contrary, the holding in *ICC V. United States ex rel. Los Angeles*, 230 U.S. 52, that the Commission lacked power to compel the railroads to construct a new passenger station, and in *United States v. Pennsylvania R. Co.*, 242 U.S. 203, that the Commission could not order a railroad to furnish tank cars for shipping oil, imply that the Commission possesses no such power.

If the Commission may not impose such regulation directly, it is equally impermissible for it to do so indirectly by attaching conditions to its approval of rate increases.

The description of industry conditions in the petition for the general rate increase was entirely accurate. It did not purport to describe the condition of each railroad in the country. The revenue needs of financially sound railroads, like the Chessie, are vastly different from those of bankrupt and near-bankrupt lines. General rate increase proceedings are not principally concerned with the revenue needs of particular railroads but serve the quite different purpose of determining whether an increase is appropriate on an industrywide or an areawide basis.

The primary concern must be with industrywide or areawide economic conditions, not with the financial condition of particular carriers. Indeed, the petition for a general rate increase in this case did not contain any representations specifically addressed to the financial condition of the Chessie, and the attached schedules contained financial statements of the Chessie of unchallenged accuracy. There was no misdescription of the industry and there was no misdescription of the Chessie.

But even if the petition had misrepresented the prosperous financial condition of the Chessie, the proper remedy would have been to suspend the rate increase as it applied to the Chessie. The reason the Commission did not take this step is that it would have forced competing railroads to lower their rates and hence would have denied them the increased revenues they need to make improvements. Thus, the Commission's position is not that conditional rate increases are necessary to maintain the integrity of the ratemaking process, but rather that they are necessary for either of two very different purposes: to prevent strong railroads from making excess profits at the rates necessary to provide a reasonable return to weak railroads; or to protect weak railroads from competition at the lower rates that would otherwise be imposed on strong railroads.

C. Rule of Rate-Making

The Transportation Act of 1920 first established a rule of rate making to guide the ICC in determining the reasonableness of proposed rates.[71] The 1920 standard was amended by the Transportation Act of 1933, which required the ICC to "give due consideration . . . to the effect of rates on the movement of traffic . . . and to the need of revenues sufficient to enable the carriers . . . to provide service." The 1933 standard also required the ICC to consider the need for rail transportation "at the lowest cost." When motor carriers came under regulation in 1935, another rule of rate making was enacted requiring the ICC, in determining just and reasonable motor carrier rates, to "give due consideration . . . to the inherent advantages of transportation by such carriers." The "inherent advantages" language provided one foundation for an ICC practice known as umbrella rate making, or setting the rate of one transportation mode to protect the traffic of another. If, for example, a commodity could move either by barge or by rail, and the railroad sought to lower its rates to compete with the unregulated barge rate, the ICC often held the rail rate higher than the lower-cost barge rate because lower costs were thought to be an inherent advantage of water movements. Thus, a rate-making standard originally intended to assure railroads a fair rate of return became the basis for protecting motor carriers, and later water carriers, from rail competition.

Since the enactment of the National Transportation Policy in 1940, it has been the task of the ICC to try to reconcile these apparently inconsistent goals. Congress, in the 1940 Act, attempted to outlaw umbrella rate making by requiring the ICC to limit its consideration of the effect of a proposed rate to the "carrier or carriers for which the rates are applied."

In the Transportation Act of 1958, the Congress, once again, amended the rule of rate making to address these issues, this time requiring that "rates of a carrier shall not be held up to a particular level to protect the traffic of any other mode . . . giving due consideration to the objectives of the national transportation policy." The relationships among minimum rate regulation, "inherent advantage" and rate of return, however, were never satisfactorily resolved.

With each progressive iteration of the rule of rate making, the role of revenue adequacy was further diminished. The concept of fair return on fair value, embodied in the original rule, disappeared entirely. No clear direction was ever provided to the ICC regarding the use of its rate-making authority to reconcile the needs of railroads to earn revenues adequate to sustain a fair rate of return with the concepts of inherent advantage, intermodal competition and low rates for shippers.

The 4R Act attempted to provide that direction. The 4R Act established an entirely new rule of rate making for railroads, refocusing the ICC's concerns on the question of adequate revenues. Section 205 of the 4R Act reads:

Commission . . . shall develop and promulgate . . . reasonable standards and procedures for the establishment of revenue levels adequate under honest, economical, and efficient management to cover total operating expenses, including depreciation and obsolescence, plus a fair, reasonable, and economic profit or return (or both) on capital. . . . Such revenue should (a) provide a flow of net income plus depreciation adequate to support prudent capital outlays, assure the repayment of a reasonable level of debt, permit the raising of needed equity capital, and cover the effects of inflation and (b) insure retention and attraction of capital.

In implementing this provision, the ICC announced that it would conduct, on a yearly basis, a proceeding designed to elicit the revenue needs of specific roads and the industry in general. The ICC also announced that "if the level of railroad revenue is inadequate, every means consistent with a just and reasonable rate structure should be used to help rectify this condition."

The ICC then took an important step toward assuring that rail revenue need will be considered in specific as well as general rate increase proceedings. It announced a new policy relating minimum and maximum rate regulation, costing and revenue adequacy.

D. Differential Pricing

SAN ANTONIO v. UNITED STATES

631 F.2d 831 (D.C. Cir. 1980)

Wilkey, Circuit Judge

This matter initially was brought before the Commission by complaint of San Antonio, requesting the Commission to prescribe a maximum just and reasonable rate for the movement of coal from Cordero Junction, Wyoming to San Antonio, Texas. . . . [72]

San Antonio, acting through its City Public Service Board, owns and operates an electric utility, which before 1972 used natural gas as a primary fuel. In that year, with the sudden, dramatic increase in the cost of natural gas, San Antonio began exploring the possibility of using coal to generate electricity. On 22 May 1974, San Antonio entered into long-term contracts to purchase coal from two suppliers in Campbell County, Wyoming, and at about the same time began construction of two coal-fired generating units. Previously, on 11 March 1974 Burlington Northern, Inc. (BN or Burlington Northern) and Southern Pacific Transportation Company (SP or Southern Pacific) had provided San Antonio with a copy of a proposed tariff setting forth a rate of $7.90 per ton for the transportation of coal by unit-train from the mines in Campbell County, Wyoming to San Antonio, but on 2 May 1974 the carriers revised their quotation to $11.90 per ton as a result of unprecedented cost increases. Approximately one year later, San Antonio, being dissatisfied with the rate proposed by the railroads, filed a complaint with the Commission seeking prescription of a just and reasonable rate.

The Commission, in a decision served 14 October 1976 (San Antonio I), established a rate of $10.98 per ton for the San Antonio movement, basing its determination primarily on evidence of rate levels for unit-train movements similar to the San Antonio service and on estimates of the fully allocated costs of service. The Commission stated that its decision was a temporary response to permit the coal movement to begin, and it invited petitions for modification of the rate when actual experience in operating the trains was gained. On petition to review the Commission's decision and order prescribing the San Antonio rate, the United States Court of Appeals for the Eighth Circuit, affirmed.

After six months of operation, the railroads petitioned the Commission in June 1977 for a modification of the rate, and in October 1977 the ICC reopened the San Antonio proceeding. One year later, on 25 October 1978 the Commission issued a decision (San Antonio II) that prescribed a rate of $16.12 per ton for the San Antonio movement. The rate was based on a computation of the full costs of the San Antonio service calculated at $12.65 per ton, and adjusted to include a 10.2% rate of return on the carriers' investment as a "revenue need" factor. Consideration of the latter criterion was intended to reflect adherence to the Railroad Revitalization and Regulatory Reform Act of 1976 (4R Act), which directs the Commission to aid the railroads in obtaining revenue levels adequate to cover total operating expenses plus a fair return on capital for the purpose of restoring the financial stability of the railway system.

Both San Antonio and the carriers petitioned the Commission for reconsideration of its decision in San Antonio II, and on one decision (San Antonio III) which established a rate of $17.23 per ton for the San Antonio movement. The increased rate reflected certain modifications in the Commission's calculation of the costs of the service as well as the use of 10.6% rate of return on capital instead of the 10.2% figure employed in San Antonio II. In addition, the Commission determined that for the railroads to achieve adequate revenue levels in accord with the 4-R Act, the carriers must be permitted to set rates exceeding full costs on some services to compensate for the fact that competition forces the carriers to set rates on other services below full costs. The Commission stated that no "simple formula" existed for ascertaining "the extent to which some shippers should subsidize others in the interest of producing a financially viable rail system." Nevertheless, that agency concluded that a rate set at 7% above full costs for the San Antonio movement (including the cost of capital figure) was reasonable as an interim solution, pending the development of more specific guidelines in another proceeding involving Western coal rates.

The several parties to this case raise two main challenges to the Commission's orders in San Antonio II and III: The carriers and San Antonio dispute several of the Commission's determinations concerning the costs of providing service for the San Antonio movement. All of the parties attack, on various grounds, the Commission's imposition in San Antonio III of a 7% additive above fully allocated costs. We find that certain of the Commission's cost calculations have no basis in the record and that the selection of the figure seven as a percentage additive above full costs is wholly without supporting rationale or justification. We accordingly set the Commission's orders aside and remand on these and other issues to be discussed.

Courts traditionally have applied a differential standard in reviewing rate determinations by an agency. Bearing in mind that the determination of the reasonableness of rates primarily is the province of the agency charged with that duty, we nonetheless have an obligation to ascertain whether the Commission's decision comports with applicable law, whether there is evidence in the record to support the Commission's findings, and whether the agency's rationale is both discernible and defensible.

Ordinarily one of the measures that the ICC uses in prescribing rates is evidence of rates from other, comparable movements, and the Commission accordingly considered this factor in its decision in San Antonio I. In establishing the maximum reasonable rate in San Antonio II and III, however, the Commission relied instead on its computations of the carriers' cost of service and the perceived revenue needs of the railroads.

Courts properly are reluctant to interfere with an agency's choice of methodology in ratemaking matters. Our review is directed to assuring only that the standards applied are reasonable. In this instance the ICC elected to rely on the costs of the service rather than evidence of rates on other movements in calculating the rate for the San Antonio traffic. The Commission's approach, provided the underlying cost calculations are substantiated in the record, is a reasonable means of arriving at a determination of the maximum reasonable rate to be prescribed. We thus find no abuse of discretion.

Section 205 of the Railroad Revitalization and Regulatory Reform Act of 1976 (4R Act) instructs the Commission to make a "continuing effort" to "assist (rail) carriers to attaining revenue levels" that are "adequate, under honest, economical, and efficient management, to cover total operating expenses . . . plus a reasonable and economic profit or return (or both) on capital employed in the business." Such revenue levels should "provide a flow of net income plus depreciation adequate to support prudent capital outlays, assure the repayment of a reasonable level of debt, permit the raising of needed equity capital, . . . cover the effects of inflation," and should ensure retention and attraction of capital "in amounts adequate to provide a sound transportation system in the United States."

To assist the carriers in attaining adequate revenue levels in accord with the mandate of the 4R Act, the Commission in San Antonio III also determined that a 7% increment above fully allocated costs (including the 10.6% rate of return on capital) was necessary. This conclusion was based on the theory of differential pricing, which postulates that rates on some services must be set at levels higher than full costs to compensate for those services on which the railroads are required to price below full costs to remain competitive.

The Commission cautioned that in the application of this theory the railroads should not be permitted to recover their entire shortfall by extracting monopoly profits from captive shippers. Stating that no "simple formula" existed for judging the extent to which some shippers should subsidize others in the interest of producing a "financially viable rail system," the Commission asserted that before it would impose a "substantial burden on some shippers," the railroads would be required to submit data on the following:

> (1) specific identification of the traffic that must be subsidized by other traffic and the reason why rates cannot be increased on that traffic; (2) the extent to which the railroads provide service on unprofitable branch lines and the reason(s) why such service cannot be made profitable or abandoned; (3) identification of commodities other than coal which could also make substantial contributions to the railroads' system revenue needs; and (4) identification and quantification of excess capacity on a carrier's system.

Until the railroads could demonstrate that they were unable to increase revenues on competitive traffic, the Commission further asserted, it would "be reluctant to approve or prescribe rates which are significantly higher than fully allocated costs(s)."

Apparently concluding that the contemplated additive did not fall within the latter category, the Commission, without benefit of the data identified above, set the San Antonio rate at seven percent above fully allocated costs. Admitting that this choice depended on no more than a "policy judgment," the Commission nonetheless asserted that its approach in the San Antonio proceeding was a reasonable measure pending the conclusion of Ex Parte No. 347, Western Coal Investigation—Guidelines for Railroad Rate Structure, which presumably would lead to the adoption of more precise guidelines. Two Commissioners dissented to what one termed the adoption of a "seven percent solution" for various reasons. Briefly, San Antonio and the State of Texas attack the Commission's whole theory of differential pricing, contending that the ICC may not require a particular movement to subsidize other traffic. Expanding on this notion, Texas also asserts that the Commission's determination to require the San Antonio service to subsidize other traffic violates section 10741 of the Interstate Commerce Act, which prescribes unreasonable discrimination against particular regions or types of traffic. For their part the carriers complain that the prescribed rate is lower than rates approved by the Commission on comparable services prior to the passage of the 4R Act. With the enactment of that Act, the carriers assert, Congress intended the railroads to have greater, rather than less, flexibility in setting rates to permit a revitalization of the railway system, and the imposition of a seven percent "ceiling" above full costs thereby frustrates congressional intent. The Department of Justice complains that the Commission's decision fails to indicate how the adoption of a seven percent additive comports with both the national policy favoring conversion to coal as a fuel source and with the Commission's own reservation concerning the extent to which captive shippers should subsidize other traffic.

Uniting these various arguments is the common objection that the Commission's decision is arbitrary and capricious in that it provides no defensible rationale for the inclusion of the seven percent increment. We base our conclusion to set aside the Commission's action on precisely this ground.

Differential pricing is "pertinent to the objective (set forth in the 4R Act) of providing an adequate overall level of earnings." Even though differential pricing thus may be a legitimate criterion for the ICC to consider in the San Antonio ratemaking proceeding, the Commission still must provide adequate justification for its choice of a particular increment above fully allocated costs. In San Antonio III, however, the ICC did no more than make the general assertion that it could not find that the railroads had achieved revenue adequacy. There is nothing in the record in the way of findings, evidence, or rationale to support the seven percent solution or any percentage solution. The Commission's general allusion to the need to consider the revenue requirements of the carriers and the economics of differential pricing is so broad as to be meaningless as a standard—this rationale could be put forth just as readily in attempt to justify 1%, 21%, 45% or even a 99% additive. The Commission here defends its action on the ground that adoption of the appropriate additive involves a policy judgment that is not susceptible to precise quantification. Concededly, the problem is a difficult one, but that does not excuse the Commission from articulating "fully and carefully the methods by which, and the purposes for which, it has chosen to act."

In San Antonio III, the Commission listed four criteria that it stated would be used to assess the extent to which particular movements should be required to subsidize other services, but the ICC then completely ignored this standard in its indiscriminate selection of the seven percent additive. Apparently, the Commission assumed that because its solution assertedly was a temporary one, it was relieved from its responsibility to follow any standard whatsoever.

Finally, the 4R Act evinces a congressional policy to "balance the needs of carriers, shippers, and the public." Neither the interest of electric consumers in lower rates nor that of the public in coal conversion dictates that the railroads must receive compensation for their services inadequate to maintain financial soundness"; still, the Commission's decision must reflect adequate consideration of all pertinent interests. As should be obvious from our discussion, the Commission has not met this obligation. From the carriers' standpoint, the ICC made no effort to determine whether the revenues that would be produced by a seven percent additive would be adequate. From the shipper's and ultimately the consumer's standpoint, the Commission professed concern that the railroads should not "make up their entire shortfall by extracting monopoly profits from captive shippers," but then failed to explain how its choice of a seven percent additive was consistent with that concern. It is undisputed that San Antonio falls into the category of a "captive shipper": it is locked into long-term contracts for the shipment of coal with no alternative means at present of transporting this coal. And with respect to the public interest in coal conversion, although the Commission in San Antonio II discussed the effect on national energy policy of including a return on equity capital as a revenue need factor, in San Antonio III it neglected to discuss what effect the imposition of an additional seven percent subsidy would have. On remand, then, the Commission is directed to explain more fully its reasons for selecting a particular increment, if any, above fully allocated costs, making sure that its decision is based on a thorough analysis of the relevant interests.

NOTE: Ramsey Pricing

A rate scheme similar to that of differential pricing (a notion approved in the *San Antonio* decision) is Ramsey pricing. Rail carriers have suggested that the ICC adopt the principles developed by British economist Frank Ramsey in assessing whether rail rates are just and reasonable. Under Ramsey pricing, shippers are charged a rate that encompasses the variable cost of providing the service plus a share of fixed costs inversely proportional to the shipper's elasticity of demand for service. Hence, a shipper of coal which enjoyed the alternatives of either coal slurry pipelines or barge transportation in addition to rail service would receive a lower rail rate than would a similarly situated shipper without such transportation alternatives.

The ICC has estimated that 78 percent of rail costs are "variable" and 22 percent are "fixed." It is argued that Ramsey pricing will benefit all shippers because price-elastic shippers will bear some of the fixed costs, which in turn will reduce the fixed cost burden for price-inelastic shippers and, theoretically, result in lower rail rates for the latter.

E. Intrastate Rate Regulation

A Department of Transportation report summarized the history of intrastate rate regulation as follows:

The Transportation Act of 1920 first gave the ICC authority to raise intrastate rates that were so low as to constitute a burden on interstate commerce. The Supreme Court ruled in 1958 that an intrastate rate could not be raised by ICC simply because by itself it was not compensatory. Rather, the entire structure of intrastate rates had to be shown to be inadequate before the ICC could adjust any one rate. The Transportation Act of 1958 reversed that decision. The Act directed the ICC not to consider the totality of intrastate operations in evaluating individual intrastate rates. Further, it permitted the ICC to institute an investigation of an intrastate rate whether or not the rate was considered by a State authority.

The 4R Act modifies the authority of the ICC to adjust intrastate rates in two respects. First, the 4R Act requires a railroad company to file a request for a rate increase with the appropriate State agency, and the agency is given 120 days to decide the matter before it could be considered by the ICC. Second, the ICC is, after that time, empowered to raise an intrastate rate to the level charged on similar traffic moving in interstate or foreign commerce. This section assures that if a railroad company cannot raise intrastate rates to interstate levels through the appropriate State agency, the ICC will be able to make the adjustment without undue delay.[73]

Under the Staggers Rail Act of 1980, a state may exercise jurisdiction over intrastate rail transportation[74] only if it submits the standards and procedures it employs in exercising such jurisdiction to the ICC[75] and the ICC certifies such standards and procedures as being consistent with those employed by the ICC.[76] Such certification shall last for five years.[77] In adding this provision to the Staggers Act, it was the intent of Congress "to ensure that the price and service flexibility and revenue adequacy goals of the Act are not undermined by state regulation of rates, practices, etc., which are not in accordance with these goals."[78]

The Bus Regulatory Reform Act of 1982 provides that intrastate passenger fares of interstate carriers may not be restricted by state law or regulation. In addition, the ICC is given jurisdiction to determine that an intrastate rate for service over an interstate route is predatory and to prescribe the applicable rate.

Under the new legislation, an intrastate rate is presumed to constitute an undue burden on interstate commerce if it (a) reflects a general increase less than the most recent general increase on interstate rate, or (b) is lower than the comparable interstate rate, or (c) fails to produce revenues exceeding the variable costs of providing the service. States must act within 120 days on the intrastate rate proposals of interstate carriers. Increase proposals which are denied by states may be appealed directly to the ICC, which has 60 days to act.

The Airline Deregulation Act of 1978 preempted all state jurisdiction over air carrier economic regulation and vested such authority in the Civil Aeronautics Board. Hence, the states may no longer exercise jurisdiction over air passenger transportation.

III. PIPELINES

A. ICC Regulation of Pipelines

1. Introduction

ICC regulation of pipelines in the early days was essentially casual.[79] The ICC was willing to consult with pipeline companies about their problems and to seek their help in devising reporting practices. There were few complaints or "ex parte" investigations before the Commission. This was understandable; the ICC's expertise was in railroad operations. No one appeared before the ICC to urge it to be heavy-handed with the pipeline carriers, and regulation was, at first, largely a formality.

Once it has been determined that a pipeline is a common carrier operating in interstate commerce, the question arises whether the rates and charges of pipeline operators are lawful. Prior to the creation of the Federal Energy Regulatory Commission, the ICC was empowered to establish a valuation and classification of pipeline property. From this base, rates allowing a return from 8 to 10 percent were upheld. Problems arose under the Elkins Act, which forbids rebates, when a pipeline subsidiary has been paying high dividends to its parent company. Is it in effect giving a rebate to its shipper-stockholder? A consent decree reached in 1941 allowed shipper-owners to receive up to an annual 7 percent return on a carrier's ICC valuation without being considered to violate the decree. This consent decree was upheld by the Supreme Court largely because the language had been interpreted to allow a dividend on the entire valuation of the property and had been adhered to by all the parties, including the Justice Department officials who drew up and administered the decree.

Like rail and truck tariffs, the charges filed are binding on carrier and shipper as a matter of law and cannot be varied or waived by either party. Any change, then, was made by application to the ICC.

In its endeavor to carry out the conflicting mandates of the National Transportation Policy, the Commission allowed railroads to reduce their rates to meet pipeline competition, or the threat of such competition. Of course, if a railroad lowered rates to head off a pipeline proposal, that may well jeopardize the revenues of competing tank truck operators. In some cases, railroad companies protested what they believed to be unreasonably low rates by pipelines. The railroads headed off some pipeline threats, but the tank car has not been the instrument of their salvation. Rather, the Southern Pacific, Burlington Northern and other railroads have gone into the pipeline business for themselves, routing the pipe alongside their rights-of-way.

"Pooling" of traffic, service and earnings had been banned to carriers since the Transportation Act of 1920. The ICC determined, however, that such pooling does not refer to joint-venture pipelines and undivided-interest pipe-line systems. Joint ventures are usually large-diameter lines owned by sev-eral oil companies and treated as if they were multiple individual lines, each completely under the control of its owners.

2. Scope of Jurisdiction over Oil Pipeline Rates

TRANS ALASKA PIPELINE RATE CASES
436 U.S. 632 (1977)

Mr. Justice Brennan delivered the opinion of the Court.

The primary question presented is whether the Interstate Commerce Commission in these cases is authorized by § 10708 "to suspend initial tariff schedules of an interstate carrier."[80] In addition, we are asked to decide whether, if the Commission is so authorized, it has additional authority summarily to fix maximum interim tariff rates which will be allowed to go into effect during the suspension period and to require carriers filing tariffs containing such rates, as a further condition of nonsuspension, to refund any amounts collected which are ultimately found to be unlawful. We hold that the Commission has statutory authority to suspend initial tariff schedules and that it has power ancillary to that authority to establish maximum interim rates and associated regulation—including refund provision—as it has done in these cases.

In 1968, massive reservoirs of oil were discovered at Prudhoe Bay in the Alaskan arctic. Two years later plans crystallized to build a pipeline from Prudhoe Bay to the all-weather port of Valdez on Alaska's Pacific coast. After protracted environmental litigation was ended by special Act of Congress, construction of the Trans Alaska Pipeline System (TAPS) began in 1974. In May and June 1977, seven of the eight owners of TAPS, anticipating completion of TAPS in mid-1977, filed tariffs with the Interstate Commerce Commission setting out the rules and rates governing transportation of oil over TAPS. These rates were met immediately by formal protests from the State of Alaska, the Arctic Slope Regional Corporation, the United States Department of Justice, and the Commission's Bureau of Investigation and Enforcement.

Acting pursuant to § 10708 of the Interstate Commerce Act, the Commission found that the protests lodged against the TAPS tariffs gave it "reason to believe the proposed rates are not just and reasonable." Trans Alaska Pipeline System, 355 I.C.C. 80, 81 (1977) (TAPS). In support of this conclusion, it cited the protestants' arguments that the filed rates allowed excessive returns on capital and that the cost data provided by the carriers were overstated. Dismissing the TAPS carriers' argument that § 10708 gave the Commission no power to suspend initial rates, the Commission suspended the TAPS rates for the full seven months allowed by law, citing protestants' showing of "probable unlawfulness," and the Commission's concern that "maintenance of excessively high rates could act as a deterrent or an obstacle to the use of the pipeline by nonaffiliated oil producers and would also delay the Alaskan interests in obtaining revenues that depend upon the well-head price of the oil."

On the other hand, the Commission found that it would not be in the public interest if TAPS had to close for a seven-month period. Accordingly, "accepting the basic data supplied by the carriers" as true, the Commission applied what it stated to be its traditional rate-of-return calculation to compute new rates that approximated what full investigation would likely reveal to be lawful rates and it stated that it would not suspend interim tariffs which specified rates no higher than those estimated. However, since the estimated rates might still "exceed reasonable levels," the Commission stated that any interim tariffs must provide for refunds of any amounts later determined to be in excess of lawful rates.

By the Act of September 18, 1940, Ch. 722, Tit. I, S 1, 54 Stat. 899, 49 U.S.C. § 10101, Congress declared the National Transportation Policy, the United States to be "to encourage the establishment and maintenance of reasonable charges for transportation services." Under the Act as passed in 1887, however, the role of the Commission in establishing "reasonable charges" was circumscribed. Although the Act provided that "all charges made for any service rendered or to be rendered in the transportation of passengers or property . . . shall be reasonable and just; and every unjust and unreasonable charge for such service is prohibited and declared to be unlawful," this Court early held that the Commission had no authority to set charges, but could only determine if charges set by the carriers were unreasonable or unjust in the context of granting reparations to injured shippers.

In 1906, Congress passed the Hepburn Act, 34 Stat. 584, which augmented the Commission's authority to condemn existing rates as unjust or unreasonable by adding express authority to set maximum rates to be observed by carriers in the future. Under the Hepburn Act, however, the Commission could not issue an order affecting a rate until it had become effective. This feature of the Hepburn Act was immediately recognized by the Commission as a major defect. It meant that the only relief against unreasonable rates lay in the reparations remedy and this could not provide a satisfactory solution.

The Commission's Annual Reports also tell us that, as early as 1907, private litigants were able to convince some federal courts to enjoin rate advances after their effective dates but before the Commission was able to complete an investigation as required by the Hepburn Act. Thus, not only did the Hepburn Act fail to protect the public against unreasonable carrier charges, but the equity litigation spawned by the Act led to discrimination in rates—much like that prohibited by the Act—in the situation in which shippers successful in court would be paying one charge while those who were unsuccessful, or who did not have the wherewithal to go to court or to post an injunction bond, were paying higher charges.

To "provide a 'means . . . for checking at the threshold new adjustments that might subsequently prove to be unreasonable or discriminatory, safeguarding the community against irreparable losses and recognizing fully that the Commission's essential task is to establish and maintain reasonable charges and proper rate relationships,' " Congress passed the Mann-Elkins Act of 1910. Section 12 of that Act amended the Interstate Commerce Act to allow the Commission to suspend "any schedule stating a new individual or joint rate, fare, or charge" for a period not to exceed 10 months. The suspension power conferred was intended to be a "particularly potent tool," giving the Commission "tremendous power."

With this background in mind, we turn to the question whether the Commission is authorized by § 10708 to suspend the initial rates of a pipeline.

Section 10708 states that "whenever there shall be filed . . . any schedule stating a *new* individual or joint rate, fare, or charge, . . . the Commission . . . may from time to time suspend the operations of such schedule" (Emphasis added). It is hard to imagine rates any more "new" than those filed for TAPS, a service which has never before been offered. And, since § 10708 applies to any new rate, there is little room to argue that Congress meant the suspension power not to apply to these cases. . . .

Petitioners' claim that the Commission is without authority to suspend initial rates is not limited to situations in which proposed initial rates are in some sense reasonable; it is a claim that a carrier can impose any rate it chooses. Nor have petitioners pointed to any mechanism which would tend to make initial rates reasonable, and Congress in 1910 concluded that the reparations provisions of the Commerce Act are an insufficient check. Moreover, in these cases, the reparations remedy is particularly ineffective since those who will ship oil over TAPS are almost exclusively parents or cosubsidiaries of TAPS owners. Thus, to an indeterminate, but possibly large extent, excess transportation charges to shipper will be offset by excess profits to TAPS owners, creating a wash transaction from the standpoint of parent oil companies. Indeed, it is telling that no shipper of oil protested the TAPS rates. Instead, as one might predict from experience under the Hepburn Act, only the public perceives that it will be injured by the proposed TAPS rates and has objected to them. . . .

Therefore, in the absence of suspension authority, unreasonable initial rates—like unreasonable increases in existing rates, will almost certainly be passed along to "a prior producer or . . . to the ultimate consumer."

Second, if the Commission has no authority to suspend initial rates, it follows that Congress cannot have meant to foreclose whatever equity power there is in the courts to enjoin carrier rates. Thus, with respect to initial rates, courts might again reach "diverse conclusions," jeopardizing "the regulatory goal of uniformity," and "causing in turn 'discrimination and hardship to the general public.' "

Accordingly, far from reaching an " 'absurd resul[t]' " which would " 'thwart the obvious purpose of the statute,' " a literal reading of the word "new" in § 10708 is necessary to curb mischief flowing from unchecked initial rates, which is in every way identical to that flowing from unchecked changes in rates to which the Mann-Elkins Act is concededly addressed.

The reason the Commission has been given power to suspend is to prevent irreparable harm to the public during the time when it has under consideration the lawfulness of a proposed rate. . . . The foundation for a suspension is the Commission's conclusion that a proposed rate is probably unreasonable or unjust. To make such a determination, the Commission is required by § 10708 to set out its reasons in writing for suspending a tariff. The usual and sufficient reason will be that the Commission has found a proposed tariff to fall on the unjust or unreasonable side of the line it has drawn, and it is a reason of precisely this sort that the Commission has given here.

Petitioners do not apparently disagree that the Commission can suspend a tariff because it falls on the wrong side of the line of reasonableness, but they would prevent the Commission in suspending a tariff from stating, as it did here, where the tentative dividing line lies. Such a statement, they say, is ratemaking. But this is untenable: No principle of law requires the Commission to engage in a pointless charade in which carriers desiring to exercise their § 10761 rights are required to submit and resubmit tariffs until one finally goes below an undisclosed maximum point of reasonableness and is allowed to take effect. The administrative process, after all, is not modeled on "The Price Is Right." What the Commission did here, therefore, far from being condemnable, is an intelligent and practical exercise of its suspension power which is thoroughly in accord with Congress' goal, to strike a fair balance between the needs of the public and the needs of regulated carriers. Indeed, the Commission might well have been derelict in its duty had it insisted on charade [sic] once it had determined that there was a way TAPS could operate without harm to the public.

Finally, petitioners contend that the Commission has no power to subject them to an obligation to account for and refund amounts collected under the interim rates in effect during the suspension period and the initial rates which would become effective at the end of such period. They point to the absence of any express authority for such refund provisions and also to the fact that § 10708 does provide expressly for refunds in a limited category of circumstances, namely, where there is an "increased rate or charge for or in respect to the transportation of property," which has become effective at the end of a suspension period. This statutory pattern, they suggested, indicates that Congress considered and rejected any broader refund scheme, thereby curtailing any ancillary power to order refund provisions that the Commission might otherwise have.

In response, we note first that we have already recognized in *Chessie* that the Commission does have powers "ancillary" to its suspension power which do not depend on an express statutory grant of authority. We had no occasion in *Chessie* to consider what the full range of such powers might be, but we did indicate that the touchstone of ancillary power was a "direct relationship" between the power asserted and the Commission's "mandate to assess the reasonableness of . . . rates and to suspend them pending investigation if there is a question as to their legality." 426 U.S. at 514. Applying this test, we found in *Chessie* a direct relationship which justified the Commission in insisting that the proceeds of proposed general railroad rate increases be used to pay for deferred maintenance. If such a use was made of the proceeds, the rates were reasonable; but they might not be reasonable if put to other purposes. We also noted that "delay through suspension would only have aggravated the already poor condition of some of the railroads." Thus, we approved the deferred maintenance condition essentially because it was necessary to strike a proper balance between the interests of the carriers and the interests of the public.

The situation here is very similar. Even a cursory glance at the pleadings before the Commission show that extended adjudicatory proceedings will be required to resolve the question of precisely what are fair rates. Accordingly, it is not apparent how the Commission could discharge its mandate under § 10708 summarily "to assess the reasonableness of (TAPS) rates," while considering the interest of the TAPS carriers in beginning operations, unless it could make gross approximations of the sort it made in this proceeding, in which it essentially accepted carrier-supplied data as true and properly included in the TAPS rate base notwithstanding protests to the contrary. But if such approximations are to be used to meet the needs of the carriers, it is plain that refund provisions are a necessary and "directly related," means of discharging the Commission's other mandate to protect the public pending a more complete determination of the reasonableness of the TAPS rates.

Thus, here as in *Chessie*, the Commission's refund conditions are a "legitimate, reasonable, and direct adjunct to the Commission's explicit statutory power to suspend rates pending investigation," in that they allow the Commission, in exercising its suspension power, to pursue "a more measured course" and to "offer an alternative tailored far more precisely to the particular circumstances" of these cases. Since, again as in *Chessie*, the measured course adopted here is necessary to strike a proper balance between the interests of carriers and the public, we think the Interstate Commerce Act should be construed to confer on the Commission the authority to enter on this course unless language in the Act plainly requires a contrary result.

For the reasons stated above, the judgment below is in all respects

Affirmed.

Mr. Justice Powell took no part in the consideration or decision of these cases.

B. Pipeline Rates

Jurisdiction over oil pipeline rates was transferred from the ICC to the Federal Energy Regulatory Commission (FERC) in 1977. At the same time, jurisdiction over natural gas pipeline rates was transferred from the former Federal Power Commission (FPC) to FERC.

Natural gas is regulated by the provisions of Section 4 of the Natural Gas

Act, which requires that "all rates and charges made, demanded, or received by any natural gas company for or in connection with the transportation or sale of natural gas subject to the jurisdiction of the Commission . . . shall be just and reasonable" and must be the "lowest reasonable rates."[81] A natural gas company may not grant any undue preference or advantage or maintain any unreasonable difference in rates or services. The FPC historically viewed the transportation and sale of natural gas as a unified transaction and was concerned with final rates rather than separate charges for transportation.

By contrast, the ICC's jurisdiction over pipelines was limited to charges for transportation. The pipelines were subject to the general provisions of the Interstate Commerce Act, including the prohibition on charging a greater rate for a short haul than a long haul and prohibitions against subjecting any shipper, locality or territory to undue or unreasonable prejudice or advantage. ICC jurisdiction over pipelines was marked by a great deal of cooperation between oil companies and the Commission in maintaining the regulatory scheme. ICC regulation of pipelines differed from its regulation of other carriers principally in its lack of jurisdiction over entry, exit or mergers. FERC has succeeded to this plenary rate jurisdiction, including suspension and investigation powers.

Recent efforts by FERC to update rate-making methodology for oil pipelines have met severe judicial criticism. See Farmers Union Exchange, Inc. v. FERC, 734 F.2d 1486 (D.C. Cir. 1984).

IV. RATES OF AIR CARRIERS

A. Regulation of Passenger Carriers

The most expensive cargo a passenger airline can fly is an empty seat.[82] Once the plane takes off, the opportunity to sell more tickets is lost forever. Hence, unsold space becomes something of an instantly perishable commodity. Filling those empty seats before takeoff has been a constant challenge to airline rate makers. The airline market is two-tiered. At one level are expense account travelers, who are not very price-sensitive. On the other level are discretionary travelers, who might drive, take a train or bus, leave their families home or decide not to go. Like most transportation companies, prior to 1983 airlines were bound by public tariffs and could not fully exploit this differential elasticity of demand by offering special deals to attract the marginal travelers. Airline fares were required to be just and reasonable, nondiscriminatory and nonpreferential. They were set at a level which allowed for a coverage of costs plus a reasonable return on their investments. The philosophy of cost-plus pricing encouraged exaggeration of the rate base, excessive overexpansion and rapid replacement of airplane fleets.

Throughout this period the Civil Aeronautics Board (CAB) failed to recognize the elasticity of demand in passenger transportation. Fares were computed on an administrative basis in which the CAB examined the industrywide cost and revenue figures and then adjusted them for a 55 percent break-even load factor. To this was added a 12 percent return on investment. Because all airlines charged similar fares for the same route, or for the same distance, some airlines were making excessive profits, while the less efficient companies were losing money on the adjusted average rate of return. In addition to general rate levels, the CAB considered the propriety of various discount fares, such as youth fares.

The CAB could regulate the intrastate fares charged by certificated interstate carriers, while the state could regulate fares of intrastate airlines. This pattern of CAB regulation of intrastate airlines prior to the Airline Deregulation Act was sometimes exclusive, sometimes concurrent with state regulation and sometimes absent.

An intrastate exemption from CAB regulation applied to any type of aircraft, provided that no interstate service was offered and no mail was carried. The commuter exemption was limited at first to planes with 22-passenger capacity, then to 30 and finally those seating 56 or fewer passengers or with cargo service of 18,000 pounds or less. These planes, whatever their routes, fell into the general aviation field, along with air taxis and other local carriers. Subsidized helicopter service was another special case. Other specialized services were the "non-skeds," or supplemental carriers, and the all-cargo airlines.

B. Deregulation of Air Freight

With few exceptions, domestic all-cargo services has been unprofitable since 1965, as opposed to the belly-cargo service performed by "combination" (freight and passenger) carriers. As a result, plane operations were down to a minimum, and most air freight was being moved on passenger aircraft, whose schedules were geared to the needs of travelers who desired to travel during the day. Most shippers by air, however, desired overnight service with early-morning arrival at destinations.

Because of the freeze on new-route applications, all-cargo carriers were prevented from adjusting their services to meet the needs of the marketplace. The CAB allowed freight rates to be set by the level of belly cargo—but in the case of the combination carriers, passengers may have already paid the costs of operating the plane, and revenue from freight is gravy to the carriers. In addition, noncertificated carriers, flying exempt lighter aircraft, were unable to get permission to substitute large aircraft for the multiple daily flights of smaller aircraft between a number of cities. The result was higher operating costs and inefficient consumption of energy.

The Ford administration had proposed deregulation of air freight as a prelude to the actual deregulation of the airline industry. It was viewed as an experiment to test the validity of deregulation as a concept. If it worked, it could be extended; if it failed, no great harm would be suffered. Air freight was viewed as a discrete example, without much effect on the rest of the transportation industry.

The air cargo business was dominated by two certificated carriers: Seaboard World Airlines and Flying Tigers. In addition, smaller operators used light planes to carry time-sensitive shipments in overnight service. The largest of these carriers was Federal Express, which used a new distribution system. Each night, Federal's jets would leave cities all over the country and fly to Memphis, Tennessee, where parcels were sorted and then flown to their destinations by morning. Federal guaranteed overnight delivery, and the service flourished.

The major constraint on Federal's system was the capacity of the Learjets. Often two or more planes had to be flown per route each night, necessitating excessive labor and fuel costs. Federal wanted to obtain 727s to handle the larger-volume shipments, but the CAB denied an exemption to Federal. Both Seaboard and Flying Tigers vigorously opposed any Federal application for operating authority from the CAB as an all-cargo carrier. The result was that Federal became one of the great enthusiasts for deregulation of air cargo transportation. The deregulation bill which emerged was popularly known as the "Federal Express Relief Act."

The Air Cargo Deregulation Act of 1977 was signed into law on November 9, 1977, as Public Law 95–163. A Senate amendment to the bill virtually eliminated CAB authority over all-cargo service and sharply reduced the Board's power to control air freight rates.[83]

Section 16 of the Act directs the Board to encourage and develop private enterprise in the all-cargo service system and to allow competitive market forces to determine the extent, variety, quality and price of air cargo services. This section takes from the Board its traditional power to suspend unreasonable rates, leaving the CAB only the power to suspend discriminatory or predatory practices.

A new Section 418 deals with the application, issuance and revocation of certificates for all-cargo air service.[84] Under Section 418, any citizen of the United States who held a valid certificate under Section 401(d)(1) of Title IV[85] and provided all-cargo air service during 1977 could apply for a new Section 418 certificate. Also, any citizen of the United States who operated pursuant to an exemption under Section 416 could apply for a Section 418 certificate immediately.[86] No later than 60 days after the application by Sections 401 and 416 carriers is submitted, the Board must issue a 418 certificate authorizing the all-cargo air service covered by the application. In other words, these cargo carriers were grandfathered into Section 419 all-cargo rights. They had one year of freedom from additional competition. Then the 418 certificate would become available to any applicant.

The year after the enactment of the new Section 418, any U.S. citizen might submit an application to the Board for an all-cargo air service certificate. The Board must issue the certificate to these non-grandfathered carriers no later than 180 days after the application is submitted, unless it finds that the applicant is not "fit, willing, and able" to provide services or comply with any rules and regulations promulgated by the Board.[87] In essence, this section required the Board to grant any all-cargo application when the applicant was able to demonstrate fitness. In ruling on the fitness of applicants, the Board focused on their finances, managerial expertise and safety records. If the Board found the applicant not fit and willing to comply with rules and regulations promulgated by the Board, then formal proceedings were instituted for the purpose of obtaining more evidence on the issue. Of the first 25 applicants under this section, only two were denied Section 418 certificates; both applicants had suffered recent fatal crashes and received Federal Aviation Administration penalties assessed for safety violations.

Section 17 reiterates the encouragement and development of an integrated transportation system relying on competitive market forces to determine the extent, variety, quality and costs in the all-cargo air service industry.[88] This section prohibits the Board from determining the points to be served by the Section 418 certificate holder and the price to be charged for these services. Instead, the carrier itself determines the optimal services it can render in a free enterprise market.

Finally, Section 17 defines all-cargo air service as "the carriage by aircraft of only property as a common carrier for compensation or hire, or mail, or both."[89] The service under this section extends to any state, territory or possession of the United States, including Puerto Rico and the Virgin Islands. Hawaii and Alaska, however, are exempted from the provisions of the deregulation law.[90]

Section 18 deals with complaints to and investigations by the CAB.[91] Fares, charges and practices are unregulated unless the Board finds that such practices are preferential, discriminatory, prejudicial or predatory. The Board is effectively limited in its scope of review because it is no longer empowered to suspend practices within the all-cargo system as being unwarranted, unreasonable or otherwise unlawful.[92] Section 18 also states that if the Board suspends a practice within its scope of power, proceedings covering the suspension must be completed within the period of suspension. The Board must act quickly or not at all.[93]

With the passage of the Air Cargo Deregulation Act, a free market began in the 48 contiguous states. The grandfathered carriers had a one-year head start. The air freight industry now has no restrictions on entry, routes or rates.[94]

The most apparent effect of deregulation of the all-cargo air industry was an increase in shipping costs. The issue of increased costs was further inflamed in March 1979, when the CAB eliminated the formal filing of rates for virtually all shipments hauled by the nation's airlines. In place of the previous rules requiring airline rates, charges and rules to be filed 60 days in advance, the Board turned to a price reporting system. Under this system, prices for the carriage of all domestic air freight shipments would be reported to the Board. The reports, however, would not be submitted in advance, but would be delivered to the Board no later than the date on which carriage at the stated charge would commence.

Under this scheme, neither shippers nor other carriers would have advance notice of upcoming rate changes. The Board felt that the filing of advance notices was anti-competitive and worked against rate reductions. The Board argued that shippers would not suffer from the lack of advance notice. Most shippers disagreed.

The shippers contend that the availability of published rates in a uniform format is essential to air cargo shipments. They claimed that shippers must know their transportation costs with reasonable certainty in advance of shipment so that they may quote prices to customers and prepare invoices reflecting the actual cost of transportation. Without advance publication, the rates and charges could change from day to day and from shipper to shipper.

In addition to rate hikes, deregulation produced other results unfavorable to shippers. Liability limits of the air carriers were reduced. Shippers warned that liability issues do not respond to the marketplace the way rates do and contended that the CAB should maintain control over the liability issue. The CAB instead felt that the increase in competition would affect liability limits in that either shippers would shop around for more favorable liability rules or the free market would encourage the growth of liability insurers. The burden of insuring cargo has passed from carrier to shipper.

Despite shipper protests, the CAB removed itself farther from the liability issue. Effective June 15, 1979, the Board stopped collecting data on freight loss and damage claims. The Board said that the old rule requiring cargo airlines to file semiannual reports was virtually useless.[95]

Again, the shippers disagreed with the Board, complaining that elimination of the reports "would deprive Congress and the public of the means to monitor the effects of deregulation on airline liability rules and practices."[96] The Board was unmoved by this argument. It explained that current regulations require all carriers conducting domestic cargo transportation to disclose, when a shipment is accepted, the limits of cargo liability insurance or the absence of such insurance. This procedure would inform the shipper of the liability coverage available so that a shipper could determine the need for additional insurance. The Board contended that claims data were not designed to analyze airline liability rules and practices, but to monitor the general trend in the number of claims received and paid.

Deregulation in the air freight business led to a sharp increase in rates. This may be because rates were formerly kept artificially low by the CAB, with the level of rates before deregulation based on belly-cargo rates of big combination carriers. Since deregulation, costs of operating aircraft have risen dramatically; the new charges reflect these rates. Possibly air freight is not very price-sensitive because its cargo generally consists of valuable, time-sensitive shipments. Here the cost of shipment is of minor concern to the consignee and has minimal effect on prices.

After several years of deregulation, many new carriers have entered the air freight business. There is no lack of competition. The number of flights and carriers have increased, but so have prices. Federal Express now flies medium-sized jets and is a major freight operator. Seaboard and Flying Tigers merged on October 1, 1980. There has been little slackening in the demand for air freight.

Events since deregulation have shown a weakening of the principle of common-carrier liability for shipments and an abandonment of the fixed tariff principle. The air freight industry is no longer considered an infant needing protection, but the consumer has no protection against high costs of shipment. Nor has the small businessman any right to equal treatment with the large shipper, who is a major consumer of the cargo airline.

NATIONAL SMALL SHIPMENTS TRAFFIC CONFERENCE v. CAB

618 F.2d 819 (1980)

J. SKELLY WRIGHT, Chief Judge:

These consolidated cases are petitions for review of three provisions of the Civil Aeronautics Board's (CAB or Board) comprehensive general regulations governing domestic air cargo transportation. ER–1080, 14 C.F.R. § 291 (1979). The challenged rules exempt domestic air cargo carriers from (1) the duty to file tariffs with the CAB showing the carrier's rates, rules, and practices for cargo transportation, imposed by Section 403(a) of the Federal Aviation Act (the Act). 49 U.S.C. § 1373(a)(1976); (2) the duty to provide air transportation service upon reasonable request—the statutory duty to carry—imposed by Section 404(a)(1) of the Act, 49 U.S.C. § 1374(a)(1) (1976); and (3) the statutory provisions relating to the filling of inter-carrier agreements affecting domestic air transportation. Pub. L. No. 95–504 §§ 28(a) and 30(a). The petitioners contend that the CAB exceeded its authority under the statute in promulgating the challenged regulations, and that the decision to adopt the regulations was arbitrary and capricious.

These cases arise against a background of fundamental changes in Congress's approach to the air transportation industry. For over forty years, under the Federal Aviation Act, the industry was subjected to a system of detailed economic regulation which this court has characterized as "severely anticompetitive." Under Section 401(a) of the Act, no person could engage in air transportation without first obtaining a certificate of public convenience and necessity from the CAB. Once certified, a carrier was obliged "to provide and furnish . . . air transportation, as authorized by its certificate, upon reasonable request therefore." . . . Carriers were required to set forth their rates, rules, and practices in tariffs filed with the CAB and to comply strictly with these tariffs. The Board was authorized to proscribe any existing or proposed rates, rules, and practices that were or would be unjust or unreasonable. Proposed changes in carrier rates had to be filed with the Board at least 30 days before the intended effective date. The Board could suspend these proposed rates for up to six months while it considered whether they were unjust or unreasonable.

Major changes in the approach to the domestic air cargo transportation industry were signaled by the enactment of the cargo deregulation legislative amendments to the Federal Aviation Act. The amendments completely overhauled the provisions of the Act pertaining to air cargo transportation. Congress stated that "encouragement and development of an integrated transportation system relying upon competitive market forces to determine the extent, variety, quality, and price of such services" is in the public interest. A new certification procedure was established, under which virtually any United States citizen could obtain authorization to provide domestic all-cargo transportation, without restrictions as to places served or rates charged. Moreover, the cargo deregulation legislation terminated the Board's authority to find interstate air cargo rates, rules, and practices unjust and unreasonable and to pre-scribe new rates, rules, and practices in their stead. However, the Board may still find rates unlawful after investigation on grounds that they are unjustly discrimi-natory, unduly preferential or prejudicial, or predatory, and the Board has the authority to suspend any such rates while it investigates them. Finally, the amend-ments empowered the Board to exempt carriers operating under the new Section 418 certificates from "section 1371(a) of this title, and any other section of this chapter which the Board by rule determines appropriate."

Pertinent for our purposes was the Board's proposal to exempt air cargo carriers from the tariff and agreement filing requirements and the duty to carry provisions of the Act. The Board pointed out:

> The Congress clearly intended Pub. L. 95-163 to substantially dereg-ulate the domestic air cargo industry. By positive statutory language, Congress completely revoked the core elements of the Board's regulatory powers over domestic air freight: its ability to control entry and exit and its ability to set or control rates by analyzing the relationship between those rates and carrier costs. To complete the task of deregulating air freight, however, Congress delegated to the Board considerable discre-tion. . . . Joint Appendix (JA)1.

The Board noted that the literal language of its exemption authority under the Act covered the proposed rules. It acknowledged that the Conference Report on the cargo deregulation legislation had stated:

> The Managers do not contemplate that the Board will exempt carriers .from the requirement of filing tariffs. Tariffs provide valuable notice of rates to users of air transportation. Tariffs will be necessary for the Board to effectively carry out its duties to determine whether rates for the transportation of property are discriminatory, preferential, prejudicial, or predatory.

H.R. Rep. No. 95-773, 95th Cong., 1st Sess. 14-15 (1977) (Conference Report). The Board reasoned, however, that "tariff filing is inconsistent with the overall scheme of the legislation which was intended to deregulate entry and pricing of air freight."

During the comment period Congress enacted the Airline Deregulation Act of 1978, which substantially revised the entire Federal Aviation Act. In light of the earlier deregulation of the domestic air cargo transportation industry, most of these revisions had little direct impact on air cargo service. However, the Act's sunset provisions will affect cargo transportation since they abolish the Board itself on January 1, 1985. In addition, the Deregulation Act substantially broadened the CAB's Section 416(b) exemption authority. Where previously the Board had been required to find that because of "an undue burden . . . by reason of the limited extent of, or unusual circumstances affecting, the operations of the carrier" enforcing the requirement "is not in the public interest," it could now grant an exemption merely upon finding that it "is consistent with the public interest" to do so. In addition, Sections 412 and 414, 49 U.S.C. §§ 1382 and 1384 (1976), were revised to provide that carriers may file agreements for Board approval, and the Board may, if it approves, relieve the parties to the agreement from antitrust liability upon finding such immunity "required in the public interest."

On November 8, 1978 the Board adopted Regulation ER–1080, Operating Rules for All-Cargo Carriers and Domestic Cargo Transportation by Section 401 and 418 Carriers, which reissued Part 291 of its Economic Regulations titled General Rules for All-Cargo Carriers, 14 C.F.R. Part 291 (1979). Insofar as is pertinent for our purposes, the Board adopted the proposal to exempt carriers from the agreement and tariff filing requirements and the statutory duty to carry.

The Board suggested that eliminating tariff filing would provide "a preliminary test of the Congressionally mandated elimination of tariffs for the passenger transportation industry in 1983" under the 1978 Act.

Finally, with respect to the exemption from the agreement filing requirement, the Board observed that the Deregulation Act of 1978 had broadened its Section 416(b) exemption authority and had "clearly directed the Board to move quickly toward a deregulated, competitive environment." The Board therefore thought it appropriate to preclude the filing of agreements and thereby to terminate the immunity from the antitrust laws which might flow from Board approval of the agreements.

The main challenge to the Board's regulation exempting carriers from the tariff filing requirement of Section 403 is presented by the seven airlines (Air Carriers) who argue that the Board exceeded its statutory authority in granting the exemption, and that the Board's conclusion that granting the exemption is "in the public interest" is not supported by substantial evidence.

We do not agree with the claim that the Board exceeded its statutory authority. Sections 416(b) and 418(c) grant the Board very broad discretion. The latter authorizes the Board to exempt all-cargo carriers from "any . . . section of this chapter which the Board by rule determines appropriate." The former permits the Board to exempt "any person or class of persons" from "the requirements of this title or any provision thereof . . . if it finds that the exemption is consistent with the public interest." Thus, as petitioners concede, the plain language of the statute authorizes the Board's action.

This case does not present an instance in which a literal interpretation of the language of the statute leads to an absurd result or conflicts with the obvious purpose of the Act. The basic purpose of the 1977 and 1978 amendments to the Act was to deregulate the air transportation industry. Authorizing the Board to grant exemptions from any provision of the Act is quite consistent with and indeed could further that goal. Thus, the literal language of the statute should control the disposition of this case.

As a reviewing court, we may not substitute our judgment for the agency's. We must affirm the Board's decisions if they are rational, based on a consideration of all the relevant factors, and adequately explained. Our review persuades us that the Board's decision to exempt carriers from the tariff filing requirement satisfies these tests.

We start by noting that the Air Carriers have not identified any flaws in the Board's reasoning. The Board's suggestion that tariff filing inhibits price competition does not seem irrational. The Senate Report on the 1978 Deregulation Act noted the anticompetitive effects of the advance filing provisions of the section.

Carriers seeking to lower their prices are unable to gain a competitive edge since they must give advance notice of price changes to their competitors. And comments submitted by the shippers, urging the Board to retain tariff filing in order to avoid inter-carrier "price wars," confirm the Board's conclusion. Also, the fact that shippers in the past relied on tariff filings for rate information is relevant but not dispositive. The crucial question is whether shippers will be able to obtain timely and accurate rate information if tariff filing is abolished. The Air Carriers have not shown that there is anything irrational about the Board's entirely reasonable prediction that carriers will not conduct business in a manner that will alienate the customers upon whom they depend for their livelihood.

Furthermore, the experience of the air taxi industry—the only segment of the air cargo transportation industry that has operated without having to file tariffs with the Board—appears to bear out the Board's prediction. Whether or not the air taxis are fully representative of the whole industry, the significant point is that only the air taxis have operated in the type of competitive setting that the exemption is designed to promote. Accordingly, it was appropriate for the Board to look to the experience of the air taxis in its attempt to predict the impact of the proposal on other carriers. Finally, we cannot challenge the Board's determination, based on its past experience in policing carrier rates, that requiring carriers to retain their rate records for one year will provide the documentation that the Board needs for investigations of allegedly discriminatory rates. For the foregoing reasons, we cannot agree with the Air Carriers' claim that the Board's decision to exempt carriers from the tariff filing requirement was arbitrary and capricious.

Because we conclude that the Board had ample authority to issue the challenged regulations and that its decision to do so was not arbitrary and capricious, we reject the petitioners' suggestion that the challenged regulations must be invalidated. Accordingly, the CAB's decision is Affirmed.

C. Deregulation of Air Passenger Fares

The Airline Deregulation Act of 1978 aimed at phasing out all regulation of rates. The Act defined the "standard industry fare level" as that which was in effect on July 1, 1977 for the particular route and service in question.[97] The suspension-free zone of reasonableness extended 5 percent above and 50 percent below this "standard industry fare level."

The Board could not suspend a rate that fell within this zone of reasonableness. If a fare lay outside this zone, it was not rendered automatically unjust or unreasonable. Such findings, however, would allow the Board to suspend or replace the fare with a lawful one if it saw fit.[98] A protestant had the burden of proof in opposing fares that fell outside the zone of reasonableness.[99]

Under the Sunset Provisions of the Airline Deregulation Act, virtually all the CAB's rate-making authority terminated on January 1, 1983. This places air transportation in a similar category as exempt agricultural and barge transportation as a fully deregulated industry. Air carriers can charge all the traffic will bear for freight and passenger rates and the invisible hand of competition will be the only regulator.

On January 1, 1985, all CAB authority over foreign air transportation was transferred to the Department of Transportation in consultation with the State Department. This included issuing certificates to U.S. carriers for foreign transportation, granting permits subject to presidential approval to non-citizen foreign air carriers and rejecting tariffs which appear to the Department to be unjust and unreasonable. The reason for different treatment of overseas air transport from domestic transportation is the fact that subsidies paid by foreign governments to their flag carriers (to encourage tourism to that country) may make it difficult for U.S. carriers to compete effectively on many routes.

The experience of deregulation has been a mixed bag. Many promotional fares have been instituted, but the basic coach fare has risen at a rate far exceeding inflation. Furthermore, the benefits of deregulation are not evenly shared throughout the country. Coast-to-coast rates and fares to Florida and other popular vacation spots offer large bargains, whereas isolated points with little airline competition pay high rates. The old principle of rates based on miles traveled has fallen by the wayside. In the future, antitrust may offer relief but only for predatory pricing by strong carriers.

V. INTERMODAL RATES

A look through the Amtrak timetable shows relatively few bus connections to off-line points.[100] Trains and buses are regarded as competitors and not complements. Even with the massive discontinuance of trains in the fall of 1979, little was done to help their passengers reach their destination by bus from a convenient intermodal terminal.

The demise of the North Coast Hiawatha provides a good example. Travelers could still use the *Empire Builder* to reach Fargo, Spokane and Sand Point but nothing in between. Yet Fargo is one of the few cities where the Amtrak and Greyhound stations are adjacent. Arrangements for through ticketing and handling of baggage could be made between the carriers, and the train traveler from Minneapolis or Chicago could continue west to Bismarck, Butte or Billings on a connecting bus. But Amtrak didn't bother, and the bus company didn't want to short-haul itself, so the connection was never made, and people along the Hiawatha route found traveling more difficult.

In such a climate, it is difficult to realize that intermodalism is the preferred policy of the U.S. government. Carriers by rail, motor and air are required to establish joint and through fares with connecting carriers of their own type but not with other modes. Section 6 of the Interstate Commerce Act originally prohibited railroads from establishing through rates or schedules with bus lines, since motor carriers were not then regulated by the ICC. Today, Amtrak fares are unregulated, but bus companies have been subject to ICC regulation of entry, exit and fares since 1935.

On passage of the Motor Carrier Act of 1935, railroads and bus companies established through routes and through ticketing. Many of the original bus companies which entered into contracts were railroad subsidiaries. Although the railroads have exited this field, as well as their regular passenger business, there are still vestigial remnants—like the Gulf Transport Company, which is owned by Illinois Central Industries, and the Bangor & Aroostook Railroad, whose passenger service is carried on by railroad-owned buses. These bus services were originally established as substitutes for local unprofitable passenger trains or as a supplement for mainline railroad service. Rather than being used to facilitate passenger travel, bus service was used for the purpose of retaining a share of passenger traffic that otherwise would go to independent bus companies. The publication of both through fares and joint fares between rail carriers and competing independent lines was rare.

Section 10703 of the Interstate Commerce Act provides that common carriers of passengers by motor vehicle may establish through routes and joint fares with railroads but does not require them to do so. It is the duty of both parties to establish just and reasonable fares and equitable divisions between the carriers. There is no requirement that the carriers establish through rates with each other or that they institute through ticketing or baggage handling arrangements. There are, however, no provisions which would preclude voluntary arrangements by the carriers.

Section 17 of the Amtrak Improvement Act of 1974 required that the Secretary of Transportation conduct a study and report to the Congress on the potential for integrating Amtrak service with other modes of transportation, such as buses, with special attention to the needs of rural areas. This survey was completed in May of 1976.

Furthermore, subsections 546(j) and (k) of the Rail Passenger Service Act, as amended in 1976, make clear the congressional policy that the establishment of through routes and joint fares between Amtrak, other railroads and bus companies is in the public interest. Carriers are encouraged, but not compelled, to make such arrangements.

The ICC was directed by the 1976 amendments to conduct a study of through routes and joint fares between Amtrak and other intercity passenger carriers. The study was to include historical perspectives, the present situation and recommendations for the future establishment of through routes and joint fares between railroads and motor carriers of passengers. The study was completed on schedule on September 30, 1977. The study contemplated the use of buses as feeders to the Amtrak system. The Transportation Department classified intermodal arrangements into four types:

1. *Dedicated service.* Under this arrangement, the bus segment of the transportation is considered an extension of the rail portion. Scheduling of connecting buses is entirely dependent on the arrival and departure time of trains. The Department believes that this is the most responsive to rail passenger demands but is also the most expensive to provide and would not be profitable in low-density areas. Such dedicated service is used today by Amtrak to reach San Francisco from its terminal in Oakland, California.

2. *Fully integrated service.* This is developed from existing schedules wherever possible. The Department of Transportation believes this to be the most cost-effective means of achieving intermodal integration. Fully integrated service involves establishing a predictable schedule connection between existing bus and rail services, which requires schedule modifications for both and possibly route modifications for bus operators. Such fully integrated service is available at New Orleans, where Amtrak and Greyhound use the same terminal and sell through tickets.

3. *Partial rail and bus integration.* This method can be accomplished at a limited cost and with minor administrative modifications. It may, for example, involve buses picking up at the railroad station. But the Department of Transportation notes that few intercity passengers would be willing to endure the associated time delays. Partial integration is presently used at Harrisburg, Pennsylvania, where Greyhound and Amtrak have used the station for years but are operated as separate entities.

4. *Coincidentally connecting service.* This is, in effect, what we have in most U.S. cities today. It is up to the passenger to obtain the schedule, purchase separate tickets and locate and transfer to the station of the other carrier. Although this is done today by passengers who have no alternative, it is not likely to attract additional intermodal passengers.

Both the ICC and the Department of Transportation have addressed the problem in publication of joint fares. Amtrak does not have to file its tariffs with the Commission and has complete freedom of scheduling and freedom to set fares—a deregulator's dream. By contrast, other rail carriers and buses must have approval of their tariffs by either the ICC or the state regulatory authority. The ICC has authority to approve the joint fare but no authority over the rail portion alone. The bus industry would like to see the Commission recapture its jurisdiction over passenger railroading. The Transportation Department sees no need for a plethora of tariffs and favors instead a through ticketing system that merely combines the existing fares of the separate carriers and does not require separate joint fare tariffs.

The 1977 report of the ICC found that the potential exists for establishing intermodal coordination that would foster public passenger transportation, promote energy conservation and provide consumers with an alternative to the automobile. Its study of the few existing intermodal arrangements at Boston, Jacksonville, New Orleans and Kalamazoo shows them to be generally successful. The ICC presently favors voluntary action by the carriers to establish intermodal interfaces in the following areas:

1. Existing terminals should be used for all surface modes whenever possible. Because railroad facilities are relatively immobile, this usually means using the railroad station, which in these days is cursed with a surplus of empty space.

2. Selection of locations for intermodal terminals should be based on market demand, availability of service and energy efficiency.

3. Unused terminals should be converted into more cost-efficient intermodal facilities. Public funds similar to those available for construction of airport terminals could continue to be used to finance intermodal terminals. Historical preservation funds could be used to renovate architecturally significant railroad stations for intermodal use.

4. Existing routes and schedules should be used whenever possible. Duplicate service should be avoided, and this use of existing patterns seems to be the most cost-effective way of achieving coordination.

5. A uniform passenger ticket honored by all carriers should be developed. This would not necessarily involve the filing of joint rates, but should be written with uniform terms, including liability for lost luggage.

6. Intermodal arrangements should continue to be on a voluntary basis. However, the ICC believes it could encourage participation by establishing a joint rail–bus master tariff. The Commission disagreed with the Department of Transportation's findings of administrative burden.

7. Rail–bus coordination should be encouraged on a national intermodal basis. With future energy shortages in mind, rail–bus travel could become the most feasible means, rather than merely an alternative to the automobile.

The 1977 report described on a state-by-state basis where Amtrak could successfully interline with independent carriers. (Greyhound and Trailways were excluded from the study.) For most cities, a single transportation terminal conveniently located and accommodating different modes of transportation would create a more efficient transportation system. In addition, intermodal centers would reduce major expenses of construction and maintenance, which must be borne by transportation companies. For these reasons, Congress established the Intermodal Passenger Terminal Program pursuant to the Amtrak Improvement Act of 1974. Several demonstration projects are currently under way to convert obsolete rail facilities into new intermodal terminals.

For a railroad station to be eligible for such assistance, the building must be capable of handling additional transportation, including intercity and local buses and airport access vehicles. The terminal must be listed on the National

Register of Historic Places, and the architectural integrity must not be violated by the conversion. Under this provision, the Department of Transportation has underwritten 60 percent of the costs of restoring these historic stations.

Although historical and other considerations might favor the renovation of existing rail terminals, some authorities, including many within the bus industry, believe that the most productive method of establishing interfaces is the construction of new facilities. This may be true in large metropolitan areas or where existing buildings are obsolete. But in small cities, the level of traffic is moderate enough that, in most cases, the capital expense necessary to build new facilities would not be justified.

Despite a slow start, intermodal passenger service has now become part of the federal government's transportation and energy policies. Recent statements by both the ICC and the Department of Transportation indicate that in the future, the government will insist that common carriers cooperate in helping passengers reach their destination. This will especially be the case if buses, as well as Amtrak, become supplicants for public largesse.

NOTES

1. 49 U.S.C. §§ 10101–11916 (Supp. IV 1980).

2. This section is adapted from Dempsey, *Rate Regulation and Antitrust Immunity in Transportation: The Genesis and Evolution of This Endangered Species*, 32 Am. U.L. Rev. 335 (1983). Copyright 1983 by the Washington College of Law, American University, reprinted by permission.

3. A tariff is a filed publication in which a carrier, or its agent, states its rates and charges. It may include rules of conditions governing the provision of transportation and related services.

4. *Id.* § 10762(a)(2), (d).

5. *Id.* § 10762(c)(3), (d).

6. *Id.* § 10762.

7. 49 U.S.C. §§ 10707(a), 10708(a) (Supp. IV 1980).

8. *Id.* § 10707(c)(1).

9. *Id.* § 10707a(3)(2)(B).

10. Southern Ry. v. Seaboard Allied Milling Corp., 442 U.S. 444 (1979) (ICC decisions not to suspend a tariff are not subject to judicial review).

11. *Id.* at 454.

12. 49 U.S.C. § 10708(c) (Supp. IV 1980).

13. *Id.* § 11701.

14. *Id.* § 10704(a)(1), (b)(1), (c)(1).

15. *Id.* § 10707(d)(1).

16. *Id.* § 10707(d)(2).

17. United States v. Chesapeake & O. Ry., 426 U.S. 600 (1976).

18. *Id.* at 513–15.

19. 436 U.S. 681 (1978).

20. *Id.* at 653.

21. 49 U.S.C. § 10761 (Supp. IV 1980).

22. *Id.* § 10741(e).

23. *Id.* § 10741(a).

24. *Id.* § 10726.

25. *Id.* § 10741(b).

26. *Id.* § 10742.

27. Southern Ry. v. Seaboard Allied Milling Corp. 422 U.S. 444 (1979).

28. Baltimore & O.R.R. v. United States, 345 U.S. 146, 150 (1952).

29. 294 U.S. 499 (1935).

30. *Id.* at 506.

31. Salt Cases of 1923, 92 I.C.C. 388, 410 (1924).

32. Burlington N., Inc. v. United States, 555 F. 2d 637, 641 (8th Cir. 1977).

33. *Id.*

34. Differential pricing involves setting certain rates at levels higher than full costs in order to compensate for losses incurred because certain services must be priced below full cost if the railroad is to be competitive. San Antonio v. United States, 631 F.2d 831, 850 (D.C. Cir. 1980).

35. Houston Lighting & Power Co. v. United States, 606 F.2d 1131, 1143 (D.C. Cir. 1979).

36. San Antonio v. United States, 631 F.2d 83 (D.C. Cir. 1980).

37. *Id.* at 352.

38. Pub. L. No. 92-296, 94 Stat. 793 (codified in scattered sections of 18 § 49 U.S.C.).

39. *See* 49 U.S.C. § 10706(d)(1) (Supp. IV 1980).

40. *Id.* § 10708(d)(2).

41. *Id.* § 10701(e).

42. Pub. L. No. 96-448, 94 Stat. 1895 (1930) (codified in scattered sections of 11,   45 & 49 U.S.C.).

43. 49 U.S.C. § 10101a (Supp. IV 1980).

44. *Id.* § 10101a(3).

45. *Id.* § 10101a(13).

46. *Id.* § 10101a(6).

47. *Id.* § 10701a(b)(1).

48. Pub. L. No. 94-210, § 202(b), 90 Stat. 31, 34 (codified at 49 U.S.C. § 10709(a) (Supp. IV 1980).

49. 49 U.S.C. § 10709(a) (Supp. IV 1980).

50. Under the ICC test, market dominance exists only where "(1) the proposed railroad carried more than 70% of the traffic in the relevant market; (2) the proponent railroad would, under the proposed rate, earn more than 160% of its variable cost of providing the service; or (3) affected shippers had made a substantial investment in rail-related facilities." Department of Transportation, Prospectus for Change in the Railroad Industry, 120–21 (1978).

51. 49 U.S.C. § 10701a(1) (Supp. IV 1980).

52. *Id.* § 10701a(c).

53. *Id.* § 10707(a)(1)(A).

54. *Id.* § 10707(a)(2)(B).

55. *Id.* § 10707a(a)(2)(B).

56. *Id.* § 10707a(b)(3).

57. *Id.* § 10707a(3).

58. *Id.* § 10707a(c)(1).

59. *Id.* § 10713(a).

60. *Id.* § 17013(b).

61. *Id.* § 10713(d)(1).

62. *Id.* § 10713(d)(2)(A).

63. *Id.* § 10713(d)(3)(B).

64. *Id.* § 10713(f).

65. 49 U.S.C. § 10713 (1980).

66. *See* 49 C.F.R. Part 1039.

67. 49 U.S.C. § 10734.

68. 49 U.S.C. § 10726.

69. *Id.* § 10727.

70. Footnotes and citations omitted.

71. Department of Transportation, A Prospectus for Change in the Freight Railroad Industry 118–24 (1978).

72. Footnotes omitted.

73. Department of Transportation, A Prospectus for Change in the Railroad Freight Industry 124 (1978).

74. 49 U.S.C. § 10501(b)(a).

75. *Id.* § 10501(b)(2).

76. *Id.* § 10501(b)(3).

77. *Id.* § 10501(b)(4).

78. N. P. Rep. 96-1430, 96th Cong., 2d Sess. 106 (1980).

79. This section is adapted from Thoms, Regulation of Oil Pipelines by the ICC, 10–11 (1979).

80. Footnotes and citations generally omitted.

81. 15 U.S.C. §§ 717c, 717d.

82. Section IV is adapted from Thoms, Deregulation: The Airline Experience. 18–20, 34–53, 68–70 (1981).

83. *See* 49 U.S.C. § 1302 (1980).

84. *Id.* § 1383.

85. *Id.* § 1386.

86. *Id.* § 1388(a)(2).

87. *Id.* § 1388(4)(b)(1)(B).

88. *Id.* § 1388(b)(2).

89. *Id.* § 1301 (11).

90. *Id.* § 1388(b)(3).

91. Pub. L. 95-163 § 17(a)(1977), adding § 418(b)(3) to the Federal Aviation Act, 91 Stat. 1285, 49 U.S.C. § 1002 (1980).

92. Pub. L. 95-163, § 18(a)(2)(1977).

93. 49 U.S.C. § 1482(g) (1980).

94. *Id.* § 1388.

95. ER-1121, Reporting Data Pertaining to Freight Loss and Damage Claims by Certified Route Carriers and Foreign Route Carriers and Foreign Route Carriers (CAB, 1979).

96. Comments of the National Freight Claims Council in Opposition to ER-1121.

97. 49 U.S.C. § 137R(d)(6)(A) (1980).

98. Dubue, *Significant Legislative Development in the Field of Aviation Law*, 45 J. Air L. 1, 26, (1979).

99. 49 U.S.C. § 1482(d)(5) (1980).

100. This section is adapted from Thoms, Intermodalism—For Passengers Too? *Trains*, Oct. 1981, at 19.

4

Antitrust and Finance Regulation

I. RATE BUREAUS

The call for regulation of railroads, like that for most utilities, arose because the public perceived that competition was imperfect. Some theorists believed that railroads, like gas and utility companies, were "natural monopolies," in which the market in a given area could best be served by one supplier.

The original Interstate Commerce Act was passed prior to the promulgation of the Sherman Antitrust Law; hence the regulatory regime is actually an older concept than antitrust. Inasmuch as railroad transactions are subject to the Interstate Commerce Act, they may be immunized from the antitrust laws. Similarly, if economic deregulation of the railroads is ever fully implemented, rail activities would presumably fall within the ambit of the antitrust laws.

A. Antitrust Immunity for Collective Rate Making

Rate bureaus (associations of two or more carriers) disseminate information regarding rates charged for transportation between various points and collectively consider the prices to be charged by participating rate bureau members.[1] Collective rate making dates back to early railroad development in the United States. Indeed, rate bureaus were formally established in the mid-nineteenth century and grew in size and number as the rail network expanded. Today there are 10 major regional motor carrier general commodity bureaus and many specialized bureaus for other sectors of the industry. In addition, the National Classification Board allows carriers to agree collectively regarding the specific classifications of particular commodities to which particular rates will apply.

The Interstate Commerce Act, as enacted in 1887, was silent on the issue of collective rate making, although it specifically prohibited pooling of traffic or revenue. Only three years later, Congress passed the Sherman Act.[2] Section 1 of the Sherman Act provides that contracts, combinations and conspiracies in restraint of trade or commerce are illegal, whereas Section 2 proscribes monopolies and attempts to monopolize, combine or conspire to monopolize trade or commerce. Such violations constitute felonies punishable by a fine of not more than $100,000 for individuals and $1 million for corporations, imprisonment for not more than three years or both.

Despite early indications from the Supreme Court that collective rate-making activities by common carriers violated the Sherman Act, for almost 50 years there were no significant federal efforts to constrain carrier rate bureaus or their collective rate making activities. The Department of Justice did not enforce the antitrust laws with respect to rate bureaus principally because the bureaus afforded their members the right of independent action. Furthermore, the Court adopted a rule of reason in interpreting antitrust violations, concluding that only unreasonable restraints of trade fell within the proscriptions of the Sherman Act.

The Clayton Act, enacted in 1914, today contains several sections relevant to common carier rate making, including prohibitions against discrimination in prices, services or facilities, as well as prohibitions against rebates and price fixing. The Interstate Commerce Commission (ICC) was given jurisdiction to enforce Section 7 of the Clayton Act, a prohibition against mergers that might substantially lessen competition, insofar as it involved rail mergers. Further, although Congress included a provision for private relief in Section 16 of the Clayton Act, it denied private parties a remedy with respect to any matter subject to the jurisdiction of the ICC.

1. Need to Shield Rate Bureaus from Antitrust Laws

A major shift in federal antitrust policy occurred in 1920, when Congress, in promulgating the Transportation Act of 1920,[3] provided antitrust immunity for certain rail mergers approved by the ICC. This shift represented the first congressional attempt to reconcile the pragmatic realities of the surface transportation industry with antitrust principals. The legislation established an exemption for activities that would otherwise violate the antitrust laws— the first in a long series of antitrust exemptions for surface carriers.

By 1940, Congress had added virtually all forms of transportation to what had become a comprehensive federal regulatory scheme. The Transportation Act of 1940[4] gave the ICC jurisdiction over mergers and acquisitions of control of all surface carriers.[5] The Act permitted the ICC to approve pooling agreements for traffic, service or earnings[6] and provided that such ICC-approved agreements were exempt from the antitrust laws.[7] Significantly, the antitrust laws did not shield the activities of rate bureaus, which were widespread prior to 1940.

In the early 1940s, the Department of Justice was no longer reticent in pursuing the antitrust remedies against regulated common carriers. In 1942, the Department convened a grand jury, which was interrupted by war, to investigate the issue. In 1944, the Department resumed its efforts and initiated litigation, contending that rate bureau activity violated the Sherman Act. That same year Georgia brought an action against several northern railroads, alleging rate discrimination and antitrust violations in price fixing. In *Georgia v. Pennsylvania Railroad*,[8] the Supreme Court held that a conspiracy "to use coercion in the fixing of rates and to discriminate against Georgia in the rates which are fixed" stated a cause of action under the antitrust laws. Justice Douglas, writing for the majority, was particularly disturbed by the allegation that the activities of the rate bureau had led to regional price discrimination. Because the relief sought was an injunction against the rate-fixing combination and conspiracy among the carriers, and not against the continuance of any tariff, the case was not within the jurisdiction of the ICC. Section 16 of the Clayton Act, therefore, did not bar Georgia from bringing the action. Nevertheless, the dissenters argued that Section 16 barred suits concerning "any matter" within the jurisdiction of the Commission. They believed that the purpose of that provision was to prevent maintenance of individual suits that would lead to the breakdown of the Commission's nationwide rate structure.

Although a bill intended to shield collective rate-making activities from such litigation had been introduced in the U.S. Senate before the Court's decision in *Georgia v. Pennsylvania Railroad*, the decision, to a large extent, prompted Congress to promulgate the Reed-Bulwinkle Act.[9] The Act shielded the rate bureaus from the application of the antitrust laws when the ICC had approved carrier rate-making agreements. The Senate report described the purposes of the Act as "harmonizing and reconciling the policy of the antitrust laws, as applicable to common carriers, with the national transportation policy in such a manner as to protect the public interest."[10] Congress recognized that it was not breaking new ground in establishing such antitrust immunity, but rather extending immunity beyond those areas that it had already designated as within the exclusive jurisdiction of the ICC. The Commission thus became the sole arbiter of whether collective rate-making agreements served the public interest. If such agreements satisfied the Commission, they were free from judicial challenge.

Under existing law, ICC approval of a rail or motor carrier rate-making agreement continues to shield such action from the antitrust laws, including the Sherman Act, the Clayton Act, Sections 73 and 74 of the Wilson Tariff Act,[11] the Act of June 19, 1936[12] and the Federal Trade Commission Act.[13] The Commission may approve rail and motor carrier rate-making agreements only when such agreements further the transportation policy of the Interstate Commerce Act. In reviewing the ICC approval of such agreements, courts have held that although the Commission does not have jurisdiction to conclude that common carriers have violated the antitrust laws, the Commission must consider the competitive effects of the proposed actions.

a. Approval of Agreements between Carriers. "Conference" pricing has been traditional in maritime, and later in the airlines industries, as a means of equalizing fares and eliminating cutthroat competition. In the railroad and the motor carrier businesses, price-fixing conferences are called rate bureaus. The Reed-Bulwinkle Act of 1948 conferred on the ICC the authority, at its discretion, to exempt railroads from the application of the antitrust laws insofar as their activities in rate bureaus are affected. Hence, agreements such as those found unlawful in *Georgia v. Pennsylvania Railroad* could, subsequent to 1948, be accorded antitrust immunity by the ICC.

The Reed-Bulwinkle Act's exemptions have been narrowed in recent years. The Railroad Revitalization and Regulatory Reform Act of 1976 (4R Act) limited participation in rate bureau discussion to those carriers which can practicably participate in the movement of the commodity, prohibited carriers from voting on single-line rates and restrained the bureaus from protesting rates independently proposed by member carriers.

Rate bureaus were further restricted by the Staggers Rail Act of 1980, which restrained the discussion of single-line rates.[14] Rate bureaus must now provide transcripts of their meetings to the ICC, which are to be held in confidence and not subject to disclosure.

Case law is uncertain about actions by the carriers which are beyond the scope of an agreement approved by the ICC. Antitrust is an underlying fabric that is applicable to agreements not authorized by the ICC, and deregulation will necessarily bring more reliance on essential antitrust principles. Whether a nonexpert and possibly politicized Justice Department can do as effective a job as a specialized regulatory agency remains to be seen.

B. Scope of Antitrust Immunity

Although the ICC can exempt rate-making agreements from the operation of the antitrust laws,[15] the federal courts have held that such antitrust immunity does not embrace activity that would eliminate the competition of another carrier.[16] Furthermore, rate making is not immune from the antitrust laws when ICC procedures are not followed.[17] Indeed, rate bureaus cannot operate validly without the protective shield of ICC approval.[18] Under the doctrine of primary jurisdiction,[19] the ICC must determine the applicability of the antitrust exemption to antitrust issues raised.[20] Various courts attempted to narrow the application of the doctrine to those situations in which the sole or dominant issue is the intent and effect of rate reduction provision included in an ICC-approved agreement. In any case, the rationale underlying the doctrine is the need for orderly administration of antitrust immunity.

Primary jurisdiction is not the only principle that the courts have used to deny relief in actions alleging antitrust violations. Efforts of private plaintiffs to recover damages under the antitrust laws were significantly stifled with the decision of the Supreme Court in *Keogh v. Chicago & Northwestern Railway*.[21] In this case, a shipper alleged, under Section 7 of the Sherman Act, that eight railroads had combined to fix freight rates. He claimed damages to the extent of the difference between the rates charged and those paid before they had been arbitrarily and unreasonably fixed. The Court stated that the federal government, through criminal proceedings, injunction and forfeiture, could redress the activities of illegal combinations of carriers to fix rates, even when the ICC had approved the rates in question. Nevertheless, the Court held that a private shipper was precluded from recovering damages under the antitrust laws, except when the Commission had concluded that rates established through such an unlawful conspiracy were unreasonably high or discriminatory under the relevant provisions of the Interstate Commerce Act. Had the Commission ruled that such rates were unlawful, the shipper could have sought damages under the Interstate Commerce Act in proceedings before either the ICC or a federal court.

In reaching its decision, the Court expressed two reasons for prohibiting private relief under such circumstances, essentially focusing on the incompatibility of such a result with the other provisions of the Interstate Commerce Act. First, the only lawful rate is that filed by the carrier on its tariff and approved by the ICC. The legal rights of a shipper are measured by that tariff, which the carrier cannot vary by contract or tort. Second, prevention of unjust discrimination might be thwarted if the party were to recover damages in an antitrust action, thereby enjoying a preference over its competitors.

Courts have refused to expand the principle of *Keogh* beyond its precise holding. In *Marnell v. United Parcel Service of America Inc.*,[22] a federal district court emphasized that antitrust exemptions are not to be implied indiscriminately. Hence, if conduct is to be shielded from antitrust scrutiny, it must not only fall within the specific parameters of the immunity provisions that Congress included in the Interstate Commerce Act, but it must also be approved by the Commission.

The ability to apply antitrust exemptions to intrastate rate bureau activities by implication has recently been questioned. In one group of decisions, a lower federal court concluded that the ICC had no jurisdiction over intrastate transportation, even though the exercise of such jurisdiction might remedy discriminatory effects on interstate commerce.[23] The court stated that Congress could have authorized the ICC to regulate intrastate rates charged by motor carriers when such transportation was in the stream of commerce and the rates were found to have substantial effect on interstate commerce. Under such reasoning, intrastate rates are not within the Commission's jurisdiction, and ICC approval of those rates does not afford antitrust immunity. The court therefore held that such rate bureau activities were not within the protection of either the state action exception to antitrust liability or the Noerr-Pennington doctrine. Moreover, the price-fixing activities of the intrastate rate bureaus constituted a per se violation of the antitrust laws. This decision, which the Court of Appeals for the Fifth Circuit affirmed, provided an indication of the potential liability to which interstate bureaus may be subject if single-line immunity is repealed.

1. Erosion of Antitrust Immunity

In 1973, the ICC instituted Ex Parte No. 297,[24] which ultimately established three rules that must be incorporated into rate bureau agreements if there is to be a continuation of antitrust immunity. First, a bureau cannot protest the independent action of its member carriers. Second, carrier members affiliated with shippers cannot serve on the bureau's board of directors, general rate committee or any other rate-making committee absent specific Commission approval. Third, a bureau cannot operate as a profit-making enterprise.

The 4R Act[25] significantly changed the principles governing the collective rate-making activities of rail carriers. It prohibited rail carriers from participating in or voting on single-line rate proposals of another carrier unless the proposals involved general rate increases or broad tariff changes.[26] Rail carriers were, however, permitted to discuss rate changes. The 4R Act limited ICC approval of rate agreements to those agreements that furthered the National Transportation Policy.[27] Because approval of the agreements continued to shield the carriers from antitrust laws,[28] such approval could be contingent on certain conditions. [29] The 4R Act also enhanced the opportunities of the Commission for monitoring rate bureaus by mandating an ICC investigation once every three years.[30]

In 1979, the ICC promulgated regulations, under Section 10505 of the Interstate Commerce Act, that removed the antitrust exemption for collective rates on the transportation of fresh fruits and vegetables.[31] In so doing, the Commission noted that "violation of the antitrust laws is a risk inherent in a deregulation environment." The next year, when Congress passed the Staggers Rail Act,[32] antitrust immunity was constricted even further: discussions of single-line rates were prohibited,[33] participation in and voting on interline rate agreements were limited to carriers participating in the interline movement[34] and immunity for agreements on general rate increases and broad tariff changes was curtailed.[35]

Similarly, the Motor Carrier Act of 1980 threatened to extinguish antitrust immunity for motor carriers acting pursuant to rate bureau agreements. Congress recognized that while rate bureaus provide an advantageous predictability in rate structures, they tend to create a rate system that compensates even the least efficient carrier, thereby causing consumers to lose the benefits of price competition. The 1980 Act was designed to implement a number of procedural reforms. Congress emphasized that the Act proposed not to eliminate rate bureaus, but to limit their consensual activities. Specifically, the legislation provides that only those carriers participating in the movements to which a rate applies may vote on a bureau proposal regarding that rate.[36] A bureau may not interfere with a carrier's right of independent action[37] or file a protest with the ICC in opposition to any tariff published by a carrier.[38] No collective discussion or voting is permitted for rates that fall within the zone of rate freedom[39] or limited liability rates.[40] The legislation also mandates total disclosure of and admission to rate bureau discussions and voting.[41] Exceptions to the prohibitions allow the Commission to approve collective agreements on general increases and decreases in rates,[42] changes in the tariff structure,[43] changes in commodity classifications[44] and ministerial bureau functions, including publishing tariffs, filing independent actions for member carriers, providing support services for members and changing rules or regulations of general application.[45]

Significantly, the Act establishes a presumption that agreements meeting the statutory requirements of the Motor Carrier Act are valid.[46] The presumption effects the purpose of the Act: to limit the discretion of the ICC to approve or disapprove rate agreements.[47] The Commission thus must validate rate agreements that meet congressionally mandated conditions unless the agreements are contrary to the National Transportation Policy.

To interpret the statutory provisions, the ICC adopted regulations that significantly affect the ability of rate bureaus to influence rate making by the member carriers.[48] The most significant regulation prohibits rate bureaus from informing the public of independent actions of member carriers that desire confidentiality. The practical effect of the requirement is that neither shippers served by the independent actor nor carriers competing with it will be apprised of the independent action before the effective date of the tariff. Hence, such shippers effectively will be precluded from filing a protest under Section 10707 or 10708 of the Interstate Commerce Act on the ground that the proposed rates are excessively high and discriminatory or excessively low and predatory. Shippers are unlikely to know that the independent actor has raised its rates until they are billed, which usually occurs several weeks subsequent to the transporting of their commodities. Shippers then will be forced not only to pay the higher rates, but also to bear the burden of proving unreasonableness if there is a formal complaint proceeding under Section 11701. The same burden of proof will be placed on competing carriers that object to a predatory rate. As a result, a tariff may become effective without the Commission's having heard opposing arguments from concerned parties.

It is important to realize that antitrust immunity for collective rate making on single-line rates expired in 1984, for Congress failed to extend its applicability. During the interim, the Motor Carrier Ratemaking Study Commission conducted comprehensive studies of public interest reasons for and against continuation of such immunity.[49] Because Congress failed to extend single-line immunity after 1984, rate bureaus ultimately are limited to the acquisition and dissemination of general cost data and the discussion of general rate increases, commodity classifications and tariff structures. To the extent that rate bureaus can survive without immunity, they essentially will become tariff-publishing agencies, much like today's rail rate bureaus that focus on tariff publishing and general revenue increases.

2. High Flying Price Fixers

After the bankruptcy of Braniff Airlines, the U.S. Department of Justice brought a civil action in federal court charging that American Airlines president Robert L. Crandall had violated the antitrust laws based on his conversation of February 1, 1982, with Howard Putnam, president of Braniff. The conversation was alleged to be essentially as follows:

CRANDALL indicated that the intensive level of competition between the two carriers was undesirable, and that continuation of such competition would result in "neither one of us making a f—— dime."

CRANDALL: There's no reason that I can see, all right, to put both companies out of business.

PUTNAM: Do you have a suggestion for me?

CRANDALL: Yes. I have a suggestion for you. Raise your goddamned fares 20 percent. I'll raise mine the next morning.

PUTNAM: Robert, we . . .

CRANDALL: You'll make more money and I will too.

PUTNAM: We can't talk about pricing.

CRANDALL: Oh, b——, Howard. We can talk about any goddamned thing we want to talk about.

Apparently, no action was taken to fix prices as a result of this conversation. The Justice Department sought a court order prohibiting Crandall from working in any responsible airline position for two years and forbidding the airline from discussing any matter concerning the pricing of service for 10 years.

II. MERGERS, CONSOLIDATIONS AND ACQUISITIONS OF CONTROL

ICC approval is required before a regulated carrier may (1) purchase, lease or enter into a contract to operate the properties of another carrier; (2) consolidate or merge with another carrier; or (3) acquire control of another carrier through stock ownership, management or otherwise.[50] In addition, Commission approval is sometimes required when a noncarrier seeks to acquire control of a carrier.[51]

Virtually every railroad listed in the *Official Guide* is a product of several mergers. The process has continued in spurts since the early 1820s but has reached new momentum since the 1960s.

The U.S. Railroad Administration operated the nation's rail system on a consolidated basis from 1917 to 1920. The purpose of temporary national-ization was to coordinate the nation's rail transportation system to provide commodities essential to support the American effort in World War I. When the rails were returned to private hands, there was some sentiment for continuing the economies of scale resulting from large railroad sys-tems. In 1920, the Transportation Act authorized the ICC to formulate a "complete plan of consolidation." The nationwide consolidation remained stillborn, but the ICC did receive authority to approve the acquisition of control by one carrier over another, if the Commission found it to be in the public interest.

Since 1940, the ICC has held authority to approve consolidations, mergers, control and other transactions. If such activities are deemed by the ICC to be consistent with the public interest, the transaction is exempt from the antitrust laws.

The public interest is, here as elsewhere in the Act, an amorphous stand-ard. If a merger is between two parallel railroads, there may be some aban-donment of redundant traffic. This could cause problems for residents and businesses along the moribund line. An end-to-end merger generally has the advantage of not restraining competition as severely as a parallel merger. There might be adverse effects on employees and communities where ter-minals and other facilities are abandoned in favor of run-through trains. Control of a railroad by a noncarrier might cause some problems if the acquiring company uses the railroad as a source of cash flow to diversify itself into a conglomerate, ignoring the railroad's public service obligations.

The merger of rail carriers into a single, strong railroad could mean disaster for a competing line struggling in a marginal position. A railroad might use its consolidation to dominate a region, as the Burlington Northern is said to have done in the Northwest. These disadvantages should be weighed against the benefits provided to the public by the merged company's more efficient operations. Until recently, railroad control of trucking companies or barge lines has been restricted because of the danger that rail control might reduce the subsidiaries to mere feeders of the rail operations.

A. ICC's Duty to Consider Anticompetitive Consequences

Pre-1920 Act. In *United States v. Southern Pac. Co.*, 259 U.S. 214 (1920), which involved a combination between the Central Pacific Railroad and the Southern Pacific Railroad, the Court found a violation of Section 1 of the Sherman Antitrust Act of 1890.[52] The combination consisted of the acquisition by Southern Pacific of the stock of the Central Pacific in 1899. Such action was found to be a combination in restraint of trade because it interfered with the free and normal flow of competition in interstate traffic and tended to create a monopoly.

There were various actions by the Congress, which secured bonds issued by Southern Pacific and Central Pacific, which allowed this transaction to be consummated, but the Court found that these actions did not justify the violation of the Sherman Act.

1920 Act. Congressional response to this decision (no doubt by way of the railroad lobby) was swift, and the Transportation Act of 1920, 41 Stat. 456, was enacted. In general, the 1920 Act marked a change in policy. Prior to the passage of the Act, Congress was concerned with preventing abuses (i.e., discriminatory rates), and emphasis on preserving free competition among carriers was part of that effort. The 1920 Act was aimed at strengthing the rail system, and the Commission was to be guided by considerations of adequacy of transportation service and the best use of transportation facilities. Specifically, Section 401 of the 1920 Act amended former Section 5 of the Interstate Commerce Act to permit, among other things, the acquisition of control of one carrier by another, when found by the Commission to be in the public interest, and expressly relieved carriers acting under such permission from the strictures of the Sherman Act and from any and all other restraints or prohibitions by law—state or federal. This antitrust exemption was formerly found in Section 5(11) and is now found in 49 U.S.C. § 11341.

The Southern Pacific quickly brought its transaction to the Commission for approval. In *Control of Central Pacific by Southern Pacific*, 76 I.C.C. 508 (1923), the Commission approved the transaction but with certain conditions designed to remove the opportunity otherwise existing for Southern Pacific to restrict competition. Thus, the Commission did consider the anticompetitive consequences of the transaction.

1935 Act. With the passage of the Motor Carrier Act of 1935, 49 Stat. 543, motor carriers came under Commission jurisdiction. Specifically, motor carrier acquisitions were to be considered under former Section 5 of the Interstate Commerce Act.

1940 Act. The Transportation Act of 1940, 54 Stat. 898, reaffirmed the concept of separation of transportation policies from antitrust policies, which concept was first developed in the 1920 Act.

The most significant case involving motor carrier acquisitions and the consideration of antitrust criteria is *McLean Trucking Co. v. United States*, 321 U.S. 67, 84–88 (1943).

The Court specifically noted that the antitrust exemption found in former Section 5(11) applied to both rail and motor consolidations and mergers. It also found that the Commission has no power to enforce the Sherman Act per se as opposed to specific and exclusive jurisdiction to enforce the Clayton Act re activities under Commission jurisdiction. The Court then engaged in an analysis of the responsibility of the Commission in considering the merits of motor acquisitions.

Beginning again in the rail area, the Court noted that antitrust laws determined "the public interest" in rail regulation in only a *qualified way* owing to the existence of the National Transportation Policy. It stated that the Commission is not to measure consolidation proposals by the standards of the antitrust laws. This appears clear because of the mere existence of Section 5(11). For why relieve such transactions from the antitrust laws if they are to be judged by such laws?

The preservation of competition was seen as being of continued value insofar as it aids in the attainment of the objectives of the National Transportation Policy. Thus, it is the Commission's duty to consider the effect of a merger on the general competitive situation in the industry in light of the objectives of the National Transportation Policy. In general, the Commission is required to weigh the effects of the curtailment of competition against such advantages as improved service, safer operation and lower costs.

It now becomes necessary to study other rail cases to obtain the judicial gloss which clarifies these broad principles. This is significant because there are no major motor cases which help to clarify the issue.

A most significant case is *Florida East Coast Railway Company v. United States*, 259 F. Supp. 993 (M.D. Fla. 1966), which followed a Supreme Court remand in *Seaboard Airline Railway Company v. United States*, 382 U.S. 154 (1965). The importance of the former decision is obvious from the following language of the court: "This case presents a head-on collision between the antitrust laws and the Interstate Commerce Act. It is incumbent upon us to seek to rationalize the statutes involved here and make of them, to the extent that what Congress has written will permit, a harmonious functional body of law."[53]

With this as a basis, it is significant that the court determined that the Commission shoud take into account the National Antitrust *Policy* of the United States. This is quite different from using the complex market analysis which is required in cases prosecuted under Section 7 of the Clayton Act or Section 1 of the Sherman Act. Market analysis is useful, however, to pinpoint the danger areas.

Such analysis alone cannot denote which transactions are "bad" and which are "good." To do so would be to ignore the National Transportation Policy and give Antitrust Policy an exalted status, which the Congress did not intend. In fact, this loading of the scales in favor of but one factor has been found by the Supreme Court to be improper in several cases, for example, *I.C.C. v. J-T Transport Co.*, 368 U.S. 81 (1961), and *Port of Portland v. United States*, 408 U.S. 811 (1972).

The last significant case in this development of the antitrust criteria is *Denver & R.G.W.R. Co. v. United States*, 387 U.S. 485 (1967). This case

involved an application to the Commission under former Section 20a, regarding the issuance of stock. That stock was to be used to carry out an
acquisition involving Railway Express Agency (REA) and Greyhound. There
was some question whether this transaction fell under Section 5 because it
was unclear whether control of REA by Greyhound would result.

The Court read the Commission's obligation to consider the "public interest" broadly. It found that the economic consequences did not differ
merely because the transaction involved an issuance of stock rather than an
acquisition on the open market. Thus, the Court concluded that the Commission is required, under its duty to determine whether the proposed
transaction is in the "public interest" (and/or for a "lawful object"), to consider
the control and anticompetitive consequences before approving stock issu-
ances under former Section 20a(2). Now comes a significant difference. Consideration of the public interest in transactions which fall under former
Section 5 arises only after the threshold fact of control[54] is established. But
no such preliminary finding is necessary to trigger the Commission's duty
to *enforce* the Clayton Act. Because of the wording of Section 7 of the Clayton
Act, a company need not acquire control of another company in order to
violate that Act. All that is necessary is the acquisition of "any part" of a
company's stock or assets if the effect "may be substantially to lessen competition, or to tend to create a monopoly."

The Commission's jurisdiction in enforcing Section 7 of the Clayton Act,
with regard to companies subject to its jurisdiction, is *exclusive*. Specifically,
Section 16 of the Clayton Act denies private persons the ability to bring
Section 7 suits for injunctive relief in all cases involving matters subject to
Commission jurisdiction. This exclusive jurisdiction was reiterated in *United
States v. Navajo Freight Lines, Inc.*, 339 F. Supp. 554 (1971).

This district court decision is the precursor to the first Commission pros-
ecution of a Section 7 Clayton violation involving a motor carrier. The Justice
Department initially brought suit under Section 7 of Clayton, claiming that
Navajo Freight Lines had violated the statute by purchasing the stock of
Garrett Freight Lines. However, as previously noted, the U.S. district court
threw the case out for lack of jurisdiction.

That action dropped the case into the Commission's hands. The Commission found that Navajo was not in unlawful *control* of Garrett (i.e., no
Section 5 jurisdiction). The first step in a Section 7 investigation is the
development of a "product market" and relevant "geographic markets," which
were developed primarily from the Justice Department's briefs and testimony.

The "product market" was found to be "transportation by regular-route
motor common carrier of general commodities, with the usual exceptions,
in LTL quantities, weighing 10,000 pounds or less." The "geographic markets" were found to be certain city-pair markets. These were Denver–Las
Vegas, San Francisco Bay area–Las Vegas, Los Angeles–Denver and San
Francisco Bay area–Denver.

Analysis of these factors led the Commission to find that the potential consolidation of Navajo and Garrett could lessen competition. Thus, the Commission found a violation of Section 7, and Navajo was ordered to divest itself of the Garrett stock it had acquired. (*Navajo Freight Lines, Inc—Invest of Control,* 122 M.C.C. 345 [1976].)

A subsequent court decision by the Court of Appeals for the Seventh Circuit found the Commission's analysis to be "insufficient" with respect to whether Navajo's conduct fell within the line extension defense of Section 7's common carrier provision. That exemption pertains to stock acquisitions by which common carriers extend their lines where there is "no substantial competition" between the carriers involved. Really, the court found the development of the pertinent product and geographic markets to be improper, as well as the conclusion that the carriers compete in the pertinent geographic markets. Thus, the Commission was unable to develop the "sophisticated antitrust market analysis" required.

We are now up-to-date on what type of analysis must be conducted by the Commission, both in investigations conducted under Section 7 Clayton and in proceedings brought pursuant to 49 U.S.C. §§ 11343–44.

1. ICC's Regulatory Posture

Until 1960, the ICC's regulatory posture could be characterized as favoring end-to-end mergers or mergers of weak railroads, rather than parallel mergers of strong railroads. The Erie and Lackawanna were allowed to merge, even though they were parallel operations, because they were financially weak carriers. The Norfolk & Western acquired the Virginian because operating efficiencies were considered to be persuasive. ICC approval of the merger of the Seaboard Air Line and Atlantic Coast Line (ACL) in 1963 departed from prior precedent inasmuch as these two were large, prosperous, competing railroads. The Florida East Coast (FEC), an intrastate railroad which had been ACL's principal Florida connection, brought the following suit to enjoin the ICC's actions approving the consolidation. (FEC, of course, would stand to lose a great deal of the ex-ACL traffic, which now would follow Seaboard rails into southern Florida.)

FLORIDA EAST COAST RY. v. UNITED STATES

259 F. Supp. 993 (M.D. Fla. 1966)

RIVES, Circuit Judge

The Interstate Commerce Commission by an order entered in December 1963, authorized the merger of the Atlantic Coast Line Railroad Company with the Seaboard Air Line Railroad Company subject to certain routing and gateway conditions and employee protective conditions. Related acquisition of control by Seaboard of carriers subsidiary to or affiliated with Atlantic, most prominently including the Louisville and Nashville Railroad Company, was also authorized. 320 I.C.C. 122 (1963). Florida East Coast Railway Company [FEC] brought suit in this Court asking that the ICC's order be enjoined, annulled and set aside.

This case presents a head-on collision between the antitrust laws and the Interstate Commerce Act. It is incumbent upon us to seek to rationalize the statutes involved here and make of them, to the extent that what Congress has written will permit, a harmonious functional body of law. Section (11344(c)) directs the Commission to approve voluntary rail mergers which it finds to be "consistent with the public interest," but reserves to the Commission power to approve the merger subject to such "terms and conditions" as it may find to be "just and reasonable." Section (11344(b)) of the Interstate Commerce Act, which sets forth certain factors which must be considered by the ICC in passing upon any proposed railroad merger or affiliation, does not expressly require that the Commission consider the antitrust laws as a factor in public interest. However, since section (13343) exempts carriers and individuals participating in an approved merger from the antitrust laws, the ICC has long been required to give weight to the antitrust policy of the Nation in approving mergers. It is the accommodation of the national transportation policy with the national antitrust policy with which this litigation is chiefly concerned.

Congress has vested the Commission with "exclusive and plenary" powers in the regulation of rail mergers. No one who reviews the history and language of the Interstate Commerce Act can doubt that Congress has entrusted the ICC with plenary power to regulate almost every aspect of the rail industry and, for that matter, almost every aspect of the transportation industry save the airlines. The ICC is in many ways a super-management, often making managerial-type decisions affecting the transportation industry, with but one overriding duty to protect the public interest. A rail carrier cannot change rates without ICC approval, and the ICC can on its own initiative investigate and alter rates after proper findings.

New services cannot be provided nor old ones discontinued without Commission approval. No new railroad may enter the field without ICC permission; the Commission may compel an existing railroad to extend its line and provide new service. We have, in effect, a government-protected monopoly for those already providing service.

The plaintiffs, and particularly the United States through the Antitrust Division of the Justice Department, vigorously attack the standards applied by the ICC in this case. They argue that the ICC failed to properly assess the dangers of this merger, because it failed to apply or misapplied the teachings of modern sophisticated antitrust principles. To understand how national antitrust policy comes into play, it is well at this point for us to review the relationship of section (11344) and section (11343) of the Interstate Commerce Act. In approving a rail merger or consolidation the ICC is required by section (11344(b)) to

> give weight to the following considerations, *among others*: (1) The effect of the proposed transaction upon adequate transportation service to the public: (2) the effect upon the public interest of the inclusion, or failure to include, other railroads in the territory involved in the proposed transaction: (3) the total fixed charges resulting from the proposed transaction: (4) the interest of the carrier employees affected [emphasis added].

Any reference to antitrust policy must be read into the words "among others" by implication, since section (1343) exempts participants in an approved merger.

> from the operation of the antitrust laws and of all other restraints, limitations, and prohibitions of law, Federal, State, or municipal, insofar

as may be necessary to enable them to carry into effect the transactions
so approved. . . . and to hold, maintain, and operate any properties and
exercise any control or franchises acquired through such transaction.

There is and could be no dispute that in determining whether a given merger is
in the public interest, the Commission should take into account the national antitrust
policy of the United States. Mr. Justice Black, speaking for the Court in *Northern
Pacific Railway Co. v. United States*, 356 U.S. 1 at 4 (1953), clearly stated the essence
of antitrust policy as follows:

The Sherman Act was designed to be comprehensive charter of economic
liberty aimed at preserving free and unfettered competition as the rule
of trade. It rests on the premise that the unrestrained interaction of
competitive forces will yield the best allocation of our economic resources, the lowest prices, the highest quality and the greatest material
progress while at the same time providing an environment conducive
to the preservation of our democratic political and social institutions.

The Congress in 1940 enacted the following "National Transportation Policy":

It is hereby declared to be the national transportation policy of the
Congress to provide for fair and impartial regulation of all modes of
transportation subject to the provisions of this Act, so administered as
to recognize and preserve the inherent advantages of each; to promote
safe, adequate, economical, and efficient service and foster sound economic conditions in transportation and among the several carriers; to
encourage the establishment and maintenance of reasonable charges for
transportation services, without unjust discriminations, undue preferences or advantages, or unfair or destructive competitive practices; to
cooperate with the several States and the duly authorized officials thereof;
and to encourage fair wages and equitable working conditions;—all to
the end of developing, coordinating, and preserving a national transportation system by water, highway, and rail, as well as other means,
adequate to meet the needs of the commerce of the United States, of
the Postal Service, and of the national defense. *All of the provisions of
this Act shall be administered and enforced with a view to carrying out
the above declaration of policy.* (49 U.S.C.A. Historical note following
table of contents [emphasis added])

The main thrust of plaintiff's argument is that this merger eliminates substantial
competition between Seaboard and Atlantic, and in some areas even creates an
effective monopoly over the transportation of certain products. This it is argued
violates not only the antitrust policy but also the transportation policy of the United
States since it fails to "preserve the inherent advantages of each" mode of transportation. Proof these allegations is sought in a resort to modern sophisticated antitrust
principles.

On remand the plaintiffs deny any intention to force the ICC to decide whether
a violation of section 7 of the Clayton Act or the Sherman Act has taken place. But
at the same time they argue that the Commission must apply modern sophisticated
antitrust market analysis.

It seems pointless to say that the Commission must employ market definition tools calculated to show whether an antitrust violation has taken place, and when it reaches the point where a conclusion may be properly drawn, it may then stop since it need not draw any conclusions.

It is argued that the ICC's failure to utilize sophisticated antitrust market definition tools is evidence that it failed to properly assess the merger. This contention must be rejected. The ICC has never applied this approach formally, and yet, in spite of the fact that Judge Learned Hand used it as early as 1916, the Supreme Court has never considered this as evidence of the ICC's failure to properly consider a merger.

It may be helpful to apply this tool in the present case. Railroads have a decided economic advantage in carrying long-haul, heavy bulk products, e.g., phosphate rock mined principally in the western portion of central Florida. In terms of antitrust analysis, we submit that this service is a separate product market and Florida is the proper geographic area.

Some illustrations should demonstrate the point. Let us assume that railroads can haul phosphate rock 50% more cheaply than the next alternative mode of transportation, trucks. This means that if a truck could haul rock at $1 per pound, railroads could carry it at 50 cents per pound. Physically both of these services are interchangeable. If both modes set the price of hauling at $1, there would be "cross-elasticity of demand" between both.

However, if the railroad companies were owned separately from the trucks and if no products were available to bring a higher return and if space were available, railroads would set their price below $1 but above 50 cents, thus taking the business away from the trucks. Railroads are a submarket of long-haul, heavy bulk products.

If there were competition by two or more railroads for the bulk business, the price would be set somewhere between $1 and 50 cents, but at such a price as would allocate the business between the roads based on market conditions. If, however, a monopoly is created, the monopoly may set the price at any level between $1 and 50 cents that will maximize its return, because it experiences no competition until the price reaches $1. The monopoly price may in fact be lower than the competitive price, depending on whether a change in the cost of transportation will appreciably affect the ultimate cost of the end product and thus increase or decrease consumption. Thus a monopolist may pass on cost savings to achieve higher profits where a competitor will take the cost savings as higher profits without passing them on. The record in the present case gives us no data on which to predict what action will be taken by railroad possessing a monopoly in the bulk-haul products market of central Florida.

It is, we think, accurate to say that railroads enjoy a decided economic advantage over all other modes of transport on heavy, long, bulk-haul products in central and western Florida.

The purpose of this example is to demonstrate that the plaintiff's briefs are correct when they analyze the market structure and conclude that the merger, if allowed, creates a monopoly in parts of Florida and that that monopoly can have significant effects. But that is all market analysis shows. A careful reading of the ICC decision shows that the ICC clearly recognized this fact. . . .

Once we accept the fact that the Commission saw this problem, we can set to one side the mechanics of antitrust law and look to the only real issue, the accommodation of the national antitrust policy with the national transportation policy.

As shown by the record, these railroads receive a substantial increment of their revenue from traffic originating in Florida. It is precisely on this traffic that the monopoly created by the merger will have its greatest impact. The Commission appears to have assumed that the equivalent of a conspiracy to fix prices in Florida already exists. The Commission said "It is to be observed that in much of Florida, Seaboard and Coast Line heretofore have had what might be described as an important monopoly. . . . At most, the rail monopoly that would result from the merger in portions of Florida would merely supplant the duopoly which has long existed there."

In *Georgia v. Pennsylvania R.R. Co.*, 324 U.S. 439, 65 S. Ct. 716, 89 L. Ed. 1051 (1945), the State of Georgia invoked the original jurisdiction of the Supreme Court with a complaint against 20 railroads. Georgia alleged that the railroads had conspired together, through the use of rate bureaus, committees, conferences, associations, etc., to establish arbitrary and unreasonable rates to and from the State of Georgia. These conspiracies, it alleged, had eliminated substantially all rail competition. The Supreme Court held that Georgia could pursue its request for an injunction. What Georgia won in the Supreme Court, it promptly lost in Congress. The Reed-Bulwinkle Act explicitly exempts rate agreements and rate bureau accords approved by the ICC from the antitrust laws.

For our purposes, it is important to remember that the Reed-Bulwinkle Act preserves the potential of competition since individual railroad initiative is a legal requirement. If the instant merger is permitted, then that initiative will be irrevocably lost. This Court has absolutely no doubt that, judged by the standards of the antitrust laws, the instant merger would fail at least as to Florida. But whether this merger violates the antitrust laws by eliminating competition or potential competition is not the question before us.

In this present case[the ICC considered the following factors:]

1. Consolidation of stations and terminals. 2. Consolidation of switching facilities and elimination of yard engines and yard diesels. 3. Consolidation would result in higher load factor on freight trains between major terminals with a concomitant reduction in the number of trains required. 4. Economy would result by combining administration. 5. Unified repair shops would result in more economical and safer operation, including the reduction of stores facilities.

The Commission concluded:

> In addition to the specific benefits above discussed, many other benefits can reasonably be expected to result from the elimination of wasteful and duplicative facilities and an overall improvement in operations. These benefits can be grouped as follows. In the area of improved service, it can be anticipated that benefits will be derived from (1) more flexible schedules and more direct routes; (2) the elimination of interchanges and delays in transit; and (3) the simplification of transit arrangements and greater flexibility in arranging standoff points. Reduction in shipping costs can be anticipated from the elimination of wasteful and unneeded transport facilities, the substitution of single-line rates on certain commodities, and the elimination of certain switching charges. A more adequate car supply, the availability of specialized equipment and more efficient utilization of equipment should result. There also are a number of advantages in dealing with a single corporate entity, such as convenience in the settlement of claims and the tracing of cars.

The Commission was given broad, plenary powers and was to look to mergers as a part of the "national" transportation problem. Thus, there could be local or limited monopolies so long as they were controlled and contributed to the attainment of the national transportation policy objectives. Therefore, a limited monopoly, such as the one in the present case, might be allowed.

The Commission is to weigh, "as an administrative matter," "the effect of the merger on competitors and on the general competitive situation in the industry." As the Supreme Court said (32 U.S. at 87):

> Resolving these considerations is a complex task which requires extensive facilities, expert judgment and considerable knowledge of the transportation industry. Congress left that task to the Commission "to the end that the wisdom and experience of that Commission may be used not only in connection with this form of transportation, but in its coordination of all other forms." . . . The wisdom and experience of that commission, not of the courts, must determine whether the proposed consolidation is consistent with the public interest. . . . If the Commission did not exceed the statutory limits within which Congress confined its discretion and its findings are adequate and supported by evidence, it is not our function to upset its order.

In the instant case, the Commission looked at and weighed all the factors. It is this weighing of factors and not the result that the statute compels. The ICC considered those areas in Florida where a monopoly would be created, including the size of the cities involved and their relative importance.

In our opinion, the ICC has clearly realized the danger zones in this merger and after analyzing the problem has chosen what it concludes to be more important public benefits.

In reaching the conclusion that this merger was in the public interest, the ICC reviewed at some length the competitive growth of other modes of transportation and their impact on the rail industry.

The ICC went on to announce its policy on intermodal competition in following terms:

> While we recognize in general the desirability of preserving intramodal rail competition, it is no longer the all-important factor that it once was in the days when the railroads had a virtual monopoly in all inter-city freight traffic. With the development of intense competition in recent years from other modes of transport, the preservation of intramodal rail competition has lost much of its significance in the furtherance of the overall national transportation policy. Even after the merger herein is approved, effective competition among railroads will continue in most of the major industrial centers.

In other regulated industries, typically gas, electric, and telephone utilities, a single company frequently serves large metropolitan areas and often even significantly larger geographic or market areas. As public utilities are affected with a public interest and are essentially monopolistic by nature, they are subjected to strict regulation and supervision by State and Federal regulatory agencies. Under regulation, their services, as a general rule, are efficient and reasonably priced despite the absence of competition. While exact comparability does not exist between railroads and public utilities generally, it must be recognized that railroads are subject to equally stringent regulation. Moreover, as railroads have the basic economic characteristics of public utilities and are subject to regulation in the public interest at both the Federal and State levels, it is not realistic to insist that intermodal rail competition must be preserved at all places, at all times, and under all circumstances. For these reasons and weighing all the factors previously discussed, plus the further consideration that railroads today encounter increasingly strong competition from other modes of transportation, we conclude and specifically find that (1) the reduction of rail competition caused by the proposed merger will not be substantial; (2) ample competitive rail service will remain after the merger throughout most of the effected areas; and (3) such reduction in competition as will result from the merger will have no appreciably injurious effect upon shippers and communities.

In short, Southern and the FEC would have us substitute our ability to predict future effects for that of the Commission. The ICC is far more experienced in this area than any one given court. The Commission, and not we, must tailor the protection to fit its expert prediction of the future. On this record, we are in no position to say that its careful study has led to capricious results. When not plainly unreasonable, we must leave to the agency vested with congressionally assumed expertise this type of decision. The question boils down to whether the ICC acted wisely in not providing more protection. Statutorily we are not the all-wise of this field, and, while our crystal ball might indicate a different result than that of the Commission, the record in this case supports its action.

2. The Merger Movement

The merger movement continued unabated through the 1960s. The Norfolk & Western expanded from a regional carrier to a major east-midwest carrier by acquiring the New York, Chicago & St. Louis (Nickel Plate Road) and leasing the Wabash. The Chesapeake & Ohio took control of the Baltimore & Ohio and Western Maryland to form the Chessie system.

This created a large imbalance in the East, with the two largest competing carriers, New York Central and Pennsylvania, left out of any of the new merger systems. The lines sought to merger with each other. The ICC, faced with their merger petition at the same time that the financially beleaguered New Haven Railroad sought to discontinue all interstate passenger service, approved the merger on the condition that the two partners include the hapless New Haven in their consolidated system.

This Penn Central system, biggest of them all, was sustained, after certain protective arrangements were made, by the Supreme Court in the Penn Central Merger and N & W Inclusion Cases.[55]

The Penn Central merger took place in 1968, and the New Haven was integrated within the system in 1969. By 1970, the system was bankrupt. In 1976, the largest consolidation to date took place, not by ICC action, but by virtue of the Regional Rail Reorganization Act of 1973, by which the Penn Central, Erie-Lackawanna, Reading, Lehigh Valley, Lehigh & Hudson River and Central of New Jersey were merged into a government-sponsored but privately owned corporation called Consolidation Rail Corporation, or Conrail.

A more successful merger, that of the so-called Northern Lines, occurred in 1970 with the consolidation of the Great Northern Railway, the Northern Pacific Railway, the Chicago, Burlington & Quincy Railroad and the Spokane, Portland and Seattle into the Burlington Northern system. The Northern Lines had long sought to merge into a single united transportation system. The Antitrust Division of the Department of Justice and the paralleling Milwaukee Road appealed, unsuccessfully, to the U.S. Supreme Court,[56] citing diminished competition and adverse effects on shippers and the public. The ICC ordered that gateways and trackage rights to Portland be conferred to the Milwaukee, but these were not enough to save the Milwaukee Road, which entered bankruptcy in 1978 and was partially dismembered in 1980. The Burlington Northern, having attained near-monopoly status in the Northwest, acquired the Frisco Lines (St. Louis–San Francisco Railroad) through ICC approval in 1980. It is now the longest railroad in the country.

If the 1970s was the decade of enthusiasm for transportation deregulation, the 1980s brought about the megamergers of railroads, coming closer and closer to the 1920 plan of Harvard professor William Z. Ripley to bring all the privately owned railways into four nationwide systems.

The competitive balance in the East, so skewered by the emergence of Conrail from the ruins of the major bankrupts, was regained by the ICC approval of the CSX Corporation, formed to acquire the railroads of the Chessie system to the north and the Seaboard-affiliated Family Lines to the south (now consolidated into the Seaboard System Railroad—formerly Seaboard Coast Line, Louisville & Nashville, Georgia Railroad, Western Railway of Alabama, Atlanta & West Point, and Clinchfield). In defense, the Norfolk & Western and the Southern Railway systems filed a consolidation petition before the ICC, which was approved in 1982. Now the Norfolk Southern Corporation, the merged system still operates with separate N & W and Southern units but is proceeding quickly toward integration of its networks. This leaves three major systems in the East, with Conrail operation mostly in the Northeast, and CSX and Norfolk Southern concentrating their efforts in the Southeast.

These mergers were effected without the traffic conditions and mandatory open gateways which the ICC usually attaches to such consolidations. As a result, each system has tended to operate as a closed system, seeking on-line traffic (or going after off-line traffic with trucking subsidiaries) and closing connections with one another. Conrail in particular has closed gateways with its Chessie Norfolk Southern connections. The ICC has maintained that its role is not to force competitive railroads to keep the gateways open.

But in the Pacific Railroad merger, which involved the Union Pacific's control of the Missouri Pacific and the Western Pacific, the Commission did impose traffic conditions. Most notable was that condition which gave the Southern Pacific access to St. Louis from Kansas City, thus saving the railroad the chore of rebuilding its ex-Rock Island trackage across the Missouri. The Rio Grande expanded to near-transcontinental status when the ICC granted the Denver-based carrier trackage rights over the Missouri Pacific's main line between Pueblo and Kansas City. Kansas City now has supplanted Chicago as the freight railroad capital of the United States. At this writing, the six major railroad companies in the United States are:

1. Burlington Northern

2. Conrail

3. Southern Pacific–Santa Fe

4. CSX (Chessie system plus Seaboard system)

5. Pacific Rail (Missouri Pacific–Union Pacific–Western Pacific)

6. Norfolk Southern

As this book goes to press, the Department of Transportation has announced its desire to sell its ownership interest in Conrail to the Norfolk–Southern Railway for approximately $1.5 billion. This will reduce to five the number of major railroads in the United States.

Numerous short lines and medium-sized railroads remain outside these behemoths and may do some scrambling to find a corporate home. One of the most interesting mergers approved by the ICC in 1982 was the acquisition of three eastern railroads by Guilford Transportation, Inc., the corporate brainchild of financier Timothy Mellon. Mellon, having acquired the Maine Central, put together enough cash for the bankrupt Boston & Maine to enable that carrier to effect an income-based reorganization. Next he turned westward to the Delaware & Hudson Railroad. Formerly a Norfolk & Western subsidiary, the D & H assumed massive loans to stave off bankruptcy and was glad to see Guilford Transportation acquire the Albany-based road. Mellon now controls a transportation system reaching from Bangor to Buffalo.

Another smaller-scale merger has been the gradual consolidation of Great Lakes area railroads into the Grand Trunk Western system. A Canadian National subsidiary, the GTW has now acquired the Detroit, Toledo & Ironton and the Detroit & Toledo Shore Line. It has attempted to acquire what is left of the Milwaukee Road. This acquisition would enable it to link the Grand Trunk mainline in Chicago with the Duluth, Winnipeg & Pacific in Duluth, thus encircling the Great Lakes on the U.S. side of the border.

Some railroads have recently increased their mileage by picking up Conrail spin-offs. The Northeast Rail Service Act of 1981 required that Conrail shed its branch lines in Rhode Island and Connecticut, which were picked up by the Providence & Worcester and the Boston & Maine, respectively. Unwanted branch lines in New York State are now operated as part of the Delaware Otsego system. So at the same time that Class I railroads are getting bigger, more and more short lines (often with local management and nonunion labor) are taking up the slack.

Two of the largest railroads did not make it into the 1980s. The Rock Island is abandoned, although about half of its freight lines are being operated by other carriers, either by acquisition or directed service orders. The east-west mainline of the Milwaukee Road has been abandoned west of Terry, Montana, and east of that point it has been acquired by South Dakota and is operated by the Burlington Northern. Most railroads not affiliated with any major system are located in the area between Chicago and the Rockies. They include the Illinois Central Gulf, the Missouri–Kansas–Texas, the Kansas City Southern, the Chicago & North Western, and the Rio Grande & Milwaukee. In the East, the Bangor & Aroostook in the North and the Florida East Coast in the South continue as mavericks.

MAINE CENTRAL R.R. V. AMOSKEAG CO., FREDERIC C. DU-MAINE & DUMAINES

360 I.C.C. 147 (1979)

By the Commission:
  Complaint
  The complaint filed by the MEC on April 21, 1974 alleged that the defendants, by reason of Amoskeag's holdings of MEC stock, possessed power to exercise control or management of the MEC. The MEC also alleged that the defendants had attempted to extend their power of control over it by purchasing additional shares of MEC stock for subsequent merger of MEC into the Bangor and Aroostook Railroad Company (BAR) which Amoskeag controls. The defendants were charged with achieving the power to control the MEC without Commission approval contrary to 49 U.S.C. 11343. The MEC sought to have the Commission order (1) the defendants to cease and desist from purchasing additional shares of MEC voting stock, (2) the voting trustee, which holds defendants' shares of MEC stock under an Independent Voting Trust Agreement, to be held accountable to the Commission, (3) the voting trustee to communicate with the defendants in writing only, with copies to the Commission, and (4) the defendants to divest themselves of all MEC stock acquired after January 1, 1973.
  Allegations of Control
  The MEC alleges several elements that it considers as amounting to power by Amoskeag, Mr. Dumaine, and DUMAINES to control it.
  Intent. The first element alleged is that the defendants possessed the intent to acquire and exercise control over MEC. It is clear that Amoskeag and the DUMAINES intended to acquire control of the MEC. The parties negotiated possible merger for several years up to the filing of the complaint. Two applications were filed by Amoskeag and DUMAINES for authority to acquire control of MEC. Even after the complaint was filed, Amoskeag's tender offer to have its subsidiary Downeast Management Corporation purchase MEC common stock clearly shows the intent to acquire control. But, as the defendants point out, having intent to control does not mean that they have the power to control.
  Largest shareholder. The second element alleged by the MEC is that Amoskeag

holds the largest block of MEC common stock, approximately 36 percent. The Commission has recognized that a minority sharehold can have power to control a carrier. The percentage of stock ownership, standing alone does not necessarily establish control. Control has been found in the owner of the largest block of shares where the remaining shares are widely diffused. Seaboard Air Line R. Co.—Merger—Atlantic Coast Line, 320 I.C.C. 122, 195 (1963). On the other hand, control has been found when the owner of a minority block of shares commands substantial influence or power over the corporation.

Besides the 36-percent interest owned beneficially by the Amoskeag, another 35 percent of the stock is aligned with the management. The remaining shares are held by several hundred owners. But the ownership of MEC stock is stable, and the stock is not widely traded. Nor is the stock readily available in the over-the-counter market. Thus we do not consider the MEC stock to be widely diffused.

Control as defined in 49 U.S.C. §10102 (formerly section 1(3)(b)) embraces the power to manage, direct, superintend, restrict, regulate, govern, administer, or oversee. No facts have been presented to show that Amoskeag has any power to manage the MEC. We have no evidence showing that the Amoskeag or its voting trustees have placed or have power to have anyone placed on the MEC board of directors.

Voting trust. The final element cited by MEC to support its complaint is the alleged attempt by the defendants to undermine the independence of the voting trustee. The use of an independent voting trust as a device to avoid a violation of 49 U.S.C. §11343 (formerly section 5(5)) has been sanctioned by the Commission and the courts, B.F. Goodrich Co. v. Northwest Industries, 303 F. Supp. 53, 61 (D. Del. 1969) affirmed 424 F. 2d 1349 (3d Cir. 1970), cert. den. 400 U.S. 822 (1971), so long as the trustee is truly independent from the settlor, Illinois Central R.R. Co. v. United States, 293 F. Supp. 421, 429 (M.D. Ill. 1966) affirmed per curiam 385 U.S. 45 (1967).

The MEC argues that the defendants sought to control it through the voting trust. The original trust was with Irving. Irving resigned in May 1973, and was replaced by Mercantile. The MEC argues that Irving resigned because the defendant had prevented it from being independent.

The MEC is correct that the voting trust agreement between defendants and Mercantile and its predecessor Irving had not been submitted to the Commission for analysis and approval. While there is no requirement that we have to approve voting trusts before they are established, carriers have been advised to seek our approval so they can be assured that the trust is lawful. But the failure to submit the agreement is not relevant to the question of the trustee's independence.

We find that the defendants attempted to undermine the independence of its voting trustee, but that both Irving and Mercantile withstood the pressure and maintained their independence. We conclude that Irving and Mercantile were independent trustees. MEC was insulated from the attempts by defendants to exert control through the trustees by the independence of Irving and Mercantile.

No evidence has been submitted showing that either one of the trustees—let alone Amoskeag—had attempted to participate in the management of the MEC. Neither trustee had been represented on the MEC board of directors, or had even sought to be represented. Neither trustee had veto power over the MEC or had any authority to control any of MEC's activities. In those instances when the trustees voted the shares held in trust, they followed their independent judgment and did not act as a rubber stamp for the defendants. See, *Illinois Central Gulf R. Co.—Acquisition—GM & O et al.*, 338 I.C.C. 805, 868–69 (1971).

Conclusions

The five elements cited by the MEC do not, in our view, show that the defendant had power to control MEC. The facts of record show that the defendant, Amoskeag, owns beneficially about 36 percent of MEC's common stock and intends to expand its stock ownership to achieve control, but have [sic] been unable to purchase control. The facts also show that the defendants have attempted to exert control over MEC through external pressure. First, they attempted, by valuating their stock interest in MEC at a low price, to pressure MEC into a merger. Secondly, they executed an agreement with CP Rail to divert traffic from the MEC and thereby diminish MEC's revenues. Thirdly, they attempted to influence their voting trustees so they would take an active interest in the MEC favoring defendants interest. Nevertheless, the defendants did not control MEC within the meaning of 49 U.S.C. § 11343.

B. Merger Procedures

1. Railroads

Congress has long been concerned about rail mergers and consolidations. Virtually every major piece of rail legislation since 1887 has addressed this question. The 4R Act is no exception.

The Conference Report summarizes the major changes in merger standards and procedures made by the 4R Act, as follows:

The most significant features of [this provision] are that the Secretary of Transportation is given a significant role as a catalyst in the studying, developing, and negotiating of railroad mergers. Further, the Secretary is authorized and under the new "expedited merger proceedings," is directed to appear before the Commission with the result of his studies.

Second, alternative merger procedures, with different standards for review by the Commission, are made available to railroads attempting to merge.

Third, strict time limits are placed upon the Commission for the completion of merger proceedings.

The 4R Act establishes time limits for filing comments, inconsistent applications and petitions for inclusion and for the completing of the evidentiary hearing and rendering of a decision by the ICC. The secretary of transportation is authorized to study and negotiate mergers and consolidations and to appear before the ICC in connection with all merger and consolidation proceedings. Employee protective arrangements provided by existing Section 11347 of the Interstate Commerce Act are also modified, and a new section is added that, in the words of the Conference Report, offers to railroads an alternative procedure for seeking approval of a merger that differs in significant functional aspects from section (11344) of the Interstate Commerce Act in that (1) the initial planning or review process is undertaken by the Secretary rather than in a hearing before the Commission (however, after the plans are finalized, they are submitted to the Commission for its approval), (2) it establishes public interest as the standard for the Commission's approval of a merger rather than the standards established under section 5(2) of the Interstate Commerce Act, and (3) the Commission is directed to approve, disapprove or modify the application before it, based on the public interest test and without concerning itself with inclusion applications. This stems from the fact that the only merger applications that are permitted to be reviewed by the Commission . . . are those that apply to the Secretary, for study, 6 months prior to applying to the Commission. Once such an application is presented to the Commission, it must be acted upon on its own merits.

The standards to be applied under Sections 11346 and 11344 are different but necessarily inconsistent. Section 11344(c) of the 4R Act provides that a consolidation proposal is to be approved when it is "consistent with the public interest" and the terms and conditions of the proposal are "just and reasonable." In determining whether this standard is met, the ICC is required, under Section 11344(b), to consider the same four factors that were enacted in the Transportation Act of 1940. In addition to those factors, the courts have required the ICC to consider the effects of the merger on competitors and on the general competitive situation in the industry, in light of the objectives of the National Transportation Policy.

The phrase "consistent with the public interest" has been construed to mean compatible with the public interest, or, at least, not contradictory or hostile to the public interest. The Rail Services Planning Office's (RSPO) recent merger report recommends that there not be a distinction between the two statutory criteria of "consistent with" the public interest and "in" the public interest: the Department of Transportation supports this view. The statute also provides that in assessing the public interest, the ICC is not restricted to the specific proposal advanced by the applicants and may also consider modifications suggested by other parties, including requests for inclusion by another railroad or railroads.

Section 11346 offers railroads an alternative procedure for seeking approval of consolidations. Under this provision, the initial analysis of the proposal is to be made by the secretary of transportation, who is directed to study each proposal with respect to nine factors:

1. Needs of rail transportation in the geographical area affected

2. Effect of such a proposed transaction on the retention and promotion of competition in the provision of rail and other transportation services in the geographic area affected

3. Environmental impact of such a proposed transaction and of alternative choices of action

4. Effect of such a proposed transaction on employment

5. Cost of rehabilitation and modernization of track, equipment and other facilities, with a comparison of the potential savings or losses from other possible choices of action

6. Rationalization of the rail system

7. Impact of such a proposed transaction on shippers, consumers and rail employees

8. Effect of such a proposed transaction on the communities in the geographic areas affected and on the geographic areas contiguous to such areas

9. Whether such a proposed transaction will improve rail service

In the event the consolidation proposal is subsequently submitted to the ICC for approval, the secretary is directed to submit a report to the ICC setting forth the results of the study of the proposal, and the ICC is directed to give "due weight and consideration" to the report in determining whether the transaction is "in the public interest." However, the standards established under Section 11344 do not govern the determination of "public interest" under Section 11346. A key distinction between review of consolidation proposals under sections 11344 and 11346 is that, unlike Section 11344 proceedings, the ICC is to review each application submitted under Section 11346 on its own merits, without concern for inconsistent applications or petitions for inclusions.

The reason for the distinction between Section 11344 and Section 11346 is detailed in the House Report:

The Committee's Subcommittee on Transportation and Commerce began this session considering various problems surrounding the bankrupt Rock Island Railroad. One of the major reasons for the plight of that railroad was that nearly twelve years elapsed before the Commission adjudicated whether or not it should be allowed to merge with a strong railroad.

The Committee recognizes that to a great extent the plight of the Rock Island is the inadequacy of existing merger provisions. Therefore, Title V of the bill provides an expedited merger procedure with prior evaluation, analysis and assistance by the secretary.

The changes made in existing law can best be illustrated by comparing existing law with the changes recommended by the Committee.

Under existing law, the Commission would handle each merger through its adjudicative process, and try to accommodate all the conflicting requests of various groups—the carriers, labor and the affected communities. Further, all railroads could petition to be included in such merger at any time during the merger proceedings.

This situation brought before the Commission a never-ending series of proposals for inclusions. Further, the Commission does not have a planning staff to study the proposed mergers and therefore remains at the mercy of the railroads, who many times would submit an infinite number of petitions for Commission consideration. The Commission would have to deal with petitions as they were filed and as the parties appeared before them, rather than attempting to have a period of time in which to study the proposed merger.

Lastly, there are no limits under existing law in which the Commission is required to complete the merger proceedings.

Therefore, in developing a new policy toward railroad mergers, the Committee created an alternative merger procedure rather than repealing the existing Section 11344 of the Interstate Commerce Act. The reason for having alternative methods for railroad mergers was to permit railroads the option of petitioning under either procedure.

a. Staggers Rail Act. The Staggers Rail Act of 1980 imposed stringent time deadlines on ICC disposition of merger applications. A "merger or control of 2 or more class I railroads" must be decided in not less than 31 months.[57] Other transactions "of regional or national transportation significance" must be decided within 10 months.[58] Finally, other transactions not deemed to be of national or regional transportation significance must be decided within six months. The ICC has construed "regional or national transportation significance" to mean only those transactions involving major market extensions.[59]

b. ICC Analysis. In the following decision, the ICC summarized the relevant statutory and regulatory criteria it assesses in analyzing proposed mergers between large rail carriers:

NORFOLK SOUTHERN CORP.—CONTROL—NORFOLK AND WESTERN RWY. CO. AND SOUTHERN RWY. CO. WY.
336 I.C.C. 171 (1982) (footnotes and citations generally omitted)
Discussion and Conclusions

Statutory Criterion: The Public Interest. Our review of the proposed consolidation of NW and Southern is governed by the basic standard of 49 U.S.C. 11344: we are required to approve the transaction if we find it to be "consistent with the public interest." Several primary sources help define and give character to this extremely broad standard.

SECTION 11344(B) FACTORS. Congress has specifically directed us to consider the following factors in determining wiether to approve a proposed consolidation as consistent with the public interest:

(1) the effect of the proposed transaction on the adequacy of transportation to the public;
(2) the effect on the public interest of including, or failing to include other rail carriers in the area involved in the proposed transaction;
(3) the total fixed charges that result from the proposed transaction;
(4) the interest of carrier employees affected by the proposed transaction and
(5) whether the proposed transaction would have an adverse effect on competition among rail carriers in the affected region.

49 U.S.C. 11344(B). The first four factors have been statutory considerations for many years. The fifth criterion—addressing the competitive effect of the transaction on rail car-

riers—was added by section 228(a)(2) of the Staggers Rail Act of 1980, Public Law 96–448 (October 14, 1980) (Staggers Act).

STATUTORY POLICIES. We are also guided in our consideration of rail consolidations, and in our regulation of the rail industry generally, by the stated policies of recent rail reform legislation and particularly by the Rail Transportation Policy of 49 U.S.C. 10101a. In this regard, the purpose of the consolidation provisions of the Railroad Revitalization and Regulatory Reform Act of 1976, Public Law 94–210 ("4R Act"), was "to encourage mergers, consolidations and joint use of facilities that tend to rationalize and improve the Nation's rail system." Staggers Act, section 2. Finally, the primary theme of 15 elements of the Rail Transportation Policy (added by the Staggers Act) is that we "ensure the development and continuation of a sound rail transportation system with effective competition among rail carriers and with other modes," 49 U.S.C. 10101a(4). Indeed, the Rail Transportation Policy emphasizes the importance of the relationship between ensuring adequacy of transportation and retention of competition. We are "to allow" competition and the demand for services to establish reasonable [rail] rates, section 10101a(1); "to foster sound economic conditions and to ensure effective competition and coordination between rail carriers and other modes, section 10101a(5); to minimize the need for Federal regulatory control over the rail transportation system, while maintaining "reasonable rates where there is an absence of effective competition," section 10101a(2),(6); and "to avoid undue concentrations of market power," section 10101a(13). We must also "encourage fair wages and suitable working conditions in the railroad industry." 49 U.S.C. 10101a(12).

ANTITRUST CONSIDERATIONS. We are required by a long line of cases to consider the policies embodied in the antitrust laws in our analysis of public interest. As the Supreme Court has observed, the antitrust laws give "understandable content to the broad statutory concept of the public interest."

In *McLean Trucking Co. v. United States*, 321 U.S. 67, 87 (1944) (*McLean*), the Supreme Court noted the proper weight to be accorded to antitrust policy in carrier consolidation proceedings:

> In short, the Commission must estimate the scope and appraise the effects of the curtailment of competition which will result from the proposed consolidation and consider them along with advantages of improved service, safer operation, lower costs, etc., to determine whether the consolidation will assist in effectuating the overall transportation policy. The wisdom and experience of that Commission, not of the courts, must determine whether the proposed consolidation is "consistent with the public interest."

Notwithstanding our consideration of competition in analyzing a proposed consolidation, we do not sit as an antitrust court in determining compliance with the Clayton, Sherman or related antitrust acts. As the Supreme Court noted in *McLean*, our statutory obligation under the public interest standard is broader. We must balance any anticompetitive effects of a consolidation against its anticipated transportation benefits. We are empowered to disapprove consolidations which would not violate the antitrust laws.

SPECIAL FINDINGS. We are required to make special, narrowly focused public interest findings (where applicable) on the following aspects of any major rail consolidation: (1) a guaranty or assumption of the payment of dividends or of fixed charges, or an increase of total fixed charges; (2) joint rail-motor operations; or (3) inclusion of rail carriers located in the area, 49 U.S.C. 11233(c).

ENVIRONMENT AND ENERGY FACTORS. Environmental and energy factors also have a bearing on the public interest. The National Environmental Policy Act of 1969 (NEPA), requires us to consider the transaction's effects on the environment. Similarly, we must consider the effects of the transaction on the conservation of energy resources, under the Energy Policy and Conservation Act (EPACA).

POLICY STATEMENT. On February 2, 1981, we issued a policy statement on rail consolidations to clarify how we incorporate the numerous elements of the public interest in evaluating specific consolidation proposals. *Railroad Consolidation Procedures*, 363 I.C.C. 784 (1981). We announced that we perform a balancing test weighing "the potential benefits to applicants and the public against the potential harm to the public." 49 CFR 1111.10(c) (1981).

Benefits from a proposed consolidation arise from operating efficiencies and marketing opportunities which can make the consolidated carrier a financially stronger competitor better able to provide adequate service on demand. 49 CRF 1111.10(d) (1981). Operating efficiencies often arise from elimination of duplicative facilities and utilization of more direct routings. Additionally, we have recognized that in some instances, consolidations may be the only feasible way for rail carriers to enter new markets. Our analysis of the potential harm from proposed consolidation focuses on two impacts highlighted by the statutes and policies discussed above: any reduction in either intramodal or intermodal competition which would likely result from the consolidation, and any harm to essential services provided by competing carriers occurring, for example, when traffic shifts expected from the consolidation are so substantial that essential service over a competing carrier's line would no longer be economically viable. 49 CRF 111.10(e)(1981).

c. ICC Policy Statement.[60]

(a) General. The Interstate Commerce Commission encourages private industry initiative that leads to the rationalization of the Nation's rail facilities and reduction of its excess capacity. One means of accomplishing these ends is rail consolidation. However, the Commission does not favor consolidations through the exercise of managerial and financial control if the controlling entity does not assume full responsibility for carrying out the controlled carrier's common carrier obligation to provide adequate service upon reasonable demand. Furthermore, the Commission does not favor consolidations that substantially reduce the transport alternatives available to shippers unless there are substantial and demonstrable benefits to the transaction that cannot be achieved in a less anticompetitive fashion. Our analysis of the competitive impacts on consolidation is especially critical in light of the congressionally mandated commitment to give railroads greater freedom to price without regulatory interference.

(b) Consolidation criteria. The Commission's consideration of mergers or controls of at least two Class I railroads is governed by the criteria prescribed in 49 U.S.C. 11344 and by the rail transportation policy set forth in 49 U.S.C. 10101a.

(1) Section 11344 directs the Commission to approve consolidations which are consistent with the public interest. In examining a proposed transaction, the Commission must consider, at a minimum: (i) The effect on the adequacy of transportation

to the public; (ii) the effect of including, or failing to include, other rail carriers in the area involved in the proposed transaction; (iii) the total fixed charges that would result; (iv) the interest of affected carrier employees; and (v) the effect on competition among rail carriers in the affected region.

(2) The Commission must also consider the impact of any transaction on the quality of the human environment and the conservation of energy resources.

(c) Public interest considerations. In determining whether a transaction is in the public interest, the Commission performs a balancing test. It weighs the potential benefits to applicants and the public against the potential harm to the public. The Commission will consider whether the benefits claimed by the applicants could be realized by means other than the proposed consolidation that pose fewer potential dangers.

(1) Potential benefits. Both the consolidated carrier and the public can benefit from a consolidation if the result is a financially sound competitor better able to provide adequate service on demand. This beneficial result can occur if the consolidated carrier is able to realize operating efficiencies and increased marketing opportunities. Since consolidations can lead to a reduction in redundant facilities and thereby to an increase in traffic density on underused lines, operating efficiencies may be realized. Furthermore, other than contractual arrangements, such as for joint use of rail facilities or run-through trains, consolidations are the only feasible new markets. In some markets where there is sufficient existing rail capacity the construction of new rail line is prohibitively expensive and does not represent a feasible means of entry into the market.

(2) Potential harm. There are two potential results from consolidations which would ill serve the public—reduction of competition and harm to essential services. In analyzing these impacts, we must consider, but are not limited by, the policies embodied in antitrust laws.

(i) Reduction of competition. If two carriers serving the same market consolidate, the result would be the elimination of competition between the two. Even if the consolidating carriers do not serve the same market, there may be a lessening of potential competition in other markets. While the reduction in the number of competitors serving a market is not in itself harmful, a lessening of competition resulting from elimination of a competitor may be contrary to the public interest. The Commission recognizes that rail carriers face not only intramodal competition, but also intermodal competition from motor and water carriers. The Commission's competitive analysis depends on the relevant market(s). In some markets the Commission's focus will be on the preservation of effective intermodal competition, while in other markets (such as long-haul movements of bulk commodities) effective intramodal competition may also be important.

(ii) Harm to essential service. Consolidations often result in shifts of market patterns. Sometimes the carrier losing its share of the market may not be able to withstand the loss of traffic. In assessing the probable impacts, the Commission's concern is the preservation of essential services, not the survival of particular carriers. A service is essential if there is a sufficient public need for the service and adequate alternative transportation is not available.

(d) Conditions. The Commission has broad authority to impose conditions on consolidations, including those that might be useful in ameliorating potential anticompetitive effects of a consolidation. However, the Commission recognizes that conditions may lessen the benefits of a consolidation to both the carrier and the public. Therefore, the Commission will not normally impose conditions on a consolidation to protect a carrier unless essential services are affected and the condition: (1) Is shown to be related to the impact of the consolidation; (2) is designed to enable shippers to receive adequate service; (3) would not pose unreasonable operating or other problems for the consolidated carrier; and (4) would not frustrate the ability of the consolidated carrier to obtain the anticipated public benefits. Moreover, the Commission believes that indemnification is ordinarily not an appropriate remedy in consolidation proceedings. Indemnification conditions can be anticompetitive by requiring the consolidated carrier to subsidize carriers who are no longer able to compete efficiently in the marketplace.

(e) Inclusion of the carriers. The Commission will consider requiring inclusion of another carrier as a condition to approval only where there is no other reasonable alternative for providing essential services, the facilities fit operationally into the new system, and inclusion can be accomplished without endangering the operational or financial success of the new company.

(f) Labor protection. The Commission is required to provide applicants' employees affected by a consolidation with adequate protection. Similarly situated employees on the applicants' system should be given equal protection. Therefore, absent a negotiated agreement, the Commission will provide for protection at the level mandated by law (49 U.S.C. 11347), unless it can be shown that because of unusual circumstances more stringent protection is necessary to provide employees with a fair and equitable arrangement. The Commission will review negotiated agreements to assure fair and equitable treatment of affected employees.

2. Motor Carriers

a. ICC Analysis. The following decision was the first major motor carrier merger analyzed by the ICC subsequent to the promulgation of the Motor Carrier Act of 1980. In it, the Commission addressed the public interest standard of the legislation.

RED BALL MOTOR FREIGHT, INC.—CONTROL AND MERGER—
SPECTOR IND., INC.
127 M.C.C. 737 (1980).

The Commission is required under 49 U.S.C. 11343 to consider whether approval of these transactions will be consistent with the public interest. The nature, as well as the number, of the issues which must be addressed in any acquisition proceeding will vary from case to case. One of these is the impact of a proposed transaction on competition, which is considered in conjunction with the furtherance of the national transportation policy.

A motor carrier acquisition consistent with the public interest will promote competition and efficiency. This may occur, for example, through substantial corporate simplification and the encouragement of the organization of stronger units in industry. Where two firms previously existed, a single entity will result, better able to provide services in a competitive marketplace. On the other hand, we must be concerned lest a particular acquisition result in a diminution of competition, contrary to the public interest.

The statutory criteria applied in rail and motor carrier consolidation proceedings are set out at 49 U.S.C. 11344. (See Appendix.) Before the passage of the Staggers Rail Act of 1980, Public Law 96-448 (Staggers Act), the four specific factors to be considered in all consolidation proceedings were contained in 49 U.S.C. 11344(b). Subsection (c) imposed a general public interest standard, authorized us to condition approval of transactions, and listed several other criteria to be applied in specific types of transactions. Section 228 of the Staggers Act amended section 11344 by limiting the provisions of subsection (b) to transactions involving the merger or control of at least two class I railroads and by codifying a fifth factor that had been considered under the case law. Subsection (c) was left unchanged. A new subsection (d) was added governing all transactions not involving control or merger of at least two class I railroads. Subsection (d) mandates approval unless:

(1) as a result of the transaction, there is likely to be substantial lessening of competition, creation of a monopoly, or restraint of trade in freight surface transportation in any region of the United States, and
(2) the anticompetitive aspects of the transaction outweigh the public interest in meeting significant transportation needs.

Thus, the Staggers Act amendments created two different standards under section 11344, one applicable to merger and control transactions involving two or more class I rail carriers and another applicable to all other consolidation proceedings.

Section 21 of the Bus Regulatory Reform Act of 1982 specifically provides that the criteria to be applied in consolidation proceedings involving motor carriers of passengers are the four criteria found in 49 U.S.C. 11344(b) prior to the Staggers Act, and the public interest standard of 49 U.S.C. 11344(c). Congress expressly excluded passenger consolidation transactions from the provisions of 49 U.S.C. 11344(d). Appendix A contains the relevant sections of amended 49 U.S.C. 11344.

While the Bus Act clarifies the criteria to be applied in motor passenger consolidations, it does not directly address the criteria to be applied in consolidations involving motor carriers of property, although other substantive changes in the law affecting motor carriers of property were enacted in the Bus Act. The legislative history of the Bus Act, however, provides some guidance.

The Bus Act reflects the work of a conference committee assigned to resolve the differences between the Senate and House of Representatives versions of the act. As pertinent here, the House bill would have subjected all motor consolidations to the pre-Staggers Act criteria. The Senate amendment, however: (1) subjected motor passenger consolidations to the pre-Staggers Act criteria; (2) made no changes to the criteria governing motor property consolidations; and (3) gave the Commission new authority to exempt certain motor property consolidations from review. With a few minor exceptions, Congress adopted the Senate amendments. The Conference committee report states that the Bus Act was intended to reinstate the pre-Staggers Act criteria for motor passenger consolidations. Congress recognized that the Staggers Act altered the criteria applicable to motor carrier consolidations. Congress also declined to act on a specific legislative proposal that would reinstate these criteria for motor property consolidations, while enacting a provision reinstating the criteria for motor passenger consolidations. Congress took this action with full knowledge of the House version of the bill which would have made this change of criteria for motor property transactions. Therefore, we conclude that Congress intended the Staggers Act criteria to govern motor property consolidations.

There is an additional reason to adopt this interpretation. The Motor Carrier Act, Staggers Act, and the Bus Act all advanced the broad policy of reducing regulation and encouraging greater reliance on market forces. Since this statement announces our intention to apply a more competitive and less regulatory approach to motor property consolidations, this interpretation conforms with these broad congressional policies.

Accordingly, in motor property consolidations, we shall apply the competition analysis of section 11344(d) and the public interest standards of section 11344(c). In motor passenger consolidations, we shall apply the four criteria in section 11344 (b)(2) and the public interest standards of section 11344(c).

Appendix A

As amended, the relevant sections of 49 U.S.C. 11344 provide:

(1) In a proceeding under this section which involves the merger or control of at least two class I railroads, as defined by the Commission, the Commission shall consider at least the following:

(A) the effect of the proposed transaction on the adequacy of transportation to the public.

(B) the effect on the public interest of including, or failing to include, other rail carriers in the area involved in the proposed transaction.

(C) the total fixed charges that result from the proposed transaction.

(D) the interest of carrier employees affected by the proposed transaction.

(E) whether the proposed transaction would have an adverse effect on competition among rail carriers in the affected region.

(2) In a proceeding under this section which involves only carriers of passengers providing transportation subject to the jurisdiction of the Interstate Commerce Commission under subchapter II of chapter 105 of this title, the Commission shall consider at least the following:

(A) the effect of the proposed transaction on the adequacy of transportation to the public.

(B) the effect on the public interest of including, or failing to include, other rail carriers in the area involved in the proposed transaction.

(C) the total fixed charges that result from the proposed transaction.

(D) the interest of carrier employees affected by the proposed transaction.

(c) The Commission shall approve and authorize a transaction under this section when it finds the transaction is consistent with the public interest. The Commission may impose conditions governing the transaction. When the transaction contemplates a guaranty or assumption of payment of dividends or of fixed charges or will result in an increase of total fixed charges, the Commission may approve and authorize the transaction only if it finds that the guaranty, assumption, or increase is consistent with the public interest. When a rail carrier, or a person controlled by or affiliated with a rail carrier, is an applicant and the transaction involves a motor carrier, the Commission may approve and authorize the transaction only if it finds that the transaction is consistent with the public interest, will enable the rail carrier to use motor carrier transportation to public advantage in its operations, and will not unreasonably restrain competition. When a rail carrier is involved in the transaction, the Commission may require inclusion of other rail carriers located in the area involved in the transaction if they apply for inclusion and the Commission finds their inclusion to be consistent with the public interest.

(d) In a proceeding under this section which does not involve the merger or control of at least two class I railroads, as defined by the Commission, the Commission shall approve such an application unless it finds that—

(1) as a result of the transaction, there is likely to be substantial lessening of competition, creation of a monopoly, or restraint of trade in freight surface transportation in any region of the United States; and

(2) the anticompetitive effects of the transaction outweigh the public interest in meeting significant transportation needs.

In making such findings, the Commission shall, with respect to any application that is part of a plan or proposed developed under section 5(a)-(d) of the Department of Transportation Act (49 U.S.C. 1654(a)-(d)), accord substantial weight to any recommendations of the Secretary of Transportation. The provisions of this subsection do not apply to any proceeding under this section which involves only carriers of passengers providing transportation subject to the jurisdiction of the Commission under subchapter II of Chapter 105 of this title.

b. Exemption Authority. The Bus Regulatory Reform Act of 1982 included a provision authorizing the ICC to exempt motor carriers of property from the merger, consolidation and acquisition of control provisions of the Interstate Commerce Act.[61] The Commission may exempt a person, class of persons or class of transactions if it finds that regulation thereof is not necessary to carry out the National Transportation Policy of 49 U.S.C. § 10101, and either that the transaction is of limited scope or that such regulation is unnecessary to protect shippers from the abuse of market power.[62] A more general exemption power exists for rail carriers but uses essentially the same criteria.[63]

c. Sale of Operating Authority. The transfer of motor carrier operating authority (with or without accompanying equipment or facilities) between carriers requires approval by the ICC. The ICC traditionally refused to authorize the transfer of dormant rights, presuming that during any substantial interruption of service, other carriers expanded their operations to fill the void.

To determine whether operating rights are dormant, the Commission has traditionally used the "test of substantiality." When a regular-route carrier has been providing service over a substantial portion of its entire system, it need not prove that it operates over every route sought to be transferred. In determining whether such operating authority is dormant, the ICC evaluates such criteria as the nature of the commodities transported, the demographic characteristics of the involved territory, and the abilities of the involved carrier.

In Central Transport, Inc.—Purchase (Portion)—Piedmont Petroleum Products, Inc.,[64] the ICC adopted a tripartite test to evaluate proposals to transfer dormant rights: (1) the applicant bears the initial burden of demonstrating a public benefit to be realized from consummation of the proposed transaction; it need "merely indicate that the transfer will in some manner improve transportation service to the public"; (2) once the applicant has sustained its burden, the burden of going forward shifts to the protestant, who must prove that there is a probability that they will be significantly harmed by the transfer; (3) if protestant's burden is satisfied, the burden of going forward shifts once again to the applicant, who must adduce evidence of public need (ordinarily in the form of supporting statements by affected shippers) sufficient to outweigh this harm.

With the eased entry standards of the Motor Carrier Act of 1980, it has become less important for carriers to buy operating authority from other trucking companies—it is far cheaper and easier to apply for additional authority. Thus, these procedures have become considerably less important. Although the Bus Regulatory Reform Act has liberalized entry in the passenger business, sale of operating rights might still be of some importance in the motor coach industry.

III. AIRLINE ANTITRUST REGULATION

A. Pre–1978

In the late 1960s, excessively optimistic CAB and industry demand projections led the industry to invest in large numbers of wide-bodied aircraft.[65] Yet the economic circumstances of the first part of the 1970s led passenger demand to fail to live up to these expectations. The diminution of disposable income engendered by the recession of the early 1970s, coupled with the tendency of air carriers to raise their prices, led load factors to drop and carrier profits to turn downward.

In response, a number of the major carriers (i.e., United, TWA, and American) agreed to a collective reduction of service provided on several of the major domestic routes. The Board continually approved these agreements betwen 1971 and 1975, first as an emergency response to overinvestment and excessive capacity and, after 1973, as a necessary response to fuel shortages which allegedly existed after the Arab oil embargo.

Although the capacity limitation agreements can, theoretically, bring about lower carrier cost and correspondingly lower fares, the latter did not materialize. The airline industry was, in fact, the only major industry which raised its prices during the recession of the early 1970s. The report of the Kennedy subcommittee concluded that "the classic regulatory response to defects in regulation is to create more regulation: the Board's response to the problem of excess capacity was to introduce capacity-restricting agreements. Yet, to do so in this highly competitive, complex industry brought the consumer the worst of both worlds, high prices, and poor service."

President Gerald Ford became firmly convinced that the air transportation industry should be substantially deregulated. In 1975, he submitted his own version of a deregulation bill to Congress and appointed John Robson chairman of the CAB. As CAB chairman, Robson reversed many of the anticompetitive regulatory features for which the Board had been soundly criticized. The route moratorium and the capacity-limitation agreements were terminated.

B. The Airline Deregulation Act of 1978

Section 408: Consolidation, Merger, and Acquisition of Control[66]: The former terms of section 408 of the Federal Aviation Act prohibited, unless approved by the Board after notice and hearing, a variety of merger and acquisition transactions involving carriers, persons engaged in any phase of aeronautics, and others. In limited cases, the Board could dispose of an application for approval without a hearing. The Board was directed to approve any transaction unless it found that the transaction would not be consistent with the public interest. The only guidance on the meaning of "public interest" in this context, apart from the Declaration of Policy in section 102, was a prohibition against approving transactions that would result in a monopoly if the result would be to restrain competition or injure a carrier not party to the transaction.

The Deregulation Act narrowed the class of transactions covered by section 408 as follows: (1) The expression "person engaged in any phase of aeronautics," which had been interpreted very broadly in the past, has been replaced by "person substantially engaged in the business of aeronautics." A large number of transactions with persons that are only incidently related to air transportation are thus removed from Board jurisdiction. (For example, the Board was once asked to pass upon the merger of two power tool companies because one of them, McCulloch, had a subsidiary which itself had a subsidiary which was an air carrier that transported prospective customers to properties develped by a real estate subsidiary. Such transactions will no longer be subject to Board scrutiny.) (2) Acquisitions of air carriers by persons who have no aviation interests have also been removed from Board jurisdiction. Supervision of these transactions is left to the antitrust laws—administered by the Department of Justice and the Federal Trade Commission.

The Board is still directed to approve a transaction unless it finds that the transaction will not be consistent with the public interest, but there is more guidance on the meaning of this term. The Declaration of Policy (section 102) has been revised to place more emphasis on competition. Also, the Board is absolutely prohibited from approving a transaction that would result in a monopoly. Moreover, the Board may not approve any transaction "the effect of which in any region of the United States may be substantially to lessen competition" (which is basically the standard under section 7 of the Clayton Act), unless it finds both (1) that the anticompetitive effects are outweighed in the public interest by the probable effect of the transaction in meeting significant transportation needs, and (2) that these needs may not be satisfied by a reasonably available alternative whose effects are materially less anticompetitive. The party challenging the transaction has the burden of proving its anticompetitive effects, while those seeking its approval have the burden of proving that it is the least anticompetitive method of meeting significant transportation needs.

The procedure for disposing, without a hearing, of applications for approval of transactions that do not involve control of a direct air carrier is retained, with the change that the Secretary of Transportation and the Attorney General may insist on a hearing without having to demonstrate that they have a substantial interest in the transaction.

Finally, there is a special procedure for merger and acquisition transactions that involve neither certificated carriers nor foreign carriers. These include, among others, air freight-forwarder mergers and acquisitions of air taxis by persons substantially engaged in a phase of aeronautics. Parties planning to enter into such transactions must notify the Board at least 45 days before the effective date of the transaction. The Board may then require the transaction to go through the regular hearing and approval process. If the Board takes no action within 45 days, however, the transaction may be consummated without approval. The transaction is subject only to the antitrust laws, with this exception: If the Board was led to take no action by fraud or misrepresentation, it can subject the transaction to the prior approval requirement.

Section 409: Interlocking Relationships: Section 409(a) formerly prohibited, unless approved by the Board, an air carrier from having interlocking directors or officers with another air carrier, common carrier, or person engaged in any phase of aeronautics. As with section 408, the expression "person engaged in any phase of aeronautics" has been replaced by "person substantially engaged in the business of aeronautics." Interlocking relationships between air carriers and persons only incidently related to air transportation are thus no longer subject to Board scrutiny.

Section 409(b) has been repealed. This section prohibited certain stock transactions by officers and directors of air carriers. It essentially reflected the common law of fiduciary duties of officers and directors, and did not give the Board any powers or duties. It was repealed because it was obsolete.

Section 412: Agreements: Formerly, agreements between air carriers affecting air transportation had to be filed with the Board. The Board was directed to disapprove agreements that it found adverse to the public interest and otherwise to approve them. Approval conferred automatic immunity from the antitrust laws. Section 412 did not establish any particular criteria for deciding whether an agreement was "adverse to the public interest."

Under the Board practice that evolved an agreement that violated the antitrust laws was considered as not adverse to the public interest, if it passed a special test. Under this test, an agreement that substantially reduced or eliminated competition could be approved if it was necessary "to meet a serious transportation need or to secure important public benefits." This has become known as the "local cartage" test, named for the Board decision that established it.

The Deregulation Act retained the existing provisions of section 412 for agreements affecting foreign air transportation, and added new provisions to govern agreements that affect only domestic transportation.

Procedurally, the major change in the treatment of domestic agreements is that filing is now voluntary. Agreements that are not filed are subject to the antitrust laws. Thus, probably the main reason a carrier would wish to file is to obtain antitrust immunity in connection with Board approval.

The other major change affecting domestic agreements is in the standards to be applied to those that are filed. The Board may not approve an agreement that limits capacity or fixes prices, except an agreement on joint rates or fares. For other agreements, the "local cartage" test has been replaced by a more stringent standard based on the approach taken in the Bank Merger Act. Even if the agreement is necessary to meet a serious transportation need or secure important public benefits, it may not be approved if the Board finds that these ends are attainable by reasonably available alternative means whose effects are materially less anticompetitive. The Board may approve if the proponent of the agreement proves that it meets a serious transportation need or has other important public benefits, and its attackers fail to prove that there are reasonably available alternatives whose effects are materially less anticompetitive. The findings on these points must be included in the Board order approving the agreement.

Finally, section 412 has been amended to disapprove any existing mutual aid agreement and establish criteria for Board approval of any new ones. These criteria are quite specific and supplement the general test discussed above. The mutual aid agreement must (A) limit payments to 60 percent of the struck carrier's direct operating expenses; (B) limit benefits to 8 weeks during any strike, with no benefits paid for losses during the first 30 days; and (C) provide that all parties to the agreement agree to submit strike issues to binding arbitration under the Railway Labor Act if requested by the striking employees.

Section 414: Antitrust Immunity: Formerly, section 414 granted carriers immunity from the antitrust and other laws for transactions and relationships that received Board approval under section 408, 409, or 412. The Deregulation Act makes the following changes: (1) It limits immunity to the antitrust laws. (2) Immunity is available only to the extent necessary to permit completion of a transaction specifically approved by the Board or contemplated by a Board order. (3) Most importantly, immunity is no longer automatic. It is discretionary with the Board, except that the Board must find that immunity is in the public interest before granting it.

On January 1, 1985, jurisdiction over sections 408, 409, 412 and 414 of the Federal Aviation Act was transferred from the CAB (which ceased to exist as of that date) to the U.S. Department of Transportation.

C. The Airline Merger Cases

1. Statutory Framework

The legislative history[67,68] of the Airline Deregulation Act (ADA) of 1978, including the airline merger provision of Section 408, clearly states the intent of Congress to increase competition in the airline industry:

Section 408 standards must now be interpreted in light of the intent of Congress to move the airline industry rapidly toward deregulation. The foundation of the new airline legislation is that it is in the public interest to allow the airline industry to be governed by the forces in the marketplace.[69]

Essentially, Congress, in the new Section 408, adopted the same merger standard found in Section 7 of the Clayton Act,[70] prohibiting any merger the effect of which may "substantially lessen competition" or "tend to create a monopoly" in any region of the United States.

The legislative history of Section 408 indicates that Congress intended more liberal standards to be applied in the airline industry in certain limited situations:

Even if a merger does not meet the antitrust standards of the Sherman and Clayton Acts, it may nonetheless be approved if it meets "significant transportation needs of the community to be served," and if there is no "reasonably available less anticompetitive alternative" to the merger.[71]

In addition, the ADA amended Section 414 of the 1958 Act. These provisions permit the CAB to grant antitrust immunity in merger cases by (1) clarifying that such immunity is specifically limited to antitrust laws; (2) providing that immunity shall be granted only to complete CAB-approved transactions; and (3) specifying that CAB immunity is discretionary and should be granted only when CAB finds the grant to be in the public interest.[72]

A final portion of the statute relevant in evaluating airline merger proposals is Section 102, the Declaration of Policy provisions. Section 102, as amended by Section 3 of the ADA, lists various factors deemed by Congress to be in the "public interest." The same "public interest" factors found in Section 102 are also used in the "public interest" portion of the airline merger policy set out in Section 408.[73]

The first CAB action taken on a merger application after the ADA became law was the approval of the merger of Southern Airways into North Central Airlines to form Republic Airlines.[74]

In North Central–Southern, the CAB considered but declined to rule on whether the Section 408 merger standard includes a separate public interest test, or whether a public interest test is included within the Section 408 antitrust test. The issue was important not only in the North Central–Southern case, but in subsequent merger cases as well, because adoption of the view that Congress intended both a public interest test and an antitrust test would pose a more difficult standard for merger applicants to meet.

The CAB found, however, that because "no party . . . offered any convincing evidence or argument that the combination of the North Central and Southern would fail under . . . the alternative interpretations," resolution of this statutory issue of first impression was reserved for subsequent decisions.

Despite sidestepping these key issues involved in interpreting the new section 408 merger standards, the Board provided some guidance in determining what is not "anticompetitive" under section 408 by adopting as authority U.S. Supreme Court interpretations of Section 7 of the Clayton Act. This section of the Clayton Act, like Section 408 of the ADA, prohibits mergers the probable effect of which may "substantially lessen competition" or "tend to create a monopoly."

To evaluate competitive effects of the merger, the Board in North Central–Southern adopted the "functional" approach used by the U.S. *Supreme Court in United States v. Brown Shoe*.[75] There, the Court outlined a method for evaluating whether a merger will "substantially lessen" competition. The Brown Shoe test involves defining geographic product markets and then examining each market so defined for such factors as market share, cross-elasticity of demand between the product and substitutes and barriers to entry.

Using a similar rationale, the CAB noted that the carrier "resulting from the present merger would not have more than a minimal effect on concentration."[76] The CAB also specifically rejected a Frontier Airlines argument that the merger would violate merger guidelines promulgated by the Justice Department in Section 7 of the Clayton Act by increasing concentration in certain regional markets. The Board reasoned that the "regional market identified [by Frontier] ignores commercial realities by excluding key points where routes of the two carriers touch each other, thus exaggerating their market shares. None of the market shares in more reasonably defined markets offend the guidelines."

Accordingly, the Board ruled that the merger opponents had not demonstrated that reasonably defined markets were highly concentrated. Largely because they failed this key test, the merger opponents were not able to meet the statutory burden of proving anticompetitive effects of the merger.

In addition to Section 408 antitrust rulings, the CAB also established a clear precedent in a merger-related question by refusing to grant antitrust immunity[77] to the merging airlines. Section 414 permits the CAB to grant antitrust immunity only to the extent necessary for the merger to go forward, unlss the CAB finds that "such exemption *is required* by the public interest" (emphasis added).[78] The CAB found "insufficient evidence of either of these requirements to form the basis of a grant of immunity."[79]

The applicants and other proponents of immunity relied principally on the argument that a strong public interest exists in finality of proceeding. They argued that while doctrines of res judicata and collateral estoppel might not preclude a Clayton Section 7[80] collateral attack, a grant of immunity would guarantee finality and fulfill the public interest.

However, the CAB was persuaded by the arguments of the opponents of immunity that the plain meaning of Section 414 allows the CAB to grant immunity only if the public interest requires such grant. The CAB reasoned that finality was not specifically listed among the public interest goals of Section 102 and further that well-settled doctrine requires deference to administrative holdings absent clear error. Consequently, the CAB held that "in this case, where there are no anticompetitive effects, little or no chance of subsequent litigation and most importantly, no basis in the record for concluding that immunity is necessary, we believe Congress intended that no immunity be granted."

A third matter the CAB considered in approving North Central–Southern was the inclusion of labor protective provisions. By imposing labor protective provisions, the CAB rejected Bureau of Pricing and Domestic Aviation arguments that ADA deregulation goals also terminate the need for such protective provisions. Still, as with other statutory issues of first impression, the CAB in North Central–Southern reserved judgment "on the question of labor protection as a policy matter."

The CAB rested its decision on the facts that (1) the record indicated that both parties litigated the case as if labor protective provisions would be imposed; (2) elimination of labor protective provisions is inconsistent with the statutory language and legislative history; and (3) the Bureau of Pricing and Domestic Aviation argument was not raised until after the hearing and therefore the issue was not fully and fairly litigated.

2. The Struggle to Control National Airlines

Although the CAB approved the applications of both Pan American and Texas International (TXI) to control National, only the Pan American–National merger actually took effect. Just before the Board granted official approval of both applications, Pan American and National agreed between themselves that Pan American would purchase control of National for $300 million. Nonetheless, the Board's decision approving TXI's application[81] provides some guidance for Board merger policy under the ADA.

In TXI–National, the CAB reversed an Administrative Law Judge (ALJ), finding that the proposed merger would substantially lessen competition in violation of Section 408. While the ALJ relied principally on market share statistics in individual city pairs, the Board adopted the broader *Brown Shoe* analysis used in the previous North Central–Southern decision. For example, the ALJ found that the existing competition would be substantially lessened in the Houston–New Orleans market. At the time of the Board's decision, TXI controlled 24 percent of the market, National held 27 percent of the market and Delta maintained 23 percent of the market. The ALJ reasoned that because a TXI–National merger would produce a 51 percent market share for the new firm, and a 74 percent market share for the top two firms (the merged firm and Delta), a TXI–National merger would violate guidelines proscribed by the U.S. Supreme Court in *United States v. Philadelphia National Bank.*[82] There, the Court found a violation of Section 7 of the Clayton Act in which the two merged firms would have had a 30 percent market share and the merged firm plus its second-ranking competitor would have controlled 59 percent of the market.

The Board noted, however, that *Philadelphia National Bank* merely raised a presumption that a 30 percent merged firm market share and a 50 percent two-firm concentration ratio violated Clayton Section 7. Moreover, the CAB cited with approval a more recent Section 7 case, *United States v. General Dynamics.*[83] There, as in *Brown Shoe*, the Supreme Curt examined all competitive factors in the industry and found no violation of Section 7, even though the market shares involved were presumptively illegal under *Philadelphia National Bank*.

The CAB opinion also favorably noted TXI statistics that 84 percent of the top 200 city pairs have two-firm concentrations in excess of 74 percent. Such markets are therefore as concentrated as Houston–New Orleans would have been after a TXI–National merger.

Thus, the Board concluded that market share data should be only one of several factors resolving whether an airline merger substantially lessens competition in violation of Section 408. The decision lists other factors, such as ease of entry and exit under deregulation, as examples of competitive factors tending to overcome a presumption of lessened competition under a Philadelphia National Bank market share analysis. The board pointed out that by the fourth quarter of 1978, TXI, a relative newcomer, had captured the largest share of the Houston–New Orleans market. More significant, the decision noted the success of Southwest Airlines, which entered the Houston–New Orleans market in February 1979 and by August 1979 accounted for 24 percent of the non-stop capacity.

Besides ruling that the loss of National would not substantially reduce actual competition in the Houston–New Orleans market, the Board also reversed an ALJ decision that a National–TXI merger would substantially reduce potential competition in 16 other city pairs.

Supporting its conclusion that the TXI–National merger would not substantially lessen potential competition, the Board cited *United States v. Marine Bancorporation*:

The potential competition doctrine has meaning only as applied to concentrated markets. That is, the doctrine comes into play only where there are dominant participants in the target market engaging in interdependent or parallel behavior and with the capacity effectively to determine price and total output of goods or services, there would be no need for concern about the prospects of long-term deconcentration of a market which is in fact genuinely competitive.[84]

The CAB noted that the *Marine Bancorporation* decision reiterated that view that concentration statistics may be rebutted by evidence of other competitive factors.

The CAB also overturned an ALJ decision in Pan American–National that such a merger would substantially lessen competition in violation of Section 408.[85] As in TXI–National, the Board held that a presumed violation of Section 408 based on a Philadelphia National Bank market share analysis was overcome in this case by other procompetitive factors: "the most crucial factors (in determining the anticompetitive effects of a merger) are those which determine the nature of competition, for example, ease of entry, traffic density, the number of actual competitors, and the likelihood of new entry."

3. The United States–Western European Market

Applying the above standards to the effect of the Pan American–National merger on the United States–Western European market, the CAB was unconvinced that the reduction of one scheduled carrier would substantially lessen competition. In particular, the CAB called attention to the large number of scheduled and charter carriers, as well as foreign and domestic carriers, now serving and willing to enter the northern transatlantic market. The Board cited a number of bilateral agreements between the United States and various nations across the Atlantic, including Germany, Israel and the Benelux countries, as further evidence of strong competitive conditions in the United States–western European market.

In addition, the Board cited ADA provisions: (1) permitting expedited procedures without oral hearing in route application cases[86]; (2) allowing incumbents more flexibility to exit markets [87]; and (3) easing the exemption requirement.[88] Clearly, evaluation of all such competitive factors is consistent with *Brown Shoe* and follows the Board precedent set in the original Section 408 case, *North Central–Southern*.

4. The Miami–London Market

Contrary to its finding in the United States–western European market, the CAB did find that competition in the London–Miami submarket would be "substantially lessened" after the merger because Pan American would be the only scheduled carrier remaining. Further, granting Pan American the Miami–London market would leave Pan American with approximately 35 percent of the United States–London market. Section 408(b) permits the CAB "to impose such terms and conditions as it shall find to be just and reasonable when approving a merger." As a result, the CAB was able to approve the National–Pan American merger on the condition that Pan American agree to divest itself of National's Miami–London route authority. Pan American was also required to maintain National's current gate facilities at London's Heathrow Airport—facilities which were in short supply and difficult to obtain—until suitable competitive service was approved by the CAB.

Finally, the CAB resolved in *Pan American–National* the issue left unresolved in *North Central–Southern*: it held Section 408 does require both a "public interest" test and an "antitrust" test, thus rejecting arguments by the Departments of Transportation and Justice that the Section 408 "public interest" and "antitrust" tests were one and the same.

The Board conceded that many of the antitrust factors are included in "public interest" considerations but emphasized that the Section 408 "public interest" tests include other factors as well. The Board's decision thus leaves open the possibility that a proposed merger could meet the antitrust test yet be rejected for failure to meet somewhat nebulous "public policy" considerations. A literal reading of Section 408—"unless . . . the Board finds that the transaction will not be consistent with the public interest or that the section 408 antitrust tests will not be fulfilled"—suggests that the CAB decision is correct.

5. CAB Rejection of Eastern–National Merger

In what now appears to be little more than a historical anomaly, a Board majority rejected the Eastern–National merger.[89] The CAB believed that a substantial reduction of competition in violation of Section 408 was likely, particularly owing to capacity restraints at certain airports along the eastern seaboard.

In disapproving *Eastern–National*, the Board endorsed an ALJ finding that the proposed Eastern–National merger would have caused substantial lessening of actual competition in the New York–Florida, Washington–Florida, New York–Washington and intra–Florida markets. The ALJ had earlier held that unavailability of slots (airside space) at Washington's National Airport and New York's LaGuardia and JFK Airports may well have posed insurmountable barriers to entry in New York–Washington, New York–Florida and Washington–Florida markets. Interestingly, with the Board's recent approval of Continental–Western II,[90] Eastern–National became the only merger proposal to be disapproved since deregulation.

6. The First Show Cause Proceeding: The Republic–Hughes Merger

On May 16, 1980, the CAB issued to the public an Order to Show Cause within 60 days why the CAB should not make final its tentative conclusion to allow Republic to acquire control of Hughes.[91] Republic's application and supporting material were sufficient to support a Board conclusion that (1) the merger would not violate Section 408 antitrust standards; and (2) the application presented no issues of material fact. On September 12, 1980, the Board formally adopted the tentative conclusions listed in the Show Cause Order and approved Republic's purchase of Hughes.[92]

In its Show Cause Order, the Board outlined standards which have evolved to date for interpreting the new Section 408. First, it emphasized that the product market has consistently been defined as scheduled air transportation, and the relevant geographic markets have been city pairs, cities, regions, and the nation. Second, the CAB affirmed applicability of the *Brown Shoe* "functional" test for each merger's individually defined markets. The CAB reaffirmed the notion that *Brown Shoe* requires examination of a relevant market's structural characteristics, including entry barriers, potential entrants, ability of merging firms to increase entry barriers, and the degree of concentration of particular markets.

Applying the above standards to *Republic–Hughes*, the CAB found that "Republic and Hughes do not engage in any single-plane competition in any city pair at the present time." The Board also found that the two carriers did engage in "a de minimus amount of single carrier competition through connecting service in three markets." Because each carrier's share was "infinitesimal," the Board believed it highly unlikely that the merger would reduce actual competition to any harmful extent.

On a regional basis, the Board found that in the six cities where the two systems met, the merger was not likely to lessen substantially actual competition because of a large number of other carriers and potential entrants.

On a national level, the Board ruled that Republic's application satisfactorily demonstrated that the merger would not violate the Justice Department Merger Guidelines: the proposed merger of Republic (12th largest carrier) and Hughes (14th largest carrier) would only result in the nation's 11th largest carrier. Therefore, the Board found that a Republic–Hughes merger was unlikely to lessen substantially actual competition in any city pair, city, region or the nation.

NOTES

1. This section is adapted from Dempsey, *Rate Regulation and Antitrust Immunity in Transportation: The Genesis and Evolution of This Endangered Species*, 32 Am. U.L. Rev. 720 (1983).

2. Ch. 647, 26 Stat. 209 (1890) (codified as amended at 15 U.S.C. §§ 1–7 (1976)).

3. Ch. 91, 41 Stat. 456 (codified as amended in scattered sections of 49 U.S.C.).

4. Ch. 722, 54 Stat. 898 (codified as amended in scattered sections of 49 U.S.C.).

5. 49 U.S.C. §§ 11341–11343 (Supp. IV 1980).

6. *Id.* §§ 11342–11343, 11914.

7. *Id.* § 11343.

8. 324 U.S. 439 (1945).

9. Ch. 491, 62 Stat. 472 (1948) (codified as amended at 49 U.S.C. § 10706 (Supp. IV 1980)).

10. S. Rep. No. 44, 80th Cong., 1st Sess. 3 (1947).

11. 15 U.S.C. §§ 8, 9.

12. *Id.* §§ 13–13b, 21a.

13. *Id.* §§ 41–51.

14. Rail carriers may not participate in agreements related to or vote on single-line rates proposed by another carrier, except for purposes of a general rate increase and broad tariff changes [49 U.S.C § 10706(b)(3)(A)].

15. This section is adapted from Dempsey, *Rate Regulation and Antitrust Immunity in Transportation: The Genesis and Evolution of This Endangered Species*, 32 Am. U.L. Rev. 725 (1983) (footnote generally omitted).

16. *See, e.g.*, Luckenbach S.S. Co. v. United States, 364 U.S. 280 (1960), *aff'd per curiam* 179 F. Supp. 605 (D. Del. 1959).

17. *See* Board of Trade v. ICC, 646 F.2nd 1187, 1193 (7th Cir. 1981).

18. Motor Carriers Traffic Ass'n v. United States, 559 F.2d 1251 (4th Cir. 1981).

19. Under the doctrine of primary jurisdiction, a court may decline to address a controversy involving a question that is within the jurisdication of an administrative agency when that agency has yet to decide the issue. This is particularly true when the question requires administrative interpretation based on the agency's special knowledge and experience in deciding technical and intricate matters of fact. *See* Luckenbach S.S. Co. v. United States, 179 F. Supp. 605, 611–13 (D. Del. 1959).

20. Luckenbach S.S. Co. v. United States, 179 F. Supp. 605, 610 (D. Del. 1959).

21. 260 U.S. 156 (1922).

22. 260 F. Supp. 391 (N.D. Cal. 1966).

23. *E.g.*, United States v. Southern Motor Carriers Rate Conference, 439 F. Supp. 29, 35 (N.D. Ga. 1977).

24. Rate Bureau Investigation, 349 I.C.C. 811 (1975).

25. Pub. L. No. 94–210, 90 Stat. 31 (codified as amended in scattered sections of 15, 31, 45, & 49 U.S.C.).

26. 49 U.S.C. § 10706(a)(3)(A)(i) (Supp. IV 1980).

27. § 10101(a).

28. *Id.* § 10706(a)(2).

29. *Id.*

30. *Id.*

31. *Id.* § 10505.

32. Pub. L. No. 96–448, 94 Stat. 1895 (1980) (codified in scattered sections of 11, 45, & 49 U.S.C.).

33. 49 U.S.C. § 10706(a)(3)(A)(i) (Supp. IV 1980).

34. *Id.* § 10706(a)(3)(A)(ii). *See also id.* § 10706(a)(3)(C).

35. *Id.* § 10706(a)(3)(A)(i).

36. *Id.* § 10706(b)(3)(i).

37. *Id.* § 10706(b)(3)(B)(ii).

38. *Id.* § 10706(b)(3)(B)(iii).

39. *Id.* § 10708(d).

40. *Id.* § 10730(b). *See id.* § 10706(b)(3)(C).

41. *Id.* § 10706(b)(3)(B)(v).

42. *Id.* § 10706(b)(3)(D)(i).

43. *Id.* § 10706(b)(3)(D)(iii).

44. *Id.* § 10706(b)(3)(D)(ii).

45. *Id.* § 10706(b)(3)(D)(iv).

46. *Id.* § 10706(b)(2).

47. *Id.*

48. Ex Parte No. 297 (Sub. No. 5), Motor Carrier Rate Bureaus, Implementation of Pub. L. 96–296, 364 I.C.C. 921 (1981). *See* C.F.R. § 1331 (1981). Ex Parte No. 297 (Sub. No. 5) imposes five additional burdens on rate bureaus: a prohibition against bureau employees initiating tariff proposals or determining whether to accept or reject such proposals; sunshine requirements for detailed public notice of meetings, which must be open to the public, and identification of tariff proponents and voting records; a requirement for detailed written proxies; specific quorum requirements; and a requirement for detailed minutes of each meeting. As of the date of this writing, these rules are on appeal before the Fifth Circuit.

49. 49 U.S.C. § 10706(b)(3)(D) (Supp. IV 1980).

50. 49 U.S.C. § 11343(a) (West Supp. 1980).

51. *Id.* § 11343(a)(4)(5).

52. Adapted from ICC, *Internal Memorandum on Commission Duty to Consider Anticompetitive Consequences in Acquisition Transactions* (1981).

53. 259 F. Suppl. at 996.

54. "Control" exists not only in applications where stock control is sought, but also in purchase and merger transactions.

55. 389 U.S. 486 (1968).

56. United States v. ICC, 396 U.S. 491 (1970).

57. *See* 49 U.S.C. §§ 11344(b), (c) and 11345(b) (West Supp. 1980).

58. *See id.* 11344(d). *See also* Norfolk & Western Ry. Co. Pur. Illinois Term. R. Co., 363 I.C.C. 882 (1981).

59. Railroad Consolidation Procedures, 366 I.C.C. 75, 79 (1982). *See* 49 C.F.R. Part IIII (1982).

60. 49 C.F.R. § 1111.10.

61. 49 U.S.C. §§ 11343, 11344 and 11345a (West Supp. 1980).

62. The Commission's rule promulgated thereunder provides that applications from exemption will be published in the *Federal Register* 60 days prior to its effective date, and that the ICC will ordinarily render its decisions 30 days after such filing. *See* Procedures for Handling Exemptions Filed by Motor Carriers of Property Under 49 U.S.C. 11343, 367 ICC 113 (1982).

63. *See* 49 U.S.C. § 10505 (West Supp. 1980).

64. 127 M.C.C. 1 (1977), 127 I.C.C. 284 (1978).

65. This section is adapted from the Dempsey, *The Rise & Fall of the Civil Aeronautics Board: Opening Wide the Floodgates of Entry*, 11 Transp. L.J. 91, 117–19 (1979).

66. Adapted from Office of the General Counsel, C.A.B., Summary of the Provisions of the Airline Deregulation Act of 1978, at 12–14 (1978) (footnotes omitted).

67. Material on the airline merger cases is adapted from Note, *The Airline Merger Cases: CAB Application of Clayton Section 7 After Deregulation*, 12 Transp. L.J. 139 (1980) (footnotes generally omitted), authored by D.U. law student, Robert Grantham.

68. H.R. Rep. No. 95–1779, 95th Cong., 2d Sess., reprinted in (1978) U.S. Code Cong. & Ad. News 3737 (hereinafter cited as H.R. Rep. No. 95–1779).

69. *Id.*

70. 15 U.S.C. § 18 (1970).

71. H.R. Rep. No. 95–1779, at 3789.

72. *Id.* at 3792.

73. 49 U.S.C. § 1302(a) (1978).

74. North Cent. Southern Merger Case, CAB Order 79–6–7 (1979).

75. United States v. Brown Shoe, 370 U.S. 294 (1961).

76. North Cent. Southern Merger Case, CAB order 79–6–7 at 10 (1979).

77. 49 U.S.C. § 1384 (1978) (as amended by the Airline Deregulation Act of 1978, Pub. L. No. 95–504, § 30, 92 Stat. 1731).

78. *Id.*

79. North Cent. Southern Merger Case, CAB Order 79–6–7 at 6 (1979).

80. 15 U.S.C. § 18 (1970).

81. Texas Int'l–National Acquisition Case, CAB Order 79–9–163 (1979).

82. 374 U.S. 321 (1963).

83. 415 U.S. 486 (1974).

84. 418 U.S. 602, 630–31 (1974).

85. Pan. Am. World Airways–National Acquisition Case, CAB Order 79–9–163 at 32 (1979).

86. 49 U.S.C. § 1371(p) (1978).

87. *Id.* § 1371(g).

88. *Id.* § 1371(b).

89. Application of Eastern Airlines for Approval of Acquisition of National, CAB Order 79–12–74 (1979).

90. Continental/Western II, CAB Order 81–3–185 (1981).

91. CAB Order 80–5–108 (1980).

92. Republic–Hughes Airwest Acquisition, CAB Order 80–9–65 (1980).

5

Liability Issues in Transportation

Common carriers have traditionally been held to a higher degree of care than have other businesses. The historic rationale has been that the carrier, being in control of the instrumentality of commerce and having accepted responsibility for the chattel, is in a better position than the shipper to minimize risk and properly care for his shipments and passengers.

Alongside this traditional view has been the minority position. When transportation innovations came into being, people who would risk their lives and fortunes to the iron horse or the flying machine were considered to have assumed the risk by riding in the contraption.

Although the strict common-carrier liability theory carried the day, there have been some changes in liability, as deregulation nears.

A. Evolution of Common Law to Carmack

The origins of common-carrier liability date back to antiquity.[1] The Roman republic first codified laws of liability around 200 B.C. and continued to refine them over several centuries. The Romans had established clear legal obligations between carriers and shippers and had introduced the idea of monetary damages in case of loss. Roman transportation contracts from around A.D. 150 have been studied, and their liability provisions are remarkably similar to those which exist today. Roman commercial law passed almost unchanged into virtually every other legal system in later European history. This was because, in medieval times, the church had the duty of trying nearly all civil cases, and the Roman mercantile laws were indispensible for fulfilling this duty. Specifically, the liability of a carrier for loss or damage to property is part of the more general law of bailments. A bailment is brought about by a transfer of property from one party to another for a special purpose. There are several kinds of bailments, depending on which party benefits from the transfer of property. At common law, a carrier is an "extraordinary bailee" because he has such complete knowledge and control of the property once it is in his possession.

The liability of a nonnegligent common carrier was established early by English courts, in the 1601 decision of *Southcote v. Bennet*. In that case, the court held the carrier liable even though he had been robbed.

The definitive statement on carrier liability was made in a famous decision by Lord Holt in *Coggs v. Bernard*. Seldom has any legal decision influenced legal practices over such a long span of time.

The decision turned on the question of the liability of a bailee offering a free service. The defendant had damaged a cask of brandy while moving it from one cellar to another. He refused to pay for the damages and the plaintiff sued, citing the decision in *Southcote v. Bennet* as authority for the carrier's absolute liability.

The judges ruled against the plaintiff and thereby overturned the rule of absolute liability for loss or damage by a gratuitous bailee. Lord Holt went beyond the immediate decision, however, and analyzed all aspects of bailments. In regard to the common carrier, Lord Holt reasoned:

The law charges this person thus entrusted to carry goods, against all events, but acts of God, and the enemies of the King. For though the force be ever so great, as if an irresistible multitude of people should rob him, nevertheless he is chargeable. And this is a politic establishment, contrived by the policy of the law, for the safety of all persons, the necessity of whose affairs oblige them to trust these sorts of persons, . . . for else these carriers might have an opportunity of undoing all persons that had dealings with them, by combining with thieves, etc., and yet doing it in such a clandestine manner as would not be possible to discover.

The American colonies adopted the common law of England, including the strict law governing the liability of common carriers. As a result, Lord Holt's rationale continues to influence matters concerning responsibility for loss or damage not only in Great Britain, but in the United States as well.

This body of law, with variations by state statutes, continued to control the liability of common carriers until 1906. When the *Act to Regulate Commerce* was initially enacted in 1887, the only provision governing carrier liability was one bringing it within federal venue. The various states remained free to enact their own laws regulating cargo liability. The resulting confusion was well documented by the Supreme Court of Georgia in *Southern Pacific Co. v. Crenshaw*, in which the court stated:

Brothers, 63 S.E. 865 (1909)
Some states allowed carriers to exempt themselves from all or a part of the common law liability, by the rule, regulation or contract; others did not, the Federal courts sitting in the various states were following the local rule. A carrier being held liable in one court when under the same set of facts he would be exempt from liability in

another, hence this branch of interstate commerce was being subject to such diversity of legislative and judicial holdings that it was practically impossible for a shipper engaged in a business that extended beyond the confines of his own state, or for a carrier whose lines were extensive, to know . . . what would be the carrier's actual responsibility as to the goods.

The federal government preempted the field with the passage of the Hepburn Rate Act of 1906. The Hepburn Act contained the Carmack Amendment, which supplanted state law related to the liability of regulated interstate rail common carriers. The Carmack Amendment adopted the common law presumption that the carrier was absolutely liable for the loss or damage of goods entrusted to it, unless the damage was due to one of the common law exceptions and the carrier was not negligent. The Amendment established a uniform standard of liability for common carriers and required them to issue bills of lading that provided that no contract, receipt, rule or regulation could exempt carriers from liability for the full actual loss sustained by the owner of the goods transported. In addition, the amendment made carriers liable for the actions of their connecting carriers.

Notwithstanding the passage of the Carmack Amendment, railroads continued to limit their liability to less than the full actual value by publishing released rates. Shippers were forced to accept a lesser declared value in return for transportation of their shipments.

The Supreme Court, in *Adams Express Co. v. Croniger*,[2] reviewed the lawfulness of liability limitations under released rates. The Court held that a carrier could, by a fair, open, just and reasonable contract, limit the amount recoverable in case of loss or damage to an agreed value for allowing the shipper to use the lower of two or more rates. The *Croniger* case was followed by a series of similar court decisions,[3] reflecting the thinking of the Supreme Court that tariffs filed with the Interstate Commerce Commission (ICC) were presumed to be part of the transportation contract and therefore binding on both shipper and carrier, including a released valuation incorporated in the bill of lading.

As a consequence of *Croniger*, carriers frequently evaded Carmack by publishing reduced rates based on released values, while settling full value rates at prohibitively high levels. Shippers effectively were denied a real choice. By 1916, this situation resulted in the passage of the First and Second Cummins Amendments to the Hepburn Act. The Second Cummins Amendment authorized carriers to limit their liability by publishing released rates. The released rates, however, had to be approved by the Commission in advance of publication and only with "value declared in writing by the shipper or agreed upon in writing as the released value of the property." This statutory scheme lasted until the passage of the Staggers Rail Act of 1980.

B. Burden of Proof

Currently, the carrier usually must prove that it was not negligent and that the proximate cause of the loss or damage was (1) an act of God, (2) the public enemy, (3) an act of the shipper, (4) an inherent characteristic of the goods or (5) the public authority. The railroads proposed that their burden of proof be lessened to proving simply that they were not negligent.

One of the distinguishing characteristics about cases involving carrier liability is the unusual burden of proof allocation. Burden of proof is a method used to resolve cases in which the evidence is such that neither party can persuade the trier of fact. In this standoff, civil law places on one of the parties the burden of persuading the jury by a preponderance of the evidence. In most negligence questions, it is the plaintiff who must prove that the defendant was negligent and thereby caused the injury; otherwise, his case is lost. This is so in cases against private carriers.

The common carrier, however, as a virtual insurer of the goods, has the common law burden to prove that the loss or damage was caused by one of the five exceptions mentioned earlier. This burden occurs after the plaintiff has presented a prima facie case against the carrier by showing that the shipment was in good condition at delivery, was in damaged condition on arrival (or was not delivered with reasonable dispatch) and the amount of damages.

There is some controversy as to what occurs next. Shippers' National Freight Claims Council, Inc., cites *Secy. of Agriculture v. U.S.*, 350 U.S. 162, 173 (1955), as holding that the carrier, in addition to proving one of the exceptions, must prove it was not negligent. Geo. A. Hormel & Co. and Institute of Scrap Iron and Steel, Inc. also cite the U.S. Supreme Court decision of *Elmore & Stahl*, 377 U.S. 134 (1964), for this holding, as does The National Industrial Traffic League. However, William Prosser, a highly respected authority on the law of torts, states:

It is generally agreed, however, that a carrier of goods, who is an insurer against everything but a few exceptional perils, has the burden of proving that the loss or damage to the goods falls within one of the exceptions, after which it is the prevailing view that the burden is upon the plaintiff to show any negligence of the carrier responsible for the harm under such circumstances. (Prosser, W. *Law of Torts*, 4th ed., 1974—sec. 38)

Several cites are given for this position, including *Oakland Meat Co. v. Railway Express Agency*, 46 Ill. App. 2d 176, 196 N.E.2d 361 (1964), and Dobie, *Bailments and Carriers*, 1914, 348–49.[4]

In either case, it remains for the carrier to show that the cause of damage or loss falls within one of the five exceptions. There are several reasons why the carrier is forced to present evidence as to the cause of the injury. A party should be required to put forth evidence or facts within its control or knowledge. It is the carrier which has sole possession of the cargo while in transit. The shipper has lost all contact with the goods and has no knowledge of what transpires during this transit.

Likewise, the Supreme Court has stated:

We are not persuaded that the carrier lacks adequate means to inform itself of the condition of goods at the time it receives them from the shipper, and it cannot be doubted that while the carrier has possession it is the only one in a position to acquire the knowledge of what actually damaged a shipment entrusted to its care. *Elmore & Stahl, supra* at 143–44.

Further support for the current burden of proof standard has been established by the courts. One has stated:

A shipper has no control over goods once he delivers them to a carrier, and no opportunity to observe how they are handled. With a rule akin to *res ipsa loquitur* a shipper would often have an intolerable task to prove negligence on the part of the carrier. *Plough, Inc. v. The Mason & Dixon Lines*, 630 F.2d 468, 472 M. 1(1980).

This res ipsa loquitur doctrine may be applied in negligence actions in which the event or injury ordinarily would not occur in the absence of negligence, the event was not caused by the plaintiff's voluntary action, the event was caused by an instrumentality within the exclusive control of the defendant and the evidence as to the true explanation of the event is more readily accessible to the defendant than to the plaintiff. If the plaintiff establishes these elements, then in the absence of an explanation by the defendant, there is reasonable evidence that the injury was caused by lack of care, or negligence. While not applicable per se in carrier liability cases, this doctrine has strikingly similar elements to that of common law liability.

C. Risk of Loss and Jurisdiction

Under current law, as stated in 49 U.S.C. 11707 (a) (1), a carrier is "liable to the person entitled to recover under the receipt or bill of lading."[5] The present system includes those who have an interest in the goods. There is a distinction, however, between who may file a claim and who may recover on a claim. The general rule is that the person who bears the loss is entitled to recover. In actual practice, the party bearing the risk of loss does not necessarily file a claim or recover. For example, a large shipper with an experienced traffic department may file claims for its customers as a courtesy or service.

Under the common law, the risk of loss generally follows the "title" to the goods. The determination of the passage of the title to goods is not a simple matter. In present-day commercial practices, sales are made under various terms:

- *F.O.B. Place of Destination.* When the term is F.O.B. destination, the seller must transport the goods to that place at his own risk and expense and tender proper delivery. Thus, the risk of loss is on the seller during transit.
- *F.O.B. Place of Origin.* Section 2–319 of the Uniform Commercial Code provides that where F.O.B. origin is specified, the seller turning transit bears the risk and expense of putting the goods in possession of the carrier. The risk of loss is then on the buyer.
- *F.A.S.* means "free along side" and requires the seller to deliver the goods to the pier or dock. Risk of loss remains in the seller until such delivery is completed.
- *C.I.F.* in a contract for the sale of goods refers to "cost, insurance and freight" and means that the price includes the freight and surface costs to the named destination. Risk of loss passes to the buyer once the seller has delivered the goods to the carrier at origin, prepaid the freight, obtained insurance and mailed the shipping documents to the buyer.
- *C. & F.* imposes the same obligations on the seller as C.I.F. except the requirement to pay for insurance.

The complexity of ascertaining when title passes is so great that it is often necessary for the parties involved to resort to litigation just to determine ownership of the goods at a particular time. Often the party holding title to the goods is not named in the bill of lading or receipt, although that party is entitled to recover for loss and damage.

The doctrine of res judicata prevents splitting a claim into individual causes of action. It requires all grounds on which a single claim is based to be asserted and included in one action. Failure to do so bars a separate suit. The question is what constitutes a single claim. As it stands now, when there is loss or damage to a consolidated carload, the receiver, shipper or each owner of the goods can sue for recovery. Thus, a person with a beneficial interest may maintain an action against a carrier regardless of whether some other person has an interest also. However, recovery will bar another suit stating the same cause of action. The plaintiff who fully recovers must in turn account to any other party with an interest.

Section 11707(d) provides that a civil action may be brought in a district court of the United States or in a state court. Because federal law prevails, claims arising under Section 11707 are "federal questions" and the provisions of the Carmack Amendment govern exclusively, regardless of whether the plaintiff asserts a federal question. The right of removal to federal court, however, is limited. The $3,000 threshold established in 1914 for removal was increased to $10,000 in 1978.

A $10,000 minimum was required to originate in federal courts. The threshold was raised to eliminate the inconsistency between removal and original jurisdiction.

A new inconsistency exists now that Congress has recently removed the $10,000 threshold for original jurisdiction in federal question cases (Pub. L. 96-486). Today, federal question cases arising under the Carmack Amendment are treated differently from other federal question controversies. *Moore's Federal Practice*, Section 0.167[4] asks, "Why pick on Carmack Amendment cases when the balance of the Interstate Commerce Act, and all other federal laws, remain free of the over $10,000 limitation?"

D. Measure of Damages

Full actual loss appears to be the preferred measure of damages with shippers, and it was the measure used in former Section 20(11).[6] Because Congress felt that "full" was surplus wording, Section 11707 now reads "actual loss." It seems clear that a plaintiff should not be in a worse position than if there had been no damage or loss. Full actual loss is consistent with the common law principle of making the plaintiff whole. Limiting the measure to market value of the transported commodity would preclude elements considered general damages by some courts. These include marginal profit on some costs, labor, administrative overhead, freight charges, interest and replacement costs.[7]

The fundamental common law decision in this matter, *Hadley v. Baxendale*,[8] allowed recovery of general damages, defined as those occurring naturally from the breach of contract. Damages in excess of this could be awarded only if they were, in the contemplation of both parties, probable consequences of a breach. In other words, special damages were awarded only when foreseeable, because the contractor could refuse to accept the contract if foreseeable damages were too great. Given the common-carrier obligation, this analogy may not be appropriate.

Each case relies on its own facts. Although courts often apply the fair market value measure for damages, other measures have been used. What is considered "general damages" may vary from court to court. Hence, the difference between special damages and general damages is not easy to define and varies with the facts and circumstances as well as the actions of the parties in each particular case.

Perhaps an example of a transportation service will be helpful. If a large company were building a new plant in a remote section of a western state, an enormous logistical exercise is necessary so that all parts, as well as the men and machines to assemble the plant, will arrive at the building site at the appropriate time. In the absence of such coordination, highly paid engineers might be left waiting for a machine part to arrive. Because of this, astute corporate executives have industrial traffic managers carefully prearrange the shipment of the factory components so that the chances of foul up are minimized. Typically, a large factory component manufactured in the

East and shipped west would require bridge and tunnel clearances as well as the procurement of special cars.

Nevertheless, a number of things could happen to the shipment: The railroad might conceivably derail the car and destroy the machine. In the meantime, the engineering company would continue to bill the receiver for its equipment and men even though they were doing nothing. It could also cost the receiver large sums for his own labor and delay, as well as contractual costs linked with arrival of the machine. So, under our current legal system, how would the courts deal with the results of the derailment, and could some of the damages awarded be defined as special or consequential?

Courts have differed on whether mere notice of these unusual circumstances to the carrier is sufficient to hold it liable for special damages. Some courts have held that the carrier must agree to accept the special conditions[9]; others do not require agreement.[10] The later holds that if a carrier is told of the special significance of a commodity and the importance of prompt delivery, it will be liable for loss of profit owing to unreasonable dispatch.

Thus, in our hypothetical situation, a court could hold that the extra effort expended by shipper and carrier alike in planning routes, obtaining special cars and getting bridge and tunnel clearances was sufficient notice to the carrier of the possibility of special damages, and therefore it could award the receiver's extra labor and contract costs as special damages. On the other hand, another court, guided only by the principle of "making the plaintiff whole," could declare these extra costs as part of the general damages. A third court might award only the cost of replacing the machine by strictly construing the common law to require a written statement on the bill of lading.

Although most courts award interest as an ordinary part of damages,[11] this is a matter left to the discretion of the courts.[12] Incidental damages which naturally and proximately arise from the loss or injury are awarded.[13]

Replacement cost is not deemed to be special damages,[14] nor are demurrage charges and expenses for separating damaged goods from undamaged.[15] Lost profits are awarded but only to the extent they were comtemplated by the parties at the time the contract of carriage was made.[16] Finally, it has been held that while remote or speculative damages are not recoverable,[17] exemplary damages are if there is gross negligence or willful breach of duty.[18]

Measurement of damages is a complex issue. Because the common law already severely limits the award of special and consequential damages, any system superceding it would require new legislation. A judge working under statutory prohibition against special damages might still make an award larger than replacement cost because he perceives the extra cost as an equitable part of general damages which should make the plaintiff "whole." Moreover, it is difficult to conceive of any legislation embracing all possible circumstances which occur without hamstringing judicial discretion.

In sum, we find that the current common law principle which allows the courts to award general damages based on the facts of the individual case, and in an amount that makes the claimant whole, appears to work as well as any system can. No alternative is any fairer or more predictable or more capable of uniform application.

E. Recent Legislation

1. Rail Carrier Liability

The Staggers Act of 1980 provides greater freedom with respect to liability issues in three ways.[19] First, carriers were permitted to establish released rates without prior Commission approval. This did away with the Commission's former practice of restricting released value rates to instances in which traffic was highly susceptible to loss or damage or in which the value of the commodity was extremely high or difficult to determine. Now released rates are readily publishable and subject only to protest or complaint alleging discrimination or rate unreasonableness, if there is market dominance. A second change made by the Staggers Act was to permit deductibles. Prior to the Staggers Act, released rates were lower than full value rates, which carried a limitation on the amount of damages recoverable in the event of loss or damage. Released rates may now specify a deductible in addition to the stated limitations on the amount recoverable.

The third significant change related to liability made by the Staggers Act is qualified freedom to contract. Before the Staggers Act was promulgated, the lawfulness of rail transportation contracts was unclear. Prior to 1978, the Commission had generally ruled them unlawful per se. The Staggers Act expressly permits rail carriers to negotiate contracts that specify all terms of the shipping transportation, including those related to liability.

The Commission has held that the new authority to publish released rates without prior approval does not detract from the rail carrier's obligation under the Interstate Commerce Act to maintain full value rates.

Former Section 20(11) of the Interstate Commerce Act provided that a common carrier was liable "for the full actual loss, damage, or injury" to property carried by it except for

transportation concerning which the carrier shall have been expressly authorized or required by order of the Interstate Commerce Commission to establish and maintain rates dependent upon the value declared in writing . . . as released value of the property, in which case such declaration or agreement shall have no other effect than to limit liability and recovery to an amount not exceeding the value so declared and released.[20]

It has been held that this section affords the shipper the opportunity to declare a higher value for his property and, consequently, incur greater shipping expense.[21] Similarly, it has been established that a common carrier cannot rely on a limited liability provision pursuant to Section 20(11) unless the shipper had an opportunity to elect greater liability for the carrier by paying a greater shipping charge.[22]

The legislative history of Section 211 of the Staggers Act supports the Commission's construction. It states: "Full value rates will of course continue in effect for the use of those shippers and receivers which choose not to utilize released rates established and filed under this provision or agree to other terms as part of a contract for services."[23]

There is other evidence of congressional intent to require that full value rates be offered. Section 213 of the Staggers Rail Act (which amends Section 10505) states that Commission exemption orders may not relieve a rail carrier from its common-carrier liability under Section 11707. The legislative history of Section 213 states that the limitation as to Section 11707 liability does not affect the ability of a carrier to offer "alternative terms."[24] Implicit in this statement is that these terms are alternatives to full value and liability required by Section 11707.

Legally, the requirement for full value rates appears to create a right without a remedy in certain instances. Since 1976, a rail carrier that has effective competition on the traffic at issue may raise its rates on that traffic to any level it chooses. The Staggers Act further limits the jurisdiction of the Commission with regard to the reasonableness of a rate: the ICC has jurisdiction to find rates unreasonable only when the rates are above a certain price-cost ratio and the rail carrier has market dominance. The result may be that while the carrier is required to offer full value rates, those rates may be set at an excessively high level in situations in which market dominance is deemed not to exist. The shipper may accept the higher rate, elect the released rate or choose another carrier with whom to do business in markets in which alternative carriage is feasible.

2. Motor Carrier Liability

The long, hard-fought and often bitter battle over truck deregulation has come to an end, at least temporarily.[25] In its wake there lies a pattern of congressional decisions regarding carrier liability for freight loss and damage which is often clear, but sometimes conflicting. Despite its overall intent to permit more competition among motor carriers and provide more freedom in rate making, Congress recognized that liability issues do not respond in the same manner as rates, and that the public interest requires retention of regulations over carrier claim and liability rules and practices.

In essence, Congress took the following actions regarding liability issues:

1. Congress exempted several new commodities from ICC controls, but it rejected proposals to free processed foods and certain other farm supplies from ICC regulations. This proposal would have included the provisions of the Carmack Amendment, which established joint and several liability on

joint-line carriers and established a uniform, minimum time limit for filing claims and suits. It would have freed truckers hauling these commodities from the Commission's loss and damage claims regulations which impose time limits on carriers' handling processing of claims and establish reasonable and uniform guidelines for settlement of claims on a nondiscriminatory basis.

Instead, Congress made it easier for owner-operators to obtain operating certificates (by filing only affidavits of "fitness") to haul processed foods. The stipulation is that at least half of the owner-operator's tonnage must consist of exempt agricultural products. The owner will be subject to all other ICC regulations for the processed foods operations, including claims liability, statutes and rules. At the same time, Congress enabled the ICC, with the cooperation of the secretary of agriculture, to prescribe minimum contract terms for agricultural movements exempt from the Commission's jurisdiction, to correct the abuses arising from agricultural transportation performed without written contracts of carriage. Under the agricultural exemption, claims are partially deducted from freight charges, a practice which frequently results in owner-operators.

2. Congress eliminated the air terminal zones concept which formerly exempted from claim regulations motor carriers operating within certain mileage radii around cities. In lieu thereof, it has extended air cargo deregulation to ground transportation when a "part of a continuous movement" by air. It also codified the Commission's present regulations authorizing exempt operations during adverse weather conditions and mechanical breakdowns. Other exempt operations include hauling newspapers, wrecked vehicles and casual operations.

These statutory exemptions will permit motor carriers to adopt the same claim and liability rules maintained by each individual airline and air freight forwarder on domestic air freight traffic.[26] The requirements for uniformity and reasonableness have been eliminated, although the standard of discrimination has not. Limitations on liability are now governed only by the common law, and air shippers' only forum is in the courts.

3. Perhaps the most significant change in carrier liability made by Congress related to the statutory limitation on carriers' ability to limit liability to a maximum value. Section 10730 of Title 49 U.S.C. required ICC approval of all released rates. The new law eliminates the statutory requirement for ICC approval of released rates and permits shippers and carriers to enter into such agreements subject, however, to all other tariff requirements. The Commission may, however, require that the carrier maintain its full value rates, offering the shipper a choice of such rates or lower released value rates.

4. Congress has defined the term "disallowance" as used in the Carmack Amendment for the purposes of preventing the unintentional outlawing of law suits caused by hidden declinations and insurance company declinations.

Previously, many carriers adopted a policy of offering a compromise settlement to a claim without specifically informing the claimant that such an offer is technically a declination of the whole claim as filed. Section 11707 provides that the two-year time limit for filing a law suit starts to run on receipt of such a disallowance. Many claimants are unaware of this technicality and permitted the time to expire while they continued their negotiations for a better settlement.

Section 11707 now provides that an offer to compromise or pay only part of a claim must be accompanied by a notice, in writing, that the remaining part of the claim is disallowed. Furthermore, reasons for the disallowance must now be given in the notice. If these two conditions are not met by a carrier, the time limit for instituting a suit shall not begin to run.

Another modification is intended to preclude insurance companies from disallowing without obtaining authority from the carrier to act on its behalf. Previously, insurers have substituted their monetary interests for the motor carrier's obligations as a bailee-for-hire. Common carriers are endowed with a public interest and must deal with all shippers indiscriminately. Therefore, liability issues must be decided by the carrier, not by its insurer.[27]

Equally significant is the House Report which accompanied H.R. 6418 (Report No. 96–1069, 96th Congr. 2nd Sess.). On three occasions the House Committee on Public Works and Transportation expressed its intent that the ICC continue to exercise its mandate to protect the public interest in carrier liability matters. This congressional intent has manifested itself in Section 12 relating to released rates,[28] Section 26 relating to disallowances,[29] and Section 29 regarding insurance.[30]

Apparently, the Congress has been sufficiently alarmed at the actions taken by the airlines under air cargo deregulation[31] and the railroads under the exemption from ICC regulations granted for fresh fruits and vegetables[32] to express its intent that no further deterioration of liability and claim regulations be permitted.[33]

3. Household Goods Liability

Today, approximately 2,650 individual carriers make up the interstate household goods moving industry. Many of these carriers do not operate under their own authority; instead, they act as agents for other authorized carriers. In the 1979 calendar year, 1,156 carriers actually engaged in operations under their own interstate authority. Together, these carriers transported 1,189,401 shipments, and their revenues for that year were about $1.4 billion. The 10 largest carriers accounted for about $1 billion, or 75 percent, of those revenues. The average revenue per shipment was $1,211.

Some carriers depend on the agents to provide the resources used in their transportation operations. The agents book the shipments; arrange for them to be weighed and provide packing, unpacking and storage services. Three of the 10 largest carriers—Allied Van Lines, Atlas Van Lines, and United

Van Lines—are owned or controlled by their agents. These three carriers share 50 percent of the market of the 10 largest carriers.

The fact that the household moving sector does business directly with individual shippers also sets it apart from the rest of the trucking industry. These shippers usually move only once or twice in their lives and, consequently, lack a thorough understanding of the industry and sufficient clout to negotiate with it. Their situation is made more vulnerable by the fact that the moves involve all of their personal possessions, which often are fragile. Further, 60 percent of the household goods moves take place between June 1 and October 1. Clearly, this condition poses operational problems which strain the industry resources.

The household goods moving industry is the single most frequent subject of consumer complaints to the ICC. During 1979, the Commission received 24,609 consumer complaints, an average of 2.1 complaints per 100 shipments transported. Basically, these complaints can be divided into three groups: 43.14 percent were related to the loss or damage of goods and the handling of complaints arising from such loss or damage; 36.36 percent were related to the failure of carriers to provide the agreed to service, including failure to pick up and deliver goods on time; and 20.50 percent were related to rates and charges, including estimates and improper weighing.

ICC MEMORANDUM ON THE HOUSEHOLD GOODS TRANSPOR-TATION ACT OF 1980 (1981)

Prior to enactment of the Transportation Act of 1980, rates for household goods transportation could only be based on the actual weight of a shipment moved, rather than on a preshipment estimate, along with other variables such as distance and the amount of accessorial work performed. Also, although the carrier had a duty to provide service with "reasonable dispatch," tariffs did not provide penalties for delay in pickup or delivery, and the shipper's remedy for damages owing to delay lay in the courts if not settled between the parties. The Commission received a large number of consumer complaints regarding the difference in rates and charges issued by a representative of the carrier prior to the move. The difference often created an extreme hardship on the individual shipper. The Commission also received a large number of consumer complaints based on carriers failing to meet the preshipment agreed pickup or delivery dates. Some carriers voluntarily reimbursed shippers for their monetary losses caused by the carriers' failure to meet the agreed pickup or delivery dates; however, some carriers would only reimburse the shipper when contacted by an employee of the Commission, (or when) the shipper threatened suit, or in some cases, settlement was only made when awarded by the courts.

DISCUSSION OF SECTIONS, SECTION BY SECTION

Section I. 4—Rates

Section 4 provides a carrier with the right to establish a rate for the transportation of household goods which is based on the carrier's written binding estimate. Carriers may charge for such estimates, but such charges must not be set collectively and are subject to the antitrust laws. The Commission will not be able to require carriers to give binding estimates. Carriers may elect to give them and can give them so long as they are based on tariff provisions, they are given on a nonpreferential basis and they do not result in predatory charges.

Section 4 provides a carrier with the right to establish rates for guaranteed pickup and delivery times and establish per diem payments or penalties for noncompliance with the specified timetable. This would come within the purview of tariff filing requirements and the carrier may charge premium rates for this service. The shipper taking advantage of such service would have the convenience of predetermined damages for cost incurred as a result of untimely pickup or delivery, without the aggravation of pursuing a claim or litigating the matter. This section grants carriers the right to establish such rates with the caveat that the Commission can require the carrier to have another rate in effect at the same time which does not guarantee specified pickup and delivery times and does not contain the per diem payments or penalties.

This section permits carriers to establish innovative price/service options and offer consumers price certainty and guaranteed service protection, two of the most common areas of consumer complaint.

Section II. 5—Agents

This section adds a new section to Title 49 dealing with agents. Sections 10934(a) and (b) substantially codify the Commission's regulations on the subject found at 49 C.F.R. 1056.19 and 1056.20, which impose burdens on principal carriers for care and selection of their agents and for responsibility for their agents' acts.

Section 10934(c) authorizes the Commission to determine the fitness of agents and to take direct enforcement action against the agent for serious violations. The agent is given the right to a hearing on the charges in a two-step process for procedural safeguards for the agent. The Commission's authority to limit, condition or prohibit an agent's participation in the household goods moving industry is clearly established. This section provides the Commission with an effective tool to discipline agents when principal carriers are unwilling or unable to do so. It also gives the Commission the power to prevent unscrupulous or unfit agents from continuing in business or from moving from one principal carrier to another.

Section III. 9—Weight Bumping

This section adds new Section 11917 to Title 49, making weight bumping for household goods transportation a specific crime. Subsection (a) defines weight bumping as the willful and knowing making or securing of a fraudulent weight on a shipment of household goods. Subsection (b) sets penalties for the offense, establishing fines of at least $1,000 but not more than $10,000, imprisonment for not more than two years or both.

4. Air Carrier Liability

NADER v. ALLEGHENY AIRLINES, INC.

626 F.2d 1031 (D.C. Cir. 1980)

ROBB, Circuit Judge:

This is an appeal by Allegheny Airlines from a judgment of the District Court awarding the plaintiff Ralph Nader compensatory and punitive damages for fraudulent misrepresentation in the sale of an airline ticket.

The facts giving rise to Nader's claim are not disputed. He was scheduled to address a rally in Hartford, Connecticut at noon on April 28, 1972. On April 25, 1972 he reserved a seat on Allegheny flight 864, scheduled to depart from Washington, D.C. for Hartford at 10:15 a.m. on April 28. His reservation was a "confirmed reservation." He arrived at the boarding and check-in area approximately five minutes before the scheduled departure time but was told by Allegheny's agent that he could not be accommodated on flight 864 because all the seats were occupied. He was offered an alternative air taxi flight by way of Philadelphia but decided not to accept it because of uncertainty as to whether he would arrive in Hartford in time for the noon rally. As a result he was prevented from attending the rally.

The Allegheny agent at the Washington check-in area tendered to Nader the Denied Boarding Form required by CAB regulations (14 C.F.R. sec. 250.9). This form notifies holders of tickets on flights that are "over-sold" that they are entitled to compensation from an airline if they are "bumped," that is denied transportation. Nader told the agent that he did not need the form because he already had one. In fact, he had received such a form when he was bumped from an American Airlines flight on April 23, 1972, two days before he made his reservation on Allegheny. Six months before that he and five other people had been bumped by Eastern Airlines. On both occasions he held a confirmed reservation.

Pursuant to CAB regulations Allegheny mailed to Nader a check in the amount of $32.41 as denied boarding compensation. Nader's attorney returned the check to Allegheny, together with a letter characterizing the denied boarding compensation as a "wholly inadequate offer of settlement."

On July 7, 1972 Nader filed suit in the District Court asserting Allegheny's liability on two theories: (1) a common law action based on fraudulent misrepresentation in that Allegheny failed to inform Nader of its "booking practices" and (2) a statutory action under section 404(b) of the Federal Aviation Act, 49 U.S.C. sec. 1374(b), arising from Allegheny's alleged failure to afford Nader the boarding priority specified in its rules, filed with the Civil Aeronautics Board pursuant to 14 C.F.R. sec. 250.3.

The District Court, sitting without a jury, entered a judgment for Nader on both claims, and awarded him a total of $10.00 in compensatory damages and $25,000.00 in punitive damages.[34] On appeal this court reversed.[35]

On remand the District Court found that Allegheny violated section 404(b) of the Act, 49 U.S.C. sec. 1374(b), by its failure to board Nader in accordance with its own priority boarding rules. For this the court awarded him $10.00 in compensatory damages. The court also found that Allegheny's failure to notify Nader of the chance that he would not be seated constituted fraudulent misrepresentation, and that "defendant Allegheny wantonly implemented its policy of nondisclosure and misrepresentation, in conscious, deliberate, and callous disregard of the effect of its policy on its passengers, including plaintiff Nader." The court awarded Nader $15,000 in punitive damages "to punish defendant Allegheny for its willful and wanton policy of non-disclosure and misrepresentation and . . . to deter defendant from engaging in such practices in the future."[36] Compensatory damages on the claim were assessed at $10.00.

On this appeal Allegheny challenges only the award of compensatory and punitive damages on the claim based upon fraudulent misrepresentation.

Nader's reservation was not honored because Allegheny had accepted more reservations for flight 864 than it could accommodate. In other words, the flight had been "overbooked." In its opinion in *Nader v. Allegheny Airlines, supra*, the Supreme Court discussed the practice of overbooking:

> Overbooking is a common industry practice, designed to ensure that each flight leaves with as few empty seats as possible despite the large number of "no-shows"—reservation-holding passengers who do not appear at flight time. By the use of statistical studies of no-show patterns of specific flights, the airlines attempt to predict the appropriate number of reservations necessary to fill each flight. In this way, they attempt to ensure the most efficient use of aircraft while preserving the flexible booking system that permits passengers to cancel and change reservation without notice or penalty. At times the practice of overbooking results in oversales, which occur when more reservation-holding passengers than can be accommodated actually appear to board the flight. When this occurs, some passengers must be denied boarding ("bumped"). The chance that any particular passenger will be bumped is so negligible that few prospective passengers aware of the possibility would give it a second thought. In April 1972, the month in which petitioner's reservation was dishonored 6.7 confirmed passengers per 10,000 enplanements were denied boarding on domestic flights. For all domestic airlines, oversales resulted in bumping an average of 5.4 passengers per 10,000 enplanements in 1972 and 4.6 per 10,000 enplanements in 1973. In domestic operations respondent oversold 6.3 seats per 10,000 in 1972 and 4.5 seats per 10,000 enplanements in 1973. Thus, based on the 1972 experience of all domestic airlines, there was only slightly more than one chance in 2,000 that any particular passenger would be bumped on a given flight.

This case presents two questions: (1) was Allegheny liable to Nader in tort for fraudulent misrepresentations? and (2) assuming such liability was the award of punitive damages proper? We first address the second question and conclude that assuming liability the award of punitive damages was clearly erroneous.

[1] The Civil Aeronautics Board in 1967 had publicly and formally expressed its approval of the practice of overbooking and had declined to issue a rule requiring notice to holders of tickets for an overbooked flight. As we observed in the first *Nader* case, 167 U.S. App. D.C. at 358, 612 F.2d at 535, the Board's determination to permit the carriers to continue the practice of non-disclosure was based on the recognition that disclosure "would create anxiety and confusion in the public to make a great number of duplicative and protective reservations, would produce a rapid turnover in reservations within the twenty-four hours before the departure of a flight and would increase the no-show problem." The Board concluded that "any rigid controls over overbooking, as now practiced, would inevitably lead to restrictions on privileges which contribute greatly to the convenience of air transportation, and have come to be relied upon by the traveling public. In addition, such controls would reduce load factors and the additional cost would ultimately have to be borne by the traveling public."[37] In summary the Board stated that the reservation systems of the carriers "in general benefit the traveling public." The Board had not modified or retreated from this position when Nader made his reservation in 1972. Allegheny's policies and practices as applied to Nader therefore carried the approval of the Board;

and Allegheny must have believed that they were approved. Under these circumstances it was clearly erroneous to find as did the District Court that Allegheny's "policy of nondisclosure" was "willful and wanton" and showed a "conscious, deliberate and callous disregard" for its passengers. An airline may not be condemned as a wanton wrongdoer for conforming to the standards set and the practices approved by the agency charged with the duty of regulating it—standards and practices that the agency has found to be in the public interest. The award of punitive damages must be set aside.

A representation may be false and fraudulent in a technical sense, although it is not so gross and wanton that it justifies an award of punitive damages. We therefore turn to the question whether Allegheny was guilty of fraudulent misrepresentation in failing to disclose to Nader that his "confirmed reservation" was subject to the contingency that he might be denied boarding if his flight was overbooked.

[2] The elements of the tort of fraudulent misrepresentation are (1) a false representation, (2) in reference to a material fact, (3) made with knowledge of its falsity, (4) and with intent to deceive, (5) with action taken in reliance upon the representation.[38]

In the first *Nader* case we reversed as clearly erroneous the District Court's finding that Allegheny affirmatively represented to Nader that he had a reservation guaranteeing him a seat. We held that Allegheny's fault, if any, was its failure to disclose that its policy of deliberate overbooking qualified the meaning of a "confirmed reservation." The District Court found that Allegheny had a duty of disclosure to Nader, that its failure to disclose amounted to false representation, and that by a preponderance of the evidence Nader had proved other elements of the tort of fraudulent mispresentation.

The record discloses that in the seventeen months preceding the Nader incident Allegheny had experienced only two oversales on flight 864, and statistical analyses had shown that in 1972 there was only slightly more than one chance in two thousand that a ticket holder would be denied boarding because of an oversale. Stated another way the chance that a holder of confirmed reservation would be boarded was approximately 99.95 out of 100. Allegheny argues that because the chance that Nader would be denied boarding was thus "so negligible as to be practically insignificant" the possibility that bumping might occur was not a material fact and the airline cannot be charged with misrepresentation in failing to disclose it. The theory of the airline is that a confirmed reservation is not a guarantee but is only a "reasonable assurance" of being flown, because any flight may be cancelled as the result of weather conditions, mechanical problems, or the like. The airlines says that Nader had that reasonable assurance of being flown; the chance of being bumped because of overbooking was too remote to affect the assurance, and silence about such a chance therefore did not amount to a false representation in reference to a material fact. As the District Court found, however, confirmation of a reservation connotes a guarantee of flight subject only to contingencies beyond the control of the airline. The possibility of being bumped because of overbooking is a factor within the airlines' control. That the possibility may be slight does not make it immaterial; it is still a factor in the equation, and as Nader's experience demonstrates, it may be an important factor. No one who has suffered the disruption of travel plans by denial of boarding would believe otherwise.

Six years after the Nader incident the Civil Aeronautics Board confirmed our opinion that the practice of overbooking is a material fact which should be brought

to the attention of those purchasing tickets. This the Board did by promulgating 14
C.F.R. sec. 250.11, 43 Fed. Reg. 24,284 (1978). This regulation requires carriers to
post in their ticket offices and include with each ticket sold a notice that "airline
flights may be overbooked, and there is a slight chance that a seat will not be available
on a flight for which a person has a confirmed reservation."

[3] Nader could not recover on his tort claim unless the evidence established that
Allegheny intended to deceive him when it failed to notify him of its overbooking
practice. The District Court found in summary fashion that Allegheny had such an
intent to deceive. The court's entire discussion of the issue:

> There can be no doubt that the nondisclosure of the existence of de-
> fendant's overbooking practice was the result of a conscious and delib-
> erate policy implemented by Allegheny in order to deprive passengers
> of information about its overbooking practice so as not to distinguish
> Allegheny's reservation practices from those of its competitors.

We think this finding is unsupported by the evidence and clearly erroneous.

As we have seen the matter of overbooking had been thoroughly explored by the
Civil Aeronautics Board in public hearings. In public comments filed in those proceedings Allegheny had acknowledged its practice of overbooking and explained its
benefits. The record discloses that the Board's Office of Consumer Affairs had issued
and distributed 400,000 copies of a booklet on consumers' rights in air travel which
covered the subject of denied boarding. Overbooking had been discussed in peri-
odicals of general circulation. The Board had promulgated rules published in the
Code of Federal Regulations and specifically designed to address situations caused
by the practice of overbooking. In short, the practice of overbooking in the air
transportation industry was public information, openly discussed by the carriers, the
Board and publications of national circulation. In light of these facts we cannot accept
the District Court's conclusion that Allegheny's failure to notify Nader of its overbooking practice was motivated by deceit and the desire to deprive him of information. The practice of overbooking was no secret, no covert operation, but was
openly carried on, and Allegheny was entitled to believe that any knowledgeable
passenger knew of the practice. The court's findings that Allegheny harbored an
intent to deceive is, we think, contrary to the evidence. An airline which intends to
deceive by concealing facts does not advertise the facts in public proceedings.

[4] Moreover, in order to recover for the tort of fraudulent mispresentation "the
false representation must have played a material and substantial part in leading the
plaintiff to adopt his particular course; and when . . . it is clear that he was not in any
way influenced by it, . . . his loss is not attributed to the defendant."

In order to be influenced by the representation, the plaintiff must of course have
relied upon it, and believed it to be true. If it appears that he knew the facts, or
believed the statement to be false, or that he was in fact so skeptical as to its truth
that he reposed no confidence in it, it cannot be regarded as a substantial cause of
his conduct.

The plaintiff Nader was an extraordinarily knowledgable passenger, an able lawyer
and a famous and distinguished advocate of consumer rights, including the rights of
airline passengers. On April 23, 1972, only two days before he made his reservation
on Allegheny flight 864, Nader was bumped from an American Airlines flight. Six
months earlier he had been bumped by Eastern Airlines. On both occasions he held

a confirmed reservation. In addition, upon being told that he could not be accommodated on flight 864 because all the seats were occupied, and being tendered the Denied Boarding Form required by CAB regulations, Nader informed the Allegheny ticket agent that he was familiar with the form. On deposition Nader explained that he told the agent he did not need the form because "I already knew what it said." In fact he had received such a form when he was bumped from the American Airlines flight. The form stated: "Tariffs filed by this carrier with the Civil Aeronautics Board provide denied boarding compensation to a passenger holding confirmed reserved space where the flight for which the passengers holds such space is unable to accommodate him and departs without him."

Therefore, the evidence demonstrates that Nader "knew the facts" that a confirmed reservation did not exclude the possibility that he might not be boarded. "One who has special knowledge, experience and competence may not be permitted to rely on statements for which the ordinary man might recover." It cannot be said that Nader relied on his confirmed reservation with Allegheny as a guarantee of passage.

The judgment for both compensatory and punitive damages is reversed.

NOTE: *Liability of Airline Carriers Following Deregulation*

By virtue of the Airline Deregulation Act, domestic airlines have not had to file tariffs for passenger fares or freight charges since January 1, 1983. Jurisdiction to issue and enforce consumer protection rules was transferred to the U.S. Department of Transportation on January 1, 1985.

Relief for any aggrieved passenger or shipper has been in the courts since 1982. This means that the courts now have to apply a body of common carrier law fashioned by Anglo-American courts in the 19th century, but which was in suspended animation since the decision by Congress to commit regulation of transportation entities to independent agencies.

Airlines will no doubt argue that acceptance of a ticket means acceptance of all the boilerplate language on the form limiting an airline's liability. Or they may try to contract away liability as the air freight companies have done, forcing the passenger to provide his own insurance. It is clear that any "contract" which might appear on a ticket form would be a contract of adhesion, which historically has been construed strictly against the party dictating the terms.

NOTES

1. This section and the next section are adapted from ICC Rail Carrier Cargo Liability Study (1981).

2. Adams Express Co. v. Croninger, 226 U.S. 491 (1913).

3. Boston & Maine R.R. Co. v. Hooker, 233 U.S. 97; Atchison T. & S.F.R. Co. v. Robinson, 233 U.S. 173, Kansas City So. Ry. Co. v. Carl, 227 U.S. 639.

4. *Also see* Am. Jur. 2d Carriers §§ 627, 630.

5. This section is adapted from ICC Rail Cargo Liability Study (1981).

6. This section is adapted from ICC Rail Cargo Liability Study (1981).

7. Vacco Indus. v. Navajo Freight Lines, 63 Cal. App. 3d 262, 133 Cal. Rptr. 628 (Ct. App. 1976), *cert. denied* 431 U.S. 916 (1976).

8. Hadley v. Baxendale, 156 Eng. Rep. 145 (1845).

9. Globe Ref. Co. v. Landa Cotton Oil Co., 190 U.S. 540 (1903).

10. L. E. Whitlock Truck Serv. v. Regal Drilling Co., 333 F.2d 488 (1964).

11. Atlantic Coast Line Ry. Co. v. Roe, 96 Fla. 429, 118 So. 155 (1928).

12. West Const. Co. v. Seaboard Airline Ry. Co., 141 Tenn. 342, 210 S.W. 633 (1919).

13. Campbell Soup v. Darling Transfer Inc., 193 F. Supp. 408.

14. Hycel, Inc. v. American Airline Inc., 328 F. Supp. 190 (1971).

15. Davis v. Clement Grain Co., 251 S.W. 545 (1923).

16. Vacco, Ind. v. Navajo Freight Lines, Inc., 63 Cal. App. 3d 273, 133 Cal. Rptr. 628 (Ct. App. 1976).

17. Texas Inst., Inc. v. Branch Motor Exp. Co., 308 F. Supp. 1228, *aff'd* 432 F.2d 564 (1970).

18. Schroeder v. Auto Drive Away Co., 114 Cal. Rptr. 22, 523 P.2d 662 (1974).

19. This section is adapted from *ICC Rail Cargo Liability Study (1981).*

20. 49 U.S.C. § 20(11) (1951).

21. Sorenson-Christian Indus. Inc. v. Railway Express Ag., Inc., 434 F.2d 867 (1970).

22. Sorenson-Christian Indus. Inc. v. Railway Express Ag. Inc., *supra.*

23. H.R. Rep. No. 96–1430, 96th Cong., 2d Sess. 102 (1980).

24. H.R. Rep. No. 96–1430, 96th Cong., 2d Sess. 105 (1980).

25. This section is adapted from W. Augello, *Cargo Liability Changes Resulting from the Motor Carrier Act of 1980* (found at the Westminster Law Library, University of Denver, Denver, Col.) (footnotes generally omitted).

26. Under air cargo deregulation, most airlines and forwarders have lowered liability limits while increasing excess value charges, have restored liability rules previously found unlawful by the CAB and, at the same time, have increased cargo rates and accessorial services by astronomical amounts. The CAB has also eliminated the requirement for publishing tariffs or adhering to rate and rules schedules.

27. Subsection (e) of Section 11707 provides that the written notice shall be received from "the carrier," not from its insurer.

28. "The Commission has complete regulatory authority over released value rates, except as provided otherwise. Vigilance should be maintained by the Commission so as to prevent unlawful discrimination. Most particularly, shippers must be fully and clearly informed about the kinds of rates and liability rules they agree to. The bill affirms the Commission's authority to require that shippers receive such information."

29. "Except where otherwise provided in the Motor Carrier Act of 1980, the Committee expects that the Commission will retain and enforce existing regulations as to the processing of loss, damage, and overcharge claims in order to protect the public interest. This is consistent with the Committee's intent that this legislation not weaken the interest and protection of shippers."

30. "The purpose of this provision is to assure that motor carriers of property providing transportation subject to the jurisdiction of the Commission maintain the minimum level of financial responsibility required by section 30 of this Act. Section 30 covers bodily injury, property damage, and environmental damage. It does not

include coverage for cargo movements. Nevertheless, the Committee expects the Commission to retain regulations governing loss or damage to cargo subject to the jurisdiction of the Commission. Furthermore, the Commission is to maintain proper staffing that will assure the continuation of reasonable regulation of cargo insurance, liability standards, and contracts of carriage under the law."

31. Air Transportation Regulatory Reform Act of 1977, Pub. L. 95–163, Nov. 9, 1977, 91 Stat. 1278.

32. Ex Parte 346 (sub. No. 1), Rail General Exemption Authority—Fresh Fruits and Vegetables, March 22, 1979.

33. *See* Testimony on Behalf of SNFCC, Senate Hearings, Serial No. 96–37, April 5, 1979, Regulation of Air Cargo Freight Transportation.

34. Nader v. Allegheny Airlines, Inc., 365 F. Supp. 128 (D.D.C. 1973).

35. Nader v. Allegheny Airlines, Inc., 167 U.S. App. D.C. 350, 512 F.2d 527 (1975).

36. Nader v. Allegheny Airlines, Inc., 445 F. Supp. 168, 178, 179 (D.D.C. 1978).

37. 32 Fed. Reg. at 461 (1967).

38. Nader v. Allegheny Airlines, Inc., 167 U.S. App. D.C. at 364 n.32, 512 F.2d at 541 n.32 (1976).

6

Government Operation of Rail Transportation Systems

I. TRADITIONAL APPROACH

Unlike other industrialized nations in the world, the United States has a tradition of private operation of railways. We have not had government ownership or operation of railroads because of the power of private rail corporations and because of a belief that competing private railroads do a better job than a government corporation, at less cost to the taxpayers.

The longest-standing government operation was the Panama Railroad, which the U.S. government acquired in 1902. Until 1978, when it passed into Panamanian hands as part of the Panama Canal treaties, it was operated as part of the government-owned Panama Canal Company and run by civilian employees responsible to the Army Corps of Engineers.

The Alaska Railroad had been owned and operated by the federal government since 1923. Providing a rail connection between the interior and the open harbors on the south coast of the Alaskan Territory was the original purpose of the rail line. When President Nixon proposed to sell the railroad to private interests, during the early 1970s, Alaskans were alarmed, noting the private railroads' lack of interest in providing passenger service and track maintenance. In 1985, the federal government transferred the Alaska Railroad to the state of Alaska.

II. STATELIZATION OF THE RAIL INDUSTRY

"Statelization" may be defined as a process whereby a state or interested party at the behest of a state secures by purchase or lease the control, ownership, or continued existence of light density rail lines, complete properties, rights-of-way or operations.[1]

The nature of each state's industrial, mineral and agricultural resources influences its policy decisions regarding the level of rail service necessary. State constitutional impediments to public investment in private enterprise often influence the methods used by the state to accomplish its goals.

When railroads were originally constructed, local governments often put up public funds. Sometimes municipal or county debt for railroad construction exceeded the assessed value of all taxable property within the political subdivision. As a result, approximately 19 states enacted laws to prohibit recurrence of this practice.[2]

State constitutional provisions prohibiting the investment of public funds in private enterprise vary in scope. For example, the Pennsylvania Constitution prohibits only the state from becoming a joint owner or stockholder in any company, corporation or association.[3] Other states, however, prohibit any government entity from pledging credit. For example, New Mexico's Constitution states: "Neither the state nor any county, school district, or municipality shall directly or indirectly lend or pledge its credit . . . for the construction of any railroad."[4] North Carolina, on the other hand, may lend its credit to a corporation in which it has controlling interest.[5]

In the mid 1970s, the bankruptcy of the Penn Central and seven other railroads in the Northeast goaded Congress into action. Facing wholesale abandonment of rail service and adverse effects to business, communities and the environment, Congress passed the Regional Rail Reorganization Act of 1973 (3R),[6] the Railroad Revitalization and Regulatory Reform Act of 1976 (4R Act),[7] and the Local Rail Service Assistance Act of 1978.[8] Federal funds made available by these acts provided an incentive for states to develop rail plans and policies and to get around state laws prohibiting investment of public money in private enterprise. Although methods used to reform these laws varied from state to state, those most frequently used are[9]:

- *Constitutional amendment.* This option is a relatively uncertain approach because voter reaction is difficult to predict.

- *Litigation in court.* This alternative is uncertain in its outcome as well as time-consuming and expensive.

- *Opinion of attorney general.* This option, although more expeditious, does not decrease the degree of risk because it can be reversed.

- *Purchase of service contracts.* Courts have generally held that the buyer-seller relationship does not contravene laws prohibiting lending of a state's credit. It is basically an "operating agreement." (For example, Conrail operates many state-owned branch lines in the East for the states, as a designated operator.)

- *Quasi-public agencies.* Quasi-public agencies may be created to be effective and yet not contravene constitutional prohibitions. The independent state agency or transit authority option appears to be the most frequently used alternative. This option is well suited to maintaining freight, commuter, and intercity rail service in congested areas in which operation of rail equipment is a necessity. This alternative, however, is frequently not profitable.

• *In-kind benefits.* Congress provided in the 4R Act, Title VIII, Section 803(g) provisions for an expanded number of in-kind benefits which states are allowed to provide instead of "matching funds."[10]

Examples of in-kind benefits include:

Forgiveness of taxes, property and trackage rights
Donation or use of land
Project improvements
Use of state- or locally owned buildings or equipment
Personal services
Materials

By providing these goods and services, states were able to avoid all but the most explicit statutory or constitutional prohibitions and to be successful in obtaining funds.

Other factors in a state's decision to become involved in the rail industry include availability and priority of state funds, the degree of importance attached to rail transport by state governments and the financial health of rail carriers within the state. The problems faced by the rail industry are unique. Unlike its competitors, a railroad's continued operation of substantial rail plant in times of lower traffic makes it difficult to adjust costs when revenue drops. The trucking industry, on the other hand, can simultaneously reduce both right-of-way cost (fuel tax) and labor costs as production units (trucks) are withdrawn from service.

The rail industry's relatively low rate of return and high fixed costs have a negative impact on its ability to attract investment or borrow when inflation raises interest rates. Predictably, the railroad's attempt to reduce costs by curtailing the pervasiveness and frequency of service has diverted traffic to other modes in a competitive service-sensitive market. This diversion of traffic is aggravated by increasingly efficient highways and waterways that reduce the operating costs of competitive modes. The rail industry's profits are thus correspondingly decreased as it lowers its rates to meet those of competitors. In addition, competition and lack of cooperation between the railways themselves have contributed to shippers' negative perception of railroad performance.

In recognition of problems facing the rail industry and in keeping with federal policy, many states assured shippers of their support and began to "rationalize" the rail industry. The rationalization process generally involves cost-benefit analysis of rail lines, followed by a variety of support mechanisms. One type of support mechanism, the subsidy, was distributed to branch lines that met federally established criteria of usage or exhibited a minimum cost-benefit ratio. States often provided some of the following "support mechanisms" for railroads to assure maintenance of service on marginally profitable rail lines:

- Interest-free or low-interest loans
- Users buy specialized equipment and lease it to the railroad at cost
- Make payments to railroad to rehabilitate or maintain track
- State purchase of equipment for operator to maintain state-owned way
- Buy specialized equipment and make payments for rehabilitation or maintenance of tracks
- Special agreements with labor
- Arrangement of increased level of service to encourage more shipments by rail with guarantees to the railroad against loss and of reasonable profit
- Operation of several light-density lines under common management
- State or local tax relief arranged through forgiveness or other legislative action
- Technical assistance to private groups to encourage the establishment of short-line railroads
- State purchase of rail and right-of-way with lease-back to the operator[11]

If all support mechanisms appear inadequate, many states have specific statutes governing the disposition of rights-of-way or "rail banking" programs.

The 1980s were ushered in with the Staggers Rail Act[12] and a spirit of deregulation. Federal funds began to dry up as the "New Federalism" set in. The intent of the Reagan administration is to improve cost-effectiveness in freight service and to see that it is supported to a larger degree by the shippers, communities and states that benefit from the services provided.

More than one state rail planner is indignant at the flux which appears to be federal transport policy. For example, an Illinois rail planner stated: "It is ironic and somehow seems a breach of the State-Federal relationship that most of the rail problems that the states must now use their own resources to try to alleviate are regional or national in scope and all too often have had their origin in federal legislation, policy or programs."[13]

It is becoming increasingly apparent, however, that the railroad industry is on the upswing:

The nation's railroads are becoming "lean and mean." For example, revenue car-loadings of the major roads have dropped from 52,271,925 in 1929 to 21,613,063 in 1981. During the same period, however, originated tonnage increased by over 100 million tons and revenue ton miles more than doubled from 447 billion to 911 billion. Some of the reasons for this increased efficiency are revealed through other data. . . . In the same 1929 to 1981 time frame, the average freight car capacity increased from 46.3 tons to 68.1, the number of cars in the average freight trains increased from 47.6 to 68.6 and the total number of locomotives dropped from 57,000 to 28,000. To complement the increased operating efficiency, railroad employment has decreased from 1.66 million in 1929 to 436,000 in 1918 and owned track dropped from 386,000 miles in 1939 to 290,000 in 1980. It may be that the railroads are spring-loaded for success with only the state of the economy restraining them.[14]

There are three primary reasons for the recent improvement in the health of American railroads: (1) mergers have provided economies of scale, (2) unprofitable rail lines have been abandoned, and (3) railroads have experienced increased profitability and ability to respond to competitive market pressures since enactment of the Staggers Rail Act of 1980. The above factors are also reasons for states to retract "statelization" efforts, leaving a basically healthy rail industry to the efficiency of the market mechanism. Countervailing reasons also exist for maintaining state involvement in the rail industry. When a formerly regulated industry is deregulated, a period of adjustment follows. As shown by airline deregulation, price cutting does not continue indefinitely. Increased user taxes for motor carriers could make trucks less cost-efficient than rail for a number of commodities. With reduced rail service, more shippers are captive (without meaningful intermodal competition for their business). Once rail rights-of-way are lost, expense of reacquisition is prohibitive.

III. AMTRAK

The idea of "Railpax" (telegraphic symbol for "railroad passenger"), a government-sponsored, although private, corporation, is credited to Professor Paul Cherington of the Massachusetts Institute of Technology, who served as assistant secretary of transportation for policy development in the Johnson administration.[15] John Burby, who served as special assistant to Secretary of Transportation Alan Boyd, states the Cherington plan was first described in a speech delivered in 1968 by Richard J. Barber, then deputy assistant secretary for policy development, before a group of railroad executives:

Barber argued that the federal government probably made the same mistake financing new airports in major cities that it made financing new highways. Expanding the capacity of New York's airports to absorb more planes would simply mean that in a few years' time planes would have restored the old levels of congestion. "Fortunately, we have a more efficient means for transporting large numbers of people between cities in densely-populated urban corridors . . . it's called a train. . . . Rail operating costs per seat-mile are low and are substantially less than short-haul costs of air transportation by conventional aircraft. . . . The economics of technology show that modern jet aircraft are most efficient over long distance, not in the sort of short-haul movement that is typical in intracorridor transportation." . . . Barber proposed establishing a "quasi-public corporation" with powers to raise capital and to construct and operate the "kind of modern rail systems that I think we should have. . . . As I see it, such a corporation should be one in which government plays a leading role and does not serve as a mere passive guarantor of obligations. It must provide the direction and the guidance." But details of operation . . . would be left to the corporation itself.[16]

In 1970, the House Commitee on Interstate and Foreign Commerce reported the Railpax bill favorably. Funding was increased. Railroads joining
the corporation would receive a tax deduction of the full amount of their
payment to the Railpax as a necessary business expense for the taxable year
in which it is made. The start-up date for Railpax was set as May 1, 1971,
and the date when trains in the basic network could be dropped was set as
January 1973. President Nixon signed the bill on October 30, 1970.[17]

The new legislation contained several curious features and more than one
ambiguity. Title I, concerning findings, purposes and definitions, read, in
part:

The Congress finds that . . . public convenience and necessity require the continuance
and improvement of such (railroad passenger) service to provide fast and comfortable
transportation between crowded urban areas and in other areas of the country; that
rail passenger service can help to end the congestion on our highways and the
overcrowding of airways and airports.

These problems exist mostly in heavily congested areas where the airlines
are in trouble and the highways are overtaxed and where rail service can
make a real contribution. But the present Amtrak system is largely composed
of long-haul service. Since Amtrak serves 45 states, long-haul trains promote
widespread political support for subsidies for rail passenger service.

The law was meant to preserve and improve intercity passenger service,
but the definition given for such service is ambiguous:

"Intercity rail passenger service" means all rail passenger service other than (A)
commuter and other short-haul service in metropolitan and suburban areas, usually
characterized by reduced-fare, multiple-ride and commutation tickets, and by morning and evening peak period operations, and (B) auto-ferry service characterized by
transportation of automobiles and their occupants where contracts for such service
have been consummated prior to enactment of this Act.

The Senate report makes it clear that the law was intended to exclude
commutation service. The Interstate Commerce Commission (ICC) has determined that "rail passenger service" means "passenger train service," rather
than "passenger service operated by railroads" (for example, by a bus
subsidiary).

Trains not operating in metropolitan and suburban areas were included
in the "intercity" classification, despite the fact that many trains which offer
passenger service were short-line or mixed train operations, with no connection with intercity trains.

Title II of the Act authorized the secretary of transportation to draw up
recommendations for a basic national railroad passenger system identifying
end points between which service shall be provided and the routes over

which trains may be operated. The statutory criteria for designation of this system are:

opportunities for provision of faster service, more convenient service, service to more centers of population, and service at lower cost, by the joint operation, for passenger service, of facilities of two or more railroad companies; the importance of a given service to overall viability of the basic system; adequacy of other transportation facilities serving the same points; unique characteristics of rail service as compared to other modes of transportation; the relationship of public benefits of given services to the costs of providing such services; and potential profitability of the service.

The familiar criteria of public convenience and necessity had apparently fallen by the wayside.

The heart of the legislation is Title III, which creates a National Railroad Passenger Corporation (NRPC). This entity

shall be a for-profit corporation, the purpose of which shall be to provide intercity rail passenger service, employing innovative operation and marketing concepts so as to fully develop the potential of modern rail service in meeting the nation's intercity passenger transportation requirements. The Corporation will not be an agency or establishment of the United States government.

The financing arrangements were described by a financial writer:

The railroads, you see, can get their unprofitable trains off their own books by buying common stock in the passenger corporation. If the roads decline to go through this maneuver, they must continue running their trains until at least 1975. That's one way to sell stock. . . . When it comes to raising other capital, the corporation has no such sales tool. It will have a high-level financial panel, which will have to come up with some clever plans to draw investors into an enterprise with bleak prospects.[18]

The Corporation is authorized to own and operate passenger trains, or contract for their operation, and carry mail and express. The carriage is a subject of contract between NRPC and the railroads. If the parties fail to agree on terms, the ICC shall set contract provisions.

The Corporation is considered a common carrier by railroad and is subject to all provisions of the Interstate Commerce Act except for regulation of fares, abandonment of trackage and discontinuance under Section 13a, with certain exceptions provided in this Act.

If the Corporation or a railroad engages in any act or policy inconsistent with the policy of the Act, the attorney general of the United States may bring an action for equitable relief in any U.S. District Court.

The Corporation is subject to the same safety regulations as a railroad and the same laws with respect to collective bargaining with employees. In view of the prevalent dissatisfaction with the Railway Labor Act and the high labor costs which result from perpetuation of certain work rules and crew standards, this provision seems to mitigate against any great savings in costs of operation for the Corporation. Any employee or employee representative may bring action against the Corporation for violation of a labor agreement.

The Corporation is exempted from any state or other law pertinent to rail passenger service, and persons contracting with the Corporation for joint use or operation of facilities necessary for passenger service are exempted from the prohibition of the antitrust laws. The Corporation must submit annual recommendations to the President and Congress for amendments to the law, including the need for financial assistance. In addition, the secretary of transportation and the ICC must submit biennial reports on the state of rail passenger service and the effectiveness of this law in meeting the requirements for a balanced national transportation system, together with any legislative recommendations.

The essentials of the Act are the "carrot-and-stick" provisions concerning assumption of passenger service by the Corporation in Title IV. The law provided that on or before May 1, 1971, or during the period from March 1, 1973, to January 1, 1975, Amtrak was to tender a contract to relieve a railroad from all responsibility for the provision of intercity rail passenger service.

In consideration for being relieved of responsibility for operating these trains, a railroad had to pay NRPC one of the following amounts: (1) 50 percent of its fully distributed passenger service deficit for 1969; (2) 100 percent of the avoidable loss on all intercity passenger service rendered in 1969; or (3) 200 percent of the avoidable loss on the intercity service provided between points on the basic national rail passenger system in 1969. The amount due was to be paid over a three-year period in case or, at NRPC's option, by a transfer of equipment or provision of future service. Disputes as to the amount owed are to be resolved by the ICC. The accounting is based on figures supplied to the ICC by the railroads in 1969, which means that if a railroad overstated its passenger losses to the ICC, it had a higher entrance fee to pay NRPC. The fact that a railroad was not operating over the NRPC route segments does not mean that it could discontinue service without paying an entrance fee to the Corporation. In exchange for the payment, the carrier may receive common stock of NRPC, but if the railroad waived its claim to stock, the payment was to be treated as a tax-deductible expense.

On May 1, 1971, the Corporation was required to begin providing intercity rail passenger service unless such service was being performed by a non-contracting railroad or by a regional transportation agency which has given satisfactory assurance of the agency's willingness or ability to cooperate with NRPC. No railroad may operate over any route which the Corporation operates without NRPC's permission, and the ICC can force a recalcitrant railroad to let NRPC operate its trains over the railroad's tracks. Combined with freedom from fare, service and antitrust regulation, this made Amtrak one of the tightest monopolies known on the continent since Hudson's Bay Company.

Section 403 is the "put up or shut up" section. It authorizes the Corporation to provide additional trains, including special excursion trains, if consistent with prudent management. Where additional service is provided for two years, that service shall be considered part of the basic system. A state, regional or local agency which feels left out may request additional service, which NRPC will have to provide if the requesting authority agrees to reimburse the Corporation two-thirds of the attributable losses incurred by the system. If the agency and NRPC are unable to agree, the matter is referred to the secretary of transportation for determination. This section, for the first time, fixes responsibility for subsidizing local service with local authorities. In a certain sense this is unfair, since when NRPC chooses one route between two cities, cities and states on the alternate route must pledge a sizable sum to get that service which citizens of the favored communities get for nothing.

A. Constitutionality

The only serious attack on the constitutionality of the Rail Passenger Service Act was by as unlikely a protestant as one could find—the Quincy College and Seminary in western Illinois. The small church-affiliated school felt that it would be deprived of contact with the outside world if the Burlington Northern was allowed to discontinue service to Quincy. Federal Judge Abraham Lincoln Marovitz saw merit enough in the school's contention to enjoin the Burlington Northern from dropping a Chicago–Quincy local, which stayed on the rails past A-Day, until the restraining order was vacated on May 10, 1971.

On June 21, 1971, a three-judge district court delivered the first opinion concerning the constitutionality of Amtrak.[19] The college and supporting plaintiffs claimed that since Chicago–Quincy was a local run within Illinois, Congress was unconstitutionally attempting to regulate intrastate commerce by this Act. The railroad patiently pointed out that the Quincy station for some time had been located across the river in West Quincy, Missouri, so the train was in interstate commerce, at least for a few hundred yards of track. The Quincy protesters then attacked Amtrak as depriving certain areas of service without due process of law, because the basic system favored metropolitan areas at the expense of small rural areas. Finally, since the Act allowed a private corporation to chart the routes and determine services, the local citizens claimed that this was an unconstitutional delegation of Congress's authority to make laws to a private group.

After considering these arguments, the district court concluded that the Rail Passenger Service Act is a rational attempt to preserve and revitalize seriously declining passenger service. Selective pruning was necessary, and thus some areas may find themselves bereft of service; but the plan was sound and well conceived for the greatest good of the greatest number. Sufficient standards and safeguards have been established by the Congress, such as authorizing the attorney general to obtain equitable relief in case of violations of the law by railroads or Amtrak itself. This decision was upheld by the U.S. Supreme Court on February 22, 1972.

B. Amtrak in the 1980s

Amtrak, representing a highly visible subsidy, has been a target for budget cutting by each administration. Nonetheless, Congress has fought each attempt to cut the system. No serious cuts were made until 1979, when some marginal routes were discontinued by Carter's secretary of transportation, Brock Adams. In 1981, Amtrak was a target for Reagan's budget cutters, but again, bolstered by local interests, labor and passenger lobbies, the passenger service survived, although 15 percent of the system was cut. No longer does Amtrak run to the Mexican border or into British Columbia.

Congress has directed that Amtrak must recover 50 cents of each expense dollar from revenues, starting in fiscal year 1982. Since then, long-haul routes must meet a criterion of 150 passenger miles per train mile with avoidable loss of less than 10.1 cents per passenger mile. Short-haul requirements are 80 passenger miles per train mile and short-term loss of 12.9 cents per passenger mile. Amtrak has had to trim its services to comply with the funding level set by the Amtrak Improvement Act of 1981,[20] and subsequent legislation without regard to statutory or corporate service criteria.

Amtrak was directed to reduce and ultimately eliminate losses on food service. The federal government now has some equity in the Corporation, as the new legislation requires that preferred stock be issued to the secretary of transportation in exchange for government grants. This preferred stock has a liquidation preference over common stock. Amtrak is also exempted from state full-crew laws and from certain local sales and property tax laws. "Put up or shut up" routes are now discretionary with Amtrak. The passenger corporation is now free from state and federal regulatory restraints. During 1982–1985, Amtrak increased its ridership and efficiency, lowered its subsidy requirements and generally mended its fences with Congress and the Reagan administration. In 1985, however, then budget director David Stockman proposed an end to all funding for Amtrak. Transportation Secretary Elizabeth Dole also called for Amtrak's end. Despite this change of political climate, the budget resolution which emerged from Congress in August 1985 called for only 15 percent reduction in Amtrak funding. Although politically safe, Amtrak still faces strong competition from low-cost airlines and needs to gain greater control of labor costs and billing from operating railroads.

IV. COMMUTER RAILROADS[21]

A paradoxical situation has beset commuter railroad operations in the United States. As participation by local government increased financially, most of it for new rolling-stock acquisitions and track rehabilitation, the nation slid economically, with the resulting loss of revenue and tax money available, forcing cutbacks in service and increases in fares. These changes, coupled with inflation, job losses and some relocation of business away from downtowns, have combined to reduce commuter train ridership.

A specific change that occurred on January 1, 1983, greatly affected commuter train service in the Northeast. Until December 31, 1982, the largest railroad passenger carrier (i.e., non-transit) on our continent was not Amtrak, VIA Rail Canada, or the Long Island Rail Road, but Consolidated Rail Corporation—Conrail. As part of the effort to get Conrail profitable for eventual sale to the private sector, CR was excused from the passenger business. In the Omnibus Budget Reconciliation Act of 1981 were numerous provisions dealing with government subsidy of railroad service, and Subtitle E—the "Northeast Rail Service Act of 1981"—was aimed at transferring the responsibility for commuter train service from Conrail to a new entity originally envisioned as an Amtrak subsidiary.

This Act set up the Amtrak Commuter Services Corporation as a contract carrier to operate trains on behalf of any commuter authority that might wish the service. The specific target was, of course, Conrail, which ran commuter trains in Connecticut, New York, New Jersey, Pennsylvania, Delaware and Maryland.

Conrail was required to run these trains through 1982, but the authorities in each state had to decide whether to run the commuter trains on their own or have Amtrak Commuter do it. As things turned out, Amtrak Commuter Services Corporation wound up with no customers, for all states except one decided to get into the railroad business directly. (The exception was Maryland.)

Effective January 1, 1983, any former Conrail passenger train had to run under the new law, with the commuter authority having acquired or leased all necessary rail properties. Amtrak and Conrail were authorized to keep trackage rights over commuter railroads, and the authorities had to negotiate trackage rights over Amtrak where applicable. Cross-subsidization of short-haul commuter service by Amtrak from intercity revenues was prohibited.

As evidenced by the strikes of spring 1983, collective bargaining rights were substantially changed by the new law. The lawmakers envisioned that Commuter Services would be operating the trains, and the new operator and the unions were to reach agreement on pay, rules and working conditions by September 1, 1982. Since they failed to do so, the President chose— according to the new law—members for an emergency board. Not a mediation or arbitration panel, the board had the power only to select the best final offer submitted. It was not quite compulsory arbitration; but if the unions refused to accept the award and struck, the employees could not receive unemployment compensation, and if the carrier refused the offer, it could not avail itself of any strike insurance or mutual assistance plan.

A. Commuter Service Provided by U.S. Railroads (1985)

PHILADELPHIA
Authority and Operator: Southeastern Pennsylvania Transportation Authority

MARYLAND
Authority: Maryland Department of Transportation
Operators: Chessie System, Amtrak

NEW JERSEY
Authority and Operator: New Jersey Transit

NEW YORK/CONNECTICUT
Authorities: Metropolitan Transit Authority, Connecticut Department of Transportation
Operators: Long Island Rail Road, Metro-North Commuter Railroad

BOSTON
Authority: Massachusetts Bay Transportation Authority
Operator: Boston & Maine Corporation

PITTSBURGH
Authority: Port Authority of Allegheny County
Operator: Chessie System

CHICAGO
Authorities: Regional Transportation Authority, Northern Indiana Commuter Transportation District
Operators: Chicago & North Western, Northeastern Illinois Railroad Corporation, Burlington Northern, Norfolk & Western, Illinois Central Gulf, Chicago South Shore & South Bend, Amtrak

SAN FRANCISCO
Authority: California Department of Transportation
Operator: Southern Pacific

V. CONRAIL

A. The Northeast Railroad Problem

Although the Northeast problem area actually runs far beyond the northeastern United States, carriers between Chicago and the eastern seaboard were the most distressed financially.[22] For example, the Jersey Central succumbed in 1967 to the paralysis of labor-intensive terminal operations in high-tax territory. The Boston & Maine, defaulting on an interest installment, was dragged forcibly to court by creditors in 1970. The Penn Central fell in June of 1970, with Lehigh Valley, dependent on Penn Central for advances no longer forthcoming, following the next month. Reading fell in 1971. The Erie-Lackawanna capitulated a year later after Hurricane Agnes tore out 135 miles of the main line.

These railroads, along with the Ann Arbor Railroad, the Lehigh and Hudson River, the Pennsylvania–Reading Seashore Lines and the tiny New Hope & Ivyland, clamored at the federal courts for protection in bac&ruptcy from their creditors.

The decline of the eastern railroads was caused by a shrinking industrial base in the east, heavy terminal costs of serving the major old cities of the country, passenger deficits, reduced use of anthracite coal as a fuel and the improved superhighways.

B. Emergence of Conrail

Proposals for the easing of the Northeast problem suggested varied remedies, but a threatened strike finally prompted legislation. A strike on the Penn Central would have disrupted lines of distribution for the automobile and steel industries. As a result of this crisis, legislation set up a United States Railway Association (USRA) to plan a new system for the Northeast.[23]

The USRA is not an association. Rather, it is a buffer agency standing between the railroads and the government. Its main role was to supervise the planning of a slimmed-down system for the Northeast. USRA, the overseer of Conrail, sends periodic reports to Congress on the adequacy of Conrail's effort. It can authorize loans to Conrail and interim assistance to localities wishing to acquire lines and to Amtrak (for the northeastern corridor) and other financially stressed railroads.[24]

Most of the Regional Rail Reorganization Act (3R Act) legislation setting up Conrail is concerned with preserving the Penn Central and other lines for freight service.

Having considered several options, USRA chose to implement a fixed-plant scheme under which the government would acquire track, fix it up and then lease it to a privately financed Conrail. On April 1, 1976, the first Conrail trains began operation on the merged system. Conrail itself, more properly termed the Consolidated Rail Corporation, is an Amtrak-like, ostensibly for-profit corporation headquartered in Philadelphia.[25] Although Conrail's common stock was owned by the creditors of the bankrupt railroads, a majority of its directors were appointed by the President with the advice and consent of the Senate. The Act originally provided for labor protection for life for former employees of old corporations who had at least five years' seniority, but the corporation could move labor around wherever desired.[26] Since 1981, Congress has moved to sharply limit Conrail's employee protection liability. (See Section III of Chapter 7).

Many similarities exist between the Amtrak and Conrail schemes. Railroad deficits are reduced by "unloading" to the government the cost of labor agreements and unwanted services, such as passenger trains, commuter lines and northeastern freight service. Both Amtrak and Conrail laws involve government-sponsored "private, for profit" corporations, whose stockholders are the "unloading" railroads[27]; both laws mandated moratoria on discontinuance of service,[28] followed by massive cutbacks by the new corporations.[29] Both aim at savings and eventual productivity through rationalization of routes and centralized operation,[30] and both contain "put up or shut up" sections by which localities that otherwise would be stranded can subsidize the cost of continued operation of routes within their areas.[31]

All lines of the bankrupts that entered Conrail are now operated by Conrail itself, abandoned or run by "designated operators." Designated operators, short-line railroads operating over lines not picked up by Conrail, usually operate over trackage acquired by states and often receive state subsidies for operations.

Conrail has successfully rehabilitated hundreds of miles of trackage and has placed most of the former New York Central and Pennsylvania main lines in prebankruptcy condition. On the other hand, it has reduced service in many areas and increased charges so as to virtually embargo traffic; it has considered closing once-vital main lines like the Erie-Lackawanna and the Lehigh Valley.

C. Conrail and Deregulation

Like the Rail Passenger Service Act, the 3R Act,[32] which established Conrail, was a harbinger of deregulation. Many features of the 3R Act involved bypassing the ICC: first the moratorium on discontinuances, then the planning process and finally the discontinuance of lines to be abandoned (or, in the euphemism of USRA, "available for subsidy"). Continuance of rail service was not based on a regulatory agency's determination of public need, but on the state's willingness to put up funding, whether for continuing commuter service to a major city or preserving a branch line to a rural area.

Oversight functions for Conrail and the other eastern roads recipient of loan guarantees are handled not by the ICC, but by the off-budget, quasi-independent USRA.

But outside of these unique factors, Conrail is treated like an ordinary carrier by the ICC. It still must submit to ICC jurisdiction concerning rates and abandonments.

The Northeast Rail Service Act of 1981[33] attempts to integrate the services performed by Conrail into the nation's privately owned freight railroad system. It requires the secretary of transportation to consult with employees, state and local officials and shippers concerning transfer of Conrail freight services to other entities. If private railroads were unwilling to take over operation of terminals in the Northeast Corridor, the secretary of transportation would arrange formation by railroads of neutral terminal companies.

The secretary of transportation was required to sell the government's common stock in Conrail, if the USRA Board determines that the railroad can be profitable. The Board made such a determination by June 1, 1983. Because Conrail was determined to be "profitable," the railroad must be sold in one piece,[34] either to its employees or to another carrier. If it were deemed hopelessly unprofitable, or if the Department of Transportation was unable to sell it in one piece, it could be sold in various segments, according to freight transfer agreements worked out between the parties.[35]

In the years 1981–1984, Conrail showed a profit and became a more attractive candidate for purchase. By late 1984, the Norfolk Southern, CSX, the Santa Fe and a coalition of Conrail's employees were all interested in purchasing the railroad. In 1985, Conrail's management, with support of congressional allies, is attempting to persuade the government not to sell off the company, but to allow sale of stock to the general public. This would enable the successful Conrail management team to continue to operate the big railroad as a separate entity. However, Secretary Dole decided in early 1985 that the Norfolk Southern corporation should acquire Conrail. The eventual fate of Conrail is far from decided at this writing (1985).

VI. BENIGN NEGLECT: THE BANKRUPT RAILROADS

On October 1, 1979, the nation's new bankruptcy act went into effect, with far-reaching consequences for insolvent railroads.[36]

Bankruptcy is a constitutional right, and the federal government is granted the powers to regulate bankruptcy proceedings. It is a technical term; no person is bankrupt unless he has been so adjudged by a federal court. Since 1898, bankruptcies of railroads were governed by Section 77 of the Bankruptcy Act, which provided for a reorganization process for railroads that could last for decades.

In November 1978, President Carter signed the "Act to Establish a Uniform Law on the Subject of Bankruptcies." But the Act did not take effect until October 1, 1979, and railroads then in reorganization continued under the old law unless the trustees had failed to file a plan of reorganization before the enactment of the new bankruptcy code. For example, the Milwaukee Road and the Rock Island began and continued their reorganizations under Section 77 but with new requirements for labor, leased lines and the public interest because various extensions carried these proceedings into Chapter 11 of the new bankruptcy law.

The new bankruptcy law is the work of the Commission on Bankruptcy Laws, created by Congress in 1970 for the purpose of modernizing and upgrading the bankruptcy laws of the United States. Since the 1898 law was last substantially revised in 1938, many changes have occurred in the laws effecting debtors and creditors, and both consumer credit and bankruptcies have steadily grown. The new law purports to streamline the bankruptcy system.

Subchapter IV of Chapter 11 deals with the reorganization of railroads. One of the first changes is that the Department of Transportation, rather than the ICC, selects a panel of five persons, from which the court chooses one to be a trustee. An essential difference between railroad reorganization and other corporate bankruptcies is that the court and trustee must take into account the public interest as well as the interests of the railroad, its creditors and stockholders. A railroad in reorganization is still subject to the ICC and other federal and state regulators, except for abandonment cases. Any order of a regulator that requires the expenditure of funds must be approved by the court. The ICC is, however, excluded from participation in the reorganization of the companies which transferred their rail properties to Conrail in 1976. Neither the court nor the trustee may change a labor agreement unilaterally, except through normal procedures of the Railway Labor Act.

A trustee in bankruptcy takes possession of property of the railroad and protects it from the creditors at the same time that he is supposed to be operating it for the public. There are a few exceptions. Equipment which is the property of a bank or other lender can be repossessed by the lender unless the trustee agrees to take on the debtor's obligations. A leased line may be rejected by the trustee, and the lessor company (which may not have operated any trains since the nineteenth century) may be stuck with the operation of the leased line instead of the bankrupt railroad.

The ICC now has only advisory authority over the abandonment of railroad lines. The trustee, if he decides to abandon a portion or all of the railroad, must file an application for abandonment, but the court will tell the ICC when the deadline is to report, and the Commission's report is merely a recommendation to the reorganization court. All the court must find is that abandonment is in the best interest of the estate (the property of the debtor railroad), is essential to the reorganization plan and is consistent with the public interest. Actual abandonment, however, may not take place until the time for filing appeals has been exhausted. This is because of the drastic nature of railroad abandonments. Railroads and pipelines are unlike any other form of transportation inasmuch as they must provide their own infrastructure. Once a rail line is abandoned, it is gone. Often the railroad merely had an easement over the land it traversed, so the right-of-way reverts to the original landowner and must be repurchased if someone else wishes to continue the service. Thus, lawmakers felt that the courts should go easy on approving abandonments which involve the actual removal of track.

Except for the public interest and abandonment provisions, railroads now are treated very much as any corporate reorganization. The trustee must come up with a reorganization plan, which might include abandonments or transfer of lines to other railroads. If the trustee cannot honestly find such a plan, he must recommend that the line be liquidated.

The old Section 77 did not authorize liquidation of a railroad under reorganization proceedings. The court would dismiss the petition for reorganization and a state court receivership would generally follow. Now if the road cannot be successfully reorganized, the railroad must be liquidated within five years and its assets sold or otherwise disposed of, with the proceeds going to the secured creditors.

If, after January 14, 1983, a person makes an offer to acquire a rail line from a carrier subject to liquidation and the trustee in bankruptcy rejects the offer, that person may submit an application to the ICC. The terms prescribed by the ICC are binding on both parties, subject to review by the court having bankruptcy jurisdiction over the carrier. The court shall approve the acquisition under the ICC's terms if the compensation is not less than that required as a constitutional minimum.[37]

On a more optimistic note, the court may confirm a reorganization plan if the creditors will get something of value equivalent to what they would get if the line were sold for scrap, if it is probable that the income from the reorganized railroad will cover fixed charges and if the plan is compatible with the public interest. If more than one such plan is submitted, the court will select the one most likely to maintain adequate service to the public.

VII. DIRECTED-SERVICE ORDERS

Directed-service orders are the ICC's way of responding to emergencies which have snarled traffic.[38] They have been used on a small scale since the ICC's inception, in cases where, say, a bridge was out or a line was blocked. The Commission uses this power to detour traffic from one railroad to another. The railroads can later settle their dispute as to who pays for what; the important objective is to keep the traffic moving.

The authority for the ICC to direct service is found in three sections of the Interstate Commerce Act. The first, Section 11123 (as now designated), provides that if the Commission finds there is an emergency requiring immediate action, it may take a number of steps, including suspending car-service rules, requiring joint use of terminals and a "reasonable distance" of main line tracks, and taking action "to promote service in the interest of the public... regardless of the ownership of a locomotive, car, or other vehicle." In other words, the ICC can order a railroad to use another line's cars or engines to help move the traffic. It makes no difference whether the emergency is an act of God or of man's doing.

More to the point in Section 11124, which states that when the ICC finds that a carrier cannot transport the traffic offered to it, the Commission may direct the handling, routing and movement of its traffic over another railroad.

The roads are suppose to work out the financial arrangements, but if they cannot, the Commission will do so for them.

Finally, extensive directed-service powers were given to the Commission in Section 11125, directing transportation over one railroad by another when the first carrier cannot handle traffic because it has been abandoned by a court order or has simply given up without any regulatory approval.

The law also provides for the takeover of a line whose "cash position makes its continuing operation impossible." The Interstate Commerce Act was addressed to short-term emergency situations, rather than the complete shutdown of a major railroad, and these provisions have remained unchanged despite the recent passage of the Staggers Act and the substantial deregulation of railroads which followed.

Although the ICC can order one road to take over the routes of another, it cannot order any actions that would impair the ability of the directed carrier to serve its own customers or meet its own obligation as a common carrier. Nor is the directed carrier responsible for the debts of the road whose line it is operating.

The railroad performing directed service does not make any changes in the operation of the inactive line. It hires the same employees under their existing work rules and collective bargaining agreement. This is a major difference between directed-service orders and designated operations, under which many short lines were formed at the time of Conrail's inception. Designated operators are new railroads; directed-service orders are stopgaps, preserving the status quo until the fate of the cashless railroad is decided and a new operator takes over. The directed-service order smooths the transition and assures temporary service for shippers and communities. In the long run, other railroads may fill the gap, the state may take over the line, another operator may be found or the line may indeed be abandoned.

Critics of directed-service orders believe that the ICC misses the point by preserving operating patterns and rules which contributed to the unsatisfactory situation. Needless to say, many of these critics are allied with creditor interests, who see their claims on the estate becoming more remote with each day of continued operation.

Directed-service orders will continue to be in the ICC's arsenal of remedies under the current legislation. The Commission and the Department of Transportation both seem presently to regard the use of these orders as temporary transition measures. The demise of the Rock Island and of the Milwaukee as a transcontinental carrier indicate that the government is unwilling to use directed-service orders as instruments for indefinite continuation of money-losing operations. Still, the use of such orders reflects a realization that once a railroad line is abandoned, it is gone for good, and that a second change may well be necessary in easing the transition to the rail system of the future.

NOTES

1. Kerian, Statelization of the Rail Industry (1983) (student paper filed at Transp. Law Office, University of North Dakota Law School, Grand Forks, N.D.).

2. H. Levine, Small Railroads 189 (1982).

3. Pa. Const. art. VIII, § 8.

4. N.M. Const. art. IX, § 14.

5. N.C. Const. art, V, § 3.

6. Pub. L. No. 93–236, Title IV, 87 Stat. 1010 (1974).

7. Pub. L. No. 94–210, Title VIII, 90 Stat. 125 (1976).

8. Pub. L. No. 95–607, 92 Stat. 3059 (1978).

9. See generally, J. Runke & M. Kannensohn, Assisting Private Enterprise: State Constitutional Issues (A Rail Program Case Study) (Council of State Governments 1977).

10. Pub. L. No. 93–236, Title VIII, § 803(g)(1), 87 Stat. § 1010 (1974).

11. See generally W. Black & J. Runke, The States and Rail Preservation 4 (Council of State Governments 1975).

12. 49 U.S.C. § 10905 (Supp. IV 1980).

13. Letter from David Denton, Illinois rail planner, to Paul Kerian (Sept. 22, 1982).

14. U.S. Dept. of Agriculture, U.S. Grain Transportation Situation (Oct. 9, 1982).

15. Adapted from W. Thoms, Reprieve for the Iron Horse 37–43 (1973).

16. J. Burby, The Great American Motion Sickness 181–82 (1971).

17. Pub. L. No. 91–518, 84 Stat. 1328 (Oct. 30, 1970), 45 U.S.C. 501, et seq. (1972).

18. Clark, Rail Passenger Corp.: Exercise in Futility? Wall Street J. May 8, 1970, editorial p. 12.

19. Thoms, Is Amtrak Legal? Trains 59 (Aug. 1972).

20. Omnibus Budget Reconciliation Act of 1981, Pub. L. No. 97–35, 401, 95 Stat. 828 (1981).

21. Thoms, Is the Clock Running Down for U.S. Rail Commuters? Trains, Oct. 1983, p. 30.

22. This section is adapted from W. Thoms, Deregulation: The Railroad Experience 1 (1981).

23. 45 U.S.C. § 711 (1980).

24. 45 U.S.C. § 721 (1980).

25. 45 U.S.C. § 741 (1980). See Blanchette v. Connecticut General U.S. Corp., 419 U.S. 102 (1974).

26. 45 U.S.C. §§ 771–779 (1980).

27. 45 U.S.C. §§ 541, 741 (1980).

28. 45 U.S.C. §§ 642, 744 (1980).

29. 45 U.S.C. §§ 564, 744(b) (1980).

30. 45 U.S.C. §§ 545(e), 742 (1980).

31. 45 U.S.C. §§ 563, 744(c) (1980).

32. 45 U.S.C. § 701 (1982).

33. Northeast Rail Service Act of 1981, 45 U.S.C. 765 (1981).

34. 45 U.S.C. 746 (1981).

35. 45 U.S.C. 763 (1981).

36. This section is adapted from Thoms, *New Rules for Bankrupt Rails*, Trains 28–30 (May 1980) (copyright 1980 by Kalmbach Publishing Co., reprinted with permission). The reader is cautioned that the 1978 Bankruptcy Act has since been declared constitutionally defective, and Congress has enacted remedial legislation.

37. Pub. L. No. 97–468 (Jan. 14, 1983).

38. This section is taken from Thoms, *Those Directed Service Orders*, Trains 48 (September 1981) (copyright 1981 by Kalmbach Publishing Co., reprinted with permission).

7

Labor Relations in the Transportation Industry

I. THE RAILWAY LABOR ACT

Railway and airline workers alike are governed by their own labor relations statute, the Railway Labor Act.[1] The Act is nationwide in scope, is not subject to any state right-to-work law and applies to any railroad subject to the Interstate Commerce Act. The Railway Labor Act, originally enacted in 1926 and extended to air carriers in 1936, is a testimony to the strength of railway labor, which was politically strong in rural states without much industrialization. Jurisdiction over air carriers is limited to those in "interstate or foreign commerce," and until recently those words were held to apply only to Civil Aeronautics Board-regulated carriers and not to intrastate airlines. With the deregulation of air traffic, these words may be given new meaning by the National Mediation Board.

Carriers are required to meet, confer and make reasonable effort to come to agreements with workers or their representatives. Neither a carrier nor a union may interfere with the other party's choice of representatives. Agreements before hire to join or not to join labor unions are forbidden, but union security clauses (equivalent to a "union shop") are allowed. An unusual provision of the Railway Labor Act is that railroad operating employees may be required to join a union but not necessarily the bargaining representative for that craft. Contracts signed between the unions and the carriers remain in effect unless changed specifically by the provisions of Section 6 of the Railway Labor Act. Section 6 requires the giving of notice to the other side, conferring and a cooling off period of 10 days after the conference has reached impasse.

Minor disputes and questions arising out of the interpretation of existing labor agreements are settled by adjustment boards. These boards, composed of labor and management members, are statutory creatures functioning on each railroad or airline system. Nationally, there is a National Railroad Adjustment Board to arbitrate these minor disputes, but no National Air Transport Adjustment Board has been established, although it is authorized by law. Instead, minor airline disputes are settled by air system adjustment boards on each airline.

The Railway Labor Act establishes a National Mediation Board to handle major disputes on railroads and airlines. Major disputes often arise during the negotiation of new contracts. If parties are unable to agree on a new contract, the National Mediation Board proffers its services.[2] As its name implies, the Board has only mediation and conciliation powers. It can recommend arbitration, but it cannot compel parties to submit their disputes to arbitration.

Carriers and unions must give the other party at least 30 days' written notice of an intended change in agreements. The parties must agree on a place for the conference within 10 days after receipt of the notice, and the conference must begin within the 30 days provided for in the notice. Neither party may change the rules or the pay until 10 days after the Mediation Board's efforts cease.

Generally in railroad disputes, the Mediation Board determines that a strike or lockout would "threaten substantially to interrupt interstate commerce to a degree such as to deprive any section of the country of essential transportation service." The Board then notifies the President of the United States, who may create an Emergency Board to study the issue and make a report of the facts of the dispute. The Emergency Boards, which are essentially fact-finding agencies, provide a cooling-off period. After the creation of such board and for 30 days after its report to the President, no change, except by agreement, may be made by the parties on the dispute.

This 60-day moratorium, when added to the built-in time frame of collective bargaining required by the Act, may be contrasted with the 80-day cooling-off period for industrial disputes under the Taft-Hartley Act. Railway Labor Act provisions refer to an emergency in "any section" of the country, whereas Taft-Hartley refers to an emergency imperiling the national health and safety. The President must order the attorney general to seek an injunction under Taft-Hartley; under the Railway Labor Act, the parties are frozen in impasse until 30 days after the Emergency Board makes its report. Thus, the emergency provisions of the Railway Labor Act are routine and predictable; under Taft-Hartley they are the exception.

The system of adjustment boards ensures the arbitration of minor disputes in the rail and airline industries. Voluntary interest arbitration is encouraged but not compelled by the Railway Labor Act. Railroad collective bargaining was handled for some time under nationwide agreements; the unions bargained for contracts with representatives of all the railroads. This created a certain amount of inflexibility in dealing with labor disputes; the same work rules applied to railroads with very different operating patterns and financial conditions. Nationwide bargaining was not enough to preserve railroad jobs, although the operating brotherhoods (many of which are now merged into the United Transportation Union) waged a tough fight to preserve jobs in a declining industry.

II. COMPULSORY ARBITRATION

The diesel locomotive fireman dispute had a long tortured history, dating back to the 1937 National Diesel Agreement. That pact retained the fireman as a lookout or helper on diesel locomotives, similar to his position on electric locomotives or steam engines with stokers or oil-fired machinery. Because of the multiple-unit potential of diesel, substantial savings were afforded the carrier by being able to use the same size crew as that of a lone steam engine to operate a multiple-unit diesel locomotive. No fireman has been required on locomotives weighing less than 45 tons, multiple-unit electric trains or single rail diesel cars. Were the carriers to eliminate the fireman in 1959, as originally contemplated, a nationwide tie-up would have resulted, with the exception of a few independent carriers.

Having exhausted the "emergency" procedures of the Railway Labor Act and the recommendations of a special Presidentail Railway Commission, the carriers were free to implement the new rules. Instead, in 1963, Congress enacted a one-shot arbitration law, which provided for a special arbitration board composed of labor and management members as well as some neutrals from outside the industry, who were to hold the balance of power. The award of the special board provided for reduction in force of firemen from freight and yard jobs (mostly by attrition), retention of a certain percentage of firemen's jobs and other changes in crew consists.

After expiration of the two-year arbitrators' award, the rails and the brotherhoods began to bargain again over the fireman and related issues. At no point in the discussion did the railroads ever propose, even as a bargaining counter, the elimination of firemen from passenger runs. Because a head-end brakeman does not ride in the cab, management agreed that safety required that a fireman be used on passenger engines.

On July 20, 1971, the fireman dispute was settled. The agreement called for the gradual phasing out of many firemen's jobs on freight and yard engines and provided that future vacancies for engineers must be filled by firemen. All firemen furloughed on that date must be recalled to service.

The fireman issue was symptomatic of the glacial pace of collective bargaining in the railroad industry—an unhealthy climate which has spurred many legislators to seriously consider reforms or substitutes for the current process of collective bargaining with its interminable negotiations and threats of strikes and lockouts. Although no changes in the Railway Labor Act have been made recently, several ad hoc laws intervening in or terminating strikes have been passed.

After the 1963 law, talk of compulsory arbitration waned. In 1964, President Johnson placed the protagonists of the railroad dispute together in a marathon session, which included pressure from the White House, to hammer out a settlement on the so-called "secondary issues" concerning work rules.

In 1967, when shopcraft unions rejected the recommendations of an Emergency Board, Congress extended the 30-day cooling-off period and appointed a special mediation panel. Its recommendations were also rejected; whereupon Congress extended the no-strike period. At the expiration of this period, the unions struck for two days on a nationwide basis. Congress again ordered the workers back on the job and set up a third board to ultimately decide the issue.

In 1969, President Nixon convened an emergency board to settle another shopworkers' strike. By December, all the unions except the Sheet Metal Workers accepted the proposal, but that union called a selective strike against certain railroads; all carriers threatened a lockout. Congress again barred the strike and in 1970 imposed the settlement on the recalcitrant Sheet Metal Workers.

In 1971, Congress halted a Signalmen's strike that had been of two days' duration. Instead of establishing an arbitration panel, Congress enacted a compromise figure and told the carriers and unions that that was the wage they were to accept.

Later in 1971 came an 18-day railroad strike by the United Transportation Union over the carriers' implementation of new work rules. Not all carriers were struck; the Union Pacific, the Southern, the Norfolk & Western and the Southern Pacific were the strike targets. Other railroads immediately implemented the contested work rule changes on their properties. The nationwide issues were settled on August 2, 1971, without congressional intervention but with heavy White House pressure. The agreement called for the institution of management-union committees on the various properties, which then had 90 days to renegotiate interdivisional crew change rules. If they could not agree, arbitrators would decide.

When Congress has been faced with a crippling rail strike, it has taken one of three paths: appoint a board of arbitration to decide the issue (as in the 1963 Firemen dispute), impose a settlement that the other unions had accepted on a holdout union (as in the 1969 Sheet Metal Workers' strike) or come up with a compromise figure of its own (as in the 1971 Signalmen's strike).

A 1982 law ending a strike by the Brotherhood of Locomotive Engineers does not go quite as far as its predecessors. The other operating unions (notably the United Transportation Union) had agreed to a no-strike condition for settling wage and benefit issues. The engineers would not go along with this (fearing the loss of the pay differential that the "eagle eyes" had always enjoyed) and struck over the issue. Congress merely mandated that the union could not strike for the pay differential and sent the engineers back to bargain with the railroads again, effectively shoving the issue under the rug.[3]

It may have been all shadow boxing. Rail labor, having lost employee protection in 1981, having seen the right to strike curtailed in 1982 and facing huge layoffs with the state takeover of Conrail commuter trains in 1983, is understandably on the defensive right now but pleased to be still working.

The aftermath of these strike threats and the subsequent patchwork laws make clear to most negotiators that Congress will not tolerate a national rail strike. The brotherhoods and management may have helped create such a situation by insistence on national treatment of issues, but there has been a gradual retreat toward local settlement of disputes rather than crisis bargaining on a nationwide scale. This has been accompanied by resurgence of the selective strike, with the carriers' accompanying right to lock out employees. In 1983, the commuter authorities operating former Conrail lines were struck by ex-Conrail trainmen over manning levels. Although the strikes lasted for months and New York- and Philadelphia-area commuters were inconvenienced, Congress did not act and the unions eventually settled for a lower level of manning and compensation than that enjoyed when Conrail ran the commuter trains.

Although no permanent compulsory arbitration of interest disputes has passed Congress, antistrike provisions exist for public employees in local transit systems. These provisions have not been enough, however, to deter the increasing number of strikes in the public sector. In addition, state ownership of a railroad apparently does not remove it from the jurisdiction of the Railway Labor Act. The Long Island Rail Road, for example, is totally owned by the state of New York, but the U.S. Supreme Court has recently held that the railroad was a common carrier under the ICC, subject to the Railway Labor Act rather than the state's Taylor Law.[4]

III. LABOR PROTECTION FOR RAILROAD EMPLOYEES

A. Introduction

Since the 1930s, employees affected by railroad mergers or consolidations have enjoyed a degree of job protection unequaled in any other industry.[5] The cost of this protection has historically been borne by the railroads; but when Congress created Conrail from the remains of the bankrupt northeast carriers, it shifted the burden of the anticipated labor protection costs to the taxpayer.

1. Origin of Labor Protection in the Rail Industry

Providing protection for employees adversely affected by mergers and consolidation gained acceptance more than 50 years ago, when railroads developed the informal practice of paying moving expenses of workers who were required to relocate. When a wave of facility consolidations in the 1930s resulted in massive unemployment, rail unions called for protection of workers. The Emergency Railroad Transportation Act of 1933 was the first statute to protect employees endangered by railroad consolidations. The Act mandated that no carrier could reduce the number of its employees below the level of May 1933 and that a carrier must pay all moving expenses and property losses incurred by employees who were forced to move.

Before the Act expired, in 1926, labor and management negotiated what remains to this day the basis for railroad labor protection—the Washington Job Protection Agreement of May 1936. That agreement has not been changed since 1936 and remains in effect. Eighty-five percent of the nation's carriers signed to the Washington Agreement, including Conrail's predecessors. The major benefits which the agreement conferred on workers affected by "co-ordination" of railroad facilities or operations included:

—For an employee deprived of employment ("displaced"), 60 percent of the employee's average monthly salary (less earnings from other railroad employment) for up to five years, depending on length of service, or a lump sum payment of up to 12 months' pay, depending on length of service.

—For an employee whose position was worsened (employee forced to hold a lower-paying job), a "displacement allowance" guarantee the same pay earned prior to the merger for up to five years, depending on length of service.

—For an employee required to move, reimbursement of moving expenses, including any loss suffered in the sale of a residence for less than its fair market value.

—For all employees, retention of fringe benefits enjoyed in previous employment.

Until 1939, a question remained as to the ICC's authority to impose labor protection conditions. That year, however, the Supreme Court ruled in *United States v. Lowden*[6] that the ICC could require protection without specific statutory authority. After this decision, the ICC began to impose conditions modeled on the Washington Agreement.

In 1940, Section 5(2)(f) was added to the Interstate Commerce Act to require the ICC to impose labor protection as a condition for approval of mergers, consolidations, acquisitions, line abandonments and other related transactions. Subsequently, the ICC promulgated various formulae for protecting employees, the most important of which were the "New Orleans Conditions."

The New Orleans Conditions, which were first prescribed in the *New Orleans Union Passenger Terminal Case*,[7] provided protection from the adverse effects of a merger or acquisition for a minimum of four years from the effective date of the Commission's order approving the transaction. During the four-year period, an employee deprived of employment as a result of the transaction receives a monthly compensation equivalent to the wage that the employee formerly received, and an employee retained in service but "bumped" to a lower-paying job as a result of the transaction receives a monthly displacement allowance to make up the difference between the new and former wages. Other benefits include reimbursement for moving costs and losses from sale of homes. After the minimum four-year period, an adversely affected employee may continue to receive benefits available under the provisions of the Washington Agreement until dismissal and displacement allowances equal the total compensation available under the agreement.

Anticipating that the ICC would prescribe similar conditions, some railroads entered into voluntary labor-protection agreements to secure labor peace. A number of these, notably the Penn Central, the Norfolk & Western and the Burlington Northern merger agreements, added a provision not previously approved—attrition protection. In effect, these agreements provided certain classes of employees a lifetime job guarantee.

In 1971, the secretary of labor certified a labor-protection arrangement under Section 405 of the Amtrak Act that became known as "Appendix C–1." The significant change in the benefits of Appendix C–1 (which are essentially the New Orleans benefits and include the upgrading of monthly compensation guarantees by subsequent general wage increases) is the increase of the protective period to six years from the date an employee was adversely affected.

The more recent protective conditions imposed by the ICC, known as "Oregon Short Line" and "New York Dock," do not differ materially from Appendix C–1 conditions. They, too, provide displacement and dismissal allowance protection upgraded by subsequent general wage increases for a six-year period. In addition, employees receive job training at the expense of the railroad. In general, the New York Dock Conditions are not the standard protective conditions imposed by the ICC.

2. Special Labor-Protection Statutes

In recent years, Congress has acted in special cases to provide unique labor-protection benefits for employees of financially troubled and bankrupt railroads. In the case of Conrail, this special legislation imposed labor protection at a level higher than normal ICC standard, and in the cases of the Milwaukee and the Rock Island, labor protection was imposed at levels lower than the ICC standard.

a. *Conrail.* As part of the reorganization of the northeast bankrupts and the creation of Conrail, Congress enacted special labor-protection provisions in Title V of the 3R Act. Title V was passed in response to rail labor's request that Congress provide for labor protection in exchange for labor's endorsement of the formation of Conrail and in recognition of the labor protection already enjoyed by most employees of the Penn Central and the Erie-Lackawanna Railroads under their respective merger protection agreements.

Title V is a product of the negotiations process which was conducted in late 1973 between representatives of rail labor and rail management. This statute became the most expensive labor-protection provision in labor history. For employees with five or more years service on January 2, 1974, Title V provided:

- Job protection until age 65
- A monthly displacement allowance ("MDA") equal to the average monthly salary received in 1974 (including overtime), upgraded to reflect general wage increases
- A severance payment up to $20,000, depending on length of service
- Maintenance of fringe benefits for both active and furloughed protected employees
- Relocation benefits

The major categories of benefits conferred by Title V are monthly displacement allowances, separation allowance and moving expenses.

b. *Milwaukee/Rock Island.* Congressional enactment of railroad labor protection in special cases did not end with Title V of the 3R Act. Faced with the abandonment of the entire Rock Island Railroad and more than half of the Milwaukee Railroad, Congress legislated labor protection for 14,000 employees of these bankrupt lines. It was recognized, however, that imposition of either Title V or New York Dock conditions on the Rock Island estate or the reorganized Milwaukee Road was not financially feasible. In the Milwaukee Railroad Restructuring Act of 1979, Congress enacted labor-protection provisions that included:

- For an employee deprived of employment prior to April 1, 1984, 80 percent of the employee's average monthly straight-time salary, not to be increased by subsequent wage increases, up to three years. An employee dismissed after that date would receive compensation up to eight months.
- A lump-sum separation payment up to $25,000
- Job training up to $3,000

For the Milwaukee, payment of these benefits is legally a liability of the railroad but is guaranteed by the federal government through the purchase of preference shares.

In the Rock Island Employees and Transition Act of 1980 (RITA), Congress provided protection for Rock Island employees similar to Milwaukee benefits. The situations differ, however, in that, whereas the Milwaukee is being reorganized, the Rock Island is undergoing liquidation. Thus, the Rock Island reorganization court refused to implement the labor-protection provisions of the Act on the ground that the cost for such protection would become a senior claim against the estate of the Rock Island and therefore would amount to an unconstitutional taking of the property of creditors and security holders.

The Supreme Court held that the uniformity requirement of the Bankruptcy Act prohibits Congress from enacting RITA because it is a bankruptcy law that applies to the affairs of only one named debtor.[8] Congress responded in January 1983 with the Bankrupt Railroad Service Preservation and Employee Protection Act of 1982.[9] The 1982 Act amends RITA to apply to any railroad which is the subject of a proceeding pending under Section 77 of the Bankruptcy Act or under Subchapter IV of Chapter 11 of Title 11.[10] The agreement shall not require the expenditure of funds in excess of amounts authorized by the 3R Act, and no benefits may be provided under this section after April 1, 1984.[11]

B. Protection for Amtrak and Conrail Employees

The 3R Act represents the high-water mark of the labor-protection movement in federal legislation.[12] Originally, labor-protection provisions were viewed as "buy-offs" for unions to support the merger or deregulation contemplated by Congress or the ICC. Labor-protection provisions are a feature of Amtrak legislation. The Rail Passenger Service Act of 1970 provides that railroads shall "provide fair and equitable arrangements to protect the interests of employees . . . affected by discontinuances of intercity rail passenger service" by the railroads or by Amtrak. Contracts between railroads and Amtrak must be certified by the secretary of labor. The result was that Amtrak was required to protect individual employees against a worsening of their employment positions. It appeared that it would cost Amtrak more to close down its system than to run it because employee-protection bills would consume a great amount of Amtrak's limited appropriation.

By 1981, the future for employee protection looked bleak. With an administration and Congress looking askance at the cost of continuing subsidies for Amtrak, Conrail and branch lines, it became less popular to champion the cause of furloughed workers. Labor's strength was gradually ebbing, and in collective bargaining, railroad labor was unable to match the gains of other industrial settlements. The congressional mood had changed to the realization that one group of employees could expect lifetime job protection while most laid-off workers had only unemployment compensation funds available.

The Budget Reconciliation Act of 1981 tells the tale. It adds Title VII to the 3R Act and directs the secretary of labor to devise a new labor-protection provision that provides termination allowances not to exceed $25,000.[13] The law specifies the manner in which Conrail may eliminate certain fireman and brakeman positions. The government may pay separation benefits up to $115,000,000 and retraining, location and other displacement costs up to $385,000,000.[14] The mandated establishment of a central hiring roster composed of Conrail, Milwaukee and Rock Island employees was to result in preferential hiring by other roads of displaced railroad employees. The new law relieves Amtrak of many labor protection costs arising from Title V of the Conrail law.[15]

It is clear that what Congress gives, it may take away. Having given an entitlement to lifetime protection to railroad employees, Congress now feels free to take back this protection. Much of this changed view is due to political realities. Organized labor now commands a mere 18 percent of the work force and little sympathy outside its ranks. The general public enthusiasm over the breaking of the air traffic controllers' strike demonstrated that a government employer can call on public sympathy in dealing even with critically sensitive employees.

IV. LABOR PROTECTION FOR AIRLINE EMPLOYEES

When an employee is discharged by a private firm, absent any discrimination or illegal intent by the employer, he has no recourse except unemployment insurance.[16] There are certain exceptions, but nowhere have the employee-protection plans been as generous as those in the railroad industry. Partly this is due to the massive displacement of employees resulting from the railroad mergers of the 1960s, the institution of Amtrak and Conrail in the 1970s and the large-scale abandonments looming in the 1980s. The Civil Aeronautics Board has in the past imposed labor-protection agreements in mergers, but large-scale layoffs were the exception rather than the rule in the airline industry. No costly payouts such as the Amtrak and Conrail settlements had occurred in the airline industry prior to deregulation.

The Airline Deregulation Act[17] directs the secretary of labor to provide to displaced airline employees protection that is at least as beneficial as the labor-protection provisions established by the Amtrak Act.

The Airline Deregulation Act provides protection for laid-off employees who have been employed by the airlines for four years or more, when a 7½ percent contraction of employment occurs in the industry because of deregulation. As part of these benefits, a laid-off employee is placed in a preferential hiring status with the airlines. Severance benefits have a maximum of six years, but the events triggering the employee-protection provisions of the Act must occur within 10 years.[18] Congress now has extended generous benefits to an industry other than the troubled railroads. These benefits may have been the price needed for organized labor's support of the deregulation bill.

V. LABOR PROTECTION FOR TRANSIT EMPLOYEES

When an urban mass transit company shifts from the private sector to the public sector, an obvious problem emerges: What happens to the employees' rights and benefits gained under collective bargaining while in the private sector?[19] This is particularly acute in those areas in which public employees do not have the right to strike or, in some cases, even the right to organize and bargain collectively.

A. Section 13(c) of the Urban Mass Transportation Act

Congress reacted to this problem by including a provision in the 1964 Act to protect employee rights.[20] Congress identified three significant areas covered under Section 13(c):

First, the determination by the secretary of labor that "fair and equitable arrangements" are made to protect the employees affected by such assistance. This has been interpreted by the secretary of labor to include all employees of established systems whose interests might be adversely affected by programs worked out under the Act.

Second, the inclusion in protective arrangements of the five areas mentioned in Section 13(c) covering preservation of rights, continuation of collective bargaining, protection of employees against worsening of their positions, assurance of employment and paid training or retraining.

Third, the requirement that such arrangements "include provisions protecting individual employees against a worsening of their positions, with respect to their employment which shall in no event provide benefits less than those established pursuant to Section 5(2)(f) of this title."

Section 13(c) incorporates by reference all the provisions of old Section 5(2)(f) of the Interstate Commerce Act into the Urban Mass Transportation Act (UMTA) of 1964. Section 5(2)(f) provides for workers of railroads which are merged or consolidated a variety of monetary benefits or, in lieu of benefits to offset the loss of jobs and earnings, compensation for unusual expenses and other equalizing compensation for periods up to five years from the change. Thus, these benefits are now available to transit workers who are affected by a change in their condition, if federal assistance to the transit operator is involved.

The administration of Section 13(c) is relatively simple in procedure. Applications for assistance under UMTA are made to the Department of Transportation. As the Department of Transportation reviews the application, it also forwards copies of the application to the Department of Labor for certification as required in Section 13(c).

B. Extent of Employee Protection

Labor has clearly seen the provision as a possible benefit. It has protected members' rights during any shift to public ownership. This has clearly been advantageous, particularly in those states in which there are no laws permitting public employee collective bargaining. However, a recent case in New York indicates that there are limits on labor's rights. This case, denying a labor union's attempt to obtain preliminary injunction in an effort to enforce an arbitration clause in Section 13(c) agreement, states that the legislative history of Section 13(c) clearly seeks only to preserve existing rights at the time of a shift to public ownership.[21] Because no interest arbitration agreement existed prior to the shift, the union was not permitted to enforce the provision. In contrast, a Tennessee district court three years later ruled, on similar facts, that there was no congressional prohibition against creation of new rights in favor of transit workers. The court held that rights created and preserved in Section 13(c) agreements may be enforced.[22] A Maryland court has defined the scope of the employees covered by a Section 13(c) agreement. The court held that absent express legislative authorization, a public transit authority may not enter arbitration of collective bargaining concerning rights of persons who were not employees of the private operating company at the time it was acquired by the public transit authority.

No longer, however, will disputes of this nature be decided in federal courts. The U.S. Supreme Court ruled in June 1982, in *Jackson Transit Authority v. Local Division 1285*, that Section 13(c) does not provide a federal cause of action for alleged breaches of Section 13(c) agreements. Instead, these disputes must be settled in state courts according to state law.[23]

Although employees generally have no voice in the takeover, they are automatically converted from employees enjoying the protection of the National Labor Relations Act to public employees who may or may not have collective bargaining rights. The unionized transit worker may now find that his right to strike has disappeared. State laws that allow bargaining usually regard city transit workers as essential, thus curbing their rights to collective action.

One problem plaguing transit bargaining is that some states forbid collective bargaining by municipal employees, or at least do not provide any mechanism for settling disputes. Although some states have comprehensive public employee relations boards with power to enforce awards through compulsory arbitration of emergency disputes, other states have no provision for collective bargaining. Practice in such jurisdictions has been for an informal type of collective bargaining to occur anyway. Contracts are signed with the bargaining representative without any clear delineation of the scope of the union's authority to represent the employees. The pattern has been that a type of de facto recognition has occurred.

VI. NATIONAL LABOR RELATIONS ACT

Unlike their colleagues in the railroad and airline industries, employees of water carriers, motor carriers, freight forwarders and pipeline companies are subject to the National Labor Relations Act (NLRA).[24] The NLRA also applies to transit operations that affect interstate commerce. Most public transit operators, however, are now owned by governmental units, and these employees are generally covered by state public employment laws.

Transportation workers covered by the NLRA have the same rights as industrial workers. They may organize, bargain collectively and strike; they also are free to refrain from such activities. They may enter into a "union-shop" or "agency-shop" agreement with their employer, except in states where a state right-to-work law forbids agreements. Employers have no right to discharge employees for union activity, and employees giving testimony to the National Labor Relations Board (NLRB) may not be discharged because of this activity.

The NLRB has jurisdiction over transportation companies and their employees in the areas of representations and complaints. In representation cases, the NLRB determines the bargaining unit, in which employees are entitled to vote for the union representative (or no union). With trucking companies and bus lines, the bargaining unit is often the drivers who operate out of a particular terminal or division, while nonoperating employees form a different unit. Most long-haul truckers are represented by the International Brotherhood of Teamsters, whereas bus, maritime and pipeline employees are represented by many unions. In complaint proceedings, either an employer or a union is cited as committing an unfair labor practice as described in Section 8 of the Act. Employer unfair practices involve interference with an employee's right to engage in union activities or employer dominance of a union, while union unfair labor practices involve such activities as illegal picketing, secondary boycotts and "hot cargo" clauses. It is also an unfair labor practice for a union to demand money for services not intended to be performed, but this sanction has been held not to apply to traditional work-preservation rules found within the transportation industry.

"Wildcat," or unauthorized, strikes are banned, but a duly authorized strike for economic reasons or to protest unfair labor practices may not be enjoined. Injunctions may be obtained only when the President determines that there is a national emergency, and the attorney general is then empowered to seek an injunction. The virtually automatic cooling-off period found in the Railway Labor Act cases is not a recurrent feature of transportation disputes outside the railroad or airline industries. During strikes, the ICC may grant temporary authority for other motor carriers to serve the area formerly served by the struck carrier.

Courts have held NLRA applicable to U.S. flag or U.S.-owned ships on the high seas. The crew of an American ship may petition to have its union certified as the bargaining representative for dealing with management.

In all NLRA cases, once the Board has certified a union as a bargaining representative, the carrier must deal with it exclusively until that union loses its mandate.

NOTES

1. 45 U.S.C. § 151 (1972).
2. 45 U.S.C. § 155 (1972).

3. Thoms, *Not Cricket to Picket*, Passenger Train Journal 13 (Nov. 1982).

4. United Transp. Union v. Long Island R.R. Co., 455 U.S. 678 (1982).

5. This section is adapted from United States Railway Ass'n, Conrail at the Crossroads: The Future of Rail Service in the Northeast 47–51 (1981).

6. 308 U.S. 225 (1939).

7. 282 I.C.C. 271 (1952).

8. Railway Labor Executives Ass'n v. Gibbons, 455 U.S. 457 (1982).

9. Pub. L. No. 97–468 (1982).

10. *Id.* § 214(a).

11. *Id.* § 106(c).

12. This section is adapted from Thoms, *What Price Labor Protection?* Trains, 47 (June 1982). (Copyright 1982 by Kalmbach Publishing Co., reprinted with permission.)

13. Pub. L. No. 97–35, § 1143, 95 Stat. 661 (1981).

14. Pub. L. No. 97–35, § 1143, 95 Stat. 663 (1981).

15. Pub. L. No. 97–35, § 1148, 95 Stat. 669 (1980).

16. This section is adapted from W. Thoms, Deregulation: The Airline Experience 82–83 (1981).

17. Pub. L. No. 95–504 (1978), amending 49 U.S.C. §§ 1301–1551 (1980).

18. *See* Ris, *Government Protection of Transportation Employees: Sound Policy or Costly Precedent*, 44 J. Air L. 509, 543 (1979).

19. This section is adapted from Thoms, Wright & Hawkins, *The Wayward Bus: Labor's Rights Under the Urban Mass Transportation Act, Public Personnel Administration* (Public Personnel Administration 3179, copyright 1982 by Prentice-Hall, reprinted with permission).

20. 49 U.S.C.A. § 5(2)(f) (Supp. 1982), amended by 49 U.S.C.A. § 11347 (1982).

21. Division 580, Amalgamated Transit Union v. Central New York Regional Transp. Auth., 556 F.2d 659, 662 (2d Cir. 1977).

22. Division 1235, Amalgamated Transit Union v. Metropolitan Transit Auth., 477 F. Supp. 1027, 1032 (M.D. Tenn. 1979), *aff'd* 650 F.2d 1389 (6th Cir. 1981).

23. Office and Professional Employees Internat'l Union v. Mass Transit Admin., The Daily Record, Baltimore, Feb. 15, 1983, at 7, col. 1 (Md. 1982).

24. 29 U.S.C. § 152 *et seq.* (1985).

8

Urban Mass Transit

I. EMERGENCE OF THE URBAN MASS TRANSPORTATION ACT

In 1827, a 12-passenger horse-drawn carriage began transporting passengers along Broadway in New York City, marking the U.S. debut of mass transportation.[1] From that humble beginning, America's urban mass transit grew through the remainder of the nineteenth century and into the twentieth moving millions of passengers by way of a patchwork of private transit operators. By the 1920s, more than a thousand cities and towns had trolley systems, operating nearly 63,000 streetcars over some 40,000 miles of track.

Mass transportation began a slow but steady decline in the mid–1930s because of neglect and perceived obsolescence. This decline was hastened in the 1940s by the growing popularity of the automobile. As America moved toward near-exclusive dependence on the auto, highway construction occupied most of the nation's attention when it came to transportation. There was no federal money for urban mass transportation as there was for highway projects, and even more important, most people in public positions believed that mass transit was not a viable alternative to the private auto.

After World War II, suburbanization, highway construction, FHA and VA home mortgage financing contributed to the decline of mass transportation. Instead of depending on fixed-route mass transit, the motoring public increasingly developed a patternless route system between distant home, work and shopping destinations. Such a system was particularly disadvantageous to poor people and the minorities, the young and the old, the handicapped and others who did not have ready access to, or could not use, automobiles.

As a result, private transit owners providing bus, trolley and other transportation services were faced with a deadly spiral of increasing costs and deferred maintenance, rising fares, declining ridership, shrinking profits, deteriorating equipment and decreasing quality of service.

As the twentieth century moved into its last three decades, however, Americans became increasingly concerned with such issues as air and noise pollution, urban sprawl and other environmental problems which seriously affect the quality of life.

As these problems became increasingly acute for urban dwellers, there was growing interest in mass transportation as an element that could favorably affect these problems. Thus, in 1961, Congress approved a program of urban mass transit assistance to state and local public bodies, which included a $25 million pilot program of mass transit demonstration grants and technical assistance and a $50 million borrowing authority to help local transit programs.

Three years later, Congress passed the Urban Mass Transportation Act,[2] establishing for the first time a comprehensive program of federal assistance for urban mass transportation. The federal program had a significant effect on the nation's mass transit, enabling public bodies to take over the financially unstable private operations and permitting much needed expansion and upgrading to take place.

This Act was legislated

to assist in the development of improved mass transportation facilities, equipment, techniques and methods, . . . to encourage the planning and establishment of area-wide urban mass transportation systems needed for economical and desirable urban development, . . . and to provide assistance to state and local governments and their instrumentalities in financing such systems, to be operated by public or private mass transportation companies as determined by local needs.[3]

II. STRUCTURE OF THE URBAN MASS TRANSPORTATION ACT

A. Introduction

The Urban Mass Transportation Act of 1964 established a program of federal matching grants (on a ⅔ federal–½ local share basis) to assist in the preservation, improvement and expansion of urban mass transportation systems in the Nation's urban centers, and also included strict requirements for local planning and labor protective provisions.[4]

A program of technical assistance also was established to help local operators plan, design and evaluate potential transit projects.

A modest research and development program authorized by the 1964 legislation was significantly augmented by a 1966 amendment that directed the U.S. Secretary of Transportation to establish a comprehensive research program that would improve the convenience, speed, safety and cleanliness of urban mass transportation. A training program for transportation managers and transportation experts also was authorized.

As operators' needs changed from public takeovers to maintaining and expanding that publicly operated service, there was general agreement in the Administration by 1968 that a new mass transportation program must be financed on a priority basis and that its essential elements should include: (1) A substantially higher program level . . . ; (2) a substantially longer period of assured federal funding . . . ; (3) a reasonable guarantee of continuing availability of federal support-contract authority . . . and (4) creation of the Urban Mass Transportation Administration in the U.S. Department of Transportation to provide consolidated management of all federal mass transit programs.

The resulting legislation, the Urban Mass Transportation Assistance Act of 1970,[5] was signed into law on October 15, 1970. Other features of the program included support for advance acquisition of right-of-way, a greater role for state governments, a greater role for private enterprise, and public hearings to assure the acceptability of the programs under consideration by local authorities.

In 1973, Federal mass transportation funding sources were significantly expanded when the Federal Aid Highway Act of 1973[6] was passed making available for the first time highway monies for urban mass transportation development. This Act authorized $3 billion from general funds in contract authority for the urban mass transportation capital grant program. . . . The federal share for these projects was increased from the ⅔ share to 80 percent of the net project cost.

The most important element of the 1973 Act was the provision permitting flexibility in the use of highway funds for transit purposes. The Act opened the Urban System program authorization (funds set aside for construction of primary highways in urbanized areas) to transit, and opened all federal highway funds to development of exclusive lanes, traffic control devices, bus shelters, parking facilities, and so forth.

On November 26, 1974, the 1964 Act was again amended when the National Mass Transportation Assistance Act of 1974[7] was signed into law, establishing (a) . . . six-year program that, for the first time included assistance for both capital and operating expenses. . . .

Of the $11.8 billion authorized for fiscal years 1975 through 1980, $7.325 billion was made available to urbanized areas for mass transportation capital and other program projects administered under existing UMTA procedures, with an additional $500 million made available for planning, demonstrations and capital activities in non-urbanized areas.

The major new provision of the Act provided for the apportionment of $3.975 billion to urbanized areas by formula for use in either mass transportation capital or operating assistance projects. The operating assistance is intended to help public transit operators meet their day-to-day operating expenses.

On November 6, 1978, the 1964 UMT Act was again amended when the Federal Public Transportation Act of 1978[8] was signed into law establishing a $16.4 billion grant and loan program for public transit capital and operating assistance, and small urban and rural transit programs through 1982. A discretionary capital grant program is authorized for 1983.

B. Funding

The Urban Mass Transportation Administration is the principal source of federal financial assistance to aid urban areas and, to some extent, non-urban

areas plan, develop and improve mass transit systems. Its financial aid programs include:

> • Technical Study Grants—to local public agencies, providing up to 80 per-
> cent of the cost for analysis and evaluation in planning for urban mass trans-
> portation systems, and for other technical studies.
> • Discretionary Capital Improvement Grants—to state and local public agen-
> cies, providing 80 percent of the total cost for new system equipment, property
> acquisition, construction and modernization of transit facilities and equipment.
> • Formula Assistance Grants—to state and local public agencies, providing
> up to 50 percent of the operating deficits or 80 percent of total capital costs,
> to improve or continue mass transportation service.
> • Managerial Training Grants—for fellowships for advanced training of per-
> sonnel employed in managerial, technical, and professional institutions com-
> bining comprehensive research and research/training in urban transportation
> problems.

The administration also conducts or sponsors a wide variety of directed
research, development and demonstration projects to improve and develop
new transit equipment; methods, systems and techniques for improved transportation planning and operations; and for studies, tests and demonstrations
of them.[9]

1. Capital Funding

Section 3 of the Urban Mass Transportation Act of 1964 authorizes the
Urban Mass Transportation Administration (UMTA) to provide capital grants
or loans to states or to local public agencies for (1) construction, acquisition
or improvement of mass transit facilities and equipment; (2) coordination of
mass transit services with highways and other transportation; (3) establishment and organization of public transit corridor development corporations.[10]

Each federal grant for a Section 3 urban mass transit project may be
awarded for up to 80 percent of the net project cost.[11] The UMTA may make
a loan for up to 100 percent of the net project cost.[12] The remaining funds
may be provided by state or local government units or from revenues derived
from operation of the mass transit systems.[13] Privately owned transportation
companies may obtain capital grant funds through leasing or other such
arrangements with public agencies receiving federal capital funds.[14]

To qualify for a Section 3 capital grant, an applicant must meet certain
criteria. First, the applicant must comply with federal labor standards.[15]
Laborers working on construction of a federally funded project must be paid
wages not less than those prevailing on similar construction in the locality,
in accordance with the Davis-Bacon Act. In addition, Section 13c protective
conditions apply to these laborers. (See Chapter 7, V.)

Second, the applicant must comply with the nondiscrimination[16] and environmental protection provisions.[17] The applicant must certify that adequate

opportunity was afforded to parties with significant economic, social or environmental interests to present their views.[18] The UMTA may not approve a project until it has determined that such an adequate opportunity was provided, that the applicant gave fair consideration to the preservation and enhancement of the environment and to the interest of the community in which the project is located, and that either no adverse environmental effect is likely to result from the project or no feasible alternative exists and the applicant has taken all reasonable steps to minimize the project's adverse effect.[19]

Third, no grant or loan may be provided unless the secretary of transportation determines that the applicant has or will have (1) the legal, technical and financial capacity to carry out the project, and (2) continuing control over the facilities and equipment.[20] The purpose of this provision is to assure that the project will become and remain operational.[21]

Fourth, the applicant may receive loans from the Secretary for acquisition of real property only upon a determination that the realty is reasonably expected to be used for a mass transit system within a reasonable time.[22]

Fifth, the applicant may not use Section 3 funds to pay operating expenses, nor may funds be used to procure equipment or facilities that use exclusionary or discriminatory specifications, such as product specifications that can be met by only one manufacturer. Sixth, an applicant may not use federal funds to acquire an interest in or compete with a private mass transit company unless the secretary of transportation finds that federal financial assistance is essential to the program, that the program provides for the participation of the private mass transit company and that just and adequate compensation will be paid to the private mass transit company.[23] In addition, the secretary of labor must certify that the assistance complies with Section 13c labor-protection conditions.[24]

Seventh, the applicant must, in most circumstances, agree not to engage in school bus operations exclusively for the transportation of students and school personnel in competition with private school bus operators.[25] The purpose of this provision is to prevent recipients of federal funds from competing with private school bus operators because Congress perceived such competition to be unfair.[26] The Court of Appeals for the Seventh Circuit has held that this provision includes regular transportation of schoolchildren not only from home to school, but also from school to school.[27]

In addition, two federal regulations have had great impact on transit planning. The first is a requirement that the federally funded program must be based on a planning process[28] outlining its investment strategy and substantially meeting the regulatory requirements.[29] The second regulation requires that the planning process include an analysis of alternative transportation system management and investment strategies.[30] The purpose of the analysis is to make more efficient use of existing transportation facilities. The process must consider all modes of transportation and must be continuing, cooperative and comprehensive to the degree appropriate to the complexity of the transportation problems.[31]

2. Formula Grants

Section 5, the formula grant program, was created in 1974 to provide federal funds that could be used not only for capital, but also for operating assistance.[32] Section 5 subsidies are not allocated on the basis of need, but are based on population and population density. The original legislation, the National Transportation Assistance Act of 1974, stated that federal funds could not be used to replace existing state and local subsidies.[33] The Surface Transportation Act of 1978, however, modified this provision by allowing farebox revenues to replace state and local subsidies.[34]

The Section 5 program comprises four tiers, two of which are discussed here.

Tier I.[35] Grants to all urban areas are apportioned on the basis of a population and density formula. Tier I funds may be used for construction or operating assistance.

Tier II.[36] These federal funds are also apportioned on the basis of a population and population density formula, but 85 percent of Tier II funds are reserved for urbanized areas with populations of 750,000 or more; the remaining 15 percent are available for urbanized areas with smaller populations. Tier II funds may be used for capital or operating assistance.

Commuter rail-fixed guideway.[37] Two-thirds of these funds are apportioned on the basis of a commuter train route-mile formula (see Section III, below, for a discussion of commuter rail). The remaining one-third is apportioned on the basis of a fixed guideway route-mile formula. The term "fixed guideway" is defined as any public transportation facility which uses and occupies a separate right-of-way for the exclusive use of public transportation service including, but not limited to, fixed rail, automated guideway transit and exclusive facilities for buses and other high-occupancy vehicles.[38] If the funding formula had been based only on passenger miles, New York City would have been eligible for nearly half of the total funding.[39] Commuter rail and fixed guideway funds may be used for construction or operating assistance.

Bus Purchase.[40] These funds may be used for the purchase of buses and related equipment or for the construction of bus-related facilities. They may not be used for operating assistance. Bus purchase monies are apportioned on the basis of a population and population density formula.

The amount of federal funding available for Section 5 funding is similar to that available for Section 3. Federal monies are available for up to 80 percent of the cost of a construction project and for up to 50 percent of the cost of operating expenses of a project.[41] These federal monies, however, are expected to supplement rather than substitute for state and local government's direct transit income, such as advertising concessions, property leases and farebox revenues.[42]

Section 5 funds are dispensed in the following manner. The governor, with the concurrence of the secretary of transportation, designates an agency to receive and dispense the apportioned funds to areas with populations of 200,000 or more. When a statewide or regional agency is responsible for the financing, construction and operation of public transportation services, the agency is the recipient to receive and dispense the federal monies. The governor dispenses the funds directly to areas with populations under 200,000.[43] Sums apportioned under Section 5 are available for designation by the governor or designated recipient for three years after the close of the fiscal year for which those monies are apportioned.[44]

The secretary of transportation has a broad mandate. He can approve a project on such terms and conditions as he may prescribe and may issue those regulations he deems necessary.[45] He may approve a plan in whole or in part and rescind an accepted application at his discretion.[46]

The applicant must meet certain criteria before the secretary may approve Section 5 funding. The secretary must find that the applicant has or will have the legal, financial and technical capacity to carry out the proposed project and to maintain continuing control over use of the project, facilities and equipment.[47] The secretary must assure that possible adverse economic, social and environmental effects have been fully considered and that the final decision on the project is made in the best overall public interest.[48] The governor or designated recipient must certify that public hearings have been held, or the opportunity for such has been offered, in compliance with the Clean Air Act, the Federal Water Control Act and other federal statutes.[49] The governor or his designated recipient must also send to the secretary a report that indicates the consideration given to the effects of the proposed project and assures that fares and services will not be substantially changed except after a public hearing.[50] The secretary must also find that the project is necessary for a unified transportation system and that the applicant has consulted public officials in the urbanized area in which the project is to be located.[51] In addition, the applicant must agree that rates charged elderly and handicapped passengers during nonpeak hours will not exceed one-half of the rates charged to other passengers at peak hours.[52]

3. Highway Funds

One additional source[53] of federal mass transit capital assistance is available under the Federal-Aid Highway Act of 1973,[54] which, for the first time, made available highway trust funds for mass transportation facilities and equipment. Assistance is available to public transit operators through two programs: Federal-Aid Urban Systems and Interstate Highway Substitutions.

Federal-Aid Urban Systems[55] (FAUS) funds can be used to support either mass transportation capital projects or urban highway network projects in urbanized areas with over 200,000 population. The funds, which can be used for fixed-rail facilities as well as for rolling stock for any transit mode, are apportioned to the states by a formula based on population.

Local officials may propose to substitute a transit project for an urban highway project, but the state must certify the project's priority within the overall urban transportation plan. If approved by the secretary of transportation, the transit project will be substituted for the highway project and will receive the same federal share (75 percent of the total project cost) as for highway construction.

Interstate Highway[56] funds also are made available for transit construction and acquisition. The state and local governments, acting together, may request that non-highway public mass transportation facilities and/or equipment be substituted for a previously approved portion of Interstate Highway System within the urban areas. Such a substitution can occur only when the secretary of transportation determines that the interstate segment is not essential to completion of a connected interstate system or will no longer be essential because of the substituted transit project, and when the state gives assurance that it will not construct a toll road in the same traffic corridor.

When a substitution is approved, the federal government will pay 85 percent of the total cost of the transit project, as long as the total federal share does not exceed the federal share of the cost of the deleted Interstate segment. Funds apportioned to a state for its Interstate activities would be reduced by an equal amount.

To date, a number of large urban areas have deleted urban Interstate segments in order to use the funds for mass transit development. Washington, D.C., for instance, deleted portions of the I–95 and I–270 highways and used the available funds for construction of the area's rapid rail transit system.

4. Funding for Nonurbanized Areas

Two sections added to the Urban Mass Transportation Act by the Federal Public Transportation Act of 1978 aid nonurbanized areas.[57] Section 18[58] provides federal subsidies for nonurbanized areas (under 50,000 population). Eligible recipients include state agencies, local public bodies, nonprofit organizations and operators of public transportation services.[59]

These Section 18 funds are apportioned through a formula based on the ratio that the population of a state's nonurbanized areas bears to the total population of nonurbanized areas in all states.[60] The federal share may be up to 80 percent of the net cost of construction projects. Operating assistance may provide up to 50 percent of the net cost. One-half of the local share must be derived from non-federal funds or mass transportation revenues.[61]

A state may use these federal monies for any project eligible under the Urban Mass Transportation Act that is appropriate to a nonurbanized area. In addition, Section 18 funds may be used to purchase service agreements with private providers of public transportation service to provide local service in nonurbanized areas.[62] The secretary of transportation may permit a state to use up to 15 percent of the apportioned sum for technical assistance. Such technical assistance may include project planning, management development, coordination of transportation programs and research that promotes effective ways of delivering public transportation to nonurbanized areas.[63]

The program must be submitted annually to the secretary of transportation for his approval and must provide for a fair and equitable distribution of funds within the state.[64] Section 18 grants are subject to such terms and conditions as the secretary may prescribe. The secretary of labor may waive Section 13(c) labor-protective conditions for recipients of Section 18 subsidies.[65]

Section 22[66] provides federal monies for the initiation, improvement or continuation of intercity bus service for rural areas and for urban areas with populations of over 5,000 but that are not urbanized areas.[67] "Intercity bus service" is defined as

transportation provided to the public as a private bus operator authorized to transport passengers in interstate commerce by the Interstate Commerce Commission or in intrastate commerce by a State regulatory commission . . . (1) between one urban place . . . and another . . . urban place; (2) between an urban place . . . and an urbanized area; or (3) between one urbanized area and other urbanized areas, through rural areas or urban places, or both.

The term does not include local service.[68] Section 22 funds may be used to subsidize up to 50 percent of the net cost of operating expenses. The local share may not be derived from farebox revenues. To the extent feasible, the secretary of transportation may distribute Section 22 funds only for privately owned intercity bus companies to subsidize deficit operations considering the profitability of the route as a whole.[69]

The secretary may subject Section 22 grants to those terms he deems necessary to promote privately owned and operated intercity bus service.[70] The labor protection provisions of 13(c) apply to recipients of these funds.[71]

Sections 18 and 22 impose a "Buy America" provision that requires domestic preference for grants of $500,000 or more. When the provision, however, is inconsistent with the public interest, or when the availability or quality of American-made products make imposition of the provision unreasonable, the secretary of transportation may waive it.[72]

C. Demonstration Projects

Section 6[73] of the Urban Mass Transportation Act authorizes the secretary of transportation to undertake research, development and demonstration projects in all phases of urban mass transit. The projects may include the development, testing and demonstration of new facilities, equipment, techniques or methods. The secretary may undertake these projects when he determines that they will assist in the reduction of transportation needs, assist in the improvement of mass transit services or contribute toward meeting total urban transportation needs at minimum cost. The secretary may undertake these projects independently or by grant or contract to public transit authorities or to transit manufacturers, suppliers and consultants.[74]

UMTA is an unusual federal agency because it is not the consumer of its Section 6 program, termed the research, development and demonstration program (RD & D). Instead, the benefits of the RD & D program go directly to providers and users of mass transit, who have the option whether to use the products of the programs.[75] RD & D's program has recently shifted emphasis from long-term high-technology projects to near-term management-oriented projects.[76] The program balances non-capital intensive projects from which research results are quickly adaptable to the transit industry with high-technology developments from which research results may prove adaptable only in the future.[77]

The Service and Methods Demonstrations Program (SMD) is a component of the RD & D program. SMD focuses on development of innovative transit service and management techniques, using existing technology to develop improvements that require low capital investment and a short implementation period. SMD demonstrates its concepts in actual use, evaluates them as to cost, impact and findings to transportation planners and operators.[78]

SMD projects are organized for four areas: (1) conventional transit service innovations, (2) pricing and service innovations, (3) paratransit services, and (4) transit services for special user groups.[79]

In the conventional transit service area,[80] SMD emphasizes efficient management of existing transit facilities. While early projects focused on increasing highway capacity by affording preferential treatment of high-occupancy vehicles, such as carpools and buses, the program now gives such treatment to urban arterial streets as a way of reducing traffic and improving bus operations in downtown areas. To improve transit service, SMD has researched route restructuring, articulated (high-occupancy) buses and computerized rider information systems. For example, SMD programs studied the feasibility of using articulated buses as replacements for conventional buses.[81] Use of the articulated bus could reduce the number of buses necessary on a given route. SMD studies revealed, however, that the increased size and unusual design of the bus created handling problems for the drivers and necessitated longer dwell times at stops than were necessary with conventional buses. The data concluded that articulated buses were cost-effective when used to replace "double-header" buses (two conventional buses running in tandem along the same route), when substituted for conventional buses at an approximate ratio of 2–for–3.

In the area of pricing and service innovations, SMD's goal is development of information that will aid local areas in setting efficient and equitable transportation pricing policies that are consistent with service objectives.[82] Recent strategies have tried to involve the private sector in financing transit service. SMD had studied, for example, user response to changes in transit and service levels and the feasibility of systemwide freefare transit during off-peak hours. Research disclosed that while ridership increased during the demonstration period, it returned to pre-freefare level within six months. In addition, the concept did not improve the mobility of the poor, the elderly and the transit dependent, nor did it significantly reduce automobile usage. The cost of the project to the two demonstration areas—Denver, Colorado, and Trenton, New Jersey—was substantial; lost revenues plus increased operating costs would have required an 11 percent increase in operating subsidies.

Paratransit service is a term for a range of transportation modes lying between single occupant automobiles and fixed-route, fixed-schedule public transit.[83] Paratransit service includes, for example, taxis, demand-responsive transit (DRT), dial-a-ride and carpools. Taxis and public DRT programs can provide transportation in those low-density areas that fixed-route buses cannot serve efficiently. In addition, they provide effective feeder service to existing conventional transit routes. A DRT service picks up and transports users at times and places specified by the riders. In Westport, Connecticut, for example, SMD tested an integrated transit system composed of a publicly operated conventional bus system and a shared-ride taxi service that used district vehicles operated under a private management contract. Studies found that the privately operated shared-ride taxi service was less costly, partly as a result of the employment of nonunion drivers. Publicly operated DRT services, on the other hand, could not maintain rider demand levels sufficient to make their use cost-effective.

The fourth area of SMD study is transportation services for special user groups.[84] A special user is one who is dependent on public transit to meet his mobility needs because of age, income, disability or lack of an automobile. To develop ways to meet the mobility needs of special users, SMD has evaluated wheelchair-accessible bus service, door-to-door service for the elderly and the handicapped, user-side subsidies for taxis and fixed-route bus service, coordination of social service agency transportation services, transportation services for disadvantaged innercity residents and public transportation services in rural areas. The user-side subsidy project has proved to be particularly cost-effective and well received. The SMD report in this area states:

User-side subsidies offer a way for local areas to provide low-cost door-to-door transportation service to their elderly and handicapped citizens by using taxis and other private transportation providers. It has been shown that, on a per-trip basis, private operators can deliver these services more efficiently and at lower cost than can a dedicated fleet of publicly operated vehicles. The SMD program has played a major role in the development and refinement of the user-side subsidy concept. Four demonstration projects in Danville, Illinois, Kingston, North Carolina, Montgomery, Alabama, and Lawrence, Massachusetts, have recently been completed. In addition, case study evaluations of locally initiated user-side subsidy programs have been conducted in Kansas City, Missouri, Milwaukee, Seattle, Los Angeles, and the San Francisco bay area. Finally, the SMD program has examined user-side subsidy programs which were elements of larger demonstrations in Pittsburgh, Milton Township, Illinois, and the state of West Virginia.

Over all, the evaluations have shown user-side subsidies to be not only feasible, but very attractive methods of delivering special needs transportation services through private providers. The programs were implemented with relatively little difficulty in a variety of settings having considerably different demographic characteristics, regulatory policies, and taxi operating practices. Moreover, the implemented programs have been generally well received by subsidized users, transportation providers, and the general public. The cost to the public to subsidize a trip through a user-side subsidy was found to be substantially less than the average per-trip cost of publicly operated specialized transportation services. Administrative costs were found to be relatively modest and largely independent of total project demand. This suggests the existence of scale economies and indicates that user-side subsidy programs may be financially viable even in larger urban areas. Moreover, private transportation providers seemed willing to absorb some of the administrative costs themselves in return for expectation of increased business.

Subsidy costs are largely a function of local policy, and were effectively controlled in the demonstrations through such mechanisms as limits on per-trip subsidy payments, eligibility restrictions, and limits on total subsidized travel. There was little or no evidence of subsidy fraud or abuse by either project users or transportation providers.

The subsidy programs seemed to attract those in the target population who were most transit dependent and most in need of subsidized transportation. Eligible individuals with other means of transportation took few, if any, subsidized trips. The principal benefits which accrued to subsidized users were a decrease in their travel costs for those taxi trips which would otherwise have been made at full-fare, and a change from less attractive transportation alternatives.[85]

The Urban Mass Transportation Act requires recipients of federal monies to meet certain requirements. Whether the statutory requirements apply to demonstration project recipients depends on the terms of each statute, as exemplified by the following case.

WESTPORT TAXI SERV. v. ADAMS
571 F.2d 697(2d Cir. 1978), *cert. denied*, 439 U.S. 829 (1978)
Circuit Judge Meskill:

The purpose of the Urban Mass Transportation Act of 1964 ("the Act") is to improve urban mass transportation systems. 49 U.S.C. sec. 1601(b). It seeks to advance this purpose by providing, among other things, financial assistance to mass transportation projects of various kinds, including so-called "demonstration projects." 49 U.S.C.

sec. 1605(a). The instant case is one in which a federally funded demonstration project to be conducted by a public mass transportation company has encountered the opposition of an existing private transportation company which, for competitive reasons, has sought to enjoin the implementation of the project.

Defendant-appellee Westport Transit District ("Transit District") is a government entity formed by Westport, Connecticut in 1969 to organize, coordinate and provide mass transportation services in Westport. In April, 1975, the Transit District applied to the federal Urban Mass Transportation Administration ("UMTA") for a $25,000 grant to study the possibility of developing an integrated and coordinated transportation system for the community. The study had two immediate goals: first, to develop a plan for a complete transportation system that would utilize and coordinate existing and potential transportation services; second, to design a demonstration project to implement and experiment with various aspects of the plan. Such studies are eligible for funding under 49 U.S.C. Sec. 1605(c). On June 26, 1975, the Administrator of the UMTA, to whom the powers of the Secretary of Transportation under the Act have been delegated, 49 C.F.R. Sec. 1.51, approved the study grant. The study was conducted, and a demonstration project was proposed. Early in 1976, the Transit District applied for a grant of roughly $610,000 to implement the project. The basic question on this appeal is whether certain of the Act's procedural requirements had to be complied with prior to the Administrator's approval of the two-year implementation grant.

Plaintiff-appellant Westport Taxi Service, Inc. ("Westport Taxi") is a small taxi company owned by two brothers. It operates under a certificate of public convenience and necessity from the Connecticut Public Utilities Control Authority ("PUCA"). The type of service offered by Westport Taxi is known as "exclusive-ride" taxi service and is governed by PUCA regulation Sec. 16–319–15, which requires that the consent of the first person to hire a taxicab be obtained before the taxi may take on additional riders. Westport Taxi's "fleet" consists of five aging taxicabs; its financial condition is precarious. The Transit District's demonstration project will provide several new types of services. Principal among them will be a "shared-ride" taxi service provided with eleven new twelve-passenger vans that will compete directly with Westport Taxi. Plaintiffs fear that their taxi company will be destroyed if the project goes forward. Given their present financial condition, these fears appear to be well founded.

Plaintiffs brought this action to enjoin the Secretary of Transportation from funding the project and the Transit District from implementing it. They argue that the Transit District failed to comply with the subsections of the Act. The first is 49 U.S.C. sec. 1602(d), which provides:

> Any application for a grant or loan under this chapter to finance the acquisition, construction, reconstruction, or improvement of facilities or equipment which will substantially affect a community or its mass transportation service shall include a certification that the applicant—
>
> (1) has afforded an adequate opportunity for public hearings pursuant to adequate prior notice, and has held such hearings unless no one with a significant economic, social, or environmental interest in the matter requests a hearing;
>
> (2) has considered the economic and social effects of the project and its impact on the environment; and

> (3) has found that the project is consistent with official plans for the comprehensive development of the urban area.
>
> Notice of any hearings under this subsection shall include a concise statement of the proposed project, and shall be published in a newspaper of general circulation in the geographic area to be served. If hearings have been held, a copy of the transcript of the hearings shall be submitted with application.

The Transit District concedes that the certification required by this subsection was not included in its application. The second is 49 U.S.C. sec. 1602(e), which provides:

> No financial assistance shall be provided under this chapter to any State or local public body or agency thereof for the purpose, directly or indirectly, of acquiring any interest in, or purchasing any facilities or other property of, a private mass transportation company, or for the purpose of constructing, improving, or reconstructing any facilities or other property acquired (after July 9, 1964) from any such company, or for the purpose of providing by contract or otherwise for the operation of mass transportation facilities or equipment in competition with, or supplementary to, the service provided by an existing mass transportation company, unless (1) the Secretary finds that such assistance is essential to a program, proposed or under active preparation, for a unified or officially coordinated urban transportation system as part of the comprehensively planned development of the urban area, (2) the Secretary finds that such program, to the maximum extent feasible, provides for the participation of private mass transportation companies, (3) just and adequate compensation will be paid to such companies for acquisition of their franchises or property to the extent required by applicable State or local laws, and (4) the Secretary of Labor certifies that such assistance complies with the requirements of section 1609(c) of this title.

All of plaintiff's claims were rejected by the district court.

* * *

Subsection (d)

The certification requirement of sec. 1602(d) applies to "[a]ny application for grant . . . under this Act to finance the acquisition, construction, reconstruction, or improvement of facilities or equipment which will substantially affect a community or its mass transportation service." . . . The defendants content and the district court held that sec. 1602(d) need not be complied with here because the Transit District's project is a demonstration project under sec. 1605, a type of project to which sec. 1602 assertedly does not apply. According to their analysis, the Act establishes discrete, mutually exclusive categories of projects, each of which is governed by a different section of the Act. Under this view, a demonstration project under sec. 1605 need not comply with any other section of the Act.

We read the Act differently. By its own terms, sec. 1602(d) applies to "[a]ny application . . . under this Act" for a grant which, if implemented, meets certain objective criteria. This language suggests the categories overlap—a demonstration project is exempt from sections other than sec. 1605 only if its nature is such that it does not meet the criteria those sections establish. Thus, a demonstration project may or may not involve "the acquisition . . . of facilities . . . which will substantially affect a community or its mass transportation service." If it does not, then sec. 1602(d) need not be complied with; if it does, however, the requirements of that subsection cannot be avoided merely because the project is a demonstration. We are confident that Congress meant what it said when it wrote "(a)ny application . . . under this Act" and set forth objective criteria. It intended each project to be treated according to its impact, not just its type.

Under our reading of the statute, therefore, the impact of each proposed mass transportation project upon the community must be evaluated. The trial judge found that the Transit District's project "is a demonstration project only and does not involve the more significant commitment of resources and more substantial effect on the community necessary to bring the hearing and certification requirements of sec. 1602(d) into play." Because this finding is based on the erroneous view that sec. 1602 and sec. 1605 are mutually exclusive, it cannot stand. It is clear that this demonstration project involves "the acquisition, construction, reconstruction, or improvement of facilities or equipment" and "will substantially affect" Westport and its mass transportation service. Indeed, it is difficult to imagine how the implementation of a $600,000 project involving the purchase of eleven twelve-passenger vans, at a cost of over $150,000, in a town of less than 30,000 inhabitants could fail to have a substantial effect on the community and its mass transportation service. In fact, that appears to have been the very intent of those who designed the project. Appellees try to minimize the impact of the project by pointing out that it is merely a two-year demonstration. We find this approach unpersuasive. The demonstration may well be the start of a long-term program. The Transit District's new vans are not going to evaporate after two years; after they are demonstrated, they will likely become a permanent part of Westport's mass transportation service. Furthermore, two years can be a very long time for some citizens of Westport. Given the present state of plaintiff's financial condition, it appears unlikely that it could survive this two-year program. It cannot be denied that elimination of one of the two independent, traditional, exclusive-ride taxi services in Westport, together with the substitution of a new $600,000 project, would constitute a "substantial" effect on the community or mass transportation of Westport. Accordingly, sec. 1602(d) must be complied with. We note, however, that on the facts of this case compliance should be a relatively simple matter. The hearings required by sec. 1602(d)(1) have already been held, and the economic, social and environmental impact of the project has been studied, as required by sec. 1602(d)(2), in great depth; the project is clearly "consistent with official plans for the comprehensive development of the urban area," sec. 1602(d)(3), for it is an integral part of Westport's own comprehensive mass transportation plan. Thus sec. 1602(d) can be satisfied merely by amending the grant application so as to include the requisite certification under sec. 1602(d).

Subsection (e)

The analysis applicable to sec. 1602(d) is also applicable to sec. 1602(e). Like subsection (d), subsection (e) applies to all "financial assistance . . . provided under this Act." However, only a "mass transportation company" may claim the protection of subsection (e). We have already held that, for standing purposes, Westport Taxi is "arguably within the zone of interests" protected by this subsection because it arguably fits the definition of a "mass transportation company." We must now decide, on the merits, whether it is in fact a "mass transportation company."

As originally enacted, the definition of "mass transportation" found in 49 U.S.C. sec. 1608(c)(5) covered "transportation by bus or rail or other conveyance, either publicly or privately owned, serving the general public (but not including school buses or charter or sightseeing service) and moving over prescribed routes." This definition clearly excluded traditional private taxi service, for taxicabs do not "move over prescribed routes." This definition proved too limited, however, because it excluded innovative, new "paratransit systems, such as "dial-a ride" or "minibus" services, which have more flexible routes. In the Housing and Urban Development Act of 1968, Pub. L. No. 90–448, sec. 702, 82 Stat. 476, 535 (1968), the definition of mass transportation was changed. It now covers "transportation by bus, rail or other conveyance, either publicly or privately owned, which provides to the public general or special service (but not including school buses or charter or sightseeing service) *on a regular and continuing basis*" (emphasis added). On its face, the definition is now broad enough to cover transportation service provided by means of a tandem bicycle, as long as it is provided "on a regular and continuing basis." In construing the definition, however, we must remember "that statutes always have some purpose or object to accomplish, whose sympathetic and imaginative discovery is the surest guide to their meaning." The purpose of the change in the definition of "mass transportation" was "to allow greater flexibility in developing and applying new concepts and systems in urban mass transportation programs." Congress does not appear to have intended to include conventional taxi service within the changed definition, for such service cannot by any stretch of the imagination be considered a "new" concept or system.

In construing the definition of "mass transportation" we also look to the interpretation given it by the UMTA. Charles F. Bingman, Acting Urban Mass Transportation Administrator, submitted to the district court an affidavit and supporting documentation in which the UMTA's interpretation of the Act is described as follows:

> UMTA has consistently included with (the) definition (of "mass transportation") any form of collective transportation service which is regularly available to the public; i.e., "any service which cannot be reserved for the private and exclusive use of particular individuals or private groups."
> . . . Hence, fixed-route bus or rail services and paratransit services such as dial-a-ride, jitney, shared-ride taxi, neighborhood transit, subscription bus service and other types of shared-ride transportation services which are available to the public or to special categories of users (such as elderly and handicapped persons) on a regular basis are considered by UMTA to be "mass transportation services." Services which can be reserved for the exclusive use of individuals or private groups, either by the operator or the first patron's refusal to permit others to be picked up, such as exclusive-ride taxi service, charter service, sight-seeing services, employer van-pool programs, car rental services, for-hire limousines and private ambulance services are not deemed to be "mass transportation" services for purposes of the UMT Act. (Emphasis added)

See also 41 Fed. Reg. 46412–13. In view of this administrative interpretation and practice, and in view of the legislative history of the 1968 amendment, we hold that a company such as Westport Taxi, operating five taxicabs under a regulation which provides that the consent of the first rider to hire a taxi must be obtained before others may be carried, is not a "mass transportation company" entitled to the protections afforded by sec. 1602(e).

D. Access for the Handicapped and the Elderly

The Urban Mass Transit Act of 1964[86] (UMT Act) was premised on congressional findings that much of the nation's population is located in urban areas, that the vitality of urban areas is being jeopardized by inadequate transportation facilities and that federal financial assistance for development of efficient and coordinated mass transportation systems is essential to the solution of these urban problems.[87]

Not until the Urban Mass Transportation Assistance Act of 1970,[88] however, was the problem of the handicapped person's difficulty in using public mass transit addressed.

1. Right to Comparable Service

The Urban Mass Transportation Assistance Act of 1970 declared that it was national policy that elderly and handicapped persons have the same right as other persons to use mass transportation facilities and services; that special efforts shall be made in planning and design of mass transportation facilities and services so that the availability to the elderly and the handicapped of mass transportation which they can effectively use will be assured. All federal programs offering assistance in the field of mass transportation should contain provisions implementing this policy.[89] In addition, the secretary of transportation was authorized to make extra loans and grants for this purpose.[90] Of the amount appropriated, 2 percent could be set aside for the benefit of the elderly and the handicapped.[91]

In 1974, the National Mass Transportation Assistance Act[92] expanded the previous law in the area of fares. To gain the secretary's approval, a project must assure that rates for the elderly and the handicapped do not exceed half of the general rates for peak hours.[93] In addition, states are not required to charge any fares for the elderly and the handicapped.[94]

In 1973, the Vocational Rehabilitation Act[95] addressed the problem of discrimination toward the handicapped. It provided in Section 504 that "(n)o otherwise qualified handicapped individual . . . shall, solely by reason of his handicap, be excluded from the participation in, be denied the benefits of, or be subjected to discrimination under any program or activity receiving Federal financial assistance."[96]

Two areas of urban mass transit law have been primary sources of litigation: (1) the type of special efforts that are sufficient to ensure accessibility for the handicapped, and (2) the quality of the handicapped person's right to use mass transportation.

In 1975, a federal district court held in *Snowden v. Birmingham–Jefferson County Transit Authority*[97] that no one, including the handicapped, had a fundamental right to public transportation and that the Constitution requires only a rational basis for discrimination. In this case, the plaintiff had sought to restrain the Department of Transportation (DOT) from appropriating further federal assistance for the local transit authority's purchase of buses not accessible to those handicapped persons confined to wheelchairs. The court reasoned that the fact that no device to load and unload wheelchair passengers had yet been devised provided a rational basis for the local transit authority to discriminate between the wheelchair handicapped and the average passenger.

The court also held that the local transit authority's plan to purchase buses inaccessible to the wheelchair handicapped did not violate Section 504 of the Rehabilitation Act of 1973. The court reasoned that even though the wheelchair handicapped person must arrange for someone to help him board and alight from the bus, he is allowed to use the bus and is, therefore, not excluded. Because the transit authority had installed grab-rails, set-well lighting and power-assisted doors, it had made the special effort required by Section 1612(a) of the UMT Act of 1970, even though this effort aided only the non-wheelchair handicapped.

In 1977, an Ohio federal court elaborated on the quality of the handicapped person's right of access to public transportation and on the meaning of special efforts. In *Vanko v. Finely*,[98] the plaintiff, who was confined to a wheelchair, sought to prevent the release of federal funds to the local transit authority for purchase of buses inaccessible to the wheelchair handicapped. The court held that Section 1612(a) of the UMT Act did not require that all mass transit vehicles provide immediate access to the elderly and the handicapped. The local transit authority is required only to provide mass transit that the handicapped can effectively use. In this instance, the transit authority had developed a separate service for the elderly and the handicapped that operated door-to-door and charged no fares during off-peak hours and only half fares during peak hours.

Section 504 does not, the court stated, require the immediate establishment of services comparable to those provided to the general public. Instead, this section's prohibition of discrimination can be satisfied by substantial good faith progress in both the planning and the implementation of transit programs for the mobility handicapped. But the court cautioned that vague plans and second-rate transit for the handicapped would be insufficient.

The court elaborated on the meaning of special efforts, as the term was used in the joint Federal Highway Administration and Urban Mass Transportation Administration guidelines and in Section 1612(a) of the UMT Act.[99] The court concluded that the requirement of special efforts contemplates "an orderly, planned process by which steps will be taken to establish transportation service for wheelchair users and other semiambulatory persons that is reasonable by comparison with the service provided to the general public."[100]

In 1978, another plaintiff sought to enjoin delivery of mass transit buses which were not equipped with facilities to accommodate the wheelchair handicapped. In *Atlantis Community, Inc., v. Adams,*[101] a federal district court held that the provisions of the UMT Act and the Rehabilitation Act governing availability of mass transportation to the elderly and the handicapped do not provide a sufficient definition of the duties of the federal transportation officials to enable the court to give directions to them. It reasoned that Congress had mandated the prescription of a particular conduct, but that a prescription of such among a wide range of possibilities is not an appropriate judicial function. The court questioned the clarity of Section 1612(a) of the UMT Act and Section 504 of the Rehabilitation Act regarding who the mobility handicapped are and what must be done to provide them with the same right as others to use mass transportation.

In 1978, Congress addressed the problem of who are the mobility handicapped. Title III of the Federal Public Transportation Act[102] defined the term "handicapped person" as

any individual who by reason of illness, injury, age, congenital malfunction, or other permanent or temporary incapacity or disability, including any person who is wheelchair bound or has semiambulatory capabilities, is unable without special facilities or special planning or design to utilize public transportation facilities and services effectively.[103]

The scope of the handicapped person's right of access to public transportation was yet to be resolved.

2. The Dilemma of the 1979 DOT Regulations

In 1976, Section 165 was added to the Federal-Aid Highway Act of 1973 (FAHA),[104] authorizing the secretary of transportation to require that a mass transit system, aided by grants from highway funds under the FAHA, "be planned, designed, constructed, and operated to allow effective utilization by elderly or handicapped persons."

In that same year, DOT issued regulations designed to implement Section 504 of the Rehabilitation Act, Section 16 of the UMT Act and Section 165 of the FAHA.[105] These regulations mandated that state and local planners make "special efforts in planning public mass transportation facilities and services that can effectively be utilized by elderly and handicapped persons." Approval of project grants was conditioned on "satisfactory special effort." The regulations were accompanied by guidelines, issued jointly by the Urban Mass Transit Administration and the Federal Highway Administration, that gave examples of the kinds of plans that would satisfy the requirement of "special efforts."[106] The guidelines allowed local authorities to choose a paratransit service that would provide a handicapped person with service comparable to that provided to the general public.

Two days before DOT's 1976 regulations were published in their final form, President Ford issued Executive Order Number 11,914.[107] The order directed the Department of Health, Education and Welfare (HEW)[108] to coordinate the implementation of Section 504 by all federal agencies by establishing guidelines and standards for determining what practices are discriminatory. In addition, President Ford required other agencies to determine regulations consistent with those to be issued by HEW.

Nearly two years later, HEW issued guidelines, which required mass transit systems receiving federal funds to integrate ("mainstream") the handicapped into the same programs available. In other words, the HEW regulations required that each mode of public transportation be accessible to the handicapped.[109] The guidelines stated that special programs, which had been an option under the 1976 DOT regulations, could be used only to fulfill the special efforts requirement when it was necessary to provide equal opportunities for the handicapped. In other words, the HEW regulations required that each mode of transportation must be accessible to the handicapped; the alternative special programs allowed under the UMTA–FAHA guidelines were no longer permissible.

DOT decided to conform its 1976 regulations to meet the mandate of HEW guidelines. Soon after the HEW guidelines were issued, DOT published its notice of proposed rule making, together with its proposed rules.[110] The notice stated that DOT felt bound by the HEW guidelines to adopt only those options that conformed with HEW's mandate to mainstream the handicapped. The final DOT regulations[111] governing provisions for handicapped persons in federally assisted mass transportation programs were adopted on May 31, 1979. The secretary of DOT considered the issue of whether buses must be made accessible to the handicapped by the addition of lifts and other specially designed devices or whether paratransit or special vehicles would be sufficient. The secretary affirmed that regularly scheduled buses should be made accessible to the handicapped.[112]

The DOT regulations contain a special waiver provision for existing subway, commuter rail and streetcar systems.[113] The waiver privilege, however, is limited in that the secretary "may grant such a petition in his . . . discretion, provided that [he] determines that local alternative service to handicapped persons will be substantially as good or better than that which would have been provided by the waived requirement."[114] This waiver provision does not apply to mass transit bus systems, but a general provision applicable to all DOT regulations authorizes DOT to allow an exemption in certain circumstances from the requirements of a regulation.[115]

In 1980, the District of Columbia Federal Court upheld these DOT regulations. In *American Public Transit Association v. Goldschmidt*,[116] a voluntary trade association brought suit to declare these DOT regulations invalid.

The federal district court upheld the regulations on the basis of three statutes:[117] Section 16 of UMT Act (local planners must make special efforts to provide transportation to the elderly and the handicapped),[118] Section 165(b) of the FAHA (transportation systems receiving highway funds should be planned, designed, constructed and operated to allow use by the elderly and the handicapped),[119] and Section 504 of the Rehabilitation Act of 1973 (no discrimination against qualified handicapped persons in programs receiving federal funds).[120] In addition, the court found that the regulations were supported by DOT's broad power to condition grants to transit systems. The court stated that the authority of the secretary of transportation to adopt regulations with respect to the handicapped derives not only from Section 504, but also from other statutes vesting in him broad authority with respect to transportation in general and transportation of the handicapped in particular.

A year later, the Court of Appeals for the District of Columbia reversed and remanded the *American Public Transit Association* decision.[121] It held that (1) Section 504 of the Rehabilitation Act of 1973 did not authorize DOT to promulgate regulations requiring that transit systems receiving federal funds make each mode of public transportation accessible to the handicapped by May 31, 1982, and (2) events surrounding the adoption of regulations by the secretary of transportation, who erroneously determined that such regulations were necessary to enforce Section 504, suggested that the secretary did not make an independent policy decision to promulgate the regulations to enforce other statutes cited in support. Remand was appropriate to give the secretary an opportunity to determine whether the regulations were based on statutes other than Section 504.

The court concluded that the DOT regulations are not a valid way to enforce Section 504. It cited *Southeastern Community College v. Davis*[122] for the proposition that Section 504 does not give federal agencies the power to impose onerous affirmative burdens on local programs.

3. Aftermath of American Public Transit

It would seem logical for the secretary to assert Sections 1612, 1604 and 1602 of the UMT Act as the basis for the valid exercise of his authority in promulgating the 1979 DOT regulations. Instead, DOT has apparently conformed its regulations to the Court of Appeals decision. This may be because of the direct influence of the Reagan administration's new policies on DOT. In any event, DOT promulgated an interim regulation[123] to replace that portion deemed invalid by the court of appeals. Two months after the ruling, DOT promulgated the interim regulation, which became effective July 20, 1981.

Explaining its rationale for the interim rule, DOT stated that early in President Reagan's administration, the Presidential Task Force on Regulatory Relief identified the accessibility requirement of 49 C.F.R. Part 27 as a costly and controversial regulation deserving review. As a result of this review, DOT established a policy on this issue: "Ensuring the provision of transportation that handicapped persons can use is an obligation of recipients of Federal assistance for mass transit, but the major responsibility for deciding how this transportation is to be provided should be returned to local communities."[124]

Generally, the interim regulation reinstates the local option to provide paratransit for the handicapped. Subsection (a) of Section 27.77 requires recipients of federal funds to certify that special efforts are being made to provide transportation that the handicapped can use. These special efforts must be made in a manner consistent with Appendix A, which is a slightly modified version of DOT's 1976 Advisory Information Appendix to 49 C.F.R. Part 613, Subpart B.[125]

The important modification is in the percentage requirement of the first option stated in the Appendix. This option provides an example of what would be sufficient to satisfy the special efforts requirement. The modified option states that "[a] program for wheelchair users and semiambulatory handicapped persons that will involve the expenditure of an average annual dollar amount equivalent to a minimum of 3.5 percent of the financial assistance that the urbanized area receives under section 5 of the UMT Act."[126] The original 1976 Appendix gave a 5 percent figure.

DOT's reasoning for the change is that the Department wants to maintain a level of effort under this interim rule equivalent to that maintained under the 1976 rules when they were actively being implemented. The 5 percent requirement was modified to 3.5 percent to take into account the effects of changes in the structure and funding level of the UMT Act's Section 5 grant program as well as the effects of inflation. DOT stated that "[t]hree and one-half percent of contemporary section 5 funding, in real dollar terms, is essentially equivalent to five percent of section five funding in fiscal year 1977, the first full fiscal year in which the 1976 UMTA regulations were in effect."[127] Actions by a local transit authority consistent with Appendix A are sufficient to meet the requirements of this section.[128]

An Appendix B derived from the 1976 Advisory Information Appendix to 23 C.F.R. Part 450, Subpart A, is added. It provides advisory information for planning transportation that the handicapped can use.[129] It restates the original definition of special effort—"genuine, good-faith progress in planning service for wheelchair users and semiambulatory handicapped persons that meets a significant fraction of the identified transportation needs of such person within a reasonable time period."[130] It also provides for representation of the handicapped and the community in general in the planning process.[131] In addition, the Appendix states that a range of alternative service improvements should be evaluated as to coverage, cost and benefit and that maximum opportunity should be given to private carriers to provide some or all of the services.[132]

Subsection (a)(2) provides that Section 18 recipients (nonurbanized areas) must certify that special efforts are being made to provide transportation that the handicapped can use, that is reasonable in comparison to the service provided to the general public and that meets a significant fraction of the transportation needs of such persons.[133] Paragraph (a)(3) establishes that a current recipient or grant applicant must make its first certification within 60 days of this amendment.[134]

With regard to buses previously approved in a UMT Act grant but as yet undelivered, UMTA will not require a prior grant amendment or a public hearing prior to acquiring buses without wheelchair lifts. Transit operators must satisfy the special efforts requirement before ordering buses without lifts. If a transit authority chooses not to implement an alternate special effort operation, it may still choose to buy wheelchair-accessible buses until one-half of its fleet is accessible.[135]

This interim regulation allows up to six months for the level of local special efforts to reach an appropriate level; the accessibility need not be immediate. DOT reasons that "[i]t is expected that by that time those areas choosing to serve handicapped persons with specialized service will have actual transportation in place, or at least have prepared draft application for any grants necessary to meet the special efforts requirement."[136]

Paragraph (a)(4) states that compliance with certification under Section 27.77 is deemed compliance with Section 504 of the Rehabilitation Act of 1963, Section 16 of the UMT Act and Section 165 of FAHA.[137]

A recipient may be found in noncompliance with this interim regulation either when he fails to certify or when he exhibits a pattern of failure to carry out special efforts. An isolated instance, such as failure of a paratransit vehicle to pick up a handicapped person, does not, however, constitute noncompliance.[138]

Subsection (c) makes explicit that a handicapped person capable of using the recipient's regular service provided to the general public cannot be denied such service on the basis of his handicap.[139]

E. The Future of Mass Transit Funding

Senator D'Amato has aptly expressed the problems facing the mass transit industry today:

One of the most significant problems facing the industry today is the immediate and growing gap between costs and revenues. . . . As a result, the single most pressing issue facing mass transit is to immediately reexamine strategies for financing capital and operating costs if public transit services are to continue to serve local and national objectives. The major sources of additional revenues consist of, first, fare increases and/or service cutbacks; second, more local assistance; third, more state assistance; or fourth, more Federal assistance. Fares now provide over 40 percent of operating costs. . . . Continued fare increases ranging from 50 percent to 100 percent are not uncommon in many areas. However, the industry generally, and many individual systems specifically, are reaching the point of diminishing returns. It is becoming apparent that little if any room is left at the fare box or in the way of service reductions to meet the kind of funding shortfalls now being forecast without bringing into play the cycle of fare increases, service cutbacks and ridership losses that brought the then privately held mass transit industry to its knees in the 1960's.

Such a cycle of increasing deficits, increased fares, and declining ridership is likely to stabilize and rebuild both the national economy as well as local urban economies. Growing documentation graphically illustrates the economic impacts of major service cutbacks, ridership losses, and even apparently marginal changes in levels of service. These declines in public transit service have a number of effects, the significance of which are being more fully documented around the country every day. As transit services are curtailed, retail sales and overall spending within local and regional economies fall, jobs are lost and as a result, urban areas are increasingly unable to support national economic recovery. In addition, transportation disadvantaged groups left without any means of mobility and increased automobile use causes congestion, air pollution, and frustrates national energy policy. Finally, increased fares and/or major service cutbacks will have substantial social impacts, as those people who have no alternative to transit and those who are least able to pay, are left to bear the brunt of major fare increases or are entirely left without service. Certainly, these effects violate the commitment to maintaining a safety net for the disadvantaged, and exacerbate the economic impacts outlined above.[140]

In 1982, two approaches for solving mass transit deficits were proposed. Senator Lugar introduced the Reagan administration's proposal, the Transit Assistance Act of 1982 (S. 2367), which centered on the concept of shifting decision making from the federal government to state and local governments.[141] A new Section 9 relates to capital assistance. Ninety percent of capital funds would be allocated by formula, with $7.4 billion of this amount slated for urbanized areas with populations of 50,000 or more. The federal share would be 75 percent. The formula capital funds would be available for capital purposes only; new rail starts and rail extensions would be ineligible. The proposed formula would be one of "revenue matching," in which each urbanized area would receive an apportionment equal to its share of total national non-federal mass transportation revenues, including state and local assistance. The administration reasoned that this formula would allow the federal government to provide funds based on transit use, transit revenues and the strength of local commitments to mass transportation. A recipient of funds from new Section 9 must prepare and publish a proposed statement of objectives and then hold at least one public hearing to obtain the views of the community. Selected designated recipients would receive and dispense funds to urbanized areas of 200,000 or more, but unlike the present Section 5 program, no public transit procedure would automatically designate recipients.[142] (In 1985, David Stockman, then Director of OMB, proposed an end to federal operating subsidies for mass transit. Funds were restored by Congress in the Budget Resolution for fiscal year 1986.)

III. THE FUTURE OF URBAN MASS TRANSIT

A. ICC Regulation

Although railroads are usually regulated by the Interstate Commerce Commission (ICC), they may apply for exemption from such regulation. For this purpose, railroads in general use Section 10505, but commuter railroads may also use Section 10504.

Section 10505[143] provides that the ICC shall exempt rail carriers that meet two requirements. First, the ICC must find that ICC regulation is not necessary to carry out transportation policy. Second, the ICC must find that either the person, transaction or service to be exempted is of limited scope or that regulation is not needed to protect shippers from abuse of market power.[144] When the ICC has found that the applicant has met both requirements, it may specify the period of time during which the exemption will be effective,[145] and it may later revoke the exemption on a finding that regulation is necessary to carry out transportation policy.[146] The ICC may not, however, relieve the rail carrier from its obligations to provide contractual terms for liability[147] and to protect the interests of its employees.[148]

The ICC frequently has exercised its authority under Section 10505. For example, in a recent proceeding,[149] the ICC exempted rail carriage of hops on the application of the Union Pacific Railroad and the Burlington Northern Railroad. The Commission reasoned that the exemption would further transportation policy because the railroads could then adjust their rates in a timely manner to compete effectively with unregulated motor carriers, thus enhancing intermodal competition. The ICC found that the service was of limited scope in that only a small tonnage and a relatively small area of four states were involved. In addition, the ICC found that little opportunity for market abuse existed because the rail market share had been declining and the service was easily divertable to motor carriage.

Commuter rails more frequently seek exemption through Section 10504.[150] This section provides that the ICC lacks jurisdiction when the applicant meets two requirements. First, the exemption is available only to rail mass transportation provided by a local public body, or an entity contracting with a local public body to provide transportation service, on a regular and continuing basis.[151] Charter and sightseeing services are specifically excluded.[152] Second, the fares charged must be subject to the approval or disapproval of the chief executive officer of the state in which the transportation is provided.

The ICC has, for example, recently exempted the Southeastern Pennsylvania Transportation Authority (SEPTA) from regulation in connection with its commuter services over former Conrail lines in Pennsylvania, New Jersey and Delaware.[153] The ICC reasoned that SEPTA's service merely provided a substitute for that service formerly provided by Conrail. The Commission decided that ICC regulation was unnecessary to protect commuters because local government agencies regulate the passenger fares.

In 1983, the ICC also granted an exemption to the Providence & Worcester Railroad for its scenic excursion passenger service in New England.[154] Although this appears to be rail mass transit, Section 10504 was not applicable; the service was for sightseeing purposes for a limited duration, and it was not provided by a public body. The railroad had requested an exemption for a round-trip scenic passenger service to be conducted on weekends and holidays for a period of six weeks. Section 10505 was the appropriate exemption statute. The ICC granted the exemption, reasoning that the service was of limited scope because it was to occur only on weekends and holidays for a limited time. In addition, the ICC found that no regulation was necessary to protect passengers from abuse of market power because their travel would be discretionary and because other modes of transportation were readily available.

B. Regional Transit Authorities

The Chicago area mass transit network is the second largest system in the United States, carrying almost a million passengers a day.[155] The Regional Transportation Authority (RTA) was established in 1974 to govern mass transportation in the six-county area ("collar counties") surrounding and including the City of Chicago. This system is composed of seven commuter railroads, bus and rapid rail operations of the massive Chicago Transit Authority (CTA), and twenty-five suburban bus companies.

The Chicago area has been involved in mass transportation since before the turn of the century. While differences exist between the Chicago system and other transit systems, many of the Chicago area's problems are not unique. Therefore, an examination of the Chicago system can provide insight into the problems of mass transportation in other cities. In order to later discuss cost problems in the Chicago system it is necessary for the reader to understand the historical background of the RTA.

The RTA was formed in 1974 as the result of an extreme financial crisis which was experienced by Chicago area transit operators in late 1973. The Chicago Transit Authority (CTA), formed out of a similar fiscal crisis in 1945, was threatening to raise fares and reduce services. Suburban bus companies were on the verge of collapse, and commuter railroads had filed for massive fare increases with the Illinois Commerce Commission.

Coinciding with the 1973 Chicago area transit crisis was the development by Congress of new Federal capital and operating subsidies, which later became provisions of the Section 5 program enacted in 1974. However, the proposed Federal legislation mandated a regional approach to mass transportation. This Federal requirement bolstered arguments by Chicago politicians who favored the establishment of a regional system which would be able to tap suburban resources to "bail out" the ailing CTA system.

As a result of Federal requirements and pressure from Chicago politicians, the Illinois General Assembly was forced to form an entity to govern mass transit in Chicago and its six "collar" counties. Federal money thus helped contribute to forcing bitter rivals (i.e., the city and the suburbs) into a single governing body.

With the establishment of the Regional Transportation Authority Act of 1974, the thirteen-member Board was given broad powers to oversee the area's mass transit system. The Board was given the power to set fares, and to distribute tax monies and subsidies derived from Federal, state, and local sources.

In addition, the Board was required to plan and coordinate mass transit, improve the level and quality of service, and to improve facilities and equipment. The Board was granted broad powers to audit member carriers and to stimulate innovation in transit management and cost control techniques.

Of the RTA's budget, approximately 39% is derived from farebox revenues. Section 5 federal subsidies amount to 9% of the total budget. Recent reductions have brought the federal operating subsidy to 7% of the total RTA budget. The Federal subsidy appears relatively low, yet is is a substantial amount of money—an amount equal to the RTA's projected short-term deficit in early 1981.

Carriers cost within the RTA are broken down as follows: 70 percent—Chicago Transit Authority (CTA); 25 percent—commuter railroads; and 5 percent—suburban bus systems. The commuter railroads are the most efficient carriers, recovering 60 percent of their costs from the farebox. Cost recovery from the farebox is 51 percent in the CTA and 42 percent in the suburban bus system. (Recent fare increases have forced the commuter railroads into recovering nearly 100 percent of their costs from the farebox.)

We now come back to our original question. Have Federal operating subsidies stimulated efficient and improved transit services at the lowest cost? In the Chicago area it appears that these funds have contributed to inefficient, rather than efficient, operations. Since 1970, costs in the RTA have risen 178 percent. Vehicle-miles for the same time period actually declined 0.8 percent. However, from 1974 to 1979, alone, the RTA operating deficit rose a whopping 205.9 percent!

Many of the cost increases can be explained by needed improvements in the system and by inflation. However, the bulk of the cost problems occurred because the RTA Board was incapable of or unwilling (primarily for political reasons) to control expenses.

Cost problems occur throughout the RTA system, but the system's overwhelming cost problem is that of labor, particularly within the Chicago Transit Authority (CTA). For fiscal 1981 labor costs amount to 77 percent of the CTA's total operating costs. Furthermore, CTA labor costs are so massive that they, alone, account for 52 percent of the total Regional Transportation Authority budget.

The labor cost problem is not simply a matter of the high levels of compensation paid. Rather, it is exacerbated by a precipitous decline in productivity experienced over the last decade. Since 1970, the workforce of the CTA has increased by only 3.7 percent, yet labor costs have increased 127 percent. In addition, for the same time period, total vehicle miles have decreased 13 percent, miles per employee have decreased 16 percent, and miles serviced per hour have dropped 10 percent. Attempts by the system to hire large numbers of part-time workers which would reduce transit costs and improve productivity have been thwarted by the transit unions.

Why have labor costs not been controlled? The answer can be found in an examination of area politics, Federal subsidy programs and Federal legislation. Looking at the political aspect, Chicago is a city where labor unions have always played a major role in local politics. Throughout the years, transit unions have been closely allied with the powerful Chicago (Cook County) Democratic Party and with Democratic mayors. As a result of this alliance, transit managers, who were political appointees themselves, were under great pressure from the political establishment to acquiesce to union demands in labor negotiations.

The Section 5 Federal subsidy program also appears to have been a stimulus to local political leaders in accommodating union demands. Such funds could be used to appease transit labor unions without imposing a financial burden on commuters or local taxpayers. The use of Federal funds for satisfying local political interests was successful in the short run, but with the acceleration of inflation in the 1970's and 1980's, labor costs rapidly outstripped the growth of government subsidies. The resulting cost burden has been the number one cause of the current mass transit fiscal crisis in the Chicago area.

The Federal government itself has contributed directly to local transit labor cost problems through legal restrictions such as section 13(c) [that] imposed regulations which protected organized labor in transit agencies receiving Federal funds. Furthermore, all grant applications submitted by local transit agencies to the U.S. Department of Transportation had to be "cosigned" by the appropriate transit union. This provision had the potential to be abused as a bargaining tool by the transit unions to pressure transit agencies for contract concessions.

Section 13(c) had been established primarily to protect the employees of private transit companies which were being purchased by State and local governments. Since many states prohibited public employee collective bargaining, the Congress wanted to ensure that employee rights previously held under private ownership maintained under public ownership.

The language of Section 13(c), however, contains no restrictions which prohibit hard bargaining between a transit system and its union. Furthermore, there is nothing in the law which prohibits the subsequent removal, reduction, modification by negotiation or state statute, or limitation enacted by the state legislature on permissible contract provisions or compensation levels.

Another factor contributing to excessive labor costs in local transit systems has been the expense of commuter railroad labor exacerbated by Federal railway labor laws. In recent years, commuter railroad services have been, for the most part, relegated to that of a public or quasi-public service under the auspices of regional public transit agencies. Yet Federal railway labor law has not been modified to reflect changes in the nature of the rail industry or to relieve the burden placed on public transit systems. Railroad corporations have been unwilling to jeopardize labor relations in their profitable freight systems to accommodate local commuter services which operated at the break-even point or at a loss.

The RTA contracts for service with seven privately-owned commuter railroads. These railroads also operate a substantial freight transportation system. The RTA is not a party to the contract negotiations of its member railroads and is thus forced to pay whatever costs accrue from national rail labor contracts. Without locally negotiated labor contracts the RTA, like other transit agencies, is powerless to control the bulk of commuter railroad costs.

The Chicago area mass transit system was constructed at the turn of the century by private entrepreneurs. Commuter railroads, the rapid rail systems, and later, bus companies competed with each other for passengers. However, with the advent of public ownership under the CTA in 1945 and the RTA in 1974, the necessity to maintain redundant, formally competitive routes ended for the most part. In addition, many of the routes which exist to this day service areas long abandoned by the bulk of industry and population.

In 1974, the State of Illinois contracted with a group of consultants to develop a logical, efficient route system for the metropolitan area. The study documented over eighty-three instances of duplicative or competing transportation services, primarily between the CTA and other carriers. While the RTA recognizes the existence of this duplication, they refused to fundamentally reform the present system's route structure.

Suburban bus operations have proven to be an especially costly and growing problem for the RTA system. Overall, suburban bus services have the poorest ridership and farebox recovery rates of all RTA carriers. The RTA continues to expand suburban operations despite this poor record and the fact that the commuter railroads remain the primary mass transportation mode of suburban commuters.

Service economies in the CTA, commuter railroads and suburban bus systems have only recently received strong public attention and have proven to be elusive. Savings have been difficult to achieve, either for political reasons or due to the restrictive labor work rules of transit unions.

The tragedy of the situation is that Federal and state subsidies continue to pay for and encourage such inefficiencies and misallocations in the system. Operating subsidy programs have not encouraged or stimulated the economies needed by mass transit systems such as those of the Chicago area.

NOTES

The authors are indebted to Susan C. Lein of the Wisconsin bar for her invaluable assistance in the preparation of this chapter.

1. Office of Public Affairs, Urban Mass Transp. Admin., U. S. Dep't of Transp., 1 Urban Mass Transportation Act of 1964, Pub. L. No. 88–365, 78 Federal Assistance for Urban Mass Transportation 1–2, 4 (Apr. 1979).

2. Urban Mass Transportation Act of 1964, Pub. L. No. 88–365, 78 Stat. 302 (codified at 49 U.S.C. § 1601 [1976]).

3. 49 U.S.C. § 1601(b).

4. Office of Public Affairs, Urban Mass Transp. Admin., U.S. Dep't of Transp., Federal Assistance for Urban Mass Transportation 4–6 (Apr. 1979).

5. Urban Mass Transportation Assistance Act of 1970, Pub. L. No. 91–453, 84 Stat. 962.

6. Federal-Aid Highway Act of 1973, Pub. L. No. 91–605, 84 Stat. 1713.

7. National Mass Transportation Assistance Act of 1974, Pub. L. No. 93–503, 88 Stat. 1565 (codified at 49 U.S.C. §§ 1601–1605 (1976 & Supp. 1982)).

8. Federal Public Transportation Act of 1978, Pub. L. No. 95–599, 92 Stat. 2735.

9. Office of Public Affairs, Urban Mass Transp. Admin., U.S. Dep't of Transp., Federal Assistance for Urban Mass Transportation 7 (Apr. 1979).

10. 49 U.S.C. § 1602(a)(1) (Supp. 1982).

11. *Id.* § 1603(a).

12. Office of Public Affairs, Urban Mass Transp. Admin., U.S. Dep't of Transp., Federal Assistance for Urban Mass Transportation 9 (Apr. 1979).

13. 49 U.S.C. § 1603(a) (Supp. 1982).

14. Office of Public Affairs, Urban Mass Transp. Admin., U.S. Dep't of Transp., Federal Assistance for Urban Mass Transportation 9 (Apr. 1979).

15. 49 U.S.C. § 1609 (1976).

16. 49 U.S.C. § 1615 (Supp. 1982).

17. *Id.* § 1610 (1976).

18. *Id.* § 1610(b).

19. *Id.* § 1610(c).

20. *Id.* § 1602(a)(2)(A) (Supp. 1982).

21. Philadelphia Council of Neighborhood Orgs. v. Coleman, 437 F. Supp. 1341, 1355 (E.D. Pa. 1977), *aff'd without opinion*, 578 F.2d 1375 (3d Cir. 1978).

22. 49 U.S.C. § 1602(a)(2)(C) (Supp. 1982).

23. 49 U.S.C. § 1602(e) (Supp. 1982) *Id.* 1602(e).

24. *Id.*

25. *Id.* § 1602(g) (1976).

26. H. Conf. Rep. No. 410, 93d Cong., 1st Sess. 87 (1973); S. Conf. Rep. No. 355, 93d Cong., 1st Sess. 87, *reprinted in* 1973 U.S. Code Cong. & Ad. News 1859.

27. Chicago Transit Auth. v. Adams, 607 F.2d 1284, 1291 (7th Cir. 1979).

28. 49 U.S.C. § 1607(c) (Supp. 1982). *See* 23 C.F.R. § 450 (1981); 49 C.F.R. § 613 (1981).

29. Parker v. Adams, Civ. No. 78–692 (W.D.N.Y. memorandum opinion filed Nov. 13, 1978).

30. 49 U.S.C. § 1607(a) (Supp. 1982). *See* 41 Fed. Reg. 41512–14 (1976).

31. 49 U.S.C. § 1607(a) (Supp. 1982).

32. National Mass Transportation Assistance Act of 1974, Pub. L. No. 93–503, 88 Stat. 1565 (codified in 49 U.S.C. §§ 1601–1605 (1976, Supp. 1982)).

33. 49 U.S.C. § 1604(f) (1976), *amended by* Pub. L. No. 95–599, § 304(c), 92 Stat. 2739.

34. Surface Transportation Act of 1978, Pub. L. No. 95–599, 92 Stat. 2689.

35. 49 U.S.C. § 1604(a)(1) (Supp. 1982).

36. *Id.* § 1604(a)(2).

37. *Id.* § 1604(a)(2).

38. *Id.* § 1608(c)(2).

39. This is due to the fact that the New York City Transit Authority is so much more extensive than the other transit systems, and uses as many subway cars as all other U.S. systems combined.

40. 49 U.S.C. § 1604(a)(4).

41. *Id.* § 1604(e) (1976).

42. *Id.* § 1604(f) (Supp. 1982).

43. *Id.* § 1604(b).

44. *Id.* § 1604(c)(4).

45. *Id.* § 1604(d) (1976).

46. *Id.* § 1604(j)(4).

47. *Id.* § 1604(g) (Supp. 1982).

48. *Id.* § 1604(h) (1976).

49. *Id.* § 1604(i) (Supp. 1982).

50. *Id.*

51. *Id.* § 1604(l) (1976).

52. *Id.* § 1604(m).

53. This section is from Office of Public Affairs, Urban Mass Transp. Admin., U.S. Dep't of Transp., Federal Assistance for Urban Mass Transportation 9–10 (Apr. 1979).

54. Federal-Aid Highway Act of 1973, Pub. L. No. 91–605, 84 Stat. 173.

55. Pub. L. No. 93–87, 87 Stat. 260–61 (codified at 23 U.S.C. § 142 (1976, Supp. 1980)).

56. Pub. L. No. 91–605, 84 Stat. 1716, § 106(b)(1) (codified at 23 U.S.C. §§ 101, 104, 139 (1976, Supp. 1980)).

57. Office of Public Affairs, Urban Mass Transp. Admin., U.S. Dep't of Transp., Federal Assistance for Urban Mass Transportation, 11–15 (1979).

58. Federal Public Transportation Act of 1978, Pub. L. No. 95–599, § 18, 92 Stat. 2748 (codified at 49 U.S.C. § 1614 [Supp. 1982]).

59. 49 U.S.C. § 1614(c) (Supp. 1982).

60. *Id.* § 1614(c).

61. *Id.* § 1614(e).

62. *Id.* § 1614(c).

63. *Id.* § 1614(d).

64. *Id.* § 1614(b).

65. *Id.* § 1614(f).

66. Federal Public Transportation Act of 1978, Pub. L. No. 95–599, § 22, 92 Stat. 2754 (codified at 49 U.S.C. § 1618 [Supp. 1982]).

67. 49 U.S.C. § 1618(a) (Supp. 1982).

68. *Id.*

69. *Id.* § 1618(b).

70. *Id.*

71. *Id.* § 1618(e).

72. Surface Transportation Assistance Act of 1978, Pub. L. No. 95–599, § 401.

73. 49 U.S.C. § 1605 (1976).

74. *Id. See* Office of Public Affairs, Urban Mass Transp. Admin., U.S. Dep't of Transp., Federal Assistance for Urban Mass Transportation 11 (Apr. 1979).

75. Office of Public Affairs, Urban Mass Transp. Admin., U.S. Dep't of Transp., Federal Assistance for Urban Mass Transportation 11 (Apr. 1979).

76. *Id.* at 12.

77. *Id.* at 13.

78. Urban Mass Transp. Admin., U.S. Dep't of Transp., Service and Methods Demonstrations Programs Summary Report 1 (Dec. 1981).

79. *Id.* at 2.

80. *Id.* at 5.

81. *Id.* at 9–10.

82. *Id.* at 14–15.

83. *Id.* at 20–21.

84. *Id.* at 27–28.

85. *Id.* at 30–31.

86. Urban Mass Transportation Act of 1964, 49 U.S.C. § 1601 (1964).

87. *Id.* § 1601(a).

88. Urban Mass Transportation Act of 1970, Pub. L. No. 91–453, 84 Stat. 962 (1970).

89. 49 U.S.C. § 1612(a).

90. *Id.* § 1612(b).

91. *Id.* § 1612(b)(2).

92. National Mass Transportation Assistance Act of 1974, Pub. L. No. 93–503, 88 Stat. 565 (1974).

93. 49 U.S.C. § 1604(m).

94. *Id.* § 1604(b).

95. Vocational Rehabilitation and Other Rehabilitation Services Act, 29 U.S.C.A. § 701 (1973).

96. *Id.* § 794.

97. Snowden v. Birmingham-Jefferson City Transit Auth., 407 F. Supp. 394 (S.D. Ala. 1985), *aff'd without opinion,* 551 F.2d 862 (5th Cir. 1977).

98. Vanko v. Finley, 440 F. Supp. 656 (N.D. Ohio 1977).

99. *See* 23 C.F.R. Part 450, Appendix B (1976).

100. 440 F. Supp. at 665–66.

101. Atlantis Community, Inc. v. Adams, 453 F. Supp. 825, 827 (D. Colo. 1978).

102. Federal Public Transportation Act of 1978, Title III, Pub. L. No. 95–599, 92 Stat. 2734 (1978).

103. 49 U.S.C.A. § 1608(c)(4) (as amended by Pub. L. No. 95–599, § 308(c) (1978)).

104. Federal-Aid Highway Act of 1973, 23 U.S.C.A. § 101, § 142 note (1976).

105. 41 Fed. 18,234 (1976).

106. 49 C.F.R. § 613.2000, Appendix (1976).

107. 41 Fed. Reg. 17,871 (1976).

108. HEW is now the Department of Health and Human Services. *See* 20 U.S.C. § 3508 (Supp. III 1979).

109. 45 C.F.R. § 85.1 (1978).

110. *See* 43 Fed. Reg. 25,016 (1976).

111. *See* 44 Fed. Reg. 31, 477–31,31,481 (1979) (codified at 49 C.F.R. § 27.81–27.119 [1979]).

112. 44 Fed. Reg. 31,456 (1979).

113. 49 C.F.R. § 27.99 (1979).

114. 44 Fed. Reg. at 31,480.

115. 49 C.F.R. § 5.11 (1978).

116. American Public Transit Ass'n v. Goldschmidt, 485 F. Supp. 811 (D.C. 1980), *rev'd sub. nom.*, 655 F.2d 1272 (D.C. Cir. 1981).

117. 485 F. Supp. at 814–15.

118. 49 U.S.C. § 142 note (1976).

119. 23 U.S.C. § 142 note (1976).

120. 29 U.S.C. § 794 (Supp. III 1979).

121. American Public Transit Ass'n v. Lewis, 655 F.2d 1272 (D.C. Cir. 1981).

122. Southeastern Community College v. Davis, 442 U.S. 397 (1979).

123. 46 Fed. Reg. 37,488 (1981) (codified at 49 C.F.R. § 27.77).

124. 45 Fed. Reg. at 37,488.

125. 49 C.F.R. § 27.77(a)(1).

126. *Id.* § 27.77, Appendix A.

127. 46 Fed. Reg. at 37,489.

128. 49 C.F.R. § 27.77, Appendix A.

129. 46 Fed. Reg. at 37,490.

130. 49 C.F.R. § 27.77, Appendix B.

131. *Id.*

132. *Id.*

133. *Id.* § 27.77(a)(2).

134. *Id.* § 27.77(a)(3).

135. *Id.* § 27.77, Appendix A.

136. 46 Fed. Reg. at 37,490.

137. 49 C.F.R. § 27.77(a)(4).

138. *Id.* § 27.77(b).

139. *Id.* § 27.77(c).

140. 128 Cong. Rec. S3599 (daily ed. Apr. 15, 1982) (Statement of Sen. D'Amato).

141. *Id.* at S3501 (daily ed. Apr. 14, 1982) (letter from Drew Lewis, secretary of transportation, to the Hon. George Bush, President of the Senate [Apr. 12, 1982], discussing the Transit Assistance Act of 1982).

142. *See* Federal Public Transportation Act of 1982, Pub. L. 97–424 (1982), 96 Stat. 2097, being Title III of the Surface Transportation Assistance Act of 1982.

143. 49 U.S.C. § 10505 (1982).

144. *Id.* § 10505(a).

145. *Id.* § 10505(c).

146. *Id.* § 10505(d).

147. *Id.* § 10505(e).

148. *Id.* § 10505(g).

149. Rail General Exemption Auth.—Hops, Ex Parte No. 346 (Sub. No. 10) (1982).

150. 49 U.S.C. § 10504 (1982).

151. *Id.* § 10504(a).

152. *See id.* § 1608(c)(6) (Supp. 1982).

153. *SEPTA Wins Exemption from ICC Regulation*, Traffic World 46 (Mar. 28, 1983) (citing Southeastern Pennsylvania Transp. Auth.—Exemption from 49 U.S.C. Subtitle IV, I.C.C. Finance 30139 (1983)).

154. *P & W Scenic Rail Exemption*, Traffic World 45–46 (Mar. 28, 1983) (citing Providence & Worcester R.R. Passenger Service Exemption from 49 U.S.C. Subtitle IV, I.C.C. Finance 30145 [1983]).

155. This section adapted from Lowenstein, *The Need for Limitations on Federal Mass Transit Operating Subsidies: The Chicago Example*, 12 Transp. L.J. 265, 267–278 (1982).

Index

About the Authors

PAUL STEPHEN DEMPSEY is Professor of Transportation Law and Director of the Transportation Law Program, University of Denver College of Law. He authored *Regulated Industries* and the study guide for *Administrative Law*. He has contributed to *American University Law Review*, *Northwestern Journal of International Law and Business*, *Transportation Law Journal*, and *Chicago Kent Law Review*.

WILLIAM E. THOMS is Professor of Law at the University of North Dakota and Director of its Aerospace Law Program and Institute for Canadian-American Law. He is the author of *Reprieve for the Iron Horse* and a frequent contributor on transportation law topics for *Trains Magazine*, *Passenger Train Journal*, and the *Transportation Law Journal*.